W9-APO-738

THE Woman's Day EVERYDAY COOKBOOK

FIRST PUBLISHED IN 2011 IN THE UNITED STATES
OF AMERICA BY FILIPACCHI PUBLISHING
1271 AVENUE OF THE AMERICAS
NEW YORK, NY 10020

DESIGN
GIORGIO BARAVALLE, DE.MO DESIGN

EDITOR
LAUREN KUCZALA

INDEXING
CATHY DORSEY

PRODUCTION
LYNN SCAGLIONE AND ANNIE ANDRES

ISBN-13:
978-1-936297-45-0

LIBRARY OF CONGRESS CONTROL NUMBER:
2010940286

PRINTED IN CHINA

THE Woman's Day EVERYDAY COOKBOOK

365 TASTY RECIPES AND MONTHLY MENUS FOR THE WHOLE YEAR

BY THE EDITORS OF WOMAN'S DAY

CONTENTS

INTRODUCTION BY ELIZABETH MAYHEW

Often I have wished for a fairy godmother, who, like the very capable lunch ladies from my grade school, would plan meals while making sure to vary the weekly repertoire and round them out in a healthy, nutritious way. Not that I would need this fairy godmother to do the cooking—I just need her to decide what I should make for dinner, which always seems to be more than half the battle. Well, consider this book your own dinnertime fairy godmother. We have taken *Woman's Day*'s very successful Month of Menus column and turned it into a year-long meal plan. So for the next 365 days, you won't have to ask the dreaded question "What should I make for dinner tonight?"

This book takes you day by day though the calendar year, giving you easy-to-make, tasty recipes with special attention paid to seasonality—come January 23 you can whip up a comforting Cornbread & Beef Skillet Pie, and on May 24 you can look forward to a delicious Spring Vegetable Frittata. We've even included week-by-week shopping lists so you know exactly what to buy and when. By taking the guesswork out of dinner planning, we hope that you will enjoy your time in the kitchen and at the table with your family even more. Now that's a wish granted!

JANUARY

JANUARY SHOPPING LIST

Week 1
JANUARY 1 TO JANUARY 7

PRODUCE
2 MEDIUM ONIONS
1 LARGE SWEET ONION
2 HEADS GARLIC (11 CLOVES)
3 MEDIUM YUKON GOLD POTATOES (ABOUT 1¼ LB)
3 MEDIUM SWEET POTATOES
4½ LB LARGE TOMATOES (ABOUT 12)
1 MEDIUM EGGPLANT (1½ LB)
3 MEDIUM ZUCCHINI
2 BELL PEPPERS
1 SPAGHETTI SQUASH (ABOUT 2½ LB)
12 OZ FRESH KALE
2 LARGE LEEKS
2 BUNCHES BASIL
1 BUNCH CHIVES
1 BUNCH PARSLEY

BAKERY
4 SLICES FOCACCIA BREAD

MEAT/POULTRY/FISH
8 OZ FULLY-COOKED SMOKED TURKEY SAUSAGE
2 LB BONELESS LEG OF LAMB OR LAMB STEW MEAT

DELI
8 PROSCIUTTO SLICES
ONE 14-LB WHOLE FRESH HAM

REFRIGERATED
1 PKG (8 OZ) FRESH WHOLE-MILK MOZZARELLA
4 OZ PART-SKIM MOZZARELLA
1 PKG (20 OZ) FOUR-CHEESE RAVIOLI

GROCERY
5 CANS (14.5 OZ) REDUCED-SODIUM CHICKEN BROTH
1 CAN (28 OZ) FIRE-ROASTED DICED TOMATOES
1 CAN (8 OZ) TOMATO SAUCE
1 CAN (6 OZ) TOMATO PASTE
1 CAN (15 OR 15.5 OZ) CANNELLINI BEANS
1 JAR (6 OZ) ARTICHOKE HEARTS
1 CONTAINER (8 OZ) OLIVE TAPENADE
8 OZ SPAGHETTI PASTA (½ A 16-OZ BOX)
¼ CUP GOLDEN RAISINS
1 PKG (6 OZ) DRIED APRICOTS
1 PKG (7 OZ) DRIED PRUNES
1 BOX (10 OZ) WHOLE-WHEAT COUSCOUS
1 PKG (6 OZ) SLIVERED ALMONDS

PANTRY
KOSHER SALT
SALT
PEPPER
EXTRA-VIRGIN OLIVE OIL
BALSAMIC VINEGAR
RED-WINE VINEGAR
DRIED OREGANO
CRUSHED RED PEPPER
CARAWAY SEEDS
PUMPKIN PIE SPICE
BAY LEAF
SUGAR
FLOUR
BROWN OR DIJON MUSTARD

Week 2
JANUARY 8 TO JANUARY 14

PRODUCE
2 MEDIUM ONIONS
1 HEAD GARLIC (3 CLOVES)
2 LB RED-SKINNED POTATOES
5 SMALL OR 2 MEDIUM ZUCCHINI (1 LB)
1 MEDIUM ZUCCHINI
1 LARGE RED OR GREEN BELL PEPPER
4 LARGE BELL PEPPERS
2 SMALL LEMONS
1 BUNCH CILANTRO
1 BUNCH CHIVES
1 BUNCH PARSLEY
1 BUNCH FRESH THYME

BAKERY
1 LOAF (8 OZ) READY-TO-HEAT GARLIC BREAD

MEAT/POULTRY/FISH
2 FLANK STEAKS (ABOUT 1½ LB EACH)
1 LB LEAN GROUND BEEF
1 ROASTING CHICKEN (ABOUT 5½ LB)
8 OZ LEAN GROUND CHICKEN
8 OZ HOT ITALIAN TURKEY SAUSAGE
1 LB SMALL FRESH FISH FILLETS (SUCH AS TILAPIA, TURBOT OR RED SNAPPER)

REFRIGERATED
2½ STICKS BUTTER
4 OZ PART-SKIM MOZZARELLA
8 OZ PEPPERJACK CHEESE
EGGS (8 LARGE)
1 CARTON (15 OZ) SOUTHWESTERN EGG BEATERS

FROZEN
1 BAG (16 OZ) BROCCOLI, CORN AND RED PEPPERS MIX
1 PKG (10 OZ) WHOLE-KERNEL CORN

GROCERY
1 CAN (14 OZ) DICED ITALIAN-SEASONED TOMATOES
1 CAN (21 OZ) RANCHERO BEANS
1 CAN (15.25 OZ) WHOLE-KERNEL CORN
1 CAN (10 OZ) ENCHILADA SAUCE
1 PKG (11 OZ) QUICK-COOKING BARLEY
1 PKG (6.5 OZ) CORNBREAD MIX

PANTRY
SALT
PEPPER
OIL
NONSTICK SPRAY
GARLIC POWDER
PAPRIKA
DRIED MARJORAM
DRIED THYME
GROUND CUMIN

Week 3
JANUARY 15 TO JANUARY 22

PRODUCE
1 LIME
1 LEMON
4 ONIONS
1 SMALL SWEET ONION
1 SMALL RED ONION
1 HEAD GARLIC (5 CLOVES)
1 PIECE FRESH GINGER
2 MEDIUM TOMATOES
4 PLUM TOMATOES
1 PT CHERRY TOMATOES
3 CARROTS
10 OZ BUTTON MUSHROOMS
4 OZ SHIITAKE OR WHITE MUSHROOMS
1 CUP FRESH CORN KERNELS
1 BAG RADISHES
2 AVOCADOS
1 BUNCH SCALLIONS (9)
1 BUNCH CELERY
1 BAG (5 OZ) BABY ARUGULA BLEND
1 BAG (10 OZ) COLESLAW MIX
1 PKG (10 OZ) CAESAR SALAD KIT
1 BUNCH PARSLEY

BAKERY
1 SMALL LOAF WHITE BREAD (FOR BREAD CRUMBS)

MEAT/POULTRY/FISH
1 FLANK STEAK (ABOUT 1 LB)
1 PORK TENDERLOIN (ABOUT 12 OZ)
1 LB CHICKEN TENDERS (ABOUT 8)
1 LB GROUND CHICKEN

DELI
1¼ LB HAM HOCK(S)
4 STRIPS BACON

REFRIGERATED
1 QT WHOLE MILK
½ CUP MILK
½ STICK BUTTER
1 CONTAINER (4 OZ) SOUR CREAM
5 OZ SHREDDED SHARP CHEDDAR
GRATED PARMESAN
EGGS (2 LARGE)

FROZEN
2 PKG (16 OZ) POTATO-ONION PIEROGIES

GROCERY
1 CAN (15 TO 16 OZ) BLACK BEANS
1 CAN (15.25 OZ) WHOLE-KERNEL CORN
1 CAN (6 OZ) LIGHT TUNA IN OIL
1 CAN (10.75 OZ) CONDENSED CREAM OF CELERY SOUP
18 JUMBO PASTA SHELLS
1 PKG (12 OZ) QUICK-COOKING GRITS
SALT-FREE SOUTHWEST CHIPOTLE SEASONING (MRS. DASH) OR CHILI POWDER
OLIVE OIL AND VINEGAR DRESSING (VINAIGRETTE)
1 LB DRIED GREEN SPLIT PEAS
3 CHICKEN BOUILLON CUBES
⅓ CUP ITALIAN-SEASONED DRIED BREAD CRUMBS
EIGHT 7- TO 8-IN. FLOUR TORTILLAS
SEASONED RICE-WINE VINEGAR
HOISIN SAUCE
1 CAN (14 OZ) BABY CORN

PANTRY
SALT
PEPPER
OLIVE OIL
DRIED THYME
PAPRIKA (OPTIONAL)

Week 4
JANUARY 23 TO JANUARY 31

PRODUCE
1 GALA APPLE
1 LEMON
3 MEDIUM ONIONS
1 SMALL ONION
1 LARGE RED ONION
3 SHALLOTS
1 HEAD GARLIC (3 CLOVES)
1 BUNCH BROCCOLI
3 CARROTS
1 CUP SHREDDED CARROTS (4 OZ)
1 RED BELL PEPPER
1 BUNCH ASPARAGUS (1 LB)
4 OZ SUGAR SNAP PEAS
1 LARGE JALAPEÑO PEPPER
4 OZ FRESH SNOW PEAS
1 KIRBY CUCUMBER
4 CUPS SHREDDED GREEN CABBAGE
1 BUNCH SCALLIONS
1 BUNCH DILL
1 BUNCH PARSLEY
1 BUNCH BASIL
1 BUNCH MINT

MEAT/POULTRY/FISH
3½-LB BOTTOM ROUND BEEF ROAST
4 WELL-TRIMMED, 1-IN.-THICK SMOKED BONE-IN PORK CHOPS (ABOUT 2 LB)
4 SHOULDER LAMB CHOPS, ¾ IN. THICK
4 BONELESS, SKINLESS CHICKEN BREASTS (5 OZ EACH)
1 PKG CHICKEN THIGHS (2 LB)
1½ CUPS SHREDDED COOKED CHICKEN
8 OZ TURKEY KIELBASA
4 SALMON FILLETS (6 OZ EACH)
12 OZ LARGE SHRIMP

REFRIGERATED
1 CUP LOWFAT SMALL-CURD COTTAGE CHEESE (2%) OR PART-SKIM RICOTTA
½ CUP SHREDDED PART-SKIM MOZZARELLA
GRATED PARMESAN

FROZEN
1 PKG (9 OZ) PETITE GREEN PEAS
1 BOX (10 OZ) LEAF SPINACH

GROCERY
2 CANS (14.5 OZ) REDUCED-SODIUM CHICKEN BROTH
2 CANS (14.5 OZ) CHICKEN BROTH
1 CAN (14.5 OZ) DICED TOMATOES
1 CAN (14.5 OZ) DICED TOMATOES WITH SWEET ONION
1 CAN CRUSHED TOMATOES
1 CAN (19 OZ) CANNELLINI BEANS
1 CAN (15.5 OZ) CHICKPEAS
12 OZ LONG FUSILLI PASTA
8 OZ LINGUINE
1 BOX (12 OZ) JUMBO PASTA SHELLS
CONVERTED WHITE RICE
1½ CUPS MARINARA SAUCE
1 BOX (5.8 OZ) ROASTED GARLIC & OLIVE OIL COUSCOUS MIX
SALT-FREE LEMON AND PEPPER SEASONING (MCCORMICK)
¼ CUP PANKO CRUMBS
¼ CUP WASABI-SOY ALMONDS
½ CUP APPLE CIDER OR JUICE
1 BAR UNSWEETENED CHOCOLATE
ASIAN SALAD DRESSING
UNSALTED PEANUTS
1 JAR (6 OZ) SOFRITO SAUCE
UNSALTED PUMPKIN SEEDS

PANTRY
SALT
PEPPER
OLIVE OIL
FLOUR
CIDER VINEGAR
PEANUT BUTTER
CARAWAY SEEDS
GROUND CUMIN
GROUND CORIANDER
GROUND CINNAMON
CRUSHED RED PEPPER

SAUSAGE & KALE SOUP

YIELD
6 servings
(makes 8 cups)

ACTIVE
10 minutes

TOTAL
35 minutes

8 OZ **FULLY-COOKED SMOKED TURKEY SAUSAGE**, SLICED

1 MEDIUM **ONION**, CHOPPED

1 TBSP MINCED **GARLIC**

6 CUPS **REDUCED-SODIUM CHICKEN BROTH**

3 MEDIUM **YUKON GOLD POTATOES** , (ABOUT 1¼ LB), PEELED AND CUT IN ½-IN. CHUNKS

12 OZ **FRESH KALE**, STEMS REMOVED AND LEAVES CHOPPED (8 CUPS)

CRUSHED RED PEPPER (OPTIONAL)

Heat a 5-qt pot over medium-high heat. Add sausage and sauté 5 minutes or until browned.

Add onion and garlic; sauté 3 minutes or until onion starts to soften. Add broth and bring to a boil.

Stir in potatoes and kale. Simmer, partially covered, 10 to 12 minutes or until potatoes and kale are tender.

Serve with crushed red pepper, if desired.

PER SERVING
CALORIES 202 **TOTAL FAT** 4G **SATURATED FAT** 1G **CHOLESTEROL** 25MG **SODIUM** 852MG **TOTAL CARBOHYDRATES** 31G **DIETARY FIBER** 4G **PROTEIN** 11G

FRESH TOMATO SOUP

YIELD
4 servings

ACTIVE
15 minutes

TOTAL
35 minutes

3 LB RIPE **TOMATOES**, COARSELY CHOPPED

¼ MEDIUM **ONION**, CHOPPED

1 TBSP EACH **EXTRA-VIRGIN OLIVE OIL** AND **BALSAMIC VINEGAR**

1½ TSP **KOSHER SALT**

1 TO 3 TSP **SUGAR**

SERVE WITH: **PROSCIUTTO & MOZZARELLA SANDWICH** (BELOW)

Put tomatoes, onion, olive oil, vinegar and salt in a large bowl; toss. Let stand at room temperature at least 20 minutes or until tomatoes release their juices, tossing occasionally. Process in food processor or blender until mixture is smooth.

Force through a fine-mesh sieve into a bowl; discard solids. Stir in 1 to 3 tsp sugar depending on ripeness of tomatoes (the less ripe, the more sugar). Serve at room temperature or chilled, drizzled with additional oil.

PROSCIUTTO & MOZZARELLA SANDWICH
Whisk 2 Tbsp each **BALSAMIC VINEGAR** and **OLIVE OIL** in a cup until blended; set aside. Drain and chop a 6-oz jar **ARTICHOKE HEARTS**; toss with ¼ cup **OLIVE TAPENADE**. Toast 4 slices **FOCACCIA BREAD**; brush one side of each with vinegar-and-oil mixture. Evenly spoon artichoke mixture onto each slice of focaccia. Top each with 2 slices **FRESH MOZZARELLA**, 2 slices **PROSCIUTTO** and a few **BASIL LEAVES**.

PER SERVING
CALORIES 64 **TOTAL FAT** 4G **SATURATED FAT** 1G **CHOLESTEROL** 0MG **SODIUM** 568MG
TOTAL CARBOHYDRATES 8G **DIETARY FIBER** 2G **PROTEIN** 1G

RATATOUILLE & WHITE BEANS

- 1 MEDIUM **EGGPLANT** (1½ LB)
- 3 MEDIUM **ZUCCHINI** (1½ LB)
- 2 **BELL PEPPERS**
- 2 LARGE **LEEKS**, CHOPPED
- 1 CAN (28 OZ) **FIRE-ROASTED DICED TOMATOES**, DRAINED
- 1 CAN (8 OZ) **TOMATO SAUCE**
- ¼ CUP **GOLDEN RAISINS**
- 2 TBSP **OLIVE OIL**
- 1 TBSP MINCED **GARLIC**
- 1 TSP **DRIED OREGANO**
- ½ TSP EACH **SALT AND PEPPER**
- 1 CAN (15 OR 15.5 OZ) **CANNELLINI BEANS**, RINSED
- ¼ CUP SLICED **FRESH BASIL LEAVES**
- 2 TBSP **RED-WINE VINEGAR**
- GARNISH: ADDITIONAL SLICED **BASIL**

YIELD
6 servings
makes 10 cups

ACTIVE
15 minutes

TOTAL
4 to 5 hours on high
or 6 to 8 hours on low

SIDE SUGGESTION
Polenta or crusty bread

Cut eggplant, zucchini and peppers into 1-in. pieces; place in a 6-qt slow cooker. Add leeks, diced tomatoes, tomato sauce, raisins, 1 Tbsp oil, garlic, oregano, salt and pepper. Toss until well mixed.

Cover and cook on low 6 to 8 hours or on high 4 to 5 hours until vegetables are tender. Add beans; cook on high 15 minutes more. Stir in remaining 1 Tbsp oil, fresh basil and vinegar.

Sprinkle with additional sliced basil, if using. Serve over polenta or with crusty bread.

PER SERVING
CALORIES 241 **TOTAL FAT** 6G **SATURATED FAT** 1G **CHOLESTEROL** 0MG **SODIUM** 718MG
TOTAL CARBOHYDRATES 40G **DIETARY FIBER** 10G **PROTEIN** 9G

RAVIOLI WITH GARLIC-HERB OIL

YIELD
5 servings

ACTIVE
10 minutes

TOTAL
20 minutes

1 PKG (20 OZ) **REFRIGERATED FOUR-CHEESE RAVIOLI**

¼ CUP **OLIVE OIL**

1 LARGE CLOVE **GARLIC**, SLICED

¼ TSP **CRUSHED RED PEPPER**

2 TBSP EACH SNIPPED **CHIVES** AND MINCED **PARSLEY**

¼ TSP **SALT**

Bring a 5- to 6-qt pot of salted water to a boil. Add ravioli and cook as package directs; gently drain and return to pot.

Meanwhile, put oil, garlic and crushed red pepper flakes in a 1-qt saucepan. Heat over medium heat until garlic turns light golden; remove from heat.

Add garlic oil mixture to pot with ravioli. Add chives, parsley and salt; toss to coat ravioli.

PER SERVING
CALORIES 454 **TOTAL FAT** 22G **SATURATED FAT** 8G **CHOLESTEROL** 65MG **SODIUM** 828MG
TOTAL CARBOHYDRATES 49G **DIETARY FIBER** 3G **PROTEIN** 15G

ROASTED FRESH HAM

YIELD
12 servings

ACTIVE
5 minutes

TOTAL
4 hours 35 minutes

- ONE 14-LB **WHOLE FRESH HAM**
- 2 TSP **CARAWAY SEEDS**
- ½ TSP EACH **SALT** AND **PEPPER**
- 2 TBSP **ALL-PURPOSE FLOUR**
- 3 TBSP **WATER**
- ¼ CUP MINCED **CHIVES** *OR* **SCALLION GREENS**
- 1 TBSP **BROWN OR DIJON MUSTARD**

SIDE SUGGESTION
Baked sweet potatoes

Place oven rack in lowest position. Heat oven to 400°F.

Cut rind and most of fat off ham, leaving only an ⅛-in.-thick layer all around. Place ham, rounded side up, directly in a roasting pan. Mix caraway seeds, salt and pepper; rub over rounded surface.

Roast ham 1 hour, then reduce oven temperature to 350°F. Roast 3 hours longer or until a meat thermometer inserted in thickest part of ham, not touching fat or bone, registers 155°F. Transfer ham to a carving board and let rest at least 30 minutes (temperature of ham will continue to rise about 5° to 160°F).

Pour pan juices into a 2-cup glass measure. Let stand until fat rises to top. Skim off fat and discard. Pour juices, along with any collected on carving board, into a medium-size saucepan. Bring to a gentle boil. Put flour in a small bowl. Gradually stir in water to make a paste. Reduce heat and whisk paste into pan juices. Simmer about 5 minutes until slightly thickened. Stir in chives and mustard.

Carve ham in thin slices against the grain toward the bone. Serve sauce at the table.

PER SERVING
CALORIES 317 **TOTAL FAT** 20G **SATURATED FAT** 0G **CHOLESTEROL** 107MG **SODIUM** 172MG **TOTAL CARBOHYDRATES** 1G **DIETARY FIBER** 0G **PROTEIN** 31G

LAMB TAGINE

1 LARGE **SWEET ONION**, SLICED

2 LB **BONELESS LEG OF LAMB OR LAMB STEW MEAT**, CUT INTO 1½-IN. PIECES, VISIBLE FAT TRIMMED

1 CUP EACH **DRIED APRICOTS** AND **PRUNES**

1 TBSP EACH **MINCED GARLIC** AND **PUMPKIN PIE SPICE**

1 TSP **KOSHER SALT**

½ TSP FRESHLY GROUND **PEPPER**

1 **BAY LEAF**

1 CAN (14.5 OZ) **REDUCED-SODIUM CHICKEN BROTH**

1 CAN (6 OZ) **TOMATO PASTE**

3 MEDIUM **SWEET POTATOES**, SCRUBBED AND RINSED

1 BOX (10 OZ) **WHOLE-WHEAT COUSCOUS**

¼ CUP TOASTED **SLIVERED ALMONDS** (OPTIONAL)

YIELD
6 servings

ACTIVE
10 minutes

TOTAL
5 to 6 hours on high *or* 7 to 9 hours on low

Mix onion, lamb, apricots, prunes, garlic, pumpkin pie spice, salt, pepper and bay leaf in a 4-qt or larger slow cooker. In a bowl, whisk broth and tomato paste until combined; pour into slow cooker. Nestle whole sweet potatoes into stew.

Cover and cook on high 5 to 6 hours or on low 7 to 9 hours until lamb and potatoes are tender.

Remove potatoes with a slotted spoon to a cutting board; discard bay leaf. Cut potatoes into wedges.

Prepare couscous as package directs; serve with stew and potatoes. Serve with almonds if desired.

PER SERVING
CALORIES 479 **TOTAL FAT** 8G **SATURATED FAT** 3G **CHOLESTEROL** 90MG **SODIUM** 822MG **TOTAL CARBOHYDRATES** 95G **DIETARY FIBER** 14G **PROTEIN** 40G

PASTA WITH SPAGHETTI SQUASH & TOMATOES

YIELD
4 servings

ACTIVE
12 minutes

TOTAL
42 minutes

1 **SPAGHETTI SQUASH** (ABOUT 2½ LB)

8 OZ **SPAGHETTI**

½ TSP **OLIVE OIL**

1 TSP MINCED **GARLIC**

4 LARGE **RIPE TOMATOES** (ABOUT 1½ LB), CUT IN BITE-SIZE PIECES

1 TSP **SALT**

¼ TSP **PEPPER**

4 OZ **PART-SKIM MOZZARELLA**, DICED (ABOUT 1 CUP)

1 CUP **FRESH BASIL LEAVES**, STACKED, ROLLED UP AND CUT CROSSWISE IN NARROW STRIPS

To cook squash in microwave: Pierce squash in 8 to 10 places with tip of a small knife. Place on a paper towel and microwave on high 6 to 7 minutes. Pierce in another 8 to 10 places, turning squash over. Microwave 6 to 7 minutes longer, until squash can be pierced easily and yields to gentle pressure.

To cook on stovetop: Place squash in a large pot with enough water to cover when held down. Bring to a boil, cover and cook 35 to 40 minutes until squash can be pierced easily.

When cool enough to handle, cut squash in half lengthwise and discard seeds and strings. With fork, scrape out spaghetti-like strands and place in a large serving bowl.

Cook pasta according to package directions. Drain and add to squash in serving bowl.

Add oil and garlic to pot and cook 1 minute over medium heat. Add tomatoes, salt and pepper, and cook 2 minutes or until hot. Add to serving bowl with the cheese and basil. Toss to mix well.

PER SERVING
CALORIES 403 **TOTAL FAT** 8G **SATURATED FAT** 0G **CHOLESTEROL** 16MG **SODIUM** 738MG **TOTAL CARBOHYDRATES** 68G **DIETARY FIBER** 0G **PROTEIN** 18G

SPICY SAUSAGE & VEGETABLE FRITTATA

1 TBSP **OIL**

8 OZ **HOT ITALIAN TURKEY SAUSAGE**, REMOVED FROM CASINGS

1 MEDIUM **ZUCCHINI**, THINLY SLICED

1 LARGE **RED OR GREEN BELL PEPPER**, OR ½ OF EACH, DICED

8 LARGE **EGGS**

4 OZ **PART-SKIM MOZZARELLA**, SHREDDED (1 CUP)

YIELD
4 servings

ACTIVE
8 minutes

TOTAL
25 minutes

Heat oil in a large nonstick skillet over medium heat. Add sausage and cook, breaking up chunks, 2 to 3 minutes until no longer pink.

Add zucchini and bell pepper, and sauté 5 minutes or until vegetables are tender.

Whisk eggs in a large bowl until well combined. Stir in cheese. Pour over sausage mixture in skillet and stir gently to distribute eggs evenly.

Heat broiler. While broiler heats, cook frittata 4 to 6 minutes until set on bottom and sides (eggs will be runny in center).

Broil 4 to 6 in. from heat source 2 minutes or until firm in center. (If the skillet handle is plastic or wood, wrap it in a double layer of foil to protect it from scorching.)

PER SERVING
CALORIES 329 **TOTAL FAT** 21G **SATURATED FAT** 6G **CHOLESTEROL** 488MG **SODIUM** 568MG
TOTAL CARBOHYDRATES 5G **DIETARY FIBER** 1G **PROTEIN** 29G

GRILLED FLANK STEAKS WITH HERB BUTTER

YIELD
12 servings

ACTIVE
12 minutes

TOTAL
35 minutes

HERB BUTTER

2 STICKS (1 CUP) **SALTED BUTTER**, SOFTENED

¼ CUP EACH CHOPPED **CHIVES** AND **PARSLEY**

2 TBSP CHOPPED **FRESH THYME**

½ TSP FRESHLY GROUND **PEPPER**

STEAKS

2 TSP EACH **GARLIC POWDER**, **PAPRIKA** AND FRESHLY GROUND **PEPPER**

½ TSP **SALT**

2 **FLANK STEAKS**, ABOUT 1½ LB EACH

SIDE SUGGESTION
Brussels sprouts

HERB BUTTER Mix herb butter ingredients in a medium bowl until well blended. Divide mixture in half. Spoon each half onto a sheet of plastic wrap and form into two 5-in. logs; wrap and refrigerate. Or spoon into a bowl or crock and serve at room temperature.

STEAKS Mix garlic powder, paprika, pepper and salt in a small bowl until blended. Sprinkle mixture all over both steaks.

Brush grill with oil or coat with nonstick grilling spray; heat grill or heat indoor grill pan over medium-high heat.

Grill steaks, turning once, 10 to 12 minutes for medium-rare. Remove to a cutting board; let rest 10 minutes before slicing across the grain. Serve hot or at room temperature with herb butter.

PLANNING TIP Herb butter can be made up to 1 week ahead. Keep double-wrapped in refrigerator until ready to use.

PER SERVING
CALORIES 303 **TOTAL FAT** 22G **SATURATED FAT** 13G **CHOLESTEROL** 79MG **SODIUM** 255MG **TOTAL CARBOHYDRATES** 1G **DIETARY FIBER** 0G **PROTEIN** 24G

PERFECT ROAST CHICKEN

2 SMALL **LEMONS**

½ STICK **BUTTER** (4 TBSP), SOFTENED

1 TBSP MINCED **GARLIC**

1 TSP EACH **DRIED MARJORAM** AND **THYME**

¼ TSP **PEPPER**

1 **ROASTING CHICKEN** (5½ LB), GIBLETS RESERVED FOR ANOTHER USE

2 LB **RED-SKINNED POTATOES**, CUT IN QUARTERS OR EIGHTHS IF LARGE

YIELD
6 servings

ACTIVE
15 minutes

TOTAL
1 hour 45 minutes

Heat oven to 400°F. Line a large roasting pan with nonstick foil. Grate enough zest from lemons to make 1 Tbsp. Cut lemons in quarters. Mix butter, garlic, lemon zest, marjoram, thyme and pepper in a small bowl.

Slide fingers under breast and as much of leg as possible to loosen skin from meat. Spread about 3 Tbsp butter mixture under skin; spread remaining over skin. Put cut-up lemons in body cavity. Tie chicken legs together. Place in roasting pan.

Roast 1 hour, covering chicken loosely with a foil tent after 20 minutes to prevent it from overbrowning.

Remove roasting pan from oven, arrange potatoes around chicken and stir to coat with drippings. Roast 30 minutes longer, or until potatoes are tender and a meat thermometer inserted in thickest part of thigh (not touching bone) registers 165°F. Remove chicken to a cutting board or serving platter; let rest 10 minutes before carving. If desired, while chicken rests, return potatoes to oven to brown further.

PER SERVING
CALORIES 773 **TOTAL FAT** 47G **SATURATED FAT** 16G **CHOLESTEROL** 228MG **SODIUM** 286MG
TOTAL CARBOHYDRATES 25G **DIETARY FIBER** 3G **PROTEIN** 56G

SANTA FE FRITTATA

YIELD
4 servings

ACTIVE
12 minutes

TOTAL
12 minutes

2 TSP **OIL**

1 BAG (16 OZ) **FROZEN BROCCOLI, CORN AND RED PEPPERS**

½ TSP **SALT**

1 CARTON (15 OZ) **SOUTHWESTERN EGG BEATERS**

4 OZ **PEPPERJACK CHEESE**, SHREDDED (1 CUP)

Position broiler rack 4 in. from heat. Heat broiler. Wrap handle of large nonstick skillet with foil (if not heatproof).

Heat oil in skillet over medium-high heat. Add frozen vegetables and salt; sauté 1 minute.

Reduce heat to medium. Pour Egg Beaters over vegetables. Cover and cook, lifting edges of frittata occasionally to let liquid run under, 8 minutes or until almost set.

Sprinkle with cheese.

PER SERVING
CALORIES 1,921 **TOTAL FAT** 9G **SATURATED FAT** 5G **CHOLESTEROL** 30MG **SODIUM** 531MG
TOTAL CARBOHYDRATES 8G **DIETARY FIBER** 2G **PROTEIN** 21G

TEX-MEX CHICKEN & BARLEY-STUFFED PEPPERS

4 LARGE **BELL PEPPERS**, HALVED LENGTHWISE THROUGH STEM, SEEDED

NONSTICK SPRAY

8 OZ **LEAN GROUND CHICKEN**

1 MEDIUM **ONION**, CHOPPED

1 CAN (10 OZ) **ENCHILADA SAUCE**

½ CUP EACH **QUICK-COOKING BARLEY** AND **FROZEN WHOLE-KERNEL CORN**

½ TSP **GROUND CUMIN**

⅓ CUP CHOPPED **FRESH CILANTRO**

YIELD
4 servings

ACTIVE
10 minutes

TOTAL
30 minutes

NOTE
Brightly colored bell peppers are a great source of antioxidants. We filled them with lean ground chicken and fiber-rich corn and barley.

Heat broiler. Line a rimmed baking sheet with nonstick foil. Put peppers cut side down in pan; coat peppers with nonstick spray.

Broil 12 to 15 minutes, turning once or twice, until lightly charred and soft.

Meanwhile, coat a large nonstick skillet with nonstick spray; heat over medium heat. Add chicken and onion, increase to medium-high heat and cook 5 minutes, breaking up chunks of chicken with a wooden spoon, until chicken and onions are lightly browned.

Add all but ¼ cup enchilada sauce, 1 cup water, the barley, corn and cumin. Bring to a boil, reduce heat, cover and simmer 10 minutes or until barley is tender. Off heat, stir in cilantro. Spoon into pepper halves; drizzle with reserved enchilada sauce.

Good with shredded romaine lettuce, avocado and tomato salad.

PER SERVING
CALORIES 251 **TOTAL FAT** 9G **SATURATED FAT** 1G **CHOLESTEROL** 47MG **SODIUM** 310MG **TOTAL CARBOHYDRATES** 32G **DIETARY FIBER** 5G **PROTEIN** 14G

ITALIAN FILLET SKILLET

YIELD
4 servings

ACTIVE
7 minutes

TOTAL
15 minutes

1 LOAF (8 OZ) **READY-TO-HEAT GARLIC BREAD**

1 MEDIUM **ONION**, THINLY SLICED

5 SMALL *OR* 2 MEDIUM **ZUCCHINI** (1 LB)

1 CAN (14 OZ) **DICED ITALIAN-SEASONED TOMATOES**

1 LB SMALL **FRESH FISH FILLETS** (SUCH AS TILAPIA, TURBOT OR RED SNAPPER), NO MORE THAN ½ IN. THICK

Put bread halves, seasoned side up, on a baking sheet. Place in oven; heat oven to 425°F.

Meanwhile, lightly coat a large nonstick skillet with nonstick spray. Heat over medium-high heat. Spread onion in skillet.

While onion cooks, cut small zucchini in ½-in.-thick rounds (or cut medium zucchini in half lengthwise, then crosswise in ½-in.-thick pieces). Stir into onions along with about half the tomatoes. Bring to a boil.

Lay fish fillets in a single layer on top. Pour remaining tomatoes over fish. Cover and cook 7 to 8 minutes, until fish is cooked through and zucchini is crisp-tender.

PER SERVING
CALORIES 478 **TOTAL FAT** 25G **SATURATED FAT** 5G **CHOLESTEROL** 52MG **SODIUM** 566MG
TOTAL CARBOHYDRATES 38G **DIETARY FIBER** 4G **PROTEIN** 24G

CORNBREAD & BEEF SKILLET PIE

YIELD
4 servings

ACTIVE
15 minutes

TOTAL
35 minutes

1 LB **LEAN GROUND BEEF**

1 CAN (21 OZ) **RANCHERO BEANS**

1 CAN (15.25 OZ) **WHOLE-KERNEL CORN**, DRAINED

1 PKG (6.5 OZ) **CORNBREAD MIX**

½ CUP **SHREDDED PEPPERJACK CHEESE**

SIDE SUGGESTION
Cucumber salad

Heat oven to 400°F.

Brown ground beef in a large skillet with heatproof handle over medium-high heat. Stir in ranchero beans and drained whole-kernel corn. Simmer 2 minutes.

Meanwhile, prepare cornbread mix as package directs.

Spoon cornbread mixture on top of beef mixture in skillet. Sprinkle with shredded pepperjack cheese.

Bake 15 minutes or until a wooden pick inserted in center of cornbread comes out clean. Cool 5 minutes.

PER SERVING
CALORIES 726 **TOTAL FAT** 28G **SATURATED FAT** 12G **CHOLESTEROL** 159MG **SODIUM** 1,515MG **TOTAL CARBOHYDRATES** 78G **DIETARY FIBER** 7G **PROTEIN** 40G

PIEROGIES

YIELD
4 servings

ACTIVE
14 minutes

TOTAL
24 minutes

2 PKG **FROZEN POTATO-ONION PIEROGIES**

4 TBSP **BUTTER**

10 OZ **BUTTON MUSHROOMS**, SLICED

1 MEDIUM **ONION,** CHOPPED

2 TBSP **SOUR CREAM**

SIDE SUGGESTION
Mixed greens and tomato salad

Cook pierogies according to package directions for boiling.

Remove pierogies from heat and strain. In a medium skillet, heat 2 Tbsp butter. Add sliced mushrooms and stir until coated with butter.

Add chopped onion to the skillet and sauté until onion is soft and mushrooms begin to give up their liquid. Remove the skillet from heat, add sour cream and stir until just combined.

In another skillet, heat remaining 2 Tbsp butter. Add the cooked pierogies to the skillet and sauté until browned. Transfer pierogies to a serving platter and spoon mushroom sauce on top.

PER SERVING
CALORIES 578 **TOTAL FAT** 53G **SATURATED FAT** 40G **CHOLESTEROL** 137MG **SODIUM** 498MG
TOTAL CARBOHYDRATES 25G **DIETARY FIBER** 3G **PROTEIN** 8G

CORN & GRITS CASSEROLE

YIELD
8 servings

ACTIVE
15 minutes

TOTAL
45 minutes

4 CUPS (1 QT) **WHOLE MILK**

1 CUP **QUICK-COOKING GRITS**

1 CAN (15.25 OZ) **WHOLE-KERNEL CORN**, DRAINED

1¼ CUP (5 OZ) **SHREDDED SHARP CHEDDAR**

6 **SCALLIONS**, CHOPPED

1 LARGE **EGG**

½ TSP **SALT**

½ TSP **DRIED THYME**

¼ TSP **PEPPER**

Heat oven to 375°F. Lightly coat a shallow 2-qt baking dish with nonstick spray.

Bring milk to a gentle boil in a 3-qt saucepan; slowly whisk in grits. Reduce heat and simmer, stirring often, 5 to 7 minutes until thickened.

Remove from heat; stir in corn, 1 cup cheese, the scallions, egg, salt, thyme and pepper. Pour into prepared dish.

Bake, uncovered, 15 minutes. Sprinkle with remaining ¼ cup cheese and bake 15 minutes more until set. Let stand 10 minutes before serving.

PLANNING TIP Can be baked up to 2 days ahead. Refrigerate covered. Bring to room temperature before reheating in microwave or oven.

PER SERVING
CALORIES 256 **TOTAL FAT** 11G **SATURATED FAT** 6G **CHOLESTEROL** 62MG **SODIUM** 404MG
TOTAL CARBOHYDRATES 28G **DIETARY FIBER** 2G **PROTEIN** 12G

SOUTHWESTERN STEAK SALAD

1 TSP **OIL**

1 CUP **FRESH CORN KERNELS**

1 LB **FLANK STEAK**

2 TSP **SALT-FREE SOUTHWEST CHIPOTLE SEASONING** (MRS. DASH) *OR* **CHILI POWDER**

1 CAN (15 TO 16 OZ) **BLACK BEANS**, RINSED

1 PT **CHERRY TOMATOES**, HALVED

1 **AVOCADO**, DICED

¼ **SWEET ONION**, THINLY SLICED

⅓ CUP **BOTTLED OLIVE OIL AND VINEGAR DRESSING**

JUICE OF HALF A **LIME**

YIELD
4 servings

ACTIVE
10 minutes

TOTAL
23 minutes

Heat ½ tsp oil in a large nonstick skillet over medium-high heat. Add corn; cook 1 minute until crisp-tender. Remove to a medium bowl.

Rub seasoning on both sides of steak. Heat remaining ½ tsp oil in skillet until hot but not smoking. Add steak and cook 6 minutes on each side for medium-rare. Transfer to a cutting board; let rest 5 minutes.

Meanwhile, add beans, tomatoes, avocado, onion, ¼ cup dressing and the lime juice to bowl with corn; toss to mix and coat.

SERVE WITH
Tortilla chips

TO SERVE Thinly slice steak across the grain. Spoon salad onto plates; top with steak. Drizzle steak with remaining dressing.

PER SERVING
CALORIES 505 **TOTAL FAT** 33G **SATURATED FAT** 8G **CHOLESTEROL** 59MG **SODIUM** 374MG **TOTAL CARBOHYDRATES** 26G **DIETARY FIBER** 6G **PROTEIN** 29G

SPLIT PEA SOUP

- 1 LB **DRIED GREEN SPLIT PEAS**
- 2 CUPS DICED **ONIONS**
- 1½ CUPS DICED **CARROTS**
- 1 CUP DICED **CELERY**
- 2 TSP MINCED **GARLIC**
- ½ TSP **PEPPER**
- 3 **CHICKEN BOUILLON CUBES**
- 1¼ LB **HAM HOCK(S)**

YIELD
4 servings

ACTIVE
15 minutes

TOTAL
6 hours on high
or 12 hours on low

Put all ingredients and 7 cups water in a 5½-qt or larger slow cooker.

Cover and cook on high 6 hours or on low 12 hours until peas are very soft and fall apart.

Remove ham. When cool enough to handle, cut meat off the bone, dice and return to soup. Serve with cornbread, or cut cornbread in cubes, toast in oven and serve as croutons.

PER SERVING
CALORIES 551 **TOTAL FAT** 8G **SATURATED FAT** 2G **CHOLESTEROL** 32MG **SODIUM** 1,528MG
TOTAL CARBOHYDRATES 84G **DIETARY FIBER** 10G **PROTEIN** 40G

CHICKEN CAESAR SALAD

YIELD
4 servings

ACTIVE
15 minutes

TOTAL
15 minutes

4 STRIPS **BACON**

1 LB **CHICKEN TENDERS** (ABOUT 8)

⅛ TSP EACH **SALT** AND **PEPPER**

2 MEDIUM **TOMATOES**

1 RIPE **AVOCADO**

1 PKG (10 OZ) **CAESAR SALAD KIT** (WITH DRESSING, CROUTONS AND PARMESAN INCLUDED)

Cook bacon in a large nonstick skillet over medium-high heat 3 minutes or until crisp. Drain on paper towels. Remove all but 1 Tbsp fat from skillet.

Season chicken with salt and pepper. Add to skillet, cover and cook over medium-high heat, turning once, 4 minutes or until golden and cooked through. Transfer to a cutting board; cut lengthwise in strips.

While chicken cooks, cut tomatoes in wedges, and halve, peel, pit and chop avocado.

Put lettuce in a large bowl and toss with the dressing. Divide among plates; top with chicken, tomatoes and avocado. Crumble on bacon; sprinkle with croutons and Parmesan.

PER SERVING
CALORIES 399 **TOTAL FAT** 25G **SATURATED FAT** 5G **CHOLESTEROL** 77MG **SODIUM** 615MG **TOTAL CARBOHYDRATES** 13G **DIETARY FIBER** 2G **PROTEIN** 32G

TUNA-STUFFED SHELLS

- 18 **JUMBO PASTA SHELLS**
- 1 CAN (6 OZ) **LIGHT TUNA IN OIL**, WELL DRAINED
- 1 CUP **FRESH WHITE BREAD CRUMBS**
- ¼ CUP FINELY CHOPPED **ONION**
- 1 LARGE **EGG**
- ¼ CUP MINCED **FRESH PARSLEY**
- 1 TSP **FRESH LEMON JUICE**
- 1 CAN (10.75 OZ) **CONDENSED CREAM OF CELERY SOUP**
- ½ CUP **MILK**
- 2 TBSP GRATED **PARMESAN**
- **PAPRIKA** (OPTIONAL)

YIELD
6 servings

ACTIVE
15 minutes

TOTAL
50 minutes

SIDE SUGGESTION
Mixed greens salad

Heat oven to 350°F. Lightly coat an 11 x 7-in. baking dish with nonstick spray.

Boil pasta as package directs until just firm-tender.

Meanwhile, mix tuna, bread crumbs, onion, egg, half the parsley and the lemon juice to blend.

Drain pasta shells. Rinse gently to cool; drain. Fill each shell with 1 Tbsp tuna mixture. Place in prepared dish.

Whisk soup and milk in a small saucepan over medium heat until hot. Remove from heat; stir in remaining parsley. Pour evenly over shells. Sprinkle with cheese and paprika. Bake 25 minutes or until hot and bubbly and serve, or cover with foil and refrigerate up to 1 day.

PER SERVING
CALORIES 270 **TOTAL FAT** 8G **SATURATED FAT** 2G **CHOLESTEROL** 50MG **SODIUM** 573MG
TOTAL CARBOHYDRATES 34G **DIETARY FIBER** 1G **PROTEIN** 16G

CHICKEN PATTIES MILANESE

YIELD
4 servings

ACTIVE
10 minutes

TOTAL
10 minutes

PATTIES

1 LB **GROUND CHICKEN**

⅓ CUP **GRATED PARMESAN**

⅓ CUP **ITALIAN-SEASONED DRIED BREAD CRUMBS**

½ TSP **SALT**

½ TSP **PEPPER**

2 TSP **OLIVE OIL**

4 CUPS (½ A 5-OZ BAG) **BABY ARUGULA BLEND**

1 CUP DICED **PLUM (ROMA) TOMATOES**

¼ CUP **BOTTLED VINAIGRETTE DRESSING**

¼ CUP SLICED **RED ONION**

SIDE SUGGESTION
Garlic bread and green beans

PATTIES Combine ingredients in a bowl; form into four ½-in.-thick patties.

Heat oil in large nonstick skillet over medium heat. Add patties and cook 6 minutes, turning once, until cooked through.

Put remaining ingredients into a bowl; toss to mix. Serve on patties.

PER SERVING
CALORIES 325 **TOTAL FAT** 19G **SATURATED FAT** 5G **CHOLESTEROL** 99MG **SODIUM** 952MG **TOTAL CARBOHYDRATES** 13G **DIETARY FIBER** 1G **PROTEIN** 25G

MOO SHU PORK PIZZA

EIGHT 7- TO 8-IN. **FLOUR TORTILLAS**

2 TSP **OIL**

1 **PORK TENDERLOIN** (ABOUT 12 OZ), TRIMMED OF EXCESS FAT, CUT CROSSWISE IN THIN SLICES, THEN EACH SLICE CUT IN ½

1 TBSP EACH MINCED **FRESH GARLIC** AND **GINGER**

4 OZ **SHIITAKE MUSHROOMS** (DISCARD STEMS) *OR* **WHITE MUSHROOMS**, SLICED

4 CUPS **COLESLAW MIX**

7 OZ **BABY CORN**, EARS CUT IN ½ LENGTHWISE (SEE NOTE)

⅓ CUP **SEASONED RICE-WINE VINEGAR**

¼ CUP **HOISIN SAUCE**

GARNISH: SLICED **RADISHES** AND **SCALLIONS**

YIELD
8 tortillas

ACTIVE
15 minutes

TOTAL
30 minutes

NOTE
Baby corn, seasoned rice-wine vinegar and hoisin sauce can be found in the Asian food section of your market.

Heat oven to 425°F. Place tortillas in a single layer on 2 large baking sheets.

Meanwhile, heat 1 tsp oil in a large nonstick skillet over medium-high heat. Add half the pork, garlic and ginger. Stir-fry 1 to 1½ minutes until pork is cooked through. Transfer to a bowl. Repeat with remaining oil, pork, garlic and ginger.

Bake tortillas 4 to 5 minutes until tinged with brown.

Meanwhile, add mushrooms to any drippings in skillet and stir-fry 2 minutes, or until lightly browned and tender. Add coleslaw mix, corn and vinegar; stir-fry 1 to 2 minutes until cabbage wilts. Stir in pork mixture; remove skillet from heat.

Remove tortillas to a wire rack (they'll get crisp). Spread with hoisin sauce and top with pork mixture. Sprinkle with radishes and scallions. Serve immediately.

PER SERVING
CALORIES 440 **TOTAL FAT** 6G **SATURATED FAT** 1G **CHOLESTEROL** 55MG **SODIUM** 1,449MG
TOTAL CARBOHYDRATES 68G **DIETARY FIBER** 4G **PROTEIN** 26G

LEMON LAMB CHOPS WITH COUSCOUS PILAF

YIELD
4 servings

ACTIVE
4 minutes

TOTAL
10 minutes

2 TSP **SALT-FREE LEMON AND PEPPER SEASONING** (MCCORMICK)

2½ TSP **GROUND CUMIN**

4 **SHOULDER LAMB CHOPS**, ¾ IN. THICK

2 TSP **OLIVE OIL**

1 CAN (15.5 OZ) **CHICKPEAS**, RINSED

1 CAN (14.5 OZ) **DICED TOMATOES WITH SWEET ONION**

1 CUP WATER

1 BOX (5.8 OZ) **ROASTED GARLIC & OLIVE OIL COUSCOUS MIX**

2 TBSP CHOPPED **FRESH MINT**

Mix lemon pepper seasoning and 2 tsp ground cumin in small cup; rub on both sides of lamb chops.

Heat oil in nonstick skillet over medium-high heat. Brown chops 3 minutes per side for medium doneness.

Meanwhile, heat chickpeas, tomatoes, water, couscous spice packet and remaining ½ tsp cumin in 2-qt saucepan until boiling. Stir in couscous, cover and remove from heat. Let stand 5 minutes; stir in mint.

PER SERVING
CALORIES 645 **TOTAL FAT** 26G **SATURATED FAT** 9G **CHOLESTEROL** 109MG **SODIUM** 668MG
TOTAL CARBOHYDRATES 64G **DIETARY FIBER** 8G **PROTEIN** 39G

TUSCAN CHICKEN & BEAN STEW

- ¼ CUP **ALL-PURPOSE FLOUR**
- ¼ TSP EACH **SALT** AND **PEPPER**
- 1 PKG (ABOUT 2 LB) **CHICKEN THIGHS**, SKINS REMOVED
- 2 TSP **OIL**
- 1 MEDIUM **ONION**, DICED
- 2 **CARROTS**, CUT INTO ½-IN. CHUNKS
- 2 CLOVES **GARLIC**, FINELY CHOPPED
- 1 CAN (14.5 OZ) **DICED TOMATOES**, DRAINED
- 1 CAN (14.5 OZ) **REDUCED-SODIUM CHICKEN BROTH**
- 1 CAN (19 OZ) **CANNELLINI BEANS**, RINSED AND DRAINED

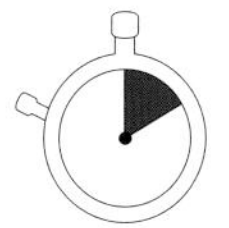

YIELD
4 servings

ACTIVE
10 minutes

TOTAL
35 minutes

Heat oven to 350°F. In a bowl, combine flour with salt and pepper. Coat chicken in flour mixture. Heat oil in Dutch oven. Add chicken and brown. Remove chicken to a plate.

Stir onion and carrots into Dutch oven with drippings. Cook, stirring, 4 minutes or until onions soften. Add garlic and cook 1 minute. Stir in diced tomatoes and top with chicken. Pour broth over chicken; bring liquid to a boil. Cover and cook in oven 20 minutes.

Mash some of the beans and stir into Dutch oven. Cover and cook for another 10 minutes, or until chicken is done.

PER SERVING
CALORIES 351 **TOTAL FAT** 8G **SATURATED FAT** 2G **CHOLESTEROL** 107MG **SODIUM** 869MG
TOTAL CARBOHYDRATES 34G **DIETARY FIBER** 7G **PROTEIN** 33G

WASABI SALMON

YIELD
4 servings

ACTIVE
5 minutes

TOTAL
15 minutes

¼ CUP **PANKO CRUMBS**

¼ CUP **WASABI-SOY ALMONDS**, CHOPPED

2 TSP **OIL**

4 **SALMON FILLETS**, 6 OZ EACH

¼ TSP **SALT**

SIDE SUGGESTION
Brown rice, soy sauce, snow peas

Heat oven to 425°F. Line a shallow baking pan with foil.

In small bowl, toss panko crumbs, chopped almonds and oil.

Place salmon, skin side down, on prepared baking pan. Sprinkle with salt. Evenly pat 2 Tbsp crumb mixture onto top of each fillet. Bake 10 to 12 minutes until fish is just cooked through and topping is browned.

PER SERVING
CALORIES 373 **TOTAL FAT** 20G **SATURATED FAT** 2G **CHOLESTEROL** 108MG **SODIUM** 276MG
TOTAL CARBOHYDRATES 7G **DIETARY FIBER** 1G **PROTEIN** 41G

FUSILLI WITH ASPARAGUS & PEAS

12 OZ **LONG FUSILLI PASTA**

1 LB **ASPARAGUS** (1 BUNCH), TRIMMED AND CUT INTO BITE-SIZE PIECES

4 OZ **SUGAR SNAP PEAS**, TRIMMED AND HALVED

1 CUP **FROZEN PEAS**

1½ TBSP **OLIVE OIL**

¾ CUP MINCED **SHALLOTS**

¼ TSP EACH **SALT** AND **PEPPER**

1 CUP **REDUCED-SODIUM CHICKEN BROTH**

1 TSP GRATED **LEMON ZEST**

⅓ CUP **GRATED PARMESAN**

YIELD
4 servings

ACTIVE
10 minutes

TOTAL
20 minutes

Bring a 5- to 6-qt pot of salted water to a boil. Add pasta and cook as package directs, adding asparagus and sugar snaps 3 minutes before pasta will be done, and peas 2 minutes before done. Drain pasta and vegetable mixture.

While pasta cooks, heat oil in a 10- to 12-in. nonstick skillet over medium heat. Add shallots, salt and pepper; sauté 5 minutes until tender. Add broth; heat.

Return pasta and vegetable mixture to pasta pot. Add shallot mixture and lemon zest; gently toss to mix and coat. Toss with Parmesan and serve.

PER SERVING
CALORIES 455 **TOTAL FAT** 8G **SATURATED FAT** 2G **CHOLESTEROL** 6MG **SODIUM** 528MG **TOTAL CARBOHYDRATES** 78G **DIETARY FIBER** 6G **PROTEIN** 19G

SMOKED PORK CHOPS WITH CABBAGE & APPLES

1 TSP **OIL**

4 WELL-TRIMMED, 1-IN.-THICK **SMOKED BONE-IN PORK CHOPS** (ABOUT 2 LB)

1 LARGE **RED ONION**, SLICED

4 CUPS SHREDDED **GREEN CABBAGE**

½ CUP EACH **APPLE CIDER OR JUICE** AND **CHICKEN BROTH**

¼ TSP EACH **SALT** AND **PEPPER**

¼ TSP **CARAWAY SEEDS** (OPTIONAL)

1 **GALA APPLE**, QUARTERED, CORED, CUT IN ½-IN.-THICK WEDGES, WEDGES HALVED

2 TBSP SNIPPED **FRESH DILL**

2 TSP **CIDER VINEGAR**

YIELD
4 servings

ACTIVE
10 minutes

TOTAL
28 minutes

Heat oil in a large nonstick skillet. Add chops and cook, turning once, 5 minutes or until browned. Remove.

Add onion to skillet; sauté 3 minutes or until golden. Add cabbage, cider, broth, salt, pepper and caraway seeds, if desired; cook, stirring often, 5 minutes or until cabbage is almost tender. Stir in apple; cook 3 minutes, stirring often, until apple is almost tender. Place chops on top.

Cover and cook over low heat 2 minutes or until cabbage and apple are tender and chops are heated through. Remove chops to plates or platter. Stir dill and vinegar into cabbage mixture. Serve with the chops.

PER SERVING
CALORIES 272 **TOTAL FAT** 12G **SATURATED FAT** 4G **CHOLESTEROL** 78MG **SODIUM** 513MG
TOTAL CARBOHYDRATES 16G **DIETARY FIBER** 3G **PROTEIN** 25G

VEGGIE-STUFFED SHELLS

- 1 BOX (12 OZ) **JUMBO PASTA SHELLS**
- 2 TSP **OLIVE OIL**
- ½ BUNCH **BROCCOLI** (7 OZ), CHOPPED (2½ CUPS)
- 1 CUP SHREDDED **CARROTS** (4 OZ)
- 1 SMALL **ONION** (4 OZ), CHOPPED
- 1 CLOVE **GARLIC**, MINCED
- 1 BOX (10 OZ) **FROZEN LEAF SPINACH**, THAWED AND COARSELY CUT
- ¼ CUP CHOPPED **FRESH BASIL**
- 1 CUP **LOWFAT SMALL-CURD COTTAGE CHEESE (2%)** *OR* **PART-SKIM RICOTTA**
- 2 TBSP **GRATED PARMESAN**
- ¼ TSP EACH **SALT** AND **PEPPER**
- 1½ CUPS **MARINARA SAUCE**
- ½ CUP **SHREDDED PART-SKIM MOZZARELLA**

YIELD
6 servings

ACTIVE
30 minutes

TOTAL
1 hour 5 minutes

Heat oven to 400°F. Cook pasta in large pot of salted boiling water, drain and cool on baking sheet as box directs.

Meanwhile, heat oil in large skillet over medium-high heat. Sauté broccoli, carrots, onion and garlic 3 minutes or until just tender. Add spinach and ½ cup water; cover and cook 2 minutes or until vegetables are tender.

Remove cover; cook until liquid is mostly evaporated. Remove from heat; stir in basil, cottage cheese, Parmesan, salt and pepper. Spread marinara sauce on bottom of 13 x 9-in. baking dish.

Spoon 1 rounded Tbsp filling into each shell; arrange in baking dish. Sprinkle with mozzarella, cover tightly with foil, and bake 35 minutes until hot and bubbly.

PER SERVING
CALORIES 382 **TOTAL FAT** 8G **SATURATED FAT** 1G **CHOLESTEROL** 11MG **SODIUM** 742MG **TOTAL CARBOHYDRATES** 60G **DIETARY FIBER** 7G **PROTEIN** 20G

GRILLED CHICKEN BREASTS WITH MOLE SAUCE

YIELD
4 servings

ACTIVE
15 minutes

TOTAL
1 hour

1½ TSP **GROUND CUMIN**

1 TSP **GROUND CORIANDER**

½ TSP FRESHLY GROUND **PEPPER**

¼ TSP **SALT**

4 **BONELESS, SKINLESS CHICKEN BREASTS** (5 OZ EACH)

1 TBSP **OLIVE OIL**

½ CUP CHOPPED **ONION**

1 LARGE **FRESH JALAPEÑO PEPPER**, MINCED, WITH SOME OF THE SEEDS (1 TBSP)

1½ TSP MINCED **GARLIC**

3 TBSP **UNSALTED PUMPKIN SEEDS**

⅛ TSP **GROUND CINNAMON**

1 CUP **CHICKEN BROTH**

⅓ CUP **CANNED CRUSHED TOMATOES**

¼ SQUARE (0.75 OZ) **UNSWEETENED CHOCOLATE**

GARNISH: **UNSALTED PUMPKIN SEEDS**

In a small heavy skillet, cook cumin and coriander over medium heat, stirring often, 2 to 4 minutes until fragrant and darker in color. Immediately tip out onto a plate to stop cooking. Put 1 tsp into a cup. Stir in ¼ tsp of the pepper and ⅛ tsp of the salt. Sprinkle mixture over both sides of chicken. Cover and refrigerate while making the sauce.

Heat oil in a heavy medium saucepan over medium heat. Add onion, jalapeño pepper and garlic, and cook 2 to 3 minutes, stirring often, until onion softens.

Add pumpkin seeds, cinnamon, the remaining toasted spices and remaining ¼ tsp pepper and ⅛ tsp salt. Cook and stir 1 minute until fragrant.

Stir in chicken broth and tomatoes. Bring to a boil, reduce heat and simmer uncovered, stirring occasionally, 15 minutes or until slightly thickened and flavors are blended. Remove from heat and stir in chocolate until melted.

Cool, then pour into food processor or blender and process until smooth. Strain back into saucepan. (Can be made ahead up to this point and refrigerated up to 3 days.)

Heat broiler, broiler pan and rack, or barbecue grill. Broil or grill chicken 4 to 5 inches from heat source, 4 to 5 minutes per side until no longer pink in center. Transfer to a warmed serving platter.

Reheat sauce and spoon over chicken. Sprinkle with pumpkin seeds.

NOTE If you can, make the sauce ahead so the flavor can mellow, and serve the finished dish with rice.

PER SERVING
CALORIES 235 **TOTAL FAT** 7G **SATURATED FAT** 0G **CHOLESTEROL** 82MG **SODIUM** 513MG
TOTAL CARBOHYDRATES 6G **DIETARY FIBER** 0G **PROTEIN** 35G

CHINESE CHICKEN & NOODLE SALAD

NOODLES

8 OZ **LINGUINE**

4 OZ **FRESH SNOW PEAS**, ENDS SNIPPED

1½ CUPS SHREDDED **COOKED CHICKEN**

1 **KIRBY CUCUMBER**, HALVED CROSSWISE, CUT LENGTHWISE IN THIN STICKS

½ CUP EACH SHREDDED **CARROT** AND SLICED **SCALLIONS**

DRESSING

½ CUP **BOTTLED ASIAN SALAD DRESSING**

2 TBSP EACH **PEANUT BUTTER** AND **HOT WATER**

¼ TSP **CRUSHED RED PEPPER**

GARNISH: CHOPPED **UNSALTED PEANUTS** AND DICED **RED BELL PEPPER**

YIELD
4 servings

ACTIVE
18 minutes

TOTAL
18 minutes

Bring a large pot of lightly salted water to a boil. Add pasta and cook 6 minutes; add snow peas and cook 2 minutes longer or until pasta and snow peas are firm-tender. Drain; rinse with cold water and drain again.

Meanwhile, whisk dressing ingredients in a large bowl until blended.

Add pasta, snow peas and remaining ingredients to bowl. Toss to mix and coat. Garnish with peanuts and bell pepper.

PER SERVING
CALORIES 452 **TOTAL FAT** 14G **SATURATED FAT** 2G **CHOLESTEROL** 47MG **SODIUM** 729MG **TOTAL CARBOHYDRATES** 54G **DIETARY FIBER** 4G **PROTEIN** 26G

EASY PAELLA

- 2 TSP **OLIVE OIL**
- 8 OZ **TURKEY KIELBASA**, SLICED
- 1 CUP CHOPPED **ONION**
- 1 CUP UNCOOKED **CONVERTED WHITE RICE**
- 1 CAN (14.5 OZ) **CHICKEN BROTH**
- 12 OZ LARGE **SHRIMP**, PEELED AND DEVEINED
- 1 JAR (6 OZ) **SOFRITO SAUCE**
- ¾ CUP THAWED **FROZEN PETITE GREEN PEAS**
- ¼ CUP CHOPPED **FRESH PARSLEY**

YIELD
4 servings

ACTIVE
10 minutes

TOTAL
25 minutes

Heat oil in a large nonstick skillet over high heat. Add kielbasa and onion; sauté 3 minutes or until onion is golden.

Add rice, broth and ½ cup water. Bring to a boil, cover and cook 17 minutes until rice is almost tender.

Add shrimp; cover and cook 2 minutes. Stir in sofrito and peas; cook, stirring, 1 minute or until rice is tender and shrimp are cooked. Remove from heat; stir in parsley.

PER SERVING
CALORIES 443 TOTAL FAT 10G SATURATED FAT 3G CHOLESTEROL 135MG SODIUM 1462MG
TOTAL CARBOHYDRATES 57G DIETARY FIBER 4G PROTEIN 29G

FEBRUARY

FEBRUARY SHOPPING LIST

Week 1
FEBRUARY 1 TO FEBRUARY 7

PRODUCE
1 ORANGE
1 SMALL PINEAPPLE
1 LEMON
2 LIMES
6 ONIONS
1 RED ONION
2 HEADS GARLIC (11 CLOVES)
2 MEDIUM YELLOW TOMATOES
2 LARGE CARROTS
1 RED BELL PEPPER
1 GREEN BELL PEPPER
1 SEEDLESS CUCUMBER
12 OZ SHIITAKE MUSHROOMS
1 BUNCH PARSLEY
1 BUNCH CILANTRO

BAKERY
4 HERO ROLLS

MEAT/POULTRY/FISH
2 LB 12 OZ LEAN BEEF CHUCK, CUT FOR STEW
1 LB LEAN GROUND BEEF
4 LAMB SHANKS (12 TO 14 OZ EACH)
1 PKG (ABOUT 13 OZ) CHICKEN SAUSAGES
1 WHOLE SALMON FILLET (ABOUT 2½ LB)

DELI
1 SLICE (¾-IN.-THICK) DELI SMOKED TURKEY (ABOUT 12 OZ)

REFRIGERATED
GRATED PARMESAN
6 OZ PINEAPPLE OR ORANGE JUICE
1 CONTAINER (2 LB) MASHED POTATOES

FROZEN
1 BAG (16 OZ) MIXED VEGETABLES

GROCERY
3 CANS (14.5 OZ) CHICKEN BROTH
1 CAN (14.5 OZ) DICED TOMATOES
1 CAN (28 OZ) CHUNKY-STYLE TOMATOES IN PURÉE
1 CAN (6 OZ) TOMATO PASTE
1 CAN (4.5 OZ) CHOPPED GREEN CHILES
3 CANS (15 TO 16 OZ EACH) ROMAN OR PINTO BEANS
2 CANS (15.5 OZ EACH) CHICKPEAS
1 JAR (12 OZ) GRAVY (WE USED HEINZ BISTRO AU JUS)
½ CUP BARLEY (NOT QUICK-COOKING)
BULGUR
¼ CUP SMOOTH PEANUT BUTTER
CINNAMON CHIPOTLE RUB (MCCORMICK GRILL MATES)
PITTED PRUNES
DRIED APRICOT HALVES
SLICED ALMONDS
1 BEER (12 OZ), OPTIONAL

PANTRY
KOSHER SALT
SALT
PEPPER
OLIVE OIL
DRIED THYME
GROUND CUMIN
GROUND CINNAMON
GROUND GINGER
CHILI POWDER

Week 2
FEBRUARY 8 TO FEBRUARY 14

PRODUCE
3 LARGE NAVEL ORANGES
RED & GREEN GRAPES (OPTIONAL)
KUMQUATS (OPTIONAL)
3 ONIONS
1 RED ONION
1 HEAD GARLIC (6 CLOVES)
1 PIECE FRESH GINGER
1 CUP GRAPE OR CHERRY TOMATOES
1 LARGE ZUCCHINI AND/OR YELLOW SQUASH (12 OZ)
1 MEDIUM ZUCCHINI
1 MEDIUM YELLOW SQUASH
1 SEEDLESS CUCUMBER
1 AVOCADO
1 BAG (6 OZ) RED RADISHES
¾ CUP SNOW PEAS
6 SCALLIONS
1 BAG (4 OZ) BABY ARUGULA OR 1 BAG (5 OZ) BABY SPINACH
1 CONTAINER ALFALFA SPROUTS
1 BUNCH MINT
1 BUNCH SAGE
1 BUNCH PARSLEY
FRESH ROSEMARY

BAKERY
4 HAMBURGER BUNS
8 SLICES MULTIGRAIN BREAD

MEAT/POULTRY/FISH
ONE 6-LB BONE-IN PORK CENTER LOIN ROAST (ABOUT ¾ IN. THICK)
1 LB CHICKEN TENDERS
12 OZ SLICED, COOKED CHICKEN (ABOUT 2 COOKED SKINLESS, BONELESS CHICKEN BREASTS)
12 OZ HOT OR SWEET ITALIAN SAUSAGE
FOUR 6-OZ STRIPED BASS, BLACK COD OR MAHI-MAHI FILLETS

DELI
8 OZ THICKLY SLICED DELI ROAST BEEF

REFRIGERATED
½ STICK BUTTER
GRATED PARMESAN
EGG (1 LARGE)
WHITE HORSERADISH

GROCERY
1 CAN (14 OZ) ROASTED GARLIC-FLAVORED CHICKEN BROTH
1 CAN (8 OZ) TOMATO SAUCE
2 CANS (15 TO 16 OZ EACH) RED KIDNEY BEANS
2 CANS (19 OZ) CANNELLINI BEANS
12 OZ SPAGHETTINI PASTA
LIGHT MAYONNAISE
LITE SOY SAUCE
CAESAR-RANCH LIGHT MAYONNAISE
¼ CUP PANKO BREAD CRUMBS OR PLAIN DRIED BREAD CRUMBS

½ CUP PLAIN DRY BREAD CRUMBS
DRIED INSTANT MINCED ONION
1 PKG (3.75 OZ) CELLOPHANE NOODLES
¼ CUP PEANUTS (OPTIONAL)
DRY WHITE WINE (OPTIONAL)
1 CUP DRIED CHERRIES
½ CUP GOLDEN RAISINS
HONEY

PANTRY
KOSHER SALT
SALT
PEPPER
OLIVE OIL
NONSTICK SPRAY
WHITE VINEGAR
SUGAR
GROUND GINGER
DRIED SAGE

Week 3
FEBRUARY 15 TO FEBRUARY 22

PRODUCE
3 LIMES
1 LEMON
1 MEDIUM ONION
2 HEADS GARLIC (14 CLOVES)
1 PIECE FRESH GINGER
4 MEDIUM CARROTS
4 RED BELL PEPPERS
1 SMALL CUCUMBER
1 MEDIUM EGGPLANT
1 BAG (12 OZ) BROCCOLI FLORETS
2 BUNCHES BROCCOLINI (ABOUT 1 LB)
1 AVOCADO
1 BAG (6 OZ) RED RADISHES
1 PKG (8 OR 10 OZ) WHOLE MUSHROOMS
12 OZ ASSORTED MUSHROOMS OR WHITE MUSHROOMS
1 HEAD BOSTON LETTUCE
5 OZ ASIAN OR OTHER SALAD BLEND
4 CUPS (6 OZ) COLESLAW MIX
6 SCALLIONS
1 BUNCH CILANTRO
1 BUNCH PARSLEY
1 BUNCH MINT

MEAT/POULTRY/FISH
4 CHICKEN THIGHS
4 DRUMSTICKS
2 CUPS (8 OZ) COOKED CHICKEN, SHREDDED
3 LINKS ITALIAN TURKEY SAUSAGE (ABOUT 10 OZ)
1½ LB SKINNED SALMON, HALIBUT, TILAPIA OR FLOUNDER FILLETS

DELI
1 ROTISSERIE CHICKEN

REFRIGERATED
¼ CUP PLAIN GREEK YOGURT
1 CUP SKIM RICOTTA
4 OZ PART-SKIM MOZZARELLA
4 OZ PEPPERJACK CHEESE
GRATED PARMESAN
EGGS (8 LARGE)

FROZEN
1 BAG (16 OZ) POTATO GNOCCHI

GROCERY
1 CAN (14.5 OZ) FAT-FREE CHICKEN BROTH
1 CAN (28 OZ) CRUSHED TOMATOES IN THICK PURÉE
1 JAR (26 OZ) MARINARA SAUCE
1 BOX (1 LB) RIGATONI PASTA
1 BOX (1 LB) ZITI PASTA
EIGHT 6- TO 7-IN. CORN TORTILLAS
BOTTLED SALSA
BOTTLED GREEK SEASONING
RED CURRY PASTE
LOW-SODIUM SOY SAUCE
ASIAN SESAME DRESSING AND MARINADE
¼ CUP CASHEWS OR PEANUTS
1 CAN (8 OZ) SLICED WATER CHESTNUTS
½ CUP WHITE WINE (OPTIONAL)

PANTRY
SALT
PEPPER
OLIVE OIL
NONSTICK SPRAY
VEGETABLE OIL
SUGAR
CRUSHED RED PEPPER
DRIED ROSEMARY

Week 4
FEBRUARY 23 TO FEBRUARY 28

PRODUCE
1 LIME
2 LARGE ONIONS
1 RED ONION
1 HEAD GARLIC (4 CLOVES)
3 LB SMALL SWEET POTATOES
2 MEDIUM TOMATOES
2 KIRBY CUCUMBERS
1 YELLOW BELL PEPPER
7 CARROTS
1 LB PARSNIPS
3 RIBS CELERY
1 AVOCADO
½ SMALL RED CABBAGE
⅓ CUP FRESH CHIVES OR GREEN PART OF SCALLIONS
1 BUNCH CILANTRO
1 BUNCH PARSLEY
3 TBSP MIXED CHOPPED FRESH HERBS (SAGE, ROSEMARY AND THYME)

BAKERY
6 SEEDED HAMBURGER BUNS
4 PITAS

MEAT/POULTRY/FISH
1 OVEN-READY, TIED FILLET OF BEEF ROAST (4 LB)
1½ LB 1-IN. CUBES BEEF CHUCK
4 BONELESS, SKINLESS, CHICKEN BREASTS (5 OZ EACH)
1 PKG (12 OZ) PRECOOKED FAJITA-STYLE CHICKEN STRIPS
4 CUPS COOKED CHICKEN

REFRIGERATED
½ CUP BUTTERMILK
½ STICK BUTTER
¾ CUP PLAIN LOWFAT YOGURT
1 CUP REDUCED-FAT SOUR CREAM
1 CUP SHREDDED MEXICAN OR TACO CHEESE BLEND
1 LARGE (10 OZ) PREBAKED THIN-CRUST PIZZA CRUST
½ CUP CREAM-STYLE HORSERADISH SAUCE

FROZEN
1¼ CUPS SOUTHWESTERN CORN BLEND

GROCERY
2 CANS (ABOUT 14 OZ EACH) BEEF BROTH
1 CAN (6 OZ) CHUNK LIGHT TUNA IN OLIVE OIL
1 JAR (8.5 OZ) OLIVE SPREAD OR 1 CAN (7.5 OZ) EGGPLANT APPETIZER (CAPONATA)
¼ CUP CHOPPED PIMIENTO-STUFFED OLIVES (OPTIONAL)
¾ CUP TACO SAUCE
12 OZ SPAGHETTI PASTA
KETCHUP
YELLOW MUSTARD
WHOLE-GRAIN DIJON MUSTARD
HONEY MUSTARD
1 TBSP RAISINS

PANTRY
KOSHER SALT
SALT
PEPPER
OLIVE OIL
EXTRA-VIRGIN OLIVE OIL
VEGETABLE OIL
CIDER VINEGAR
SUGAR
FLOUR
GROUND CUMIN
CURRY POWDER

BEEF, SHIITAKE & BARLEY SOUP

YIELD
6 servings

ACTIVE
15 minutes

TOTAL
1 hour

3 TSP **OIL**, DIVIDED

12 OZ **LEAN BEEF CHUCK** FOR STEW, CUT INTO BITE-SIZE PIECES

1 LARGE **ONION**, CHOPPED

2 LARGE **CARROTS**, DICED

12 OZ **SHIITAKE MUSHROOMS**, STEMS DISCARDED AND CAPS SLICED

2 TSP MINCED **GARLIC**

4 CUPS **CHICKEN BROTH**

2 CUPS **WATER**

½ CUP **BARLEY** (NOT QUICK-COOKING)

¾ TSP **KOSHER SALT**, OR TO TASTE

¼ TSP FRESHLY GROUND **PEPPER**

Heat 1 tsp oil in a 5-qt pot over medium-high heat. Add beef; cook 4 to 5 minutes until browned. With slotted spoon, transfer beef to plate.

Add remaining 2 tsp oil to pot. Sauté onion and carrots 3 minutes. Add mushrooms and garlic; sauté 3 minutes more.

Return beef to pot. Add broth, water, barley, salt and pepper; bring to a boil. Reduce heat and simmer, covered, 30 minutes or until meat and barley are tender. Season with salt to taste.

PER SERVING
CALORIES 206 **TOTAL FAT** 8G **SATURATED FAT** 2G **CHOLESTEROL** 37MG **SODIUM** 640MG
TOTAL CARBOHYDRATES 19G **DIETARY FIBER** 5G **PROTEIN** 15G

CHICKEN SAUSAGE, PEPPER & ONION HEROS

YIELD
4 servings

ACTIVE
15 minutes

TOTAL
15 minutes

1 TBSP **OIL**

1 PKG (ABOUT 13 OZ) **CHICKEN SAUSAGES**

1 EACH **RED** AND **GREEN BELL PEPPER**

1 MEDIUM **ONION**

4 **HERO ROLLS**

Heat oil in a large nonstick skillet over medium-high heat. Arrange sausages on one side of pan, cover and cook 4 minutes. Meanwhile, cut peppers into thin strips. Add to other side of pan; cook 2 minutes.

While sausages cook, cut onion in half lengthwise, then in long, thin strips. Add to peppers; turn sausages. Cook all 6 minutes, stirring occasionally, until sausages are lightly charred and cooked through and vegetables are lightly browned and tender.

Place a sausage on each roll and top with pepper and onion.

PER SERVING
CALORIES 412 **TOTAL FAT** 20G **SATURATED FAT** 5G **CHOLESTEROL** 74MG **SODIUM** 1,335MG **TOTAL CARBOHYDRATES** 39G **DIETARY FIBER** 3G **PROTEIN** 20G

SHEPHERD'S PIE

1 LB **LEAN GROUND BEEF**

1 MEDIUM **ONION**, CHOPPED

2 CLOVES **GARLIC**, MINCED

1 TSP **DRIED THYME LEAVES**

¼ TSP **PEPPER**

3 CUPS **FROZEN MIXED VEGETABLES**

1 CAN (14.5 OZ) **DICED TOMATOES**, DRAINED

1 JAR (12 OZ) **GRAVY** (WE USED HEINZ BISTRO AU JUS)

1 CONTAINER (2 LB) **REFRIGERATED MASHED POTATOES**

2 TBSP **GRATED PARMESAN**

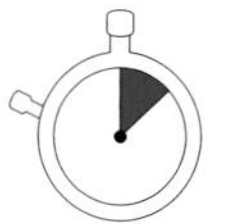

YIELD
5 servings

ACTIVE
8 minutes

TOTAL
18 minutes

Heat broiler. Heat ovenproof nonstick skillet over medium-high heat. Add ground beef, onion, garlic, thyme and pepper; cook, breaking up meat, 5 minutes or until browned. Stir in vegetables, tomatoes and gravy; simmer, covered, 5 minutes.

Meanwhile, heat potatoes in microwave as package directs. Drop spoonfuls of potatoes on top of beef mixture; sprinkle with Parmesan. Place under broiler for 3 to 5 minutes until topping is browned.

PER SERVING
CALORIES 549 **TOTAL FAT** 26G **SATURATED FAT** 12G **CHOLESTEROL** 89MG **SODIUM** 1,194MG
TOTAL CARBOHYDRATES 46G **DIETARY FIBER** 7G **PROTEIN** 25G

CITRUS-INFUSED SALMON

3 TBSP **CINNAMON CHIPOTLE RUB** (MCCORMICK GRILL MATES)

2 TSP GRATED **LIME ZEST**

1 TSP **GROUND CUMIN**

1 **WHOLE SALMON FILLET** (ABOUT 2½ LB)

¾ CUP (6 OZ) **PINEAPPLE** *OR* **ORANGE JUICE**

2 TBSP **LIME JUICE**

GARNISH: **PINEAPPLE** AND **LIME SLICES**, **FRESH PINEAPPLE LEAVES**

YIELD
8 servings

ACTIVE
5 minutes

TOTAL
25 minutes

Mix rub, lime zest and cumin in small bowl.

Put salmon in a large glass baking dish or 2-gallon ziptop bag. Add juices; cover or seal. Marinate 15 minutes at room temperature.

Heat oven to 450°F. Line a large rimmed baking sheet with foil. Place salmon skin-side down on foil; discard marinade. Evenly sprinkle spice mixture over salmon.

Bake salmon 15 to 20 minutes until opaque at thickest part. Lift with 2 large spatulas to serving platter, leaving skin behind.

PER SERVING
CALORIES 182 **TOTAL FAT** 5G **SATURATED FAT** 1G **CHOLESTEROL** 66MG **SODIUM** 352MG **TOTAL CARBOHYDRATES** 3G **DIETARY FIBER** 0G **PROTEIN** 28G

SMOKED TURKEY & BULGUR SALAD

1 CUP UNCOOKED **BULGUR**

2 CUPS BOILING **WATER**

1 SLICE (¾-IN.-THICK) **DELI SMOKED TURKEY** (ABOUT 12 OZ)

2 MEDIUM **YELLOW TOMATOES**

1 **SEEDLESS CUCUMBER**

½ SMALL **RED ONION**

⅓ CUPS CHOPPED **PARSLEY**

LEMON-CUMIN DRESSING

¼ CUP **LEMON JUICE**

2 TBSP **OLIVE OIL**

½ TSP **GROUND CUMIN**

¼ TSP EACH **SALT** AND **PEPPER**

YIELD
4 servings

ACTIVE
30 minutes

TOTAL
30 minutes

SIDE SUGGESTION
Hummus

Put bulgur in a medium bowl. Add boiling water; cover and let soak 30 minutes.

Meanwhile, cut smoked turkey into ¾-in. pieces and coarsely chop tomatoes. Cut cucumber lengthwise in quarters, then into ½-in. slices. Finely chop red onion. Gently mix turkey, tomatoes, cucumber, onion and parsley in a large bowl.

Meanwhile, make dressing: Whisk lemon juice, olive oil, cumin, salt and pepper in a small bowl until blended.

Drain bulgur well; add to turkey mixture. Toss with dressing until evenly coated.

PER SERVING
CALORIES 298 **TOTAL FAT** 10G **SATURATED FAT** 2G **CHOLESTEROL** 36MG **SODIUM** 961MG
TOTAL CARBOHYDRATES 36G **DIETARY FIBER** 8G **PROTEIN** 21G

MOROCCAN LAMB SHANKS

2 CANS (15.5 OZ EACH) **CHICKPEAS**, RINSED

1 CUP EACH **PITTED PRUNES** AND **DRIED APRICOT HALVES**

1 CUP FINELY CHOPPED **ONION**

1 TBSP MINCED **GARLIC**

1 CUP **CHICKEN BROTH**

¼ CUP **FRESH ORANGE JUICE**

1 TBSP FRESHLY GRATED **ORANGE ZEST**

½ TSP EACH **SALT**, **GROUND CINNAMON**, **CUMIN** AND **GROUND GINGER**

4 **LAMB SHANKS** (12 TO 14 OZ EACH)

GARNISH: TOASTED **SLICED ALMONDS** AND CHOPPED **PARSLEY**

YIELD
4 servings

ACTIVE
20 minutes

TOTAL
10 to 12 hours on low

SIDE SUGGESTION
Couscous

Mix all ingredients except lamb in an oval 5½-qt or larger slow cooker. Add lamb; spoon some mixture over shanks.

Cover and cook on low 10 to 12 hours until lamb is very tender.

Remove lamb to serving plates; spoon out chickpeas and fruit with a slotted spoon and add to plates. Pour liquid into a bowl, skim off fat and pour juices into a gravy boat. Serve with the lamb; garnish plates with almonds and parsley.

PER SERVING
CALORIES 850 **TOTAL FAT** 31G **SATURATED FAT** 11G **CHOLESTEROL** 196MG **SODIUM** 931MG **TOTAL CARBOHYDRATES** 74G **DIETARY FIBER** 12G **PROTEIN** 69G

CHUNKY BEEF CHILI

2 LB **LEAN BEEF CHUCK**, CUT FOR STEW

1 CAN (28 OZ) **CHUNKY-STYLE TOMATOES IN PURÉE**, UNDRAINED

1½ CUPS CHOPPED **ONIONS**

12 OZ **BEER** *OR* 1½ CUPS **WATER**

1 CAN (4.5 OZ) **CHOPPED GREEN CHILES**

¼ CUP **TOMATO PASTE**

3 TBSP **CHILI POWDER**

1½ TBSP MINCED **GARLIC**

2 TSP **GROUND CUMIN**

1¼ TSP **SALT**

¼ TSP **GROUND CINNAMON**

¼ CUP **SMOOTH PEANUT BUTTER**

3 CANS (15 TO 16 OZ EACH) **ROMAN OR PINTO BEANS**, RINSED

⅓ CUP CHOPPED **CILANTRO**

YIELD
8 servings

ACTIVE
10 minutes

TOTAL
7 to 9 hours on low

Mix all ingredients except peanut butter, beans and cilantro in a 4-qt or larger slow cooker.

Cover and cook on low 7 to 9 hours until beef is tender. Stir in peanut butter until blended, then stir in beans.

Cover and cook 5 minutes, or until beans are hot. Stir in cilantro.

SIDE SUGGESTION
Sour cream, chopped red onion, shredded Cheddar

PER SERVING
CALORIES 377 **TOTAL FAT** 14G **SATURATED FAT** 4G **CHOLESTEROL** 74MG **SODIUM** 1,145MG
TOTAL CARBOHYDRATES 32G **DIETARY FIBER** 8G **PROTEIN** 32G

ASIAN BEAN BURGERS

BURGERS

2 CANS (15 TO 16 OZ EACH) **RED KIDNEY BEANS**, RINSED

½ CUP **PLAIN DRY BREAD CRUMBS**

⅓ CUP MINCED **SCALLIONS**

1 LARGE **EGG**

1 TBSP **LITE SOY SAUCE**

1 TSP EACH **GROUND GINGER** AND **MINCED GARLIC**

1 TBSP **OIL**

SAUCE

¼ CUP **LIGHT MAYONNAISE**

1 TBSP **PREPARED WHITE HORSERADISH**

1 TBSP MINCED **SCALLIONS**

1 TSP **LITE SOY SAUCE**

4 **HAMBURGER BUNS**

LETTUCE AND SLICED **TOMATO** AND **CUCUMBER**

YIELD
4 servings

ACTIVE
10 minutes

TOTAL
18 minutes

SIDE SUGGESTION
Oven fries

BURGERS Mash beans in a medium bowl with a potato masher or fork. Stir in remaining burger ingredients until well blended. Form into 4 patties.

Heat oil in a large nonstick skillet over medium heat. Cook patties 3 to 4 minutes per side until heated through and crusty, and internal temperature registers 160°F on an instant-read thermometer inserted from side into middle.

SAUCE Mix ingredients in a small bowl.

Serve the burgers on buns with lettuce, tomato, cucumber and the sauce.

PER SERVING
CALORIES 436 **TOTAL FAT** 14G **SATURATED FAT** 2G **CHOLESTEROL** 58MG **SODIUM** 958MG **TOTAL CARBOHYDRATES** 59G **DIETARY FIBER** 10G **PROTEIN** 18G

TUSCAN BASS WITH SQUASH & BEANS

1 TBSP **OLIVE OIL**

1 CUP SLICED **ONION**

12 OZ **ZUCCHINI** *AND/OR* **YELLOW SQUASH**

2 CLOVES **GARLIC**, SLICED

1 CAN (19 OZ) **CANNELLINI BEANS**, RINSED AND DRAINED

1 CAN (8 OZ) **TOMATO SAUCE**

½ CUP **WATER**

1½ TSP CHOPPED **FRESH ROSEMARY**

¼ TSP **PEPPER**

FOUR 6-OZ **STRIPED BASS, BLACK COD** *OR* **MAHI-MAHI FILLETS** (ABOUT ¾ IN. THICK)

YIELD
4 servings

ACTIVE
10 minutes

TOTAL
22 minutes

Heat 1½ tsp of the oil in a large nonstick skillet. Add onion; sauté 3 minutes. Add squash; sauté 2 minutes. Add garlic; sauté 1 minute or until fragrant.

Add beans, tomato sauce, water, rosemary and pepper; stir and bring to a boil. Reduce heat; place fish on top. Cover and simmer 7 to 8 minutes until fish is just cooked through.

Spoon bean mixture on plates; top with fish. Drizzle with remaining 1½ tsp olive oil.

PER SERVING
CALORIES 340 **TOTAL FAT** 8G **SATURATED FAT** 1G **CHOLESTEROL** 136MG **SODIUM** 632MG
TOTAL CARBOHYDRATES 28G **DIETARY FIBER** 8G **PROTEIN** 37G

CALIFORNIA CHICKEN SANDWICH

YIELD
4 servings

ACTIVE
8 minutes

TOTAL
8 minutes

8 SLICES **MULTIGRAIN BREAD**

½ CUP **BOTTLED CAESAR-RANCH LIGHT MAYONNAISE**

12 OZ SLICED **COOKED CHICKEN** (ABOUT 2 COOKED SKINLESS, BONELESS CHICKEN BREASTS)

1 **AVOCADO**, SLICED

1 **RED ONION**, SLICED

1 CUP **RED RADISHES**, SLICED

1 CUP **ALFALFA SPROUTS**

SIDE SUGGESTION
Baked potato chips

Spread multigrain bread slices with Caesar-ranch light mayonnaise.

Top each of 4 slices with ¼ of the chicken, ¼ of a thinly sliced avocado, 1 thin slice red onion, ¼ cup red radishes and ¼ cup alfalfa sprouts.

Cover with rest of bread.

PER SERVING
CALORIES 471 **TOTAL FAT** 23G **SATURATED FAT** 4G **CHOLESTEROL** 92MG **SODIUM** 592MG **TOTAL CARBOHYDRATES** 36G **DIETARY FIBER** 6G **PROTEIN** 34G

"FRIED" CHICKEN FINGERS WITH VEGETABLE SAUTÉ

CHICKEN FINGERS

¼ CUP **PANKO BREAD CRUMBS** (SEE NOTE) *OR* **PLAIN DRIED BREAD CRUMBS**

2 TSP **GRATED PARMESAN**

2 TSP **DRIED INSTANT MINCED ONION**

¼ TSP **SALT**

1 LB **CHICKEN TENDERS**

NONSTICK SPRAY

VEGETABLE SAUTÉ

1 TBSP **OLIVE OIL**

1 EACH MEDIUM **ZUCCHINI** AND **YELLOW SQUASH**, SLICED

1 CUP **GRAPE** *OR* **CHERRY TOMATOES**

1 TSP MINCED **GARLIC**

⅛ TSP EACH **SALT** AND **PEPPER**

YIELD
4 servings

ACTIVE
15 minutes

TOTAL
25 minutes

NOTE
Coarse, white panko bread crumbs are used in Japanese cooking for coating food before frying. Look for them in the Asian or bread crumb section of your supermarket.

CHICKEN FINGERS Place oven rack in lowest position. Heat oven to 475°F. Line a rimmed baking sheet with nonstick foil.

On a sheet of wax paper, mix crumbs, cheese, instant onion and salt. Press tenders in mixture to coat. Place on lined sheet. Coat chicken with nonstick spray.

Bake 7 minutes or until bottoms of tenders turn light golden. Remove baking sheet from oven; turn chicken and coat with nonstick spray. Bake 5 minutes more, until golden and cooked through.

VEGETABLE SAUTÉ While chicken bakes, heat oil in a large nonstick skillet over medium-high heat. Add squashes and sauté 5 minutes or until lightly colored and crisp-tender. Add remaining ingredients; sauté 1 minute or until garlic is fragrant and tomatoes are hot.

PER SERVING
CALORIES 210 **TOTAL FAT** 7G **SATURATED FAT** 1G **CHOLESTEROL** 66MG **SODIUM** 324MG
TOTAL CARBOHYDRATES 8G **DIETARY FIBER** 1G **PROTEIN** 29G

THAI BEEF & NOODLE SALAD

YIELD
4 servings

ACTIVE
15 minutes

TOTAL
15 minutes

1 PACKAGE (3.75 OZ) **CELLOPHANE NOODLES**

¾ CUP HALVED **SNOW PEAS**

4 CUPS **BOILING WATER**

¼ CUP **WHITE VINEGAR**

2 TBSP **SUGAR**

1 TSP GRATED **GINGER**

½ TSP **KOSHER SALT**

8 OZ **THICKLY SLICED DELI ROAST BEEF**, CUT IN STRIPS

1½ CUPS SLICED **SEEDLESS CUCUMBER**

½ CUP SLICED **FRESH MINT**

¼ CUP CHOPPED **PEANUTS** (OPTIONAL)

Put noodles and snow peas in a large bowl. Pour in boiling water and let sit 10 minutes until noodles are tender. Drain; rinse under cold running water and drain again. Shake colander to remove excess water, then return to bowl.

Combine vinegar, sugar, ginger and salt in a jar; shake to dissolve sugar.

Pour dressing over noodles and snow peas; add remaining ingredients (except peanuts) and toss to coat. Sprinkle each serving with peanuts if desired.

PER SERVING
CALORIES 200 **TOTAL FAT** 2G **SATURATED FAT** 1G **CHOLESTEROL** 25MG **SODIUM** 536MG
TOTAL CARBOHYDRATES 34G **DIETARY FIBER** 2G **PROTEIN** 12G

WHITE BEANS, SAUSAGE & ARUGULA PASTA

YIELD
4 servings

ACTIVE
5 minutes

TOTAL
15 minutes

12 OZ **SPAGHETTINI PASTA**

12 OZ **HOT** *OR* **SWEET ITALIAN SAUSAGE**, CASING REMOVED

1 MEDIUM **ONION**, QUARTERED, THINLY SLICED

1 CAN (14 OZ) **ROASTED GARLIC-FLAVORED CHICKEN BROTH**

1 CAN (19 OZ) **CANNELLINI BEANS**, RINSED

1 BAG (4 OZ) **BABY ARUGULA** *OR* 1 BAG (5 OZ) **BABY SPINACH**

GARNISH: **GRATED PARMESAN**

Cook pasta in a large pot of lightly salted boiling water as package directs. Drain; return to pot.

Meanwhile, heat a large nonstick skillet over medium-high heat. Add sausage and onion and, breaking up sausage with a wooden spoon, sauté 6 minutes or until no longer pink. Add broth and beans; bring to a boil. Reduce heat; simmer 3 minutes to blend flavors.

Pour over pasta, add arugula and toss to mix and coat. Top with Parmesan.

PER SERVING
CALORIES 748 **TOTAL FAT** 29G **SATURATED FAT** 10G **CHOLESTEROL** 66MG **SODIUM** 1,256MG **TOTAL CARBOHYDRATES** 89G **DIETARY FIBER** 10G **PROTEIN** 31G

PORK LOIN WITH CHERRY-ORANGE COMPOTE

YIELD
12 servings

ACTIVE
35 minutes

TOTAL
2 hours 35 minutes

RUB

2 TBSP **ZEST GRATED FROM 3 LARGE NAVEL ORANGES** (RESERVE ORANGES)

¼ CUP MINCED **GARLIC**

2 TBSP **DRIED SAGE**

1 TBSP **OIL**

1½ TSP EACH **SALT** AND FRESHLY GROUND **BLACK PEPPER**

6-LB **BONE-IN PORK CENTER LOIN ROAST** (SEE TIP)

FRUIT COMPOTE

3 TBSP **BUTTER**

1 CUP FINELY CHOPPED **ONION**

1 CUP **DRY WHITE WINE** *OR* **FRESH ORANGE JUICE**

1 CUP **DRIED CHERRIES**

½ CUP **GOLDEN RAISINS**

2 TBSP **HONEY**

¼ TSP **SALT**

RESERVED 3 ORANGES

GARNISH: SPRIGS OF **SAGE** AND **PARSLEY**, **RED AND GREEN GRAPES**, AND **KUMQUATS**

Place oven rack in lowest position. Heat oven to 350°F.

RUB Mix ingredients in a small bowl. Press mixture firmly onto pork.

Place pork, bones up, on a rack in a shallow roasting pan. Roast 2 hours or until a meat thermometer inserted into center of meat, not touching bone, registers 150°F for medium, 160°F for well-done.

While pork roasts, make **COMPOTE**: Melt butter in a medium saucepan. Add onion; sauté until transluscent. Add wine, cherries, raisins, honey and salt. Bring to a boil; reduce heat, cover and simmer gently 15 minutes or until fruits are soft. Remove pan from heat.

Cut off white part and any peel remaining on reserved oranges. Holding oranges over a bowl, cut between membranes to release sections. Squeeze juices from membranes into bowl; cover and reserve.

When pork is done, place on a large serving platter; cover loosely with foil and let rest 15 minutes (temperature will continue to rise 5 to 10°F).

Add ½ cup water to roasting pan. Place pan over 2 burners and stir, scraping up browned bits on bottom. Pour into a small bowl or 1- to 2-cup glass measure. Let stand until fat rises to top. Skim fat off to reserve drippings on bottom.

Stir drippings, the oranges and juice into compote. Heat over medium-low heat (don't boil or orange sections will break up).

Garnish platter with herbs and fruit; serve compote from a bowl.

TIP Have your butcher crack the roast's chine (backbone) and, for an elegant presentation, french the ribs (trim meat from ends of bone).

PER SERVING
CALORIES 432 **TOTAL FAT** 21G **SATURATED FAT** 8G **CHOLESTEROL** 109MG **SODIUM** 451MG **TOTAL CARBOHYDRATES** 23G **DIETARY FIBER** 2G **PROTEIN** 34G

THAI FISH CAKES

SWEET & SOUR SAUCE

4 TBSP **LIME JUICE**

1 TBSP EACH **LOW-SODIUM SOY SAUCE** AND **SUGAR**

¼ TSP **CRUSHED RED PEPPER**

FISH CAKES

½ MEDIUM **RED BELL PEPPER**

⅓ CUP PACKED **FRESH CILANTRO**

1 CLOVE **GARLIC**

1 SLICE (½ IN. THICK) **FRESH GINGER**

2 TSP **RED CURRY PASTE**

1 TSP EACH GRATED **LIME ZEST** AND **SUGAR**

1½ LB **SKINNED SALMON, HALIBUT, TILAPIA** *OR* **FLOUNDER FILLETS**, CUT IN CHUNKS

1 TBSP **VEGETABLE OIL**

YIELD
4 servings

ACTIVE
20 minutes

TOTAL
25 minutes

SIDE SUGGESTION
Riçe noodles

SAUCE Stir all ingredients in a small bowl until well blended.

FISH CAKES Pulse all ingredients except fish and oil in food processor until just blended. Add fish; pulse until fish is just blended.

Shape level ¼-cupfuls fish mixture into twelve 3-in. patties. (At this point, fish cakes may be refrigerated, loosely covered, up to 4 hours.)

Heat oil in large nonstick skillet over medium-high heat. Cook fish cakes in two batches, 1 minute on each side, or until just cooked through. Drain on paper towels. Drizzle fish cakes with Sweet & Sour Sauce.

PER SERVING
CALORIES 304 **TOTAL FAT** 14G **SATURATED FAT** 2G **CHOLESTEROL** 93MG **SODIUM** 260MG
TOTAL CARBOHYDRATES 8G **DIETARY FIBER** 1G **PROTEIN** 35G

RIGATONI BOLOGNESE

1 BOX (1 LB) **RIGATONI PASTA**

2 MEDIUM **CARROTS** (4 OZ), HALVED

1 MEDIUM **ONION** (6 OZ), QUARTERED

1 PKG (8 OR 10 OZ) **WHOLE MUSHROOMS**

2 CLOVES **GARLIC**, PEELED

2 TSP **OLIVE OIL**

3 LINKS **ITALIAN TURKEY SAUSAGE** (ABOUT 10 OZ), CASINGS REMOVED

½ TSP CRUSHED **ROSEMARY**

¼ TSP EACH **SALT** AND **PEPPER**

½ CUP **WHITE WINE** (OPTIONAL)

1 CAN (28 OZ) **CRUSHED TOMATOES IN THICK PURÉE**

YIELD
6 servings

ACTIVE
20 minutes

TOTAL
35 minutes

Cook pasta in a large pot of salted boiling water as box directs. Meanwhile, put carrots, onion, mushrooms and garlic in a food processor; pulse until finely chopped.

Heat oil in a large nonstick skillet over medium-high heat. Sauté chopped vegetables 6 minutes.

Add turkey sausage and cook, breaking up clumps, 4 minutes or until no longer pink. Stir in rosemary, salt, pepper and wine, if using; boil 1 minute.

Stir in crushed tomatoes, reduce heat and simmer, covered, 5 minutes. Spoon over drained pasta.

PER SERVING
CALORIES 460 **TOTAL FAT** 8G **SATURATED FAT** 2G **CHOLESTEROL** 25MG **SODIUM** 698MG
TOTAL CARBOHYDRATES 75G **DIETARY FIBER** 5G **PROTEIN** 22G

SESAME CHICKEN SALAD

$\frac{1}{3}$ CUP **ASIAN SESAME DRESSING AND MARINADE**

2 TBSP **FRESH LIME JUICE**

2 CUPS (8 OZ) **COOKED CHICKEN**, SHREDDED

4 CUPS (6 OZ) **COLESLAW MIX**

1 SMALL **CUCUMBER**, HALVED LENGTHWISE, SEEDS SCRAPED OUT, THINLY SLICED

1 SMALL **RED BELL PEPPER**, QUARTERED AND CUT IN NARROW STRIPS

$\frac{1}{4}$ CUP COARSELY CHOPPED **FRESH CILANTRO**

$\frac{1}{4}$ CUP COARSELY CHOPPED **FRESH MINT LEAVES**

5 OZ **ASIAN OR OTHER SALAD BLEND**

$\frac{1}{4}$ CUP **CASHEWS** *OR* **PEANUTS**, CHOPPED

YIELD
4 servings

ACTIVE
15 minutes

TOTAL
15 minutes

Whisk dressing and lime juice in a large bowl. Add chicken, coleslaw, cucumber, pepper, cilantro and mint; toss to mix and coat.

Serve over greens; sprinkle with nuts.

PER SERVING
CALORIES 248 **TOTAL FAT** 11G **SATURATED FAT** 2G **CHOLESTEROL** 63MG **SODIUM** 832MG **TOTAL CARBOHYDRATES** 23G **DIETARY FIBER** 3G **PROTEIN** 19G

STOVETOP ZITI

YIELD
6 servings

ACTIVE
10 minutes

TOTAL
25 minutes

1 LB **ZITI PASTA**

1 BAG (12 OZ) **BROCCOLI FLORETS**

SAUCE

1 JAR (26 OZ) **MARINARA SAUCE**

1 CUP **SKIM RICOTTA**

4 OZ **PART-SKIM MOZZARELLA**, DICED

⅓ CUP CHOPPED **FRESH PARSLEY**

¼ CUP **GRATED PARMESAN**

Cook pasta in a large pot of lightly salted boiling water as package directs, adding broccoli 4 minutes before pasta is done.

Mix marinara sauce and about ½ the ricotta in a large saucepan. Cook over medium-low heat until hot.

Drain pasta and broccoli; return to pot. Add sauce mixture; toss to mix and coat. Immediately add mozzarella and about ½ the parsley and Parmesan. Stir until mozzarella melts.

Transfer to serving bowl; sprinkle with remaining parsley and Parmesan. Top with dollops of remaining ricotta.

PER SERVING
CALORIES 478 **TOTAL FAT** 10G **SATURATED FAT** 3G **CHOLESTEROL** 14MG **SODIUM** 1,257MG
TOTAL CARBOHYDRATES 74G **DIETARY FIBER** 5G **PROTEIN** 25G

ASIAN CHICKEN SALAD LETTUCE CUPS

YIELD
4 servings

ACTIVE
12 minutes

TOTAL
12 minutes

1 **DELI ROTISSERIE CHICKEN**

1 CUP SHREDDED **CARROTS**

1 CAN (8 OZ) **SLICED WATER CHESTNUTS**, HALVED

6 **SCALLIONS**, DIAGONALLY SLICED

¼ CUP **PLAIN GREEK YOGURT**

¼ CUP **ASIAN SESAME SALAD DRESSING**

1 HEAD **BOSTON LETTUCE**, SEPARATED INTO LEAVES

GARNISH: **CRUSHED RED PEPPER** (OPTIONAL)

Remove and discard chicken skin and pull meat off bones. Tear or cut meat into bite-size pieces. Place in a large bowl with carrots, water chestnuts and scallions.

In a small bowl, whisk yogurt with salad dressing; toss with chicken mixture.

Spoon into lettuce leaves. Sprinkle with hot pepper flakes, if desired.

PER SERVING
CALORIES 236 **TOTAL FAT** 8G **SATURATED FAT** 2G **CHOLESTEROL** 67MG **SODIUM** 578MG
TOTAL CARBOHYDRATES 16G **DIETARY FIBER** 4G **PROTEIN** 28G

HUEVOS RANCHEROS

YIELD
4 servings

ACTIVE
10 minutes

TOTAL
20 minutes

EIGHT 6- TO 7-IN. **CORN TORTILLAS**

NONSTICK COOKING SPRAY

1 TSP **VEGETABLE OIL**

8 LARGE **EGGS**

4 OZ **MONTEREY JACK CHEESE WITH JALAPEÑO PEPPERS** (ALSO CALLED PEPPERJACK), SHREDDED (1 CUP)

1 RIPE **AVOCADO**, HALVED, PITTED, PEELED AND SLICED

½ CUP THINLY SLICED **RADISHES**

¼ CUP MINCED **CILANTRO**

ACCOMPANIMENT: **BOTTLED SALSA**

Heat oven to 350°F. Spray tortillas on both sides with nonstick cooking spray. Arrange on baking sheet and bake 8 to 10 minutes until crisp.

Heat oil in a large nonstick skillet. Carefully break eggs into skillet, cover and cook over low heat 3 to 5 minutes until whites are set and yolks shake slightly when pan is jiggled.

Remove tortillas to serving platter. Sprinkle with cheese, top each with an egg, then avocado, radishes and cilantro, equally divided. Spoon on salsa at table.

PER SERVING
CALORIES 474 **TOTAL FAT** 31G **SATURATED FAT** 0G **CHOLESTEROL** 455MG **SODIUM** 405MG **TOTAL CARBOHYDRATES** 30G **DIETARY FIBER** 0G **PROTEIN** 23G

OVEN-ROASTED GREEK CHICKEN

- 4 **THIGHS** AND 4 **DRUMSTICKS**
- 1 MEDIUM **EGGPLANT**, CUT IN 1½-IN. CHUNKS
- 2 **RED BELL PEPPERS**, EACH CUT IN 12 STRIPS
- 8 CLOVES **GARLIC**
- 2 TBSP **OIL**
- 2 TBSP **FRESH LEMON JUICE**
- 1 TBSP **BOTTLED GREEK SEASONING**
- ½ TSP EACH **SALT** AND **PEPPER**
- GARNISH: **FRESH MINT**

YIELD
4 servings

ACTIVE
10 minutes

TOTAL
40 minutes

Heat oven to 450°F. Line 2 rimmed baking sheets with nonstick foil.

Divide chicken, vegetables and garlic evenly between baking sheets. Drizzle with oil; sprinkle with lemon juice, Greek seasoning, salt and pepper. Turn with a rubber spatula to mix and coat. Spread into a single layer.

Roast side by side on middle oven rack, turning chicken and vegetables once, 25 to 30 minutes, until an instant-read thermometer inserted in thickest part of thigh, not touching bone, registers 170°F and vegetables are browned at the edges and tender. Remove to serving platter, add mint, if desired, and serve.

PER SERVING
CALORIES 427 **TOTAL FAT** 27G **SATURATED FAT** 7G **CHOLESTEROL** 139MG **SODIUM** 1,058MG
TOTAL CARBOHYDRATES 13G **DIETARY FIBER** 3G **PROTEIN** 32G

GNOCCHI WITH BROCCOLINI & MUSHROOMS

YIELD
4 servings

ACTIVE
20 minutes

TOTAL
35 minutes

3 TBSP **OLIVE OIL**

12 OZ **ASSORTED MUSHROOMS** (SEE TIP) *OR* **WHITE MUSHROOMS**, SLICED

1 TSP **SALT**

1 TBSP MINCED **GARLIC**

1 CUP **FAT-FREE CHICKEN BROTH**

2 BUNCHES **BROCCOLINI** (ABOUT 1 LB), ENDS TRIMMED, HALVED CROSSWISE

¼ TSP **CRUSHED RED PEPPER**

1 BAG (16 OZ) **FROZEN POTATO GNOCCHI**

GARNISH: **GRATED PARMESAN**

Bring a large pot of lightly salted water to a boil.

Heat 1 Tbsp oil in a large nonstick skillet over medium heat. Add mushrooms and, stirring occasionally, cook 4 to 5 minutes until tender (mushrooms will release their liquid). Increase heat to medium-high, add salt and cook 4 to 5 minutes until liquid evaporates and mushrooms are golden brown. Remove to serving bowl. Reduce heat to medium.

Heat remaining 2 Tbsp oil and garlic in skillet about 1 minute or until garlic is fragrant. Add broth, broccolini and crushed red pepper; cover and simmer 8 to 10 minutes until stems are tender.

Meanwhile, add gnocchi to pot; cover just until water returns to a boil. Uncover; cook as package directs. Drain; add to serving bowl along with broccolini; toss to mix. Sprinkle servings with Parmesan.

TIP If including shiitakes, discard stems.

PER SERVING
CALORIES 431 **TOTAL FAT** 12G **SATURATED FAT** 2G **CHOLESTEROL** 17MG **SODIUM** 1,544MG
TOTAL CARBOHYDRATES 66G **DIETARY FIBER** 6G **PROTEIN** 17G

PULLED CHICKEN SANDWICHES WITH RED CABBAGE SLAW

4 CUPS **COOKED CHICKEN**, SHREDDED (SEE NOTE)

¾ CUP **KETCHUP**

⅓ CUP **PREPARED YELLOW MUSTARD** (SUCH AS FRENCH'S)

2 TBSP **CIDER VINEGAR**

RED CABBAGE SLAW

½ CUP **BUTTERMILK**

1 TSP **SUGAR**

¼ TSP EACH **SALT** AND **PEPPER**

½ SMALL **RED CABBAGE**, CORED AND THINLY SLICED

1 **CARROT**, GRATED

⅓ CUP MINCED **FRESH CHIVES** *OR* **GREEN PART OF SCALLIONS**

6 **SPLIT, SEEDED HAMBURGER BUNS**

YIELD
6 servings

ACTIVE
25 minutes

TOTAL
25 minutes

SIDE SUGGESTION
Pickles and tortilla chips

Combine chicken, ketchup, mustard and vinegar in a medium saucepan. Cover and cook over medium-low heat, stirring occasionally, until hot.

RED CABBAGE SLAW Meanwhile, mix buttermilk, sugar, salt and pepper in a large bowl. Toss in remaining ingredients.

Arrange open buns on plates. Mound chicken mixture on bottom halves. Top with some of the slaw; cover with bun tops. Serve remaining slaw on the side.

NOTE You can use purchased cooked chicken or prepare one yourself. To cook: Put a 4- to 4½-lb chicken, cut into pieces, and 1½ cups water or chicken broth in a large saucepan or deep skillet. Bring to a gentle boil, reduce heat to a simmer, cover and cook 20 to 25 minutes, or just until meat is cooked through. Let cool, then remove the skin and pull the meat off the bones.

PER SERVING
CALORIES 375 **TOTAL FAT** 10G **SATURATED FAT** 3G **CHOLESTEROL** 84MG **SODIUM** 975MG **TOTAL CARBOHYDRATES** 37G **DIETARY FIBER** 3G **PROTEIN** 33G

MEXICAN PIZZA

YIELD
6 servings

ACTIVE
4 minutes

TOTAL
10 minutes

1 LARGE (10-OZ) **PREBAKED THIN-CRUST PIZZA CRUST**

¾ CUP **TACO SAUCE**

1 PKG (12 OZ) **PRECOOKED FAJITA-STYLE CHICKEN STRIPS**

1¼ CUPS **FROZEN SOUTHWESTERN CORN BLEND**

1 CUP **SHREDDED MEXICAN OR TACO CHEESE BLEND**

½ CUP DICED **AVOCADO**

2 TBSP CHOPPED **CILANTRO**

Heat oven to 500°F. Spread crust with taco sauce, leaving ½-in. border around edge.

Sprinkle with chicken, frozen corn blend and cheese. Place directly on middle oven rack.

Bake 6 minutes or until crust is crisp and cheese melts. Sprinkle with avocado and cilantro; cut in wedges.

PER SERVING
CALORIES 318 **TOTAL FAT** 12G **SATURATED FAT** 5G **CHOLESTEROL** 52MG **SODIUM** 943MG
TOTAL CARBOHYDRATES 30G **DIETARY FIBER** 3G **PROTEIN** 24G

BEEF STEW CASSEROLE

- 1½ LB **1-IN. CUBES BEEF CHUCK** (FOR STEW)
- ¼ CUP **ALL-PURPOSE FLOUR**
- 1½ TBSP **VEGETABLE OIL**
- 2 CANS (ABOUT 14 OZ EACH) **BEEF BROTH**
- 1 LARGE **ONION**, SLICED
- 1 TBSP MINCED **GARLIC**
- 3 LB SMALL **SWEET POTATOES**
- 1 LB EACH **CARROTS** AND **PARSNIPS**
- 3 RIBS **CELERY**
- 1 TBSP **BUTTER**
- ¼ TSP **SALT**

YIELD
8 servings

ACTIVE
45 minutes

TOTAL
1 hour 35 minutes

Position racks to divide oven in thirds. Heat oven to 325°F.

Coat beef with flour. Heat oil in a Dutch oven over medium-high heat. Add beef and brown. Add broth, onion and garlic; bring to a boil. Cover tightly and place stew on one oven rack, potatoes on other rack. Bake 30 minutes.

Cut carrots, parsnips and celery into 1-in. lengths; stir into stew. Cover and bake 45 minutes or until vegetables are tender when pierced.

Peel potatoes and mash with butter and salt. Bake and serve, or cool, cover separately and refrigerate up to 3 days.

TO SERVE Heat oven to 400°F. Skim fat off stew, then spoon into a shallow 3½-qt baking dish; spread potatoes over top. Bake 50 minutes or until bubbly around edges and hot in center.

PER SERVING
CALORIES 488 **TOTAL FAT** 22G **SATURATED FAT** 8G **CHOLESTEROL** 56MG **SODIUM** 550MG **TOTAL CARBOHYDRATES** 50G **DIETARY FIBER** 9G **PROTEIN** 20G

SICILIAN PASTA WITH TUNA

12 OZ **SPAGHETTI PASTA**

2 TSP **OLIVE OIL**

1 LARGE **ONION**, SLICED

1 JAR (8.5 OZ) **OLIVE SPREAD** *OR*
1 CAN (7.5 OZ) **EGGPLANT APPETIZER (CAPONATA) PLUS ¼ CUP CHOPPED PIMIENTO-STUFFED OLIVES**

1 CAN (6 OZ) **CHUNK LIGHT TUNA IN OLIVE OIL**, DRAINED

1 TBSP **RAISINS**

¼ TSP **PEPPER**

GARNISH: CHOPPED **PARSLEY**

YIELD
4 servings

ACTIVE
15 minutes

TOTAL
22 minutes

Bring a large pot of lightly salted water to a boil. Add pasta and cook as package directs.

Meanwhile, heat oil in a large nonstick skillet over medium-high heat. Add onion and sauté 7 minutes until golden and tender. Reduce heat to medium, add remaining ingredients and stir gently until heated through.

Remove ½ cup pasta cooking water. Drain pasta; return to pot. Add olive mixture and reserved pasta water; toss to mix and coat. Sprinkle with chopped parsley.

PER SERVING
CALORIES 542 **TOTAL FAT** 17G **SATURATED FAT** 2G **CHOLESTEROL** 15MG **SODIUM** 945MG
TOTAL CARBOHYDRATES 76G **DIETARY FIBER** 3G **PROTEIN** 20G

TANDOORI CHICKEN BREASTS ON PITAS

¼ CUP **ALL-PURPOSE FLOUR**

2 TBSP **CURRY POWDER**

¼ TSP EACH **SALT** AND **PEPPER**

4 **BONELESS, SKINLESS CHICKEN BREASTS** (5 OZ EACH), VISIBLE FAT TRIMMED

1 TBSP **OIL**

YOGURT SAUCE

¾ CUP **PLAIN LOWFAT YOGURT**

1 TBSP FINELY CHOPPED **RED ONION**

1 TSP MINCED **GARLIC**

¼ TSP EACH **GROUND CUMIN** AND **SALT**

1 **YELLOW BELL PEPPER**

2 EACH MEDIUM **TOMATOES** AND **KIRBY (PICKLING) CUCUMBERS**

4 **PITAS**

GARNISH: **LIME WEDGES** AND CHOPPED **CILANTRO**

YIELD
4 servings

ACTIVE
15 minutes

TOTAL
15 minutes

Mix flour, curry powder, salt and pepper in a plastic food bag. Add chicken, close bag and shake to coat. Remove chicken; shake off excess flour.

Heat oil in a large nonstick skillet over medium-high heat. Add chicken and cook, turning once, 10 minutes or until golden and cooked through. Remove to a cutting board.

While chicken cooks, mix **SAUCE** ingredients in a bowl, coarsely chop bell pepper, tomatoes and cucumbers, and toast pitas.

Cut chicken diagonally in ½-in.-wide strips. Place a pita on each plate. Top with pepper, tomato and cucumber, then chicken. Spoon on sauce; garnish with limes and cilantro.

PER SERVING
CALORIES 453 **TOTAL FAT** 7G **SATURATED FAT** 1G **CHOLESTEROL** 85MG **SODIUM** 740MG
TOTAL CARBOHYDRATES 52G **DIETARY FIBER** 5G **PROTEIN** 43G

ROASTED HERB FILLET OF BEEF WITH HORSERADISH SAUCE

HERB FILLET OF BEEF

¼ CUP **WHOLE-GRAIN DIJON MUSTARD**

3 TBSP MIXED CHOPPED **FRESH HERBS** (**SAGE**, **ROSEMARY** AND **THYME**)

1 TBSP **EXTRA-VIRGIN OLIVE OIL**

VEGETABLE OIL, FOR BROWNING

1 OVEN-READY, TIED **FILLET OF BEEF ROAST** (4 LB)

1 TSP **KOSHER SALT**

FRESHLY GROUND **PEPPER**

HORSERADISH SAUCE

1 CUP **REDUCED-FAT SOUR CREAM**

½ CUP **CREAM-STYLE HORSERADISH SAUCE**

1½ TBSP CHOPPED **PARSLEY**

1½ TSP **HONEY MUSTARD**

PEPPER

YIELD
12 servings

ACTIVE
35 minutes

TOTAL
1 hour 15 minutes

PLANNING TIP
Horseradish sauce can be made up to 2 days ahead and refrigerated.

Heat oven to 450°F. In a small bowl, mix mustard, herbs and olive oil.

Heat a large Dutch oven over medium-high heat. Add enough vegetable oil to just coat bottom of pan. Pat beef dry with paper towel and season with salt. Sear beef, turning every 3 minutes, until all sides are well browned, about 12 minutes total. Transfer beef to a roasting rack set in a shallow roasting pan and brush with the mustard mixture.

Roast the beef 15 to 20 minutes until an instant-read thermometer inserted in center registers 125°F, for medium-rare. Let beef rest on a cutting board, loosely tented with foil, 15 to 20 minutes.

Meanwhile, to make **HORSERADISH SAUCE**, whisk all ingredients in a medium bowl until blended.

Slice beef into thick slices. Serve warm or at room temperature with horseradish sauce.

PER SERVING
CALORIES 440 **TOTAL FAT** 34G **SATURATED FAT** 13G **CHOLESTEROL** 13MG **SODIUM** 389MG **TOTAL CARBOHYDRATES** 4G **DIETARY FIBER** 1G **PROTEIN** 29G

MARCH

MARCH SHOPPING LIST

Week 1
MARCH 1 TO MARCH 7

PRODUCE
3 ROYAL GALA OR OTHER RED APPLES
1 LARGE ONION
1 MEDIUM RED ONION
2 SWEET ONIONS
1 HEAD GARLIC (3 CLOVES)
4 MEDIUM SWEET POTATOES (ABOUT 2 LB)
1½ LB EGGPLANT
1 YELLOW BELL PEPPER
2 RED BELL PEPPERS
1 HEAD CAULIFLOWER
12 OZ SHIITAKE MUSHROOM CAPS
8 SCALLIONS
1 BUNCH PARSLEY
1 BUNCH CILANTRO

BAKERY
BREAD (FOR ¾ CUP FRESH BREAD CRUMBS)

MEAT/POULTRY/FISH
1 LB LEAN GROUND BEEF
ONE 12-OZ PORK TENDERLOIN
1 LB HOT OR SWEET ITALIAN PORK SAUSAGE
4 SMALL WHOLE CHICKEN LEGS (2 LB)
1 LB RAW LARGE SHRIMP

DELI
2 HAM STEAKS (7 TO 8 OZ EACH)
4 STRIPS BACON
10 PITTED KALAMATA OLIVES

REFRIGERATED
3 OZ CRUMBLED FETA CHEESE
¼ CUP GRATED ROMANO OR PARMESAN
EGG (1 LARGE)

FROZEN
1 BAG (16 OZ) SLICED PEACHES

GROCERY
2 CANS (19.75 OZ EACH) PORK & BEANS
1 CAN (16 OZ) BLACK BEANS
3 CANS (15 TO 16 OZ EACH) BEANS (ANY KIND—CHICKPEAS, PINTO, KIDNEY BEANS)
1 JAR (26 OZ) MARINARA SAUCE
1½ CUPS BARILLA SWEET PEPPERS & GARLIC PASTA SAUCE
8 OZ LOW-CARB OR WHOLE-WHEAT SPAGHETTI PASTA
1 LB PENNE RIGATE OR OTHER PASTA
1 JAR (9 OZ) HOT OR SWEET MANGO CHUTNEY
2 TBSP CHOPPED MANGO CHUTNEY OR ORANGE MARMALADE
2 TBSP BARBECUE SAUCE
SOY SAUCE
WORCESTERSHIRE SAUCE
4 BURRITO-SIZE 99%-FAT-FREE TORTILLAS
GARLIC-FLAVOR NONSTICK SPRAY
½ CUP DRY WHITE OR RED WINE (OPTIONAL)

PANTRY
SALT
PEPPER
OLIVE OIL
CIDER VINEGAR
MOLASSES
DRIED ROSEMARY
DRIED OREGANO
CURRY POWDER
FENNEL SEEDS (OPTIONAL)

Week 2
MARCH 8 TO MARCH 14

PRODUCE
1 MEDIUM ONION
1 SMALL ONION
2 HEADS GARLIC (8 CLOVES)
3 LARGE POTATOES (ABOUT 1½ LB)
1 RED BELL PEPPER
1 LARGE YELLOW BELL PEPPER
2 CUBANELLE PEPPERS
1 SMALL JICAMA
1 AVOCADO
1 PKG (10 OZ) SLICED MUSHROOMS
4 CUPS BAGGED COLESLAW MIX
3 SCALLIONS
1 BUNCH PARSLEY
1 BUNCH CHIVES
1 BUNCH CILANTRO

BAKERY
6 HAMBURGER BUNS WITH SESAME SEEDS

MEAT/POULTRY/FISH
1 LB CUBE STEAKS (ABOUT 4)
1 PORK TENDERLOIN (ABOUT 1¼ LB)
2 LB GROUND PORK
1 LB BONELESS, SKINLESS CHICKEN BREASTS
1 LB LARGE PEELED COOKED SHRIMP

DELI
5 STRIPS LOWER-SODIUM BACON

REFRIGERATED
2 CUPS FAT-FREE HALF-AND-HALF
3 TBSP BUTTERMILK, MILK OR SOUR CREAM
1 TBSP UNSALTED BUTTER
GRATED PARMESAN
1 CARTON (15 OZ) CHEESE AND CHIVE EGG BEATERS
ONE 15-OZ BOX PIE CRUSTS
½ CUP MILD SALSA (PREFERABLY REFRIGERATED FRESH)

FROZEN
1 BAG (24 OZ) BROCCOLI, CARROTS, CAULIFLOWER AND CHEDDAR SAUCE

GROCERY
1 CAN (14.5 OZ) DICED TOMATOES IN SAUCE
12 OZ SHORT FUSILLI OR CELLENTANI PASTA
1 LB SPINACH FETTUCINE OR LINGUINE
⅓ CUP LIGHT MAYONNAISE
BARBECUE SAUCE
1 CUP MIXED MARINATED OLIVES

PANTRY
SALT
PEPPER
OLIVE OIL
CIDER VINEGAR
NONSTICK SPRAY

FLOUR
SUGAR
DRIED ITALIAN SEASONING
CRUSHED RED PEPPER
GROUND NUTMEG
GROUND CUMIN

Week 3

MARCH 15 TO MARCH 22

PRODUCE
3 MEDIUM ONIONS
1 RED ONION
2 HEADS GARLIC (8 CLOVES)
5 POTATOES (ABOUT 2 LB)
1 LB RED-SKINNED POTATOES
3 CARROTS (ABOUT 1 LB)
2 BUTTERNUT SQUASH (2 LB)
2 LARGE EGGPLANTS
1 RED BELL PEPPER
2 CUPS GREEN BEANS
8 OZ COLESLAW MIX (ABOUT 4 CUPS)
1 BUNCH CILANTRO
1 BUNCH PARSLEY

BAKERY
1 LOAF ITALIAN BREAD (ABOUT 1 LB)
BREAD (FOR 1/4 CUP FRESH BREAD CRUMBS)

MEAT/POULTRY/FISH
8-RIB RACK OF LAMB (1 1/2 TO 2 LB)
8 CHICKEN DRUMSTICKS (2 1/4 LB)

DELI
1 THIN-CUT CORNED BEEF BRISKET (ABOUT 2 3/4 LB)
1 READY-TO-COOK BONE-IN SMOKED HAM HALF (8- TO 10-LB), PREFERABLY SHANK END
6 OZ THINLY SLICED REDUCED-SODIUM HAM

REFRIGERATED
1/2 CUP PLAIN LOWFAT YOGURT
GRATED PARMESAN

FROZEN
1 BAG (12 OZ) MEDIUM SHRIMP

GROCERY
1 JAR (24 OZ) PUTTANESCA SAUCE
2 CUPS JARRED MARINARA SAUCE
12 OZ LINGUINE FINI
2 BOXES (12 OZ EACH) CREAMY CHEESE-SAUCE-AND-SHELL PASTA
1 BAG (17 OZ) DRIED LENTILS
1 JAR (12 OZ) ROASTED RED PEPPERS
LIGHT MAYONNAISE
1 CUP JARRED SALSA
1 JAR (12 OZ) APRICOT PRESERVES
1/4 CUP APPLE JELLY

PANTRY
SALT
PEPPER
OLIVE OIL
WINE VINEGAR
CIDER VINEGAR
HONEY-DIJON MUSTARD
2 TBSP GRAINY DIJON MUSTARD (SUCH AS MAILLE)
SWEET-HOT OR HONEY MUSTARD
LIGHT BROWN SUGAR
DRIED ITALIAN HERB SEASONING
WHOLE CLOVES

Week 4

MARCH 23 TO MARCH 31

PRODUCE
4 NAVEL ORANGES
1 LIME
5 ONIONS
1 RED ONION
1 HEAD GARLIC (5 CLOVES)
1 PIECE FRESH GINGER
9 MEDIUM PLUM TOMATOES (ABOUT 1 1/2 LB)
2 CARROTS
1 RED BELL PEPPER
1 YELLOW BELL PEPPER
2 MEDIUM ZUCCHINI (ABOUT 12 OZ)
1 MEDIUM YELLOW SQUASH (ABOUT 6 OZ)
1 AVOCADO
1 LB WHOLE PORTOBELLO MUSHROOMS
1 HEAD ROMAINE LETTUCE
1 MEDIUM HEAD CABBAGE
1 LB BOK CHOY
1 BUNCH (ABOUT 5 OZ) ARUGULA
1 BUNCH CILANTRO
FRESH THYME

BAKERY
2 SLICES FIRM WHOLE-WHEAT OR WHITE BREAD

MEAT/POULTRY/FISH
4 BONELESS, SKINLESS CHICKEN BREASTS (ABOUT 5 OZ EACH)
1 LB BONELESS, SKINLESS CHICKEN THIGHS
1 BONELESS, SKINLESS TURKEY BREAST (ABOUT 2 1/2 LB)
12 OZ GROUND TURKEY
1 LB LEAN SWEET ITALIAN TURKEY SAUSAGE
FOUR 3/4- TO 1-IN.-THICK PIECES COD FILLET (ABOUT 5 OZ EACH)
4 SALMON FILLETS (ABOUT 1 1/4 IN. THICK, 5 TO 6 OZ EACH)

DELI
6 SLICES REDUCED-SODIUM BACON

REFRIGERATED
1/2 STICK BUTTER
1 CONTAINER (8 OZ) REDUCED-FAT SOUR CREAM
4 OZ (HALF AN 8-OZ BRICK) 1/3-LESS-FAT CREAM CHEESE (NEUFCHÂTEL)
2 OZ PART-SKIM SHREDDED MOZZARELLA
5 OZ SMOKED MOZZARELLA
CHUNK OF PARMESAN
1/2 CUP GRATED PARMESAN
EGGS (9 LARGE)
1 TUBE (10 OZ) PIZZA CRUST

FROZEN
1 BOX (10 OZ) LEAF SPINACH

GROCERY
1 CAN (14.5 OZ) CHICKEN BROTH
1 CAN (8 OZ) TOMATO SAUCE
1 CAN (8.75 OZ) WHOLE-KERNEL CORN
1 CAN (15.5 OZ) BLACK BEANS
1 CAN (14.5 OZ) SLICED POTATOES
2 CUPS MARINARA SAUCE
1 CUP REDUCED-FAT MUSHROOM ALFREDO SAUCE
2 CUPS JARRED SALSA
1/2 CUP SMOOTH CHIPOTLE SALSA
WHITE RICE
1 CUP LONG-GRAIN RICE
8 CORN TORTILLAS
1/4 CUP DARK RAISINS
1/4 CUP PISTACHIOS
1/4 CUP DRIED CRANBERRIES
1/4 CUP DRIED SNIPPED APRICOTS
HOISIN SAUCE
HONEY
1/3 CUP DRY WHITE WINE

PANTRY
SALT
PEPPER
OLIVE OIL
CANOLA OIL
NONSTICK SPRAY
BALSAMIC VINEGAR
CIDER VINEGAR
BROWN SUGAR
FLOUR
CORNSTARCH
CHILI POWDER
GROUND CUMIN

PENNE WITH MUSHROOM "BOLOGNESE"

YIELD
6 servings

ACTIVE
3 minutes

TOTAL
20 minutes

- 1 LB **PENNE RIGATE** OR OTHER PASTA
- 12 OZ **SLICED SHIITAKE MUSHROOM CAPS**
- 2 LARGE CLOVES **GARLIC**
- 2 TSP **OLIVE OIL**
- ½ CUP **DRY WHITE** *OR* **RED WINE** (OPTIONAL)
- 1 JAR (26 OZ) **MARINARA SAUCE**
- ½ TSP CRUSHED **DRIED ROSEMARY**
- 2 TBSP CHOPPED **FRESH PARSLEY**

SERVE WITH
Grated Parmesan

Bring a large pot of lightly salted water to a boil. Add pasta and cook as package directs.

Meanwhile, pulse mushrooms and garlic in food processor until finely chopped.

Heat oil in a large nonstick skillet. Add mushroom mixture; sauté over medium-high heat 3 minutes or until lightly browned.

Stir in wine (if using); boil 1 minute. Stir in sauce and rosemary, bring to boil, reduce heat and simmer 2 minutes to blend flavors. Stir in parsley; spoon onto pasta. Serve with Parmesan.

PER SERVING
CALORIES 394 **TOTAL FAT** 7G **SATURATED FAT** 1G **CHOLESTEROL** 0MG **SODIUM** 779MG **TOTAL CARBOHYDRATES** 72G **DIETARY FIBER** 5G **PROTEIN** 13G

SWEET & SOUR HAM STEAKS

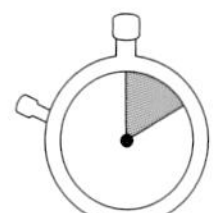

YIELD
4 servings

ACTIVE
10 minutes

TOTAL
15 minutes

½ TSP **OIL**

2 **HAM STEAKS** (7 TO 8 OZ EACH), CUT IN HALF

1 BAG (16 OZ) **FROZEN SLICED PEACHES**, THAWED, CUT BITE-SIZE

1 JAR (9 OZ) **HOT OR SWEET MANGO CHUTNEY**

GARNISH: CHOPPED **CILANTRO**

SIDE SUGGESTION
Steamed broccoli

Heat oil in a large nonstick skillet over medium-high heat. Add ham and cook 4 minutes, turning once, until lightly browned. Remove to a serving platter.

Add peaches and chutney to skillet and cook, stirring, just until hot. Spoon over ham. Garnish with chopped cilantro, if desired.

DIFFERENT TAKES

- Stir some curry powder into the chutney and peach mixture.
- Substitute fresh pineapple chunks for the peaches and add some sliced scallions.
- When in season, use fresh peaches or nectarines. Then grill the ham and serve the sauce cold as a salsa.

PER SERVING
CALORIES 385 **TOTAL FAT** 6G **SATURATED FAT** 2G **CHOLESTEROL** 47MG **SODIUM** 1,988MG **TOTAL CARBOHYDRATES** 60G **DIETARY FIBER** 2G **PROTEIN** 20G

PASTA WITH SHRIMP & EGGPLANT

2 TSP **OLIVE OIL**

1½ LB **EGGPLANT**, CUT IN ¾-IN. CUBES

8 OZ **LOW-CARB** *OR* **WHOLE-WHEAT SPAGHETTI PASTA**

1 EACH **RED** AND **YELLOW BELL PEPPER**, CUT IN THIN STRIPS

1 MEDIUM **RED ONION**, THINLY SLICED

1 TSP **DRIED OREGANO**

1 LB **RAW LARGE SHRIMP**, PEELED AND DEVEINED

10 **PITTED KALAMATA OLIVES**, HALVED

¾ CUP (3 OZ) **CRUMBLED FETA CHEESE**

GARNISH: CHOPPED **PARSLEY**

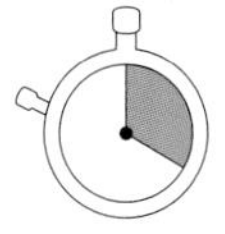

YIELD
4 servings

ACTIVE
20 minutes

TOTAL
25 minutes

Bring a large pot of lightly salted water to a boil.

Heat oil in a large nonstick skillet over medium-high heat. Add eggplant; sauté 6 minutes or until almost soft.

Stir pasta into boiling water. Cook as package directs. Ladle off ½ cup cooking water; reserve. Drain pasta, return to pot and add reserved water.

Meanwhile, add pepper strips, onion and oregano to eggplant. Sauté 6 minutes until crisp-tender. Stir in shrimp, cover and steam, stirring once, 2 to 4 minutes, until shrimp are just done. Add to pasta in pot; toss to mix and coat. Pour into a serving bowl. Add olives and cheese; sprinkle with parsley. Toss again just before serving.

PER SERVING
CALORIES 474 **TOTAL FAT** 13G **SATURATED FAT** 4G **CHOLESTEROL** 159MG **SODIUM** 998MG **TOTAL CARBOHYDRATES** 63G **DIETARY FIBER** 8G **PROTEIN** 32G

SAUSAGE & PEPPERS MEAT LOAF

1½ CUPS **BARILLA SWEET PEPPERS & GARLIC PASTA SAUCE**

1 LB **HOT OR SWEET ITALIAN PORK SAUSAGE**, REMOVED FROM CASINGS

1 LB **LEAN GROUND BEEF**

¾ CUP **FRESH BREAD CRUMBS**

¾ CUP FINELY CHOPPED **ONION**

¼ CUP GRATED **ROMANO OR PARMESAN**

1 LARGE **EGG**

2 TSP MINCED **GARLIC**

2 TSP **FENNEL SEEDS** (OPTIONAL)

½ TSP EACH **SALT** AND **PEPPER**

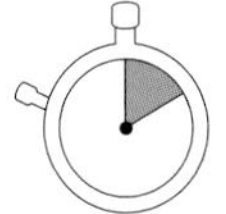

YIELD
8 servings

ACTIVE
10 minutes

TOTAL
5 to 8 hours on low

TIP
Leftover meat loaf makes great sandwiches.

SIDE SUGGESTION
Pasta salad

To ease removal of loaf from cooker, fold two 24-in.-long pieces foil in half lengthwise twice. Place strips across each other, forming a "+" in bottom of a 3½-qt or larger slow cooker. Press strips against inside of cooker, letting ends hang over outside.

Mix ½ cup pasta sauce with remaining ingredients in a large bowl until well blended. Form into a 7½ x 4½ x 2½-in. loaf. Place in cooker.

Cover and cook on low 5 to 8 hours or until a meat thermometer inserted in center of loaf registers 165°F.

Heat rest of sauce; serve at table.

PER SERVING
CALORIES 410 **TOTAL FAT** 32G **SATURATED FAT** 12G **CHOLESTEROL** 115MG **SODIUM** 893MG
TOTAL CARBOHYDRATES 8G **DIETARY FIBER** 1G **PROTEIN** 21G

BARBECUED PORK WITH SWEET POTATOES & APPLES

GARLIC-FLAVOR NONSTICK SPRAY

2 TBSP **BARBECUE SAUCE**

2 TBSP **CHOPPED MANGO CHUTNEY** OR **ORANGE MARMALADE**

2 TSP **SOY SAUCE**

ONE 12-OZ **PORK TENDERLOIN**

2 **ROYAL GALA OR OTHER RED APPLES**, QUARTERED, CORED AND CUT IN ¾-IN. WEDGES

¾ TSP **CURRY POWDER**

¼ TSP **SALT**

2 MEDIUM **SWEET POTATOES** (ABOUT 1 LB), PEELED, CUT IN HALF CROSSWISE, THEN THINLY SLICED LENGTHWISE

8 **SCALLIONS**, ENDS TRIMMED

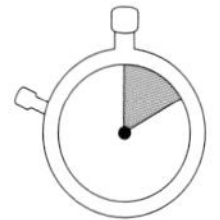

YIELD
4 servings

ACTIVE
10 minutes

TOTAL
27 minutes

Heat oven to 500°F. Line 2 rimmed baking sheets with foil; coat foil with garlic spray.

Mix barbecue sauce, chutney and soy sauce; spread over pork. Place pork on one side of one lined pan, apples on other side. Coat apples with garlic spray; sprinkle with ¼ tsp curry powder and ⅛ tsp salt.

Spread sweet potatoes in other pan; coat with garlic spray, then sprinkle with remaining curry powder and salt.

Roast 12 minutes or until potatoes are tender. Remove potatoes to a serving platter; cover to keep warm. Put scallions in pan with pork; coat with garlic spray. Roast 5 minutes or until meat thermometer inserted in thickest part of pork registers 160°F and scallions and apples are tender.

Slice pork; add to platter along with apples and scallions.

PER SERVING
CALORIES 308 **TOTAL FAT** 6G **SATURATED FAT** 2G **CHOLESTEROL** 56MG **SODIUM** 521MG **TOTAL CARBOHYDRATES** 44G **DIETARY FIBER** 5G **PROTEIN** 20G

SKILLET "BAKED" BEANS

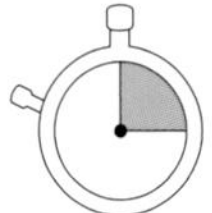

YIELD
8 servings

ACTIVE
15 minutes

TOTAL
1 hour 10 minutes

4 **STRIPS BACON**, CUT IN 1½-IN. PIECES

2 CUPS CHOPPED **SWEET ONION**

3 CANS (15 TO 16 OZ EACH) **BEANS**, RINSED (ANY KIND—WE USED CHICKPEAS, PINTO AND KIDNEY BEANS)

2 CANS (19.75 OZ EACH) **PORK & BEANS**

2 TBSP PACKED **DARK BROWN SUGAR**

2 TBSP **WORCESTERSHIRE SAUCE**

2 TBSP **CIDER VINEGAR**

2 TBSP **MOLASSES**

Cook bacon in a deep, medium skillet until crisp. Drain on paper towels. Pour off all but 2 Tbsp drippings from pan. Add onion and cook over low heat, stirring occasionally, 15 minutes, or until golden.

Stir in remaining ingredients. Bring to a boil, reduce heat and simmer, stirring often, 25 minutes, or until mixture thickens. Sprinkle with bacon and serve.

PER SERVING
CALORIES 308 **TOTAL FAT** 8G **SATURATED FAT** 2G **CHOLESTEROL** 15MG **SODIUM** 816MG
TOTAL CARBOHYDRATES 52G **DIETARY FIBER** 12G **PROTEIN** 20G

CURRY ROAST CHICKEN & VEGGIES

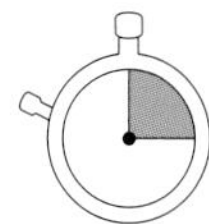

YIELD
4 servings

ACTIVE
15 minutes

TOTAL
50 minutes

1 HEAD **CAULIFLOWER**, CUT INTO FLORETS

2 MEDIUM **SWEET POTATOES** (1 LB), CUT INTO 8 WEDGES, THEN HALVED CROSSWISE

1 LARGE **GALA APPLE**, CORED, CUT INTO 12 WEDGES

4 SMALL **WHOLE CHICKEN LEGS** (2 LB), CUT TO SEPARATE THIGHS AND DRUMSTICKS

4 TSP **OIL**

1 TBSP **CURRY POWDER**

GARNISH: **PARSLEY LEAVES** (OPTIONAL)

Position oven racks to divide oven into thirds. Heat oven to 450°F. Line two rimmed baking pans with foil.

Place half the vegetables, apple wedges and chicken on each of the two pans. Drizzle 2 tsp oil over each, then sprinkle each with 1½ tsp curry powder. Toss to coat evenly.

Roast 15 minutes, toss, then roast 15 to 20 minutes more until chicken is cooked through and vegetables are tender. Sprinkle with parsley leaves, if desired.

PER SERVING
CALORIES 449 **TOTAL FAT** 21G **SATURATED FAT** 5G **CHOLESTEROL** 107MG **SODIUM** 190MG **TOTAL CARBOHYDRATES** 33G **DIETARY FIBER** 8G **PROTEIN** 35G

CHEDDAR-VEGETABLE QUICHE

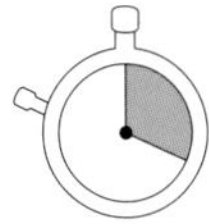

YIELD
6 servings

ACTIVE
19 minutes

TOTAL
59 minutes

1 **REFRIGERATED PIE CRUST** (FROM A 15-OZ BOX OF TWO)

1 BAG (24 OZ) **FROZEN BROCCOLI, CARROTS, CAULIFLOWER AND CHEDDAR SAUCE**

1 CARTON (15 OZ) **CHEESE AND CHIVE EGG BEATERS**

GARNISH: **CHIVES**

Heat oven to 400°F. Lightly coat a 9-in. pie plate with nonstick spray.

Fit crust into pie plate, turn edges under and crimp or flute. Prick crust in several places. Press a sheet of foil directly on crust. Bake 12 to 14 minutes until edges are lightly browned. Remove foil; cool crust on a wire rack while preparing vegetables.

Microwave vegetables and cheese sauce as bag directs. Stir in Egg Beaters and pour into crust.

Bake 15 minutes; reduce heat to 350°F and bake 20 to 25 minutes until a knife inserted near center of quiche comes out clean. If desired, garnish with chives.

PER SERVING
CALORIES 251 **TOTAL FAT** 12G **SATURATED FAT** 6G **CHOLESTEROL** 13MG **SODIUM** 735MG
TOTAL CARBOHYDRATES 26G **DIETARY FIBER** 2G **PROTEIN** 9G

PASTA CACCIATORE

3 TBSP **OLIVE OIL**

1 LB **BONELESS, SKINLESS CHICKEN BREASTS**, CUT IN BITE-SIZE PIECES

3/4 TSP **SALT**

12 OZ **SHORT FUSILLI** *OR* **CELLENTANI PASTA**

1 MEDIUM **ONION**, CHOPPED

1 LARGE **YELLOW BELL PEPPER**, CUT IN 3/4-IN. PIECES

1 PKG (10 OZ) **SLICED MUSHROOMS**

1 TBSP MINCED **GARLIC**

3/4 TSP **DRIED ITALIAN SEASONING**

1/4 TSP **CRUSHED RED PEPPER**

1 CAN (14.5 OZ) **DICED TOMATOES IN SAUCE**

1 CUP **MIXED MARINATED OLIVES**, PITTED AND HALVED

1/3 CUP CHOPPED **PARSLEY**

GARNISH: **GRATED PARMESAN**

YIELD
6 servings

ACTIVE
15 minutes

TOTAL
30 minutes

Bring a large pot of lightly salted water to a boil.

Meanwhile, heat 2 Tbsp oil in a large skillet over medium-high heat. Sprinkle chicken with 1/4 tsp salt. Add to skillet and sauté 2 to 3 minutes until lightly browned, but not fully cooked. Remove to a plate.

Stir pasta into boiling water; cook as package directs.

Meanwhile, add remaining 1 Tbsp oil, the onion, bell pepper, mushrooms, garlic, seasoning, crushed red pepper and remaining 1/2 tsp salt to skillet. Cook, stirring often, 5 minutes, or until liquid evaporates and vegetables begin to brown. Add 3/4 cup cooking water from pasta pot to skillet. Stir in tomatoes and olives. Bring to a simmer and cook, uncovered, 8 minutes.

Drain pasta. Add parsley and chicken to skillet and simmer 2 to 3 minutes or until chicken is cooked through. Return pasta to pot, add chicken sauce and toss to coat. Serve with grated Parmesan.

PER SERVING
CALORIES 480 **TOTAL FAT** 17G **SATURATED FAT** 2G **CHOLESTEROL** 44MG **SODIUM** 1,586MG **TOTAL CARBOHYDRATES** 55G **DIETARY FIBER** 4G **PROTEIN** 27G

LITE FETTUCINE ALFREDO

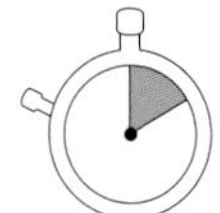

YIELD
6 servings

ACTIVE
10 minutes

TOTAL
20 minutes

- 1 LB **SPINACH FETTUCINE** *OR* **LINGUINE**
- 1 TBSP **UNSALTED BUTTER**
- 2 CLOVES **GARLIC**, MINCED
- 3 TBSP **FLOUR**
- 2 CUPS **FAT-FREE HALF-AND-HALF**
- ¼ TSP EACH **SALT**, **PEPPER** AND **GROUND NUTMEG**
- ¼ CUP **GRATED PARMESAN**

Cook pasta in large pot of lightly salted boiling water as package directs.

Meanwhile, melt butter in a medium saucepan. Add garlic; cook over low heat 1 minute or until fragrant.

Whisk in flour, then slowly whisk in half-and-half until well combined. Whisk in salt, pepper and nutmeg, and bring to a boil, whisking frequently.

Reduce heat and simmer 5 minutes or until thickened. Remove from heat and stir in cheese until melted.

Drain pasta; return to pot. Add sauce and toss to mix and coat.

PER SERVING
CALORIES 371 **TOTAL FAT** 6G **SATURATED FAT** 3G **CHOLESTEROL** 13MG **SODIUM** 382MG **TOTAL CARBOHYDRATES** 65G **DIETARY FIBER** 3G **PROTEIN** 14G

SOUTHERN BBQ PORK BURGERS

SLAW

⅓ CUP **LIGHT MAYONNAISE**

3 TBSP **BUTTERMILK, MILK OR SOUR CREAM**

2 TBSP SNIPPED **FRESH CHIVES**

1 TBSP **CIDER VINEGAR**

¼ TSP EACH **SUGAR**, **SALT** AND FRESHLY GROUND **PEPPER**

4 CUPS **BAGGED COLESLAW MIX**

BURGERS

2 LB **GROUND PORK**

⅓ CUP **BARBECUE SAUCE**

1 SMALL **ONION**, GRATED

½ TSP FRESHLY GROUND **PEPPER**

¼ TSP **SALT**

6 **HAMBURGER BUNS WITH SESAME SEEDS**

NONSTICK SPRAY

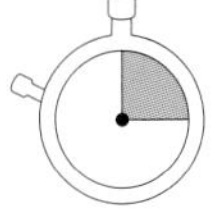

YIELD
6 servings

ACTIVE
15 minutes

TOTAL
1 hour 30 minutes

SLAW Whisk mayonnaise, buttermilk, chives, vinegar, sugar, salt and pepper in a bowl until blended. Add coleslaw; toss to coat. Refrigerate 1 hour, stirring a few times.

BURGERS Gently mix ingredients in a large bowl. Shape into six 1-in.-thick burgers.

Heat outdoor grill. Toast buns on grill; remove to a platter. Cover loosely with foil to keep warm.

Coat burgers with nonstick spray. Grill, turning once, 10 to 12 minutes until an instant-read thermometer inserted from side to middle registers 160°F. Place on buns; top with slaw. Serve remaining slaw on the side.

PER SERVING
CALORIES 530 **TOTAL FAT** 28G **SATURATED FAT** 9G **CHOLESTEROL** 102MG **SODIUM** 762MG
TOTAL CARBOHYDRATES 33G **DIETARY FIBER** 3G **PROTEIN** 33G

SOUTHWESTERN SHRIMP

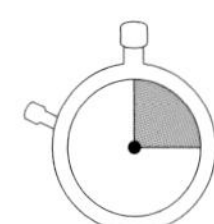

YIELD
4 servings

ACTIVE
15 minutes

TOTAL
15 minutes

1 LB LARGE **PEELED COOKED SHRIMP**

1 CUP DICED **JICAMA**

½ CUP **MILD SALSA** (PREFERABLY REFRIGERATED FRESH)

1 TBSP **OLIVE OIL**

⅓ CUP CHOPPED **CILANTRO**

¼ TSP **GROUND CUMIN**

1 RIPE **AVOCADO**, SLICED

SIDE SUGGESTION
Warm corn or flour tortillas and lime wedges

Put shrimp, jicama, salsa, oil, cilantro and cumin in a medium bowl; toss to mix. Add avocado; gently toss to mix.

PER SERVING
CALORIES 218 **TOTAL FAT** 7G **SATURATED FAT** 2G **CHOLESTEROL** 221MG **SODIUM** 370MG **TOTAL CARBOHYDRATES** 7G **DIETARY FIBER** 4G **PROTEIN** 25G

GRILLED CUBE STEAKS & PEPPERS WITH POTATO PLANKS

⅔ CUP **OIL**

1 TBSP MINCED **GARLIC** (3 CLOVES)

1¼ TSP **GROUND CUMIN**

½ TSP **SALT**

¼ TSP **PEPPER**

2 TBSP **RED-WINE** *OR* **CIDER VINEGAR**

1 LB **CUBE STEAKS** (ABOUT 4), HALVED

1½ LB **POTATOES** (3 LARGE), SCRUBBED AND CUT IN ½-IN. LENGTHWISE SLICES

1 **RED BELL PEPPER**, HALVED LENGTHWISE

2 **CUBANELLE PEPPERS**, HALVED LENGTHWISE

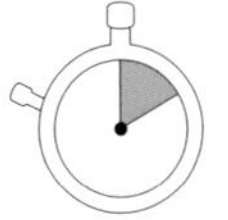

YIELD
4 servings

ACTIVE
10 minutes

TOTAL
35 minutes

Whisk oil, garlic, cumin, salt and pepper in small bowl until blended; remove 4 tbsp to large ziptop bag. Add vinegar and steaks. Marinate 15 minutes at room temperature or at least 2 hours in refrigerator.

Pour remaining oil mixture into another large ziptop bag. Add potato slices and pepper halves. Shake to coat with marinade; refrigerate 1 hour.

Heat outdoor grill or stovetop grill pan. Remove potatoes and peppers from bag, saving marinade. Grill potatoes 18 minutes, turning once. Grill peppers 8 minutes, turning once. Slice peppers into strips; toss with reserved marinade.

Remove steaks from bag; discard steak marinade. Grill steaks 3 minutes, turning once. Spoon peppers on top of steaks; serve with potato planks.

PER SERVING
CALORIES 565 **TOTAL FAT** 34G **SATURATED FAT** 4G **CHOLESTEROL** 68MG **SODIUM** 274MG
TOTAL CARBOHYDRATES 35G **DIETARY FIBER** 5G **PROTEIN** 31G

BACON-WRAPPED PORK TENDERLOIN

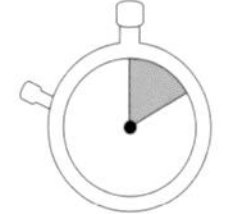

YIELD
5 servings

ACTIVE
10 minutes

TOTAL
40 minutes

1 **PORK TENDERLOIN** (ABOUT 1¼ LB)

3 **SCALLIONS**, TRIMMED AND CUT LENGTHWISE IN STRIPS

5 STRIPS **LOWER-SODIUM BACON**

½ TSP **PEPPER**

1 TBSP **SUGAR**

SIDE SUGGESTION
Steamed carrots

Heat oven to 425°F. Make a long slit lengthwise down center of pork, being careful not to cut all the way through. Open like a book. Place scallions on one cut side of pork; fold pork back over to close.

Wrap bacon slices around pork to cover completely. Place in small roasting pan. Rub pepper and sugar over bacon. Roast 20 minutes or until instant-read thermometer inserted in center reads 150°F. Let stand 10 minutes before slicing.

DIFFERENT TAKES

- Spread pork with Dijon mustard before wrapping with bacon.
- Rub bacon with brown sugar instead of granulated sugar.
- Substitute fresh chopped herbs for the scallions.

PER SERVING
CALORIES 172 **TOTAL FAT** 6G **SATURATED FAT** 2G **CHOLESTEROL** 69MG **SODIUM** 134MG **TOTAL CARBOHYDRATES** 4G **DIETARY FIBER** 0G **PROTEIN** 25G

HAM & COLESLAW HERO

COLESLAW

½ CUP **PLAIN LOWFAT YOGURT**

2 TBSP **LIGHT MAYONNAISE**

1 TBSP **WINE VINEGAR**

2 TSP **HONEY-DIJON MUSTARD**

¼ TSP FRESHLY GROUND **PEPPER**

8 OZ **COLESLAW MIX** (ABOUT 4 CUPS)

1 **LOAF ITALIAN BREAD** (ABOUT 1 LB)

6 OZ **THINLY SLICED REDUCED-SODIUM HAM**

1 JAR (12 OZ) **ROASTED RED PEPPERS,** WELL-DRAINED AND CUT IN STRIPS

¾ CUP THINLY SLICED **RED ONION**

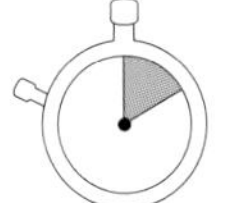

YIELD
4 servings

ACTIVE
10 minutes

TOTAL
10 minutes

COLESLAW Whisk yogurt, mayonnaise, vinegar, mustard and pepper in a medium bowl. Add coleslaw mix and toss to coat well.

Split Italian bread horizontally. Arrange ham on bottom half, then peppers and onion. Cover with coleslaw and bread top. Cut loaf in four portions to serve.

PER SERVING
CALORIES 443 **TOTAL FAT** 8G **SATURATED FAT** 2G **CHOLESTEROL** 25MG **SODIUM** 1,314MG
TOTAL CARBOHYDRATES 70G **DIETARY FIBER** 5G **PROTEIN** 20G

EGGPLANT ROLLATINI

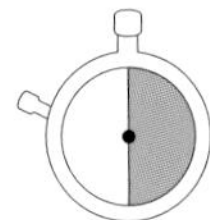

YIELD
6 servings

ACTIVE
30 minutes

TOTAL
1 hour

1 JAR (24 OZ) **PUTTANESCA SAUCE**

2 LARGE **EGGPLANTS**

2 TBSP **OIL**

12 OZ **LINGUINE FINI**

Heat oven to 400°F. Line 2 large baking sheets with nonstick foil.

Spread ½ cup puttanesca sauce in a 13 x 9-in. baking dish. Cut each eggplant lengthwise in 6 slices, trimming to make slices even. Brush both sides with oil. Place on baking sheets. Coarsely chop trimmings; add to sheets. Bake 20 minutes; turn and bake 10 minutes more or until tender.

Bring a large pot of lightly salted water to a boil. Add pasta and cook as package directs. Drain and return to pot. Stir chopped eggplant trimmings into remaining sauce, remove 1 cup sauce and reserve. Toss rest of sauce with the pasta.

Top each slice eggplant with ¼ cup pasta and roll up. Spread remaining pasta in baking dish; top with rollatini, seam side down. Spread with the 1 cup reserved sauce; cover with foil. Bake 30 minutes or until hot and bubbly.

PER SERVING
CALORIES 340 **TOTAL FAT** 9G **SATURATED FAT** 1G **CHOLESTEROL** 0MG **SODIUM** 507MG
TOTAL CARBOHYDRATES 58G **DIETARY FIBER** 7G **PROTEIN** 11G

GLAZED CORNED BEEF

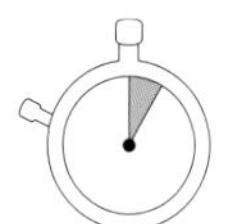

YIELD
6 servings

ACTIVE
5 minutes

TOTAL
4 hours

1 **THIN-CUT CORNED BEEF BRISKET** (ABOUT 2¾ LB), FAT TRIMMED

¼ CUP **APPLE JELLY**

¼ CUP **SWEET-HOT** OR **HONEY MUSTARD**

SIDE SUGGESTION
Boiled cabbage and carrots

Heat oven to 350°F. Put corned beef in a Dutch oven, add water to cover and bring to a boil.

Cover and bake 3½ to 4 hours until fork-tender. Remove from oven.

Heat broiler. Line a rimmed baking sheet with nonstick foil. Place beef on sheet.

Whisk jelly and mustard in a bowl until smooth. Spoon about ½ the glaze over beef.

Broil 2 minutes or until glaze bubbles. Remove to a cutting board; thinly slice across the grain. Serve with remaining glaze.

DIFFERENT TAKES

- Instead of cooking corned beef in oven, simmer in slow cooker 10 to 11 hours on low. Glaze and broil as directed.
- Add some pickling spices to the cooking water.
- Make Reuben wraps with leftovers: Spread sandwich wraps with Russian dressing. Top with sliced corned beef, Swiss cheese and sauerkraut; roll up.

PER SERVING
CALORIES 275 **TOTAL FAT** 14G **SATURATED FAT** 4G **CHOLESTEROL** 89MG **SODIUM** 2,674MG **TOTAL CARBOHYDRATES** 14G **DIETARY FIBER** 0G **PROTEIN** 24G

ROAST DRUMSTICKS & VEGETABLES

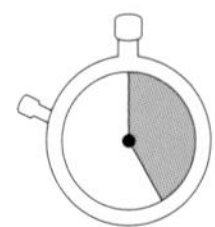

YIELD
4 servings

ACTIVE
25 minutes

TOTAL
1 hour 10 minutes

8 **CHICKEN DRUMSTICKS** (2¼ LB)

1½ LB **ALL-PURPOSE POTATOES**, SCRUBBED AND QUARTERED

1 LB **CARROTS**, CUT IN 2-IN. PIECES

2 LB **BUTTERNUT SQUASH**, PEELED, SEEDED AND CUT IN 1-IN.-WIDE SLICES

2 MEDIUM **ONIONS**, EACH CUT IN 8 WEDGES

5 CLOVES **GARLIC**, HALVED

2 TBSP **OIL**

1 TBSP **ITALIAN HERB SEASONING**

1½ TSP **SALT**

1 TSP FRESHLY GROUND **PEPPER**

Position racks to divide oven in thirds. Heat oven to 425°F.

Put all ingredients in a large bowl; stir to mix and coat. Arrange in a single layer on 2 rimmed baking sheets.

Roast, switching position of pans and turning vegetables halfway through roasting, 45 minutes or until chicken is cooked through and vegetables are tender.

PER SERVING
CALORIES 649 **TOTAL FAT** 22G **SATURATED FAT** 5G **CHOLESTEROL** 139MG **SODIUM** 1,088MG
TOTAL CARBOHYDRATES 74G **DIETARY FIBER** 11G **PROTEIN** 41G

SEASIDE MAC & CHEESE

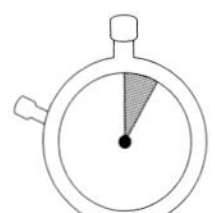

YIELD
4 servings

ACTIVE
5 minutes

TOTAL
12 minutes

2 BOXES (12 OZ EACH) **CREAMY CHEESE-SAUCE-AND-SHELL PASTA**

1 BAG (12 OZ) **FROZEN MEDIUM SHRIMP**, COOKED, PEELED AND DEVEINED

1 CUP **BOTTLED SALSA**

GARNISH: CHOPPED **CILANTRO**

SIDE SUGGESTION
Mixed greens salad

Cook pasta shells in a large pot of lightly salted boiling water as package directs. Two minutes before pasta is done, add frozen shrimp. Cook, stirring often, 2 minutes or until shrimp are hot.

Drain pasta and shrimp in a colander; return to pot. Stir in cheese sauce from packets. Pour into serving dish. Top servings with salsa and garnish with cilantro.

PER SERVING
CALORIES 646 **TOTAL FAT** 20G **SATURATED FAT** 8G **CHOLESTEROL** 203MG **SODIUM** 2,146MG
TOTAL CARBOHYDRATES 72G **DIETARY FIBER** 3G **PROTEIN** 39G

RACK OF LAMB

BREADING

¼ CUP EACH **FRESH BREAD CRUMBS, CHOPPED PARSLEY** AND **GRATED PARMESAN**

1 TBSP PLUS 1 TSP **OLIVE OIL**

1 TBSP MINCED **GARLIC**

¼ TSP EACH **SALT** AND **PEPPER**

2 TBSP **DIJON MUSTARD**

8-RIB **RACK OF LAMB** (1½ TO 2 LB), FAT TRIMMED OFF TOP OF RIBS LEAVING A THIN LAYER

1 LB **RED-SKINNED POTATOES**, SCRUBBED, CUT IN 1-IN. CHUNKS

1 TBSP **OLIVE OIL**

½ TSP EACH **SALT** AND **PEPPER**

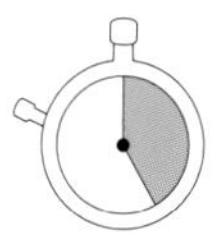

YIELD
4 servings

ACTIVE
25 minutes

TOTAL
1 hour 5 minutes

Heat oven to 425°F. Coat half of a shallow roasting pan with nonstick spray.

Mix BREADING ingredients in a small bowl. Spread mustard on both sides of lamb; pat on breading. Place bone side down on sprayed side of pan. Toss potatoes with remaining ingredients. Spread in a single layer next to lamb.

Roast 30 to 35 minutes, turning potatoes once, until tender and golden brown and a meat thermometer inserted in thickest part of meat, not touching bone, registers 150°F for medium-well chops at ends of rack, medium-rare at center. Let lamb rest 10 minutes before cutting into chops.

PER SERVING
CALORIES 341 **TOTAL FAT** 18G **SATURATED FAT** 5G **CHOLESTEROL** 60MG **SODIUM** 791MG **TOTAL CARBOHYDRATES** 21G **DIETARY FIBER** 2G **PROTEIN** 22G

APRICOT-GLAZED SMOKED HAM

1 **READY-TO-COOK BONE-IN SMOKED HAM HALF** (8- TO 10-LB), PREFERABLY SHANK END

WHOLE CLOVES

3 CUPS **WATER**

GLAZE

1 JAR (12-OZ) **APRICOT PRESERVES**

¼ CUP **LIGHT BROWN SUGAR**
2 TBSP **GRAINY DIJON MUSTARD** (WE USED MAILLE)

1 TBSP **CIDER VINEGAR**

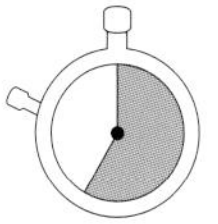

YIELD
8 servings with leftovers

ACTIVE
35 minutes

TOTAL
3 hours

PLAN AHEAD
Let ham come to room temperature, covered, about 2 hours before baking.

Position oven rack in bottom third of oven; heat to 325°F.

Cut off thick rind on ham to expose the fat layer underneath, leaving about 5 inches of the rind intact covering the narrow shank end. Using a sharp knife, score fat in diamond pattern. Press 1 clove into center of each diamond. Place ham in a shallow roasting pan; pour water in pan. Cover loosely with heavy-duty foil. Roast ham 1½ hours.

Meanwhile, mix **GLAZE** ingredients. Remove ham from oven; brush with ⅓ of the glaze. Continue to bake, uncovered, 1 hour, brushing with remaining glaze every 20 minutes, or until internal temperature registers 160°F on an instant-read thermometer.

Let ham rest 20 minutes. Transfer to platter. Serve ham hot, warm or at room temperature.

PER 4-OZ SERVING
CALORIES 284 **TOTAL FAT** 13G **SATURATED FAT** 4G **CHOLESTEROL** 85MG **SODIUM** 965MG
TOTAL CARBOHYDRATES 17G **DIETARY FIBER** 0G **PROTEIN** 26G

ITALIAN LENTIL & VEGETABLE STEW

1½ CUPS **DRIED LENTILS**

3 CUPS **WATER**

3 CUPS **BUTTERNUT SQUASH**, CUT IN 1-IN. CHUNKS

2 CUPS **BOTTLED MARINARA SAUCE**

2 CUPS **GREEN BEANS**, ENDS TRIMMED AND BEANS CUT IN HALF

1 **RED BELL PEPPER**, CUT IN 1-IN. PIECES

1 LARGE **ALL-PURPOSE POTATO**, PEELED AND CUT IN 1-IN. CHUNKS

¾ CUP CHOPPED **ONION**

1 TSP MINCED **GARLIC**

1 TBSP **OLIVE OIL**, PREFERABLY EXTRA-VIRGIN

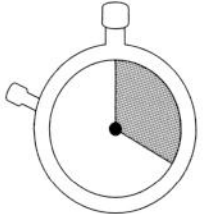

YIELD
5 servings

ACTIVE
20 minutes

TOTAL
8 to 10 hours on low

SERVE WITH
Grated parmesan

Mix lentils and 3 cups water in a 3-qt or larger slow cooker. In a large bowl, mix remaining ingredients except olive oil; place over lentils.

Cover and cook on low 8 to 10 hours until vegetables and lentils are tender. Stir in the oil. Serve in soup plates or bowls.

PER SERVING
CALORIES 383 **TOTAL FAT** 7G **SATURATED FAT** 1G **CHOLESTEROL** 0MG **SODIUM** 644MG **TOTAL CARBOHYDRATES** 66G **DIETARY FIBER** 12G **PROTEIN** 21G

SAUSAGE & POTATO FRITTATA

4 TSP **OIL**

1 LB **LEAN SWEET ITALIAN TURKEY SAUSAGE**, CASINGS REMOVED

1 MEDIUM **ZUCCHINI** (ABOUT 6 OZ), THINLY SLICED

8 LARGE **EGGS**

1 CAN (14.5 OZ) **SLICED POTATOES**

1 CAN (8.75 OZ) **WHOLE-KERNEL CORN**

4 OZ (HALF AN 8-OZ BRICK) **⅓-LESS-FAT CREAM CHEESE (NEUFCHÂTEL)**, DICED

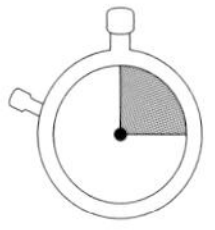

YIELD
6 servings

ACTIVE
15 minutes

TOTAL
30 minutes

Heat 2 tsp oil in a nonstick 10-in. skillet over medium-high heat. Add sausage and zucchini. Cook, stirring and breaking up sausage with a wooden spoon, 5 to 6 minutes until sausage is cooked through and zucchini is tender. Let cool.

Meanwhile, whisk eggs in a medium bowl, and drain the potatoes and corn. Stir sausage, zucchini, potatoes and corn into eggs, then stir in cream cheese. Wipe skillet clean.

Heat broiler (see Note). Heat remaining 2 tsp oil in skillet over medium-low heat, tilting skillet to coat bottom and halfway up sides.

Add egg mixture, cover and cook 12 minutes or until eggs are set on bottom. Slide under broiler and cook just until eggs on top have set.

NOTE If the skillet handle is plastic or wood, wrap it in a double layer of foil to protect it from scorching when placed under the broiler.

PER SERVING
CALORIES 354 **TOTAL FAT** 22G **SATURATED FAT** 7G **CHOLESTEROL** 337MG **SODIUM** 721MG
TOTAL CARBOHYDRATES 15G **DIETARY FIBER** 1G **PROTEIN** 25G

CHICKEN WITH TOMATOES & ARUGULA

CHICKEN

2 TBSP **ALL-PURPOSE FLOUR**

¼ TSP **SALT**

¼ TSP **PEPPER**

4 **BONELESS, SKINLESS CHICKEN BREASTS** (ABOUT 5 OZ EACH)

1 TSP **OLIVE OIL**

¼ CUP **WATER**

½ CUP CHOPPED **ONION**

1 TSP MINCED **GARLIC**

9 MEDIUM **PLUM TOMATOES** (ABOUT 1½ POUNDS), CUT IN BITE-SIZE PIECES

½ TSP **SALT**

¼ TSP **PEPPER**

1 TBSP **BALSAMIC VINEGAR**

1 BUNCH (ABOUT 5 OZ) **ARUGULA**, RINSED AND PATTED DRY

PARMESAN CURLS (ABOUT 1 OZ), SHAVED FROM A CHUNK OF CHEESE WITH A VEGETABLE PEELER

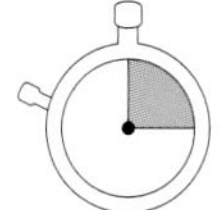

YIELD
4 servings

ACTIVE
15 minutes

TOTAL
30 minutes

CHICKEN Mix flour, salt and pepper in a large ziptop food bag. Add half the chicken; close bag and shake until evenly coated. Remove, shaking off excess flour. Repeat with remaining chicken.

Heat oil in a large nonstick skillet over medium-high heat. Add chicken and cook 6 to 8 minutes, turning once, until golden-brown and no longer pink at center. Remove to cutting board; cut each breast in half lengthwise. Place on a warm serving platter; cover loosely with foil to keep warm.

Place water, onion and garlic in same skillet. Cook until onions are soft, about 3 minutes. Add tomatoes, salt and pepper. Cook until juices released from tomatoes start to boil. Stir in vinegar, then add arugula. Toss with tongs or 2 large spoons until well mixed. Pour over chicken. Scatter cheese over the top.

PER SERVING
CALORIES 257 **TOTAL FAT** 5G **SATURATED FAT** 0G **CHOLESTEROL** 87MG **SODIUM** 787MG
TOTAL CARBOHYDRATES 14G **DIETARY FIBER** 0G **PROTEIN** 38G

TEX-MEX STUFFED CABBAGE

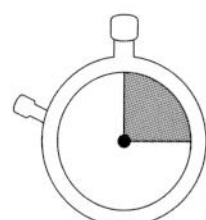

YIELD
4 servings

ACTIVE
15 minutes

TOTAL
21 minutes

FILLING

2 TSP **OIL**

12 OZ **GROUND TURKEY**

½ CUP FINELY CHOPPED **ONION**

1 TBSP EACH **CHILI POWDER**, PACKED **BROWN SUGAR** AND **CIDER VINEGAR**

1 CAN (8 OZ) **TOMATO SAUCE**

1 CUP COOKED **WHITE RICE**

¼ CUP **DARK RAISINS**

2 TSP **GROUND CUMIN**

¾ TSP **SALT**

1 MEDIUM HEAD **CABBAGE**

¾ CUP **WATER**

ACCOMPANIMENTS: **BOTTLED SALSA** AND **REDUCED-FAT SOUR CREAM**

Heat oven to 375°F. Heat oil in a large nonstick skillet over medium-high heat. Add turkey and onion, and cook, breaking up meat, 4 minutes or until no longer pink. Stir in remaining FILLING ingredients; heat 2 to 3 minutes.

Meanwhile, core and rinse cabbage. Wrap in wax paper and microwave on high 4 minutes or until 8 large outer leaves can be removed easily (save rest of cabbage for another use). Cut thick ribs from leaves. If leaves are still not pliable, wrap in wax paper and microwave about 2 minutes more.

Put ⅓ cup filling on each leaf. Fold in sides and roll up starting with the core end. Place seam side down in an 11 x 17-in. baking dish; add water. Cover tightly with foil.

Bake 45 minutes or until tender. Serve with red or green salsa and reduced-fat sour cream.

PER SERVING
CALORIES 294 **TOTAL FAT** 10G **SATURATED FAT** 2G **CHOLESTEROL** 62MG **SODIUM** 903MG
TOTAL CARBOHYDRATES 35G **DIETARY FIBER** 5G **PROTEIN** 19G

COD WITH ORANGES

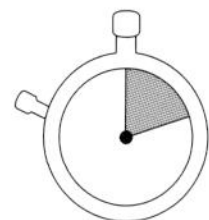

YIELD
4 servings

ACTIVE
12 minutes

TOTAL
30 minutes

4 **NAVEL ORANGES**

FOUR ¾- **TO 1-IN.-THICK PIECES COD FILLET** (ABOUT 5 OZ EACH)

¼ TSP EACH **SALT** AND **PEPPER**

1 TBSP **OIL**

1 CUP **THINLY SLICED RED ONION**

SIDE SUGGESTION
Couscous and green beans

Cut peel from 2 oranges to the flesh; section oranges and squeeze juice from membranes into a 2-cup measure. Squeeze juice from remaining oranges (you should have 1 cup).

Season fish with salt and pepper. Heat oil in a large nonstick skillet over medium-high heat. Add fish and cook 6 to 8 minutes, turning once, until lightly browned and cooked through. Remove to a platter; cover loosely with foil to keep warm.

Add onion to skillet; cook over low heat until lightly browned.

Add juice to pan, bring to a boil; cook until reduced to about ½ cup and slightly thickened. Stir in orange segments; pour over fish.

PER SERVING
CALORIES 223 **TOTAL FAT** 5G **SATURATED FAT** 1G **CHOLESTEROL** 61MG **SODIUM** 225MG
TOTAL CARBOHYDRATES 18G **DIETARY FIBER** 2G **PROTEIN** 27G

GRILLED VEGGIE PIZZAS ALFREDO

1 TUBE (10 OZ) **REFRIGERATED PIZZA CRUST**

1 LB **WHOLE PORTOBELLO MUSHROOMS**, STEMS REMOVED

1 EACH **RED** AND **YELLOW BELL PEPPER**, QUARTERED AND CORED

1 EACH (ABOUT 6 OZ EACH) MEDIUM **ZUCCHINI** AND **YELLOW SQUASH**, CUT LENGTHWISE IN ½-IN.-THICK SLICES

NONSTICK SPRAY

¾ TSP **SALT**

1 CUP **REDUCED-FAT MUSHROOM ALFREDO SAUCE**

5 OZ **SMOKED MOZZARELLA**, SHREDDED (1¼ CUPS)

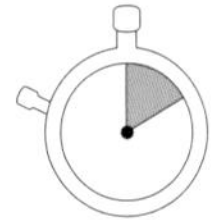

YIELD
4 servings

ACTIVE
10 minutes

TOTAL
31 minutes

Heat barbecue grill. Lightly dust 2 baking sheets with flour.

On a lightly floured surface, press dough into a 15 x 11-in. rectangle. Cut in quarters; place 2 on each baking sheet.

Lightly coat veggies with nonstick spray; sprinkle with salt.

Grill vegetables, turning once: mushrooms and peppers 10 to 12 minutes (mushrooms should be tender and peppers charred), squashes 8 to 10 minutes until tender. Cut mushrooms and peppers in slices, squashes in half crosswise.

Grill 2 pieces pizza dough at a time, 1 minute or until undersides are browned. Using tongs, turn dough over and grill 30 seconds or until undersides stiffen. Return to baking sheets; repeat with remaining dough. Spread crusts with sauce. Top with vegetables and cheese.

Grill 2 pizzas at a time, covered, 2 to 3 minutes until cheese melts, making sure undersides of pizzas don't burn.

PER SERVING
CALORIES 396 **TOTAL FAT** 15G **SATURATED FAT** 7G **CHOLESTEROL** 40MG **SODIUM** 1,725MG **TOTAL CARBOHYDRATES** 50G **DIETARY FIBER** 4G **PROTEIN** 20G

CRANBERRY-PISTACHIO-STUFFED TURKEY BREAST WITH GRAVY

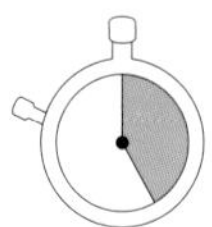

YIELD
6 servings

ACTIVE
25 minutes

TOTAL
1 hour 45 minutes

TURKEY/STUFFING

2 TBSP **BUTTER**

2 CUPS CHOPPED **ONIONS**

2 SLICES **FIRM WHOLE-WHEAT OR WHITE BREAD**, CUT IN ¼-IN. CUBES

¼ CUP EACH CHOPPED **PISTACHIOS, DRIED CRANBERRIES** AND SNIPPED **APRICOTS**

1 TBSP CHOPPED **FRESH THYME** *OR* 1 TSP **DRIED**

¼ CUP **CHICKEN BROTH**

1 **BONELESS, SKINLESS TURKEY BREAST** (ABOUT 2½ LB)

6 STRIPS **REDUCED-SODIUM BACON**

GRAVY

1½ CUPS **CHICKEN BROTH**

⅓ CUP **DRY WHITE WINE**

1 TBSP **CORNSTARCH**

1 TSP CHOPPED **FRESH THYME** *OR* ¼ TSP **DRIED**

GARNISH: **HERB SPRIGS** AND **DRIED CRANBERRIES**

TURKEY/STUFFING Heat oven to 375°F. Oil a large roasting pan.

Melt butter in a large nonstick skillet over medium heat. Add onions; cover and cook 12 minutes, stirring occasionally, until golden. Off heat, stir in bread, pistachios, cranberries, apricots and thyme. Stir in broth; toss until moist.

Place turkey breast skinned side down with one long side facing you between double layers of plastic wrap. Pound meat at thickest parts to ½ in. thick. Remove wrap on top; mound stuffing crosswise down middle. Fold sides of turkey over stuffing into a tight roll. Skewer with toothpicks to help keep stuffing enclosed. Place pick side down in pan; wrap bacon crosswise around meat, tucking ends under.

Roast 60 to 70 minutes until thermometer inserted in center registers 160°F. Transfer to a cutting board; cover loosely with foil and let rest while preparing gravy (internal temperature will rise to 165°F).

GRAVY Discard fat from roasting pan. Place pan on stove over 2 burners. Add 1¼ cups chicken broth and the wine. Cook over medium-high heat, scraping up browned bits on bottom of pan until boiling. Boil 1 minute.

Mix remaining broth and cornstarch in a small cup until smooth. Stir along with the thyme into pan. Cook, stirring often, until boiling. Boil 1 minute until slightly thickened and clear.

TO SERVE Remove toothpicks from turkey. Cut in ½-in.-thick slices. Place on serving platter; garnish. Pour gravy into gravy boat and serve alongside.

PLANNING TIP Stuffing and turkey can be prepared up to 1 day ahead. After wrapping with bacon, cover and refrigerate, then roast when ready.

PER SERVING
CALORIES 400 **TOTAL FAT** 11G **SATURATED FAT** 4G **CHOLESTEROL** 133MG **SODIUM** 436MG
TOTAL CARBOHYDRATES 19G **DIETARY FIBER** 3G **PROTEIN** 52G

SPINACH-RICE CAKES

2 TSP **OIL**

½ CUP CHOPPED **ONION**

2 CLOVES **GARLIC**, MINCED

1 BOX (10 OZ) **FROZEN LEAF SPINACH**, THAWED AND COARSELY CUT

2¼ CUPS **WATER**

1 CUP **LONG-GRAIN RICE**

½ CUP **GRATED PARMESAN**

¼ TSP **PEPPER**

1 LARGE **EGG**

2 OZ **PART-SKIM MOZZARELLA**, SHREDDED

2 CUPS **MARINARA SAUCE**

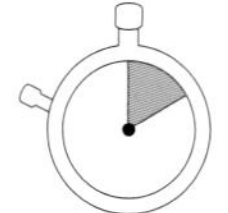

YIELD
4 servings

ACTIVE
10 minutes

TOTAL
50 minutes

Heat oil in a large nonstick skillet over high heat. Sauté onion and garlic 2 minutes. Add spinach and water; bring to a boil.

Stir in rice; cover and simmer 20 minutes or until water is absorbed. Heat oven to 350°F. Line a large baking sheet with nonstick foil.

Transfer rice to bowl; stir in Parmesan and pepper. Mix in egg. For each cake, scoop and flatten ¼ cup rice mixture onto baking sheet.

Bake 20 minutes or until firm. Sprinkle tops with mozzarella; return to oven 1 minute to melt. Serve with warmed marinara.

PER SERVING
CALORIES 562 **TOTAL FAT** 22G **SATURATED FAT** 8G **CHOLESTEROL** 100MG **SODIUM** 1,406MG **TOTAL CARBOHYDRATES** 66G **DIETARY FIBER** 6G **PROTEIN** 25G

TOSTADOS

8 **CORN TORTILLAS**

NONSTICK COOKING SPRAY

1 LB **BONELESS, SKINLESS CHICKEN THIGHS**

1½ TSP **GROUND CUMIN**

2 TSP **OIL**

1 FIRM-RIPE **AVOCADO**

2 TBSP **LIME JUICE**

1 CAN (15.5 OZ) **BLACK BEANS**, RINSED

¼ CUP CHOPPED **CILANTRO**

½ CUP **SMOOTH CHIPOTLE SALSA**

3 TO 4 CUPS CHOPPED **ROMAINE LETTUCE**

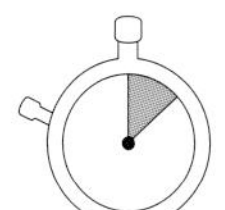

YIELD
4 servings

ACTIVE
8 minutes

TOTAL
15 minutes

Heat oven to 450°F. Coat corn tortillas with nonstick spray. Place directly on oven rack; bake 8 minutes to crisp.

Meanwhile, cut chicken into 1-in. pieces; toss with 1 tsp cumin. Heat oil in large nonstick skillet over medium-high heat. Cook chicken 5 minutes, or until browned and cooked through.

Cut avocado into chunks. Toss with lime juice, black beans, cilantro and remaining ½ tsp cumin.

Stir salsa into chicken; remove from heat. Serve corn tortillas topped with lettuce, bean mixture and chicken. Serve with additional salsa.

PER SERVING
CALORIES 468 **TOTAL FAT** 16G **SATURATED FAT** 3G **CHOLESTEROL** 94MG **SODIUM** 509MG
TOTAL CARBOHYDRATES 50G **DIETARY FIBER** 15G **PROTEIN** 34G

GINGER SALMON OVER BOK CHOY

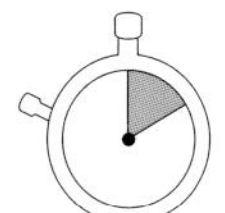

YIELD
4 servings

ACTIVE
10 minutes

TOTAL
20 minutes

3 TBSP **HOISIN SAUCE**

4 TSP MINCED **FRESH GINGER**

1 TBSP **HONEY**

4 **SALMON FILLETS** (ABOUT 1¼ IN. THICK, 5 TO 6 OZ EACH)

2 TSP **CANOLA OIL**

2 TSP MINCED **GARLIC**

1 LB **BOK CHOY**, HALVED LENGTHWISE, THEN SLICED CROSSWISE IN 1-IN. STRIPS

1 CUP SHREDDED **CARROTS**

¼ TSP **SALT**

Heat broiler. Line a rimmed baking pan with nonstick foil.

In a small cup, mix hoisin, 2 tsp of the ginger, and the honey. Set aside 2 Tbsp for serving later. Place salmon skin-side down on baking sheet. Spoon, then spread about 1½ tsp hoisin mixture onto each fillet.

Broil 7 to 9 minutes until salmon is just cooked through (opaque at center).

Meanwhile, heat oil in a large nonstick skillet. Add remaining 2 tsp ginger and the garlic; cook over low heat a few seconds until fragrant.

Increase heat to medium-high. Add bok choy, carrots and salt; toss. Cover and cook 4 to 6 minutes, stirring occasionally, until bok choy and carrots are tender.

Spoon bok choy mixture onto serving plates; top with salmon and drizzle with reserved hoisin mixture.

PER SERVING
CALORIES 368 **TOTAL FAT** 15G **SATURATED FAT** 2G **CHOLESTEROL** 108MG **SODIUM** 516MG **TOTAL CARBOHYDRATES** 16G **DIETARY FIBER** 3G **PROTEIN** 41G

APRIL

APRIL SHOPPING LIST

Week 1

APRIL 1 TO APRIL 7

PRODUCE

1 ORANGE
2 LIMES
1 HEAD GARLIC (4 CLOVES)
1 LARGE BEEFSTEAK TOMATO
2 ZUCCHINI
FRESH ROSEMARY
8 SAGE LEAVES (OR 2 TSP DRIED)
1 BUNCH BASIL
1 BUNCH CILANTRO

BAKERY

4 LARGE SLICES ITALIAN BREAD
4 SPLIT SEEDED KAISER OR HAMBURGER ROLLS

MEAT/POULTRY/FISH

1 FLANK STEAK (1½ LB)
8 CHICKEN THIGHS (ABOUT 2 LB)
1 PRECOOKED 7- TO 8-LB SPIRAL-SLICED BONE-IN HALF HAM (SHANK OR BUTT)
FOUR ¾- TO 1-IN.-THICK PIECES SWORDFISH STEAK (6 OZ EACH)

DELI

4 OZ BAKED HAM

REFRIGERATED

½ STICK BUTTER
1 CONTAINER (8 OZ) REDUCED-FAT SOUR CREAM
¾ CUP SHREDDED MOZZARELLA AND ASIAGO CHEESE WITH ROASTED GARLIC OR ¾ CUP SHREDDED MOZZARELLA
2½ CUPS SHREDDED CHEDDAR AND MONTEREY JACK CHEESE BLEND

FROZEN

½ CUP CUT GREEN BEANS
½ CUP GREEN BELL PEPPER
1 BOX (10 OZ) BROCCOLI

GROCERY

1 CAN (14.5 OZ) NO-SALT-ADDED DICED TOMATOES IN JUICE
1 CAN (15 TO 16 OZ) BLACK-EYED PEAS
1 CAN (15 TO 16 OZ) RED KIDNEY BEANS
1 CAN (12 OZ) EVAPORATED MILK
1½ CUPS JARRED MARINARA SAUCE
¼ CUP JARRED ROASTED RED PEPPERS
1 JAR (9.5 OZ) HOT-PEPPER SPREAD OR JELLY
1 CUP THICK-AND-CHUNKY SALSA
¾ LB ELBOW MACARONI (3 CUPS)
LIGHT MAYONNAISE
WORCESTERSHIRE SAUCE
1 BOX (6 OZ) CORNBREAD STUFFING MIX
1½ CUPS DRY RED WINE

PANTRY

SALT
PEPPER
OLIVE OIL
RED-WINE VINEGAR
CORNSTARCH
LIGHT-BROWN SUGAR
DIJON MUSTARD
DRIED OREGANO
CRUSHED RED PEPPER
CHILI POWDER

Week 2

APRIL 8 TO APRIL 14

PRODUCE

2 SMALL ONIONS
2 MEDIUM ONIONS
1 HEAD GARLIC (5 CLOVES)
1 SMALL CARROT
1 RED, YELLOW OR ORANGE BELL PEPPER
1 YELLOW SQUASH (ABOUT 8 OZ)
1 ZUCCHINI (ABOUT 8 OZ)
2 AVOCADOS
1 HEAD ROMAINE LETTUCE
6 CUPS BABY SPINACH
4 CUPS BAGGED CLASSIC COLESLAW MIX
1 BUNCH FRESH BASIL OR PARSLEY

MEAT/POULTRY/FISH

4 LB COUNTRY-STYLE PORK RIBS
4 BONELESS, SKINLESS CHICKEN BREASTS (ABOUT 4 OZ EACH)
4 TURKEY BREAST CUTLETS (ABOUT 4 OZ EACH)
3 LINKS (ABOUT 8 OZ) ITALIAN TURKEY SAUSAGE

DELI

8 OZ SLICED 97%-FAT-FREE HONEY-ROASTED & SMOKED TURKEY BREAST
4 OZ THINLY SLICED REDUCED-FAT, LOW-SODIUM SWISS CHEESE

REFRIGERATED

½ CUP MILK
1 CONTAINER (8 OZ) SOUR CREAM
2 CONTAINERS (15 OZ) PART-SKIM RICOTTA
½ CUP SHREDDED MOZZARELLA WITH PARMESAN
GRATED PARMESAN
EGGS (4 LARGE)
1 TUBE (ABOUT 16 OZ) POLENTA

FROZEN

1 PKG (12 OZ) CHICKEN BURGERS (4 BURGERS), PREFERABLY SPICY SALSA AND CHEDDAR FLAVOR (WE USED CASUAL GOURMET)
2¼ CUPS (8 OZ) CUT-LEAF SPINACH, FROM A 10-OZ BAG
2 CUPS (10 OZ) GREEN PEAS

GROCERY

1 CAN (14.5 OZ) CHICKEN BROTH
1 CAN (14.5 OZ) CHUNKY TOMATOES, PASTA-STYLE
1 CAN (ABOUT 16 OZ) CRUSHED TOMATOES
1 CAN (4.5 OZ) CHOPPED GREEN CHILES
1 JAR (28 OZ) MARINARA SAUCE
1 JAR (15.5 OZ) SALSA
1 BOX (8 OR 9 OZ) OVEN-READY LASAGNA NOODLES
4 BURRITO-SIZE (8 IN.) FLOUR TORTILLAS
FOUR 8-IN. PLAIN OR WHOLE-WHEAT FLOUR TORTILLA WRAPS
3 PKG (ABOUT 3 OZ EACH) ANY FLAVOR RAMEN NOODLE SOUP
FAT-FREE THOUSAND ISLAND DRESSING

1 CUP HOT 'N SPICY BARBECUE SAUCE
1/3 CUP SEASONED DRIED BREAD CRUMBS

PANTRY
SALT
PEPPER
OLIVE OIL
FLOUR
CHILI POWDER
FENNEL SEEDS

Week 3
APRIL 15 TO APRIL 22

PRODUCE
2 APPLES
1 CONTAINER (20 OZ) PEELED AND CORED FRESH PINEAPPLE
2 LEMONS
2 ONIONS
4 RED ONIONS
1 HEAD GARLIC (7 CLOVES)
8 PLUM TOMATOES (ABOUT 2 LB)
1 MEDIUM CUCUMBER
6 BELL PEPPERS (ANY COLOR)
2 RED BELL PEPPERS
1 EGGPLANT (1½ LB)
3 SMALL ZUCCHINI
2 LARGE ZUCCHINI (ABOUT 1¼ LB)
1 YELLOW SQUASH (ABOUT 6 OZ)
1 AVOCADO
1 LB MUSHROOMS
1 HEAD GREEN LETTUCE
1 PKG (5 OZ) MIXED SALAD GREENS
2 BAGS (4.5 OZ EACH) WALNUT & CRANBERRY SPRING MIX SALAD
1 BUNCH FRESH MINT
1 BUNCH BASIL
1 BUNCH CILANTRO

BAKERY
2 SLICES 7-GRAIN OR OTHER WHOLE-GRAIN BREAD
4 PITAS
4 PORTUGUESE OR KAISER ROLLS

MEAT/POULTRY/FISH
12 OZ GROUND BEEF
1 PORK TENDERLOIN (ABOUT 12 OZ)
FOUR ¼-IN.-THICK PORK CUTLETS (ABOUT 12 OZ)
12 OZ GROUND PORK
6 OZ FULLY COOKED CHORIZO SAUSAGE (2 LINKS)

DELI
ONE 12-OZ CHUNK SMOKED TURKEY
8 THIN SLICES SWISS CHEESE
8 THIN SLICES VIRGINIA HAM
½ CUP SLICED DILL PICKLES

REFRIGERATED
1 CUP PLAIN YOGURT
4 OZ CHEDDAR
GRATED PARMESAN
EGG (1 LARGE)

FROZEN
1 BAG (16 OZ) CORN, BLACK BEAN, TOMATO, GREEN PEPPER AND ONION MIXTURE (LATINO BLEND)
2 BAGS (8.5 OZ EACH) HONEY CHIPOTLE SHRIMP

GROCERY
1 CAN (15 OZ) BLACK BEANS
1 JAR (28 OZ) MARINARA SAUCE
1 JAR (6.5 OZ) OIL-CURED OLIVES
1 LB LINGUINE OR SPAGHETTI PASTA
CONVERTED (PARBOILED) WHITE RICE
BOTTLED HONEY-MUSTARD DRESSING
1 BOX (6 OZ) FALAFEL MIX
ITALIAN-STYLE DRIED BREAD CRUMBS
JERK SEASONING
GARLIC-FLAVOR NONSTICK SEASONING SPRAY

PANTRY
SALT
PEPPER
OLIVE OIL
BALSAMIC VINEGAR
WHITE VINEGAR
SUGAR
ITALIAN SEASONING
DRIED OREGANO
GROUND CUMIN

Week 4
APRIL 23 TO APRIL 30

PRODUCE
1 APPLE (OPTIONAL)
1 LEMON
1 MEDIUM VIDALIA OR SWEET ONION
1 HEAD GARLIC (5 CLOVES)
4 SWEET POTATOES (ABOUT 7 OZ EACH)
5 MEDIUM TOMATOES
1 PT GRAPE OR CHERRY TOMATOES
1 BAG (12 OZ) FRESH BROCCOLI FLORETS
1 BAG (12 OZ) MICROWAVE-IN-THE-BAG FRESH GREEN BEANS
1 AVOCADO
1 BAG (5 OZ) BABY ARUGULA
1 BAG (9 OZ) MICROWAVABLE BABY SPINACH
1 BUNCH PARSLEY
1 BUNCH CILANTRO
1 BUNCH BASIL
FRESH SAGE

BAKERY
6 CIABATTA ROLLS

MEAT/POULTRY/FISH
ONE 3-LB BEEF BOTTOM ROUND OR RUMP ROAST
2 RACKS BABY-BACK RIBS (ABOUT 3¾ LB)
4 CENTER-CUT BONELESS PORK LOIN CHOPS (5 TO 6 OZ EACH)
4 BONELESS, SKINLESS CHICKEN BREASTS (5 OZ EACH)
1 LB CHICKEN TENDERS
4 TILAPIA FILLETS (ABOUT 5 OZ EACH)

DELI
4 THIN SLICES PROSCIUTTO (ABOUT ½ OZ EACH)

REFRIGERATED
½ STICK BUTTER
4 OZ GOAT CHEESE

GROCERY
1 CAN (14.5 OZ) FAT-FREE CHICKEN BROTH
1 CAN (19 OZ) CANNELLINI BEANS
1 CAN (15 TO 16 OZ) CANNELLINI BEANS
1 CAN (15 OZ) BLACK BEANS
1 CAN (11 OZ) WHOLE-KERNEL CORN
2 CANS (5 TO 6 OZ EACH) SOLID LIGHT TUNA IN OLIVE OIL
¼ CUP JARRED ROASTED RED PEPPERS
1 JAR (11 OZ) PEPPERONCINI PEPPERS
½ CUP PITTED KALAMATA OLIVES
1 CUP SALSA
1 LB FARFALLE (BOW-TIE) PASTA
BARBECUE SAUCE
1 POUCH (0.7 OZ) BASIL VINAIGRETTE OR ITALIAN SALAD DRESSING & RECIPE MIX
1 PKT (1.12 OZ) FAJITA SEASONING MIX
¼ CUP CHOPPED WALNUTS

PANTRY
SALT
PEPPER
OLIVE OIL
EXTRA-VIRGIN OLIVE OIL
NONSTICK SPRAY
RED-WINE VINEGAR
DIJON MUSTARD
FLOUR
SUGAR
SEASONED SALT
GROUND GINGER
GROUND CINNAMON
PUMPKIN PIE SPICE
CRUSHED RED PEPPER
GARLIC POWDER
SALT-FREE CHILI POWDER
ONION POWDER
DRIED BASIL
DRIED MARJORAM

OPEN-FACE ZUCCHINI SANDWICHES

YIELD
4 servings

ACTIVE
10 minutes

TOTAL
15 minutes

1 TBSP **OLIVE OIL**

2 **ZUCCHINI**, SLICED ¼ IN. THICK

4 LARGE SLICES **ITALIAN BREAD** (FROM CENTER OF A ROUND LOAF), TOASTED

1 LARGE **BEEFSTEAK TOMATO**, CUT IN 8 SLICES

¾ CUP **SHREDDED MOZZARELLA AND ASIAGO CHEESE WITH ROASTED GARLIC** *OR* ¾ CUP **SHREDDED MOZZARELLA**

½ TSP **DRIED OREGANO**

¼ TSP EACH **SALT** AND **PEPPER**

½ CUP FRESH **BASIL LEAVES**

Heat oil in a large nonstick skillet. Add zucchini; cook over high heat 4 minutes, turning once, until golden and tender.

Meanwhile, top each slice of bread with 2 slices tomato and 3 Tbsp cheese.

Sprinkle zucchini with oregano, salt and pepper; lift from skillet with a slotted spoon onto the bread. Scatter basil over top.

PER SERVING
CALORIES 285 **TOTAL FAT** 10G **SATURATED FAT** 4G **CHOLESTEROL** 15MG **SODIUM** 650MG
TOTAL CARBOHYDRATES 36G **DIETARY FIBER** 4G **PROTEIN** 12G

GRILLED SWORDFISH WITH RED PEPPER–MUSTARD SAUCE

SAUCE

¼ CUP **JARRED ROASTED RED PEPPERS**

2 TBSP **LIGHT MAYONNAISE**

2 TBSP **REDUCED-FAT SOUR CREAM**

1 TBSP **DIJON MUSTARD**

1 TSP FRESHLY GRATED **ORANGE ZEST**

¼ TSP **SALT**

⅛ TSP FRESHLY GROUND **PEPPER**

FOUR ¾- TO 1-IN.-THICK PIECES **SWORDFISH STEAK** (ABOUT 6 OZ EACH)

2 TBSP **OLIVE OIL**

½ TSP **SALT**

¼ TSP FRESHLY GROUND **PEPPER**

YIELD
4 servings

ACTIVE
4 minutes

TOTAL
14 minutes

SIDE SUGGESTION
Sautéed fresh spinach, purchased or homemade tabbouleh

SAUCE Put ingredients in food processor or blender. Process until well blended and smooth. Scrape into a small serving dish.

Heat outdoor grill or ridged iron grill pan. Brush swordfish with oil and sprinkle with salt and pepper.

Grill, turning over once, 8 to 10 minutes until just cooked through. Serve with the sauce.

PER SERVING
CALORIES 288 **TOTAL FAT** 16G **SATURATED FAT** 4G **CHOLESTEROL** 64MG **SODIUM** 737MG **TOTAL CARBOHYDRATES** 2G **DIETARY FIBER** 0G **PROTEIN** 30G

WINE-GLAZED CHICKEN THIGHS

8 **CHICKEN THIGHS** (ABOUT 2 LB), SKIN AND VISIBLE FAT REMOVED

¼ TSP **SALT**

⅛ TSP **PEPPER**, OR TO TASTE

1 TBSP EACH **OLIVE OIL** AND **BUTTER**

2 TBSP CHOPPED **FRESH ROSEMARY** OR 2 TSP DRIED, CRUMBLED

8 LARGE LEAVES **FRESH SAGE** OR 2 TSP DRIED, CRUMBLED

1½ CUPS **DRY RED WINE**

3 TSP **MINCED GARLIC**

PINCH OF **CRUSHED RED PEPPER**

GARNISH: **FRESH SAGE** CUT IN NARROW STRIPS

YIELD
4 servings

ACTIVE
5 minutes

TOTAL
45 minutes

SIDE SUGGESTION
Mashed potatoes, green and wax beans

Season chicken with salt and pepper. Heat oil and butter in a large, heavy nonstick skillet over medium heat. Add chicken, rosemary and sage, and cook, turning chicken occasionally, 15 minutes or until golden brown.

Spoon off fat, leaving about 2 tsp in skillet. Add ¼ cup of the wine, the garlic and crushed pepper.

Cook 20 minutes longer, turning chicken occasionally and spooning on all but 2 Tbsp of the wine as pan juices evaporate, until chicken is cooked through and coated with a deep brown glaze. Remove to warm serving plates.

Add remaining 2 Tbsp wine to skillet and cook, stirring in browned drippings from bottom of pan. Spoon pan juices over chicken and garnish with sage.

PER SERVING
CALORIES 200 **TOTAL FAT** 7G **SATURATED FAT** 2G **CHOLESTEROL** 117MG **SODIUM** 259MG
TOTAL CARBOHYDRATES 3G **DIETARY FIBER** 0G **PROTEIN** 28G

SWEET & SPICY GLAZED SPIRAL-SLICED HAM & SAUCE

GLAZE & SAUCE

1 JAR (9.5 OZ) **HOT-PEPPER SPREAD OR JELLY** (¾ CUP; SEE NOTE)

¼ CUP FIRMLY PACKED **LIGHT-BROWN SUGAR**

2 TBSP CHOPPED **CILANTRO**

2 TBSP **FRESH LIME JUICE**

1 TSP MINCED **GARLIC**

1 **PRECOOKED 7- TO 8-LB SPIRAL-SLICED BONE-IN HALF HAM** (SHANK OR BUTT)

YIELD
12 servings

ACTIVE
5 minutes

TOTAL
1 hour 30 minutes

Heat oven to 325°F.

GLAZE & SAUCE Microwave ingredients in a bowl just until jelly melts. Transfer 1 cup to a serving bowl; reserve to use as sauce.

Bake ham as package directs, or place ham, cut side down, in a large roasting pan and add ¼ in. water. Cover pan tightly with foil; bake 12 minutes per pound.

Remove ham from oven. Brush with remaining glaze and bake, uncovered, 30 minutes, or until an instant-read thermometer inserted in thickest part registers 135°F. Serve with reserved sauce.

PLANNING TIP The glaze and sauce can be made up to 1 day ahead. Refrigerate covered.

NOTE If you can't find hot-pepper spread or jelly, stir 4 to 6 tsp jalapeño hot sauce into ¾ cup apple jelly.

PER SERVING
CALORIES 215 **TOTAL FAT** 8G **SATURATED FAT** 3G **CHOLESTEROL** 50MG **SODIUM** 1,282MG
TOTAL CARBOHYDRATES 15G **DIETARY FIBER** 0G **PROTEIN** 19G

TWO-BEAN SLOPPY JOES

BEAN MIXTURE

1 CAN EACH (15 TO 16 OZ) **BLACK-EYED PEAS** AND **RED KIDNEY BEANS**, RINSED

1½ CUPS **BOTTLED MARINARA SAUCE**

1 CAN (14.5 OZ) **NO-SALT-ADDED DICED TOMATOES** IN JUICE, DRAINED

½ CUP EACH **FROZEN CUT GREEN BEANS** AND **CHOPPED GREEN BELL PEPPER**

1 TBSP **WORCESTERSHIRE SAUCE**

2 TSP **RED-WINE VINEGAR**

1½ TSP **CHILI POWDER**

4 **SPLIT SEEDED KAISER OR HAMBURGER ROLLS**, TOASTED

YIELD
4 servings

ACTIVE
5 minutes

TOTAL
20 minutes

BEAN MIXTURE Bring all ingredients to a boil in a 10- or 12-in. nonstick skillet over medium-high heat. Reduce heat, partially cover skillet and simmer, stirring occasionally, 10 to 15 minutes until green pepper is tender.

Spoon onto roll bottoms; replace tops.

PER SERVING
CALORIES 433 **TOTAL FAT** 8G **SATURATED FAT** 1G **CHOLESTEROL** 0MG **SODIUM** 1,429MG
TOTAL CARBOHYDRATES 75G **DIETARY FIBER** 9G **PROTEIN** 20G

MAC & CHEESE WITH BROCCOLI & HAM

- 4 CUPS **WATER**
- 3/4 LB **ELBOW MACARONI** (3 CUPS)
- 1 CAN (12 OZ) **EVAPORATED MILK**
- 1 TSP **CORNSTARCH**
- 1 TSP **DIJON MUSTARD**
- 1/4 TSP **SALT**
- 1 BOX (10 OZ) **FROZEN BROCCOLI**, THAWED
- 4 OZ **BAKED HAM**, DICED
- 2 1/2 CUPS **SHREDDED CHEDDAR AND MONTEREY JACK CHEESE BLEND**

YIELD
6 servings

ACTIVE
5 minutes

TOTAL
22 minutes

Bring water, macaroni and 1 cup milk to a boil in a 5-qt Dutch oven, stirring frequently. Reduce heat to medium-high and boil 7 to 8 minutes, stirring, until macaroni is just al dente.

Stir remaining milk, cornstarch, mustard and salt in a bowl to blend.

Add broccoli and ham to pot. Cover and cook 2 minutes. Reduce heat to medium and stir in milk mixture. Simmer 1 minute, stirring constantly. Remove pot from heat; stir in cheeses.

PER SERVING
CALORIES 456 **TOTAL FAT** 15G **SATURATED FAT** 11G **CHOLESTEROL** 53MG **SODIUM** 741MG **TOTAL CARBOHYDRATES** 54G **DIETARY FIBER** 3G **PROTEIN** 27G

MEXICAN ROLLED FLANK STEAK

YIELD
5 servings

ACTIVE
25 minutes

TOTAL
8 to 10 hours on low

1 **FLANK STEAK** (1½ LB)

1 BOX (6 OZ) **CORNBREAD STUFFING MIX**

1 CUP BOILING **WATER**

1 CUP **THICK-AND-CHUNKY SALSA**

¼ CUP CHOPPED **FRESH CILANTRO**

SIDE SUGGESTION
Steamed green beans

Ask your butcher to butterfly the flank steak, or you can do it yourself: Lay meat on a cutting board with the grain running vertically. Using a long, sharp knife, cut the meat almost in half, opening it like a book but stopping before going all the way through. Cut several 12-in. pieces of kitchen twine and space evenly under steak.

Toss cornbread stuffing with 1 cup boiling water and ½ cup salsa until moistened; stir in cilantro. Spread over steak, leaving about 1 in. along edges. Roll steak starting from a long side, jelly-roll style; tie with twine.

Place seam side down in a 6-qt oval slow cooker. Spoon remaining ½ cup salsa over meat. Cover and cook on low 8 to 10 hours.

Remove steak to a cutting board; let rest 10 minutes. Discard cooking liquid. Remove string and cut steak into ½-in.-thick slices. Serve with additional salsa, if desired.

PER SERVING
CALORIES 370 **TOTAL FAT** 12G **SATURATED FAT** 5G **CHOLESTEROL** 57MG **SODIUM** 936MG
TOTAL CARBOHYDRATES 28G **DIETARY FIBER** 2G **PROTEIN** 33G

SKILLET CHICKEN PARMESAN WITH CRISP POLENTA

1 LARGE **EGG**

⅓ CUP **SEASONED DRIED BREAD CRUMBS**

4 **BONELESS, SKINLESS CHICKEN BREASTS** (ABOUT 4 OZ EACH)

2 TBSP **OLIVE OIL**

1 TUBE (ABOUT 16 OZ) **POLENTA**, CUT IN 12 SLICES

½ CUP PACKAGED **SHREDDED MOZZARELLA WITH PARMESAN**

1½ CUPS **JARRED MARINARA SAUCE**

GARNISH: CHOPPED **FRESH BASIL** *OR* **PARSLEY**

YIELD
4 servings

ACTIVE
5 minutes

TOTAL
18 minutes

Lightly beat egg in a shallow dish. Spread crumbs on a sheet of wax paper. Dip breasts in egg, then crumbs to coat.

Heat 1 Tbsp oil in a large nonstick skillet over medium-high heat. Add chicken; cook 3 to 4 minutes per side or until golden and cooked through. Remove chicken.

Wipe out skillet with paper towel; add remaining 1 Tbsp oil and heat. Add polenta and cook 3 minutes until bottoms of slices are golden. Sprinkle tops with ¼ cup cheese; turn slices over and cook 2 minutes until bottoms are golden and crisp. Remove to a serving platter.

Pour marinara sauce into skillet; bring to a simmer. Add chicken; sprinkle with remaining ¼ cup cheese. Cover and cook 1 minute until cheese melts. Serve with polenta.

PER SERVING
CALORIES 417 **TOTAL FAT** 16G **SATURATED FAT** 4G **CHOLESTEROL** 121MG **SODIUM** 1,232MG **TOTAL CARBOHYDRATES** 33G **DIETARY FIBER** 4G **PROTEIN** 33G

SLOW COOKER BBQ RIBS

YIELD
5 servings

ACTIVE
5 minutes

TOTAL
6 to 8 hours on low

2 MEDIUM **ONIONS**

4 LB **COUNTRY-STYLE PORK RIBS**

1 CUP **HOT 'N SPICY BARBECUE SAUCE** (OR YOUR FAVORITE SAUCE)

SIDE SUGGESTION
Coleslaw, cornbread

Halve, then thinly slice onions. Place onions, then ribs and barbecue sauce in a 5-qt or larger slow cooker.

Cover and cook on low 6 to 8 hours or until ribs are tender.

DIFFERENT TAKES

- Add 1 lb rinsed fresh sauerkraut to cooker before adding ribs.
- Give ribs an Asian twist by adding minced garlic and ginger to teriyaki-flavor barbecue sauce.
- Stir canned baked beans into sauce in cooker 30 minutes before ribs will be done.

PER SERVING
CALORIES 549 **TOTAL FAT** 39G **SATURATED FAT** 13G **CHOLESTEROL** 142MG **SODIUM** 461MG
TOTAL CARBOHYDRATES 10G **DIETARY FIBER** 1G **PROTEIN** 36G

FAJITA BURGERS

YIELD
4 servings

ACTIVE
7 minutes

TOTAL
15 minutes

2 TBSP **OIL**

1½ TSP **CHILI POWDER**

1 **RED, YELLOW OR ORANGE BELL PEPPER**, QUARTERED

1 PKG (12 OZ) **FROZEN CHICKEN BURGERS** (4 BURGERS), PREFERABLY SPICY SALSA AND CHEDDAR FLAVOR (WE USED CASUAL GOURMET)

4 BURRITO-SIZE (8 IN.) **FLOUR TORTILLAS**

8 MEDIUM LEAVES **ROMAINE LETTUCE**

ACCOMPANIMENTS: **SOUR CREAM**, SLICED **AVOCADOS** AND **SALSA**

Heat outdoor grill. Mix oil and chili powder.

Grill pepper, turning once, 12 minutes or until charred and crisp-tender. Grill burgers as package directs. Remove burgers to a plate, pepper to a cutting board; thinly slice pepper.

Brush 1 side of each tortilla with the chili oil. Grill oil side down 1 minute. Turn over; cook 1 minute until grill-marked. Transfer to serving plates.

For each fajita: Put 2 lettuce leaves, a burger and ¼ the pepper slices on half of oiled side of a tortilla. Fold over other half. Serve with accompaniments.

NOTE Grilling times given are approximate. If using a gas grill, bear in mind that when cooking food with the lid closed, even a quick peek can cool the grill enough to require an increase in cooking time.

PER SERVING
CALORIES 296 **TOTAL FAT** 14G **SATURATED FAT** 3G **CHOLESTEROL** 65MG **SODIUM** 639MG
TOTAL CARBOHYDRATES 23G **DIETARY FIBER** 2G **PROTEIN** 19G

LASAGNA ROLLS

YIELD
12 servings

ACTIVE
25 minutes

TOTAL
1 hour 20 minutes

1 SMALL **ONION**, COARSELY CHOPPED

1 SMALL **CARROT**, COARSELY CHOPPED

3 LINKS (ABOUT 8 OZ) **ITALIAN TURKEY SAUSAGE**

2 TSP MINCED **GARLIC**

½ TSP EACH **SALT** AND **FENNEL SEEDS**, CRUSHED

2¼ CUPS (8 OZ) **FROZEN CUT LEAF SPINACH**, THAWED AND SQUEEZED DRY

1 CUP **PART-SKIM RICOTTA**

⅓ CUP **GRATED PARMESAN**

8 **OVEN-READY LASAGNA NOODLES** (FROM AN 8- OR 9-OZ BOX)

2½ CUPS **BOTTLED MARINARA SAUCE**

¾ CUP **CHICKEN BROTH**

Put onion and carrot in food processor and pulse until finely chopped. Remove sausage from casing, add to processor and pulse until well blended.

Heat a large nonstick skillet over medium heat; coat with cooking spray. Add sausage mixture and cook 5 to 7 minutes, breaking up clumps, until no longer pink. Add garlic, salt and fennel seeds; cook 3 minutes, or until garlic is fragrant. Transfer to a bowl; let cool slightly. Add spinach, ricotta and Parmesan; stir until well blended.

Fill a 9 x 5-in. loaf pan with hot water. Add noodles one at a time. Let soak 8 to 10 minutes until soft.

Mix marinara sauce and chicken broth in a 13 x 9-in. baking dish.

TO ASSEMBLE Place a paper towel on work surface. Remove 2 lasagna noodles from water and place on towel, end to end, overlapping by ¾ in. Spread ¼ of the sausage mixture (about ¾ cup) on noodles, leaving ¾ in. at one end. Beginning at other end, roll up. Cover with a damp paper towel to keep roll moist. Repeat with remaining noodles and sausage mixture. Cut each roll crosswise in thirds. Place cut-side up in sauce in baking dish.

Heat oven to 375°F. Bake 45 minutes, or until hot and bubbly.

PLANNING TIP Can be prepared and assembled in baking dish up to two days ahead. Cover with plastic wrap, then foil; refrigerate. To bake, remove plastic wrap and cover with foil, then bake as instructed above.

PER SERVING
CALORIES 326 **TOTAL FAT** 13G **SATURATED FAT** 5G **CHOLESTEROL** 36MG **SODIUM** 1,370MG **TOTAL CARBOHYDRATES** 37G **DIETARY FIBER** 4G **PROTEIN** 19G

RICOTTA FRITTATA

YIELD
6 servings

ACTIVE
5 minutes

TOTAL
32 minutes

2 CUPS (10 OZ) **FROZEN GREEN PEAS**

3 PACKAGES (ABOUT 3 OZ EACH) ANY FLAVOR **RAMEN NOODLE SOUP** (YOU'LL NEED ONLY 2 SEASONING PACKETS)

1 CONTAINER (15 OZ) **PART-SKIM RICOTTA**

3 LARGE **EGGS**

½ CUP **MILK**

½ CUP **GRATED PARMESAN**

¼ TSP **PEPPER**

1 CAN (14.5 OZ) **CHUNKY TOMATOES, PASTA-STYLE**

Heat oven to 400°F. Lightly grease a 13 x 9-in. baking dish.

Bring a half-filled 4- to 6-qt pot of water to a boil. Add frozen peas and return to a boil. Break up noodles as directed on package and add to pot. Cook 3 minutes, stirring occasionally, or until noodles and peas are tender. Drain in a colander.

Meanwhile, stir ricotta, eggs, milk, Parmesan, pepper and the 2 seasoning packets in a large bowl until blended. Stir in noodles and peas.

Transfer mixture to prepared baking dish and spread evenly. Bake about 20 minutes or until set.

Heat tomatoes in a saucepan or microwave until hot. Spoon over frittata. Cut in squares to serve.

PER SERVING
CALORIES 436 **TOTAL FAT** 19G **SATURATED FAT** 0G **CHOLESTEROL** 136MG **SODIUM** 1,214MG
TOTAL CARBOHYDRATES 44G **DIETARY FIBER** 0G **PROTEIN** 22G

REUBEN WRAPS

YIELD
4 servings
makes 4 wraps

ACTIVE
25 minutes

TOTAL
40 minutes

- FOUR 8-IN. **PLAIN OR WHOLE-WHEAT FLOUR TORTILLA WRAPS**
- 4 TBSP **FAT-FREE THOUSAND ISLAND DRESSING**
- 6 CUPS **BABY SPINACH**
- 8 OZ **SLICED 97%-FAT-FREE HONEY-ROASTED & SMOKED TURKEY BREAST** (SUCH AS HEALTHY CHOICE)
- 4 OZ **THINLY SLICED REDUCED-FAT, LOW-SODIUM SWISS CHEESE** (SUCH AS LORRAINE)
- 4 CUPS **BAGGED CLASSIC COLESLAW MIX**

SIDE SUGGESTION
Tomato soup

Spread each tortilla with 1 Tbsp dressing. Top each to within 1 in. of an edge with ¼ the spinach, turkey, cheese and coleslaw mix. Roll up tightly from side with fillings.

Wrap each in plastic wrap and refrigerate at least 15 minutes. Cut diagonally in halves or thirds.

NOTE Healthy spinach, coleslaw and lowfat turkey breast stand in for high-sodium sauerkraut and corned beef in this version of the classic sandwich.

PER SERVING
CALORIES 397 **TOTAL FAT** 10G **SATURATED FAT** 5G **CHOLESTEROL** 47MG **SODIUM** 978MG **TOTAL CARBOHYDRATES** 48G **DIETARY FIBER** 7G **PROTEIN** 25G

TURKEY CUTLETS WITH SOUTH-OF-THE-BORDER SAUCE

3 TBSP **FLOUR**

1/4 TSP EACH **SALT** AND **PEPPER**

4 **TURKEY BREAST CUTLETS** (ABOUT 4 OZ EACH)

2 TSP **OIL**

1 EACH **YELLOW SQUASH** AND **ZUCCHINI** (ABOUT 8 OZ EACH), CUT IN 1/2-IN. CHUNKS

1/2 CUP CHOPPED **ONION**

1 TBSP MINCED **GARLIC**

1 1/2 TSP **CHILI POWDER**

1 CAN (ABOUT 16 OZ) **CRUSHED TOMATOES**

1 CAN (4.5 OZ) **CHOPPED GREEN CHILES**

YIELD
4 servings

ACTIVE
10 minutes

TOTAL
25 minutes

Mix flour, salt and pepper on a plate. Dredge cutlets in mixture; shake off excess.

Coat a large nonstick skillet with nonstick spray. Heat over medium heat; add 1 tsp oil and swirl to coat bottom of skillet. Add half the cutlets and cook 1 minute per side or until lightly browned and cooked through. Transfer to a plate. Repeat with remaining oil and cutlets.

Add squashes and onion to any drippings in skillet. Sauté 4 to 5 minutes until browned. Stir in garlic and chili powder; cook 1 minute. Add tomatoes and chiles; bring to a boil, reduce heat, cover and simmer 5 minutes or until squashes are tender. Return cutlets to skillet just to heat through.

PER SERVING
CALORIES 233 **TOTAL FAT** 4G **SATURATED FAT** 0G **CHOLESTEROL** 70MG **SODIUM** 592MG
TOTAL CARBOHYDRATES 18G **DIETARY FIBER** 3G **PROTEIN** 32G

SMOKED TURKEY & SPINACH SALAD WITH CROUTONS

YIELD
4 servings

ACTIVE
10 minutes

TOTAL
10 minutes

12-OZ CHUNK **SMOKED TURKEY**, CUT IN THIN STRIPS

2 BAGS (4.5 OZ EACH) **WALNUT & CRANBERRY SPRING MIX SALAD**

2 **APPLES**, CUT IN THIN WEDGES

4 OZ **CHEDDAR**, DICED

½ CUP SLICED **RED ONION**

½ CUP **BOTTLED HONEY-MUSTARD DRESSING**

2 SLICES **7-GRAIN OR OTHER WHOLE-GRAIN BREAD**, TOASTED, STACKED AND CUT IN ½-IN. CROUTONS

Put turkey, greens from salad mix, apples, cheese, onion and dressing in large bowl; toss to mix and coat.

Sprinkle with dried cranberries and walnuts (from packets in salad mix) and croutons.

PER SERVING
CALORIES 477 **TOTAL FAT** 25G **SATURATED FAT** 8G **CHOLESTEROL** 70MG **SODIUM** 1,366MG
TOTAL CARBOHYDRATES 38G **DIETARY FIBER** 5G **PROTEIN** 26G

ITALIAN MEATBALLS WITH MARINARA SAUCE

12 OZ **GROUND BEEF**

12 OZ **GROUND PORK**

1/4 CUP CHOPPED **ONION**

2 CLOVES **GARLIC**, FINELY CHOPPED

2 TSP **ITALIAN SEASONING**

1/4 CUP **ITALIAN-STYLE DRIED BREAD CRUMBS**

1 LARGE **EGG**, LIGHTLY BEATEN

1 JAR (28 OZ) **MARINARA SAUCE**

YIELD
6 servings

ACTIVE
50 minutes

TOTAL
6 to 7 hours on low

TIPS
To make perfectly round meatballs, use a small ice cream scoop. If you use your hands, be sure not to over-handle the meat, or it will become too tightly packed to let the sauce sink in.

Instead of pasta, try meatballs on a bed of polenta. If you prefer the classic spaghetti approach, though, give thicker, chewier pastas like perciatelli or bucatini a try.

Heat oven to 375°F. Line a 15 x 10 x 1-in. baking pan with aluminum foil; coat with nonstick cooking spray.

Mix all ingredients except the marinara sauce in a bowl until well combined. Shape mixture into 24 balls about 1½ in. in diameter (see Tip 1). Place in baking pan.

Bake 30 to 35 minutes, until meat is no longer pink in the center. Place meatballs in a 3½- to 4-qt slow cooker. Pour marinara sauce over meatballs.

Cover and cook on low 6 to 7 hours to blend flavors.

Serve with pasta (see Tip 2).

PER SERVING
CALORIES 329 **TOTAL FAT** 17G **SATURATED FAT** 6G **CHOLESTEROL** 103MG **SODIUM** 693MG **TOTAL CARBOHYDRATES** 16G **DIETARY FIBER** 3G **PROTEIN** 28G

ANTIPASTO PLATTER

YIELD
12 servings

ACTIVE
1 hour 25 minutes

TOTAL
2 hours 30 minutes

¼ CUP PLUS 3 TBSP **OLIVE OIL**

6 **BELL PEPPERS** (ANY COLOR), HALVED LENGTHWISE, STEMS, MEMBRANES AND SEEDS REMOVED

1½ LB **EGGPLANT**, SLICED IN ¼-IN.-THICK ROUNDS

3 SMALL **ZUCCHINI** (ABOUT 1 LB), ENDS TRIMMED, CUT DIAGONALLY IN ¼-IN.-THICK SLICES

1 LB **MUSHROOMS**, WIPED CLEAN AND SLICED

⅓ CUP **BALSAMIC VINEGAR**

2 TBSP **FRESH LEMON JUICE**

½ CUP LOOSELY PACKED **FRESH MINT**, COARSELY CHOPPED (2 TBSP)

½ CUP LOOSELY PACKED **BASIL**, COARSELY CHOPPED (2 TBSP)

1 TSP **SALT**

½ TSP COARSELY GROUND **PEPPER**

8 CUPS LOOSELY PACKED **MIXED SALAD GREENS**

1 JAR (6.5 OZ) **OIL-CURED OLIVES**

Heat broiler. Line broiler pan with foil for easy cleanup. Brush 2 jelly-roll pans or baking sheets with ½ Tbsp of the oil.

Place pepper halves on broiler-pan rack, cut sides down. Broil 4 to 5 in. from heat source 12 to 15 minutes until skins are mostly charred. Remove peppers to a saucepan and cover.

Turn off broiler. Position racks to divide oven in thirds. Heat to 425°F.

Arrange eggplant rounds on prepared pans in a single layer. Brush with 2 Tbsp of the olive oil. Roast, switching position of pans and turning eggplant slices over after 10 minutes. Roast 8 to 10 minutes longer or until soft. Remove slices to a large bowl.

Meanwhile, bring a 3-qt pot of water to a boil. Add zucchini and boil 5 to 7 minutes until tender. Drain, rinse under cold running water and pat dry with paper towels. Add to eggplant.

Pull charred skin from peppers (some will remain). Cut halves lengthwise in quarters. Add to bowl with vegetables. Add mushrooms, balsamic vinegar, remaining ¼ cup oil, the lemon juice, 1 Tbsp each of the chopped mint and basil, and the salt and pepper. Toss to coat; let stand at room temperature 30 minutes, or cover and refrigerate up to 1 day.

TO SERVE Bring vegetables to room temperature. Line a large serving platter with the mixed greens. Carefully remove vegetables from bowl and arrange in groups on greens. Scatter olives over vegetables. Sprinkle with remaining basil and mint.

PLANNING TIP The vegetables can be marinated up to 1 day ahead.

PER SERVING
CALORIES 174 **TOTAL FAT** 14G **SATURATED FAT** 0G **CHOLESTEROL** 0MG **SODIUM** 699MG
TOTAL CARBOHYDRATES 13G **DIETARY FIBER** 0G **PROTEIN** 3G

GRILLED PORK TENDERLOIN WITH RICE & PINEAPPLE SALSA

PORK

1 **PORK TENDERLOIN** (ABOUT 12 OZ)

1 TBSP **JERK SEASONING**

RICE

¾ CUP **CONVERTED (PARBOILED) WHITE RICE**

1 CAN (15 OZ) **BLACK BEANS**, RINSED

2 TBSP CHOPPED **CILANTRO**

¼ TSP **PEPPER**

SALSA

1 CONTAINER (20 OZ) **PEELED AND CORED FRESH PINEAPPLE**, CHOPPED; JUICES RESERVED

¼ CUP EACH CHOPPED **CILANTRO** AND FINELY CHOPPED **RED ONION**

⅛ TSP **SALT** AND **PEPPER**

1 **AVOCADO**, PEELED, PITTED AND SLICED

YIELD
4 servings

ACTIVE
10 minutes

TOTAL
45 minutes

Lightly oil, then heat a ridged grill pan or outdoor barbecue grill.

PORK Rub with jerk seasoning. Grill, browning all sides, 25 to 30 minutes until a meat thermometer inserted in center registers 160°F. Let rest 8 to 10 minutes before cutting in ⅓-in.-thick slices.

Meanwhile prepare **RICE**: Cook as box directs but omit oil or butter. Stir black beans, cilantro and pepper into remaining rice.

SALSA Mix ingredients plus ⅓ cup reserved pineapple juice. Serve with sliced pork and avocado; accompany with rice and beans.

PER SERVING
CALORIES 433 **TOTAL FAT** 13G **SATURATED FAT** 3G **CHOLESTEROL** 54MG **SODIUM** 221MG **TOTAL CARBOHYDRATES** 56G **DIETARY FIBER** 5G **PROTEIN** 23G

FALAFEL PLATE

- 1 BOX (6 OZ) **FALAFEL MIX** (WE USED NEAR EAST)
- 1 CUP **PLAIN YOGURT**
- 1 MEDIUM **CUCUMBER**, PEELED, SEEDED AND SHREDDED
- 2 TSP **WHITE VINEGAR**
- 1 CLOVE **GARLIC**, MINCED
- ¼ TSP EACH **PEPPER**, **SALT** AND **SUGAR**
- 1 SMALL **RED ONION**, THINLY SLICED
- 1 CUP **GREEN LETTUCE**
- 2 **PLUM TOMATOES**, THINLY SLICED
- 4 **PITAS**

YIELD
4 servings

ACTIVE
15 minutes

TOTAL
35 minutes

Heat oven to 375°F. Prepare falafel according to package directions for baking.

In a medium bowl, combine yogurt, cucumber, vinegar, garlic, pepper, salt and sugar. Set aside.

Place onion in a glass bowl with water to cover. Microwave for 1 minute or until onion softens. Drain.

Arrange falafel on a platter with cucumber sauce, lettuce, onions, tomatoes and pitas.

PER SERVING
CALORIES 350 **TOTAL FAT** 4G **SATURATED FAT** 1G **CHOLESTEROL** 8MG **SODIUM** 1,204MG
TOTAL CARBOHYDRATES 63G **DIETARY FIBER** 9G **PROTEIN** 21G

CUBAN PORK SANDWICHES

YIELD
4 servings

ACTIVE
8 minutes

TOTAL
8 minutes

1 TSP **GROUND CUMIN**

1 TSP **DRIED OREGANO**

¼ TSP EACH **SALT** AND **PEPPER**

FOUR ¼-IN.-THICK **PORK CUTLETS** (ABOUT 12 OZ)

1 MEDIUM **ONION**, SLICED

GARLIC-FLAVOR NONSTICK SEASONING SPRAY

4 **PORTUGUESE OR KAISER ROLLS**, SPLIT

8 **THIN SLICES SWISS CHEESE**

8 **THIN SLICES VIRGINIA HAM**

½ CUP **SLICED DILL PICKLES**

Heat barbecue grill (see Tip). Mix the cumin, oregano, salt and pepper; sprinkle over both sides of pork cutlets.

Coat cutlets and onion with seasoning spray. Grill 3 minutes, turning cutlets and onion slices over once, until cutlets are cooked through and onions are slightly charred and crisp-tender.

Fill each roll with 2 slices each cheese and ham, 1 cutlet and ¼ of the onions and pickles. Return to grill for 1 or 2 minutes to melt cheese, if desired.

TIP If you don't have a grill (or can't be bothered to heat it) but want your food to look and taste grilled, use a ridged grill pan. Most have a baked-on black finish that resists sticking and, when heated, leaves "grill" marks that would fool the best barbecue chef. The ridges also keep foods above any fat that may drip off. When the grill pan is hot, lightly coat it with oil before adding food. Stovetop grilling can be smoky, so turn on your stove's hood fan.

PER SERVING
CALORIES 507 **TOTAL FAT** 22G **SATURATED FAT** 9G **CHOLESTEROL** 95MG **SODIUM** 1,240MG
TOTAL CARBOHYDRATES 36G **DIETARY FIBER** 2G **PROTEIN** 39G

SMOKY SHRIMP & CHORIZO

YIELD
5 servings

ACTIVE
5 minutes

TOTAL
20 minutes

2 TSP **OIL**

6 OZ **FULLY COOKED CHORIZO SAUSAGE** (2 LINKS), CUT IN ¼-IN. SLICES

1 BAG (16 OZ) **FROZEN CORN, BLACK BEAN, TOMATO, GREEN PEPPER AND ONION MIXTURE** (LATINO BLEND)

2 BAGS (8.5 OZ EACH) **FROZEN HONEY CHIPOTLE SHRIMP**

SIDE SUGGESTION
Rice, lime wedges, cilantro

Heat oil in large skillet over medium heat. Add chorizo to skillet; sauté 3 minutes or until browned.

Add frozen vegetables and ¼ cup water to skillet. Cover, reduce heat and simmer 10 minutes or until tender and heated through.

Meanwhile, microwave each bag of shrimp as package directs. Remove skillet from heat. Add shrimp and their liquid to skillet; stir.

PER SERVING
CALORIES 404 **TOTAL FAT** 22G **SATURATED FAT** 8G **CHOLESTEROL** 166MG **SODIUM** 778MG **TOTAL CARBOHYDRATES** 22G **DIETARY FIBER** 4G **PROTEIN** 29G

LINGUINE WITH ROASTED VEGETABLES

1½ LB **PLUM TOMATOES**, CUT IN ¾-IN. CHUNKS

2 LARGE **ZUCCHINI** (ABOUT 1¼ LB), QUARTERED LENGTHWISE, CUT CROSSWISE IN ¾-IN. PIECES

1 **YELLOW SQUASH** (ABOUT 6 OZ), QUARTERED LENGTHWISE, CUT CROSSWISE IN ¾-IN. PIECES

2 **RED BELL PEPPERS**, CUT IN ½ -IN. PIECES

1 MEDIUM **RED ONION**, COARSELY CHOPPED

3 TBSP **OLIVE OIL**

1½ TBSP MINCED **GARLIC**

1 TSP **SALT**

½ TSP FRESHLY GROUND **PEPPER**

1 LB **LINGUINE OR SPAGHETTI PASTA**

½ CUP **GRATED PARMESAN**

⅓ CUP CHOPPED **BASIL** *OR* **PARSLEY**

GARNISH: **GRATED PARMESAN**

YIELD
6 servings

ACTIVE
20 minutes

TOTAL
45 minutes

Adjust oven racks to divide oven into thirds. Heat oven to 450°F. Bring a large pot of lightly salted water to a boil.

Put all ingredients except the Parmesan and basil in a large bowl. Toss to mix and coat. Spread in 2 rimmed baking sheets. Roast, switching position of pans once, 20 to 25 minutes until vegetables are tender.

Meanwhile, stir pasta into the boiling water and cook as package directs.

Remove and reserve ½ cup pasta cooking water. Drain pasta; return to pot. Add vegetables (scraping baking pans with a rubber spatula to include any juices), reserved cooking water, the cheese, and basil or parsley. Toss to mix. Sprinkle with grated Parmesan if desired.

PER SERVING
CALORIES 437 **TOTAL FAT** 11G **SATURATED FAT** 2G **CHOLESTEROL** 5MG **SODIUM** 794MG
TOTAL CARBOHYDRATES 71G **DIETARY FIBER** 5G **PROTEIN** 16G

CHICKEN SALTIMBOCCA WITH BEANS & SPINACH

1⁄3 CUP **ALL-PURPOSE FLOUR**

1⁄8 TSP EACH **SALT** AND **PEPPER**

4 **BONELESS, SKINLESS CHICKEN BREASTS** (5 OZ EACH), TRIMMED OF VISIBLE FAT

1 TBSP **OIL**

1 TSP **DRIED SAGE** OR CHOPPED FRESH

4 **THIN SLICES PROSCIUTTO** (ABOUT 1⁄2 OZ EACH)

1⁄2 CUP **CANNED FAT-FREE CHICKEN BROTH**

1 TBSP **FRESH LEMON JUICE**

1⁄2 TBSP **BUTTER**

BEANS

1 CAN (19 OZ) **CANNELLINI BEANS**, RINSED

1⁄4 CUP CHOPPED **JARRED ROASTED RED PEPPERS**

1 TBSP **OIL**

1⁄8 TSP EACH **SALT** AND **PEPPER**

1 BAG (9 OZ) **MICROWAVABLE BABY SPINACH**

GARNISH: **FRESH SAGE LEAVES**

YIELD
4 servings

ACTIVE
15 minutes

TOTAL
15 minutes

Mix flour, salt and pepper in a plastic food bag. Add chicken, close bag and shake to coat. Remove chicken; shake off excess flour.

Meanwhile heat oil in a large nonstick skillet over medium-high heat. Add chicken, cover and cook, 5 minutes on each side, or until golden and cooked through. Remove to plates, sprinkle with sage and top each with prosciutto.

Add broth and lemon juice to pan. Increase heat to high and boil until reduced by half. Whisk in butter until melted. Drizzle over chicken.

Meanwhile combine **BEANS** ingredients in a microwave-safe bowl, cover and microwave until hot, then microwave spinach as bag directs. Serve with the chicken. Garnish with sage leaves.

PER SERVING
CALORIES 435 **TOTAL FAT** 13G **SATURATED FAT** 3G **CHOLESTEROL** 99MG **SODIUM** 896MG **TOTAL CARBOHYDRATES** 32G **DIETARY FIBER** 9G **PROTEIN** 47G

PORK WITH SWEET POTATOES & BROCCOLI

1 BAG (12 OZ) **FRESH BROCCOLI FLORETS**

2 TSP **BUTTER**

4 **SWEET POTATOES** (ABOUT 7 OZ EACH), SCRUBBED AND PIERCED WITH A FORK

½ TSP EACH **GROUND GINGER** AND **SALT**

¼ TSP EACH **GROUND CINNAMON** AND **PEPPER**

4 **CENTER-CUT BONELESS PORK LOIN CHOPS** (5 TO 6 OZ EACH)

NONSTICK SPRAY

FRESH APPLE SLICES (OPTIONAL)

YIELD
4 servings

ACTIVE
8 minutes

TOTAL
11 minutes

Heat a ridged grill pan that's at least 17½ x 11½ in. or a barbecue grill.

Meanwhile, place broccoli in a single layer on a 14-in.-long sheet of foil; fold up sides. Add ⅓ cup water; dot broccoli with butter. Cover with another sheet of foil; fold sides of top and bottom sheets together twice to seal.

Microwave sweet potatoes until tender when pierced.

Meanwhile, mix ginger, salt, cinnamon and pepper; sprinkle on both sides of chops. Spray chops with nonstick spray. Place chops at one side of grill pan or barbecue grill and grill 5 minutes.

Turn chops over. Place foil packet on other side of grill pan or barbecue grill and grill 5 to 6 minutes until chops are barely pink in the middle and broccoli is crisp-tender when packet is pierced. Open packet carefully to let steam escape; serve with chops, potatoes and apple slices.

PER SERVING
CALORIES 470 **TOTAL FAT** 18G **SATURATED FAT** 7G **CHOLESTEROL** 99MG **SODIUM** 419MG
TOTAL CARBOHYDRATES 38G **DIETARY FIBER** 6G **PROTEIN** 38G

LOW & SLOW RIBS

YIELD
8 servings

ACTIVE
10 minutes

TOTAL
3 hours

1 TBSP EACH **SEASONED SALT** AND **SUGAR**

1½ TSP EACH **SALT-FREE CHILI POWDER** AND **ONION POWDER**

½ TSP **PUMPKIN PIE SPICE**

2 RACKS **BABY-BACK RIBS** (ABOUT 3¾ LB)

½ CUP **WATER**

½ CUP **BARBECUE SAUCE**

Heat oven to 300°F. In a cup, mix seasoned salt, sugar, chili and onion powders, and pumpkin pie spice. Rub all over ribs; place ribs rounded side up on a rack in a large roasting pan.

Pour water into bottom of roasting pan; cover with foil and bake 2½ to 3 hours until ribs are very tender.

Heat outdoor grill. Brush ribs with half the barbecue sauce. Grill 5 minutes or until lightly charred, turning as needed and brushing with remaining sauce. Cut into individual ribs to serve.

TIP The ribs can be cooked 2 days ahead, then covered and refrigerated. To serve, let ribs sit out on the counter for 10 minutes (while the grill heats), then follow last step above.

PER SERVING
CALORIES 324 **TOTAL FAT** 23G **SATURATED FAT** 9G **CHOLESTEROL** 100MG **SODIUM** 800MG **TOTAL CARBOHYDRATES** 9G **DIETARY FIBER** 0G **PROTEIN** 19G

TUNA & WHITE BEAN SALAD

1 BAG (12 OZ) **MICROWAVE-IN-THE-BAG FRESH GREEN BEANS**

2 CANS (5 TO 6 OZ EACH) **SOLID LIGHT TUNA IN OLIVE OIL**, UNDRAINED

3 TBSP **RED-WINE VINEGAR**

1 TSP **DIJON MUSTARD**

¼ TSP EACH **SALT** AND **PEPPER**

1 CAN (15 TO 16 OZ) **CANNELLINI BEANS**, RINSED AND DRAINED

1 MEDIUM **TOMATO**, CUT INTO WEDGES

½ CUP **PITTED KALAMATA OLIVES**

GARNISH: CHOPPED **PARSLEY**

YIELD
4 servings

ACTIVE
10 minutes

TOTAL
20 minutes

Microwave green beans according to package directions. Remove from microwave and let cool slightly.

Meanwhile, make dressing: Drain olive oil from tuna into a liquid measuring cup (you should have ¼ cup). Add vinegar, mustard, salt and pepper, and stir with a fork to blend.

In a large serving bowl, gently combine green beans, cannellini beans, tomato and olives. Break tuna into chunks using a fork and place on top of salad. Drizzle dressing over salad and garnish with parsley, if desired.

PER SERVING
CALORIES 347 **TOTAL FAT** 14G **SATURATED FAT** 3G **CHOLESTEROL** 53MG **SODIUM** 1,103MG **TOTAL CARBOHYDRATES** 25G **DIETARY FIBER** 7G **PROTEIN** 29G

BEEF DIP SANDWICHES

ONE 3-LB **BEEF BOTTOM ROUND OR RUMP ROAST**, TRIMMED OF VISIBLE FAT

1 MEDIUM **VIDALIA OR SWEET ONION**, THINLY SLICED

1 JAR (11 OZ) **PEPPERONCINI PEPPERS**, SLICED (RESERVE ½ CUP JUICE)

¼ CUP EACH **OIL** AND **WATER**

1 POUCH (0.7 OZ) **BASIL VINAIGRETTE OR ITALIAN SALAD DRESSING & RECIPE MIX** (WE USED GOOD SEASONS)

1 TBSP MINCED **GARLIC**

6 **CIABATTA ROLLS**

2 MEDIUM **TOMATOES**, SLICED

1 BAG (5 OZ) **BABY ARUGULA**

YIELD
6 servings

ACTIVE
10 minutes

TOTAL
5 to 6 hours on high
or 8 to 10 hours on low

Place beef and onion in a 3½-qt or larger slow cooker. Mix pepper juice, oil, water, dressing mix and garlic in a small bowl until blended. Pour over beef. (If you have time, cover the crock and place in refrigerator to let beef marinate the night before, turning occasionally.)

Cover and cook on low 8 to 10 hours or on high 5 to 6 hours until beef is tender.

Cut rolls lengthwise in half and brush cut sides with some of the cooking liquid. Pour remaining liquid into a serving bowl.

Transfer beef to cutting board; let rest 15 minutes, then slice thinly. Layer beef, onions, sliced pepperoncini, tomatoes and arugula on bottom half of rolls. Cover with top. Serve with reserved cooking liquid for dipping.

PER SERVING
CALORIES 635 **TOTAL FAT** 20G **SATURATED FAT** 4G **CHOLESTEROL** 123MG **SODIUM** 1,576MG
TOTAL CARBOHYDRATES 55G **DIETARY FIBER** 3G **PROTEIN** 60G

BAKED TILAPIA WITH AVOCADO & TOMATO

YIELD
4 servings

ACTIVE
5 minutes

TOTAL
15 minutes

4 **TILAPIA FILLETS** (ABOUT 5 OZ EACH)

2 TBSP **OLIVE OIL** (PREFERABLY EXTRA-VIRGIN)

¼ TSP EACH **PEPPER**, **GARLIC POWDER**, **DRIED BASIL** AND **DRIED MARJORAM**

½ TSP **SALT**

2 RIPE MEDIUM **TOMATOES**, SEEDED AND DICED

1 RIPE **AVOCADO** (PREFERABLY HASS, THE VERY DARK-SKINNED VARIETY), PEELED AND DICED

Heat oven to 350°F. Line a rimmed baking sheet with foil (for easy cleanup).

Brush both sides of fish with 1 Tbsp oil; place on lined pan. Sprinkle fish with ⅛ tsp pepper, the garlic powder, basil and marjoram, and ¼ tsp salt.

Bake 7 to 10 minutes until fish is just barely opaque at center.

Meanwhile, put tomato and avocado into a medium bowl, add remaining 1 Tbsp olive oil, ¼ tsp salt and ⅛ tsp pepper. Toss to mix and coat. Serve over the fish.

PER SERVING
CALORIES 294 **TOTAL FAT** 18G **SATURATED FAT** 2G **CHOLESTEROL** 0MG **SODIUM** 374MG **TOTAL CARBOHYDRATES** 7G **DIETARY FIBER** 2G **PROTEIN** 28G

FAJITA-STYLE CHICKEN TENDERS WITH CORN & BLACK BEANS

YIELD
4 servings

ACTIVE
3 minutes

TOTAL
7 minutes

2 TSP **OLIVE OIL**

1 LB **CHICKEN TENDERS**

1 PKT (1.12 OZ) **FAJITA SEASONING MIX**

2 TBSP **WATER**

1 CAN (15 OZ) **BLACK BEANS**, RINSED

1 CAN (11 OZ) **WHOLE-KERNEL CORN**

1 CUP **SALSA**

3 TBSP CHOPPED **FRESH CILANTRO**

Heat oil in a large nonstick skillet. Add tenders and cook over medium-high heat, turning once, 3 minutes or until lightly colored. Sprinkle with fajita seasoning and water; toss over medium heat 1 minute until coated and chicken is cooked through.

While tenders cook, combine beans, corn and salsa in a medium saucepan or microwave dish. Heat until hot. Remove from heat and stir in cilantro. Serve with the tenders.

PER SERVING
CALORIES 295 **TOTAL FAT** 5G **SATURATED FAT** 1G **CHOLESTEROL** 66MG **SODIUM** 1,535MG
TOTAL CARBOHYDRATES 29G **DIETARY FIBER** 4G **PROTEIN** 32G

FARFALLE WITH PESTO, GOAT CHEESE & GRAPE TOMATOES

YIELD
6 servings

ACTIVE
10 minutes

TOTAL
25 minutes

1 LB **FARFALLE (BOW-TIE) PASTA**

SAUCE

¼ CUP **CHOPPED WALNUTS**

¼ CUP **EXTRA-VIRGIN OLIVE OIL**

2 CUPS **FRESH BASIL LEAVES**

2 SMALL CLOVES **GARLIC**, SMASHED

½ TSP **CRUSHED RED PEPPER**

½ TSP **SALT**

4 OZ **GOAT CHEESE**

1 PT **GRAPE OR CHERRY TOMATOES**, CUT IN HALF

Cook pasta in a large pot of lightly salted boiling water as package directs.

Meanwhile, put walnuts, oil, basil, garlic, crushed red pepper and salt in a blender; process until puréed.

Remove and reserve ¼ cup pasta cooking water. Drain pasta; transfer to serving bowl. Add ½ the goat cheese and the tomatoes. Toss to mix. Add basil mixture and reserved cooking water; toss to coat. Spoon remaining goat cheese over top.

PER SERVING
CALORIES 477 **TOTAL FAT** 20G **SATURATED FAT** 6G **CHOLESTEROL** 15MG **SODIUM** 559MG
TOTAL CARBOHYDRATES 61G **DIETARY FIBER** 4G **PROTEIN** 16G

MAY

MAY SHOPPING LIST

Week 1
MAY 1 TO MAY 7

PRODUCE
2 NAVEL ORANGES
1 LEMON
2 ONIONS
1 SMALL SWEET ONION
1 HEAD GARLIC (2 CLOVES)
1 PT GRAPE TOMATOES
2 MEDIUM CARROTS
1 BAG (1 LB) BABY CARROTS
1½ CUPS BROCCOLI FLORETS
1 BELL PEPPER
2 CUBANELLE PEPPERS
8 OZ FRESH ASPARAGUS
1 LARGE LEEK
12 OZ BABY BOK CHOY
4 SCALLIONS
FRESH TARRAGON
1 BUNCH CILANTRO
1 BUNCH DILL

MEAT/POULTRY/FISH
FOUR ¾-IN.-THICK BONELESS SHELL STEAKS (ABOUT 6 OZ EACH)
ONE 12-OZ PORK TENDERLOIN
4 BONELESS, SKINLESS CHICKEN BREASTS (ABOUT 6 OZ EACH)
1½ LB BONELESS, SKINLESS CHICKEN THIGHS
8 OZ TURKEY BREAKFAST SAUSAGE
4 SALMON STEAKS OR PIECES OF FILLET (ABOUT 1 IN. THICK AND 6 OZ EACH)

FROZEN
1 BOX (10 OZ) PEAS

REFRIGERATED
1¼ CUPS FAT-FREE OR REGULAR HALF-AND-HALF
1 CONTAINER (16 OZ) FAT-FREE SOUR CREAM
1 CUP LOWFAT PLAIN YOGURT
¼ CUP FETA CHEESE
2 OZ PEPPERJACK CHEESE

GROCERY
1 CAN (16 OZ) BLACK BEANS
1 CUP CANNED COOKED PUMPKIN
1 JAR (12 OZ) CHICKEN GRAVY
1 LB RADIATORE PASTA
¾ CUP GOYA ALCAPARRADO (MANZANILLA OLIVES, PIMIENTOS AND CAPERS)
4 BURRITO-SIZE 99%-FAT-FREE TORTILLAS
STIR-FRY SAUCE
HONEY
1 SLOW COOKER LINER (WE USED REYNOLDS)
⅓ CUP DRY WHITE WINE

PANTRY
SALT
PEPPER
CANOLA OIL
OLIVE OIL
NONSTICK SPRAY
FLOUR
CORNSTARCH
BROWN SUGAR
SALT-FREE CHILI POWDER
CURRY POWDER
PUMPKIN PIE SPICE

Week 2
MAY 8 TO MAY 14

PRODUCE
1 LIME
2 MEDIUM ONIONS
1 RED ONION
1 HEAD GARLIC (2 CLOVES)
1 LB THIN-SKINNED POTATOES
1½ PINTS CHERRY OR GRAPE TOMATOES
1 HASS AVOCADO
1 BAG (6 OZ) RADISHES
1 SPAGHETTI SQUASH (ABOUT 3½ LB)
1 LARGE ZUCCHINI (ABOUT 1 LB)
1 HEAD LETTUCE
SMALL SEEDLESS CUCUMBERS (OPTIONAL)
1 BUNCH MINT
1 BUNCH CILANTRO

BAKERY
8 SANDWICH BUNS

MEAT/POULTRY/FISH
ONE 3½-LB BOTTOM ROUND BEEF ROAST
ONE 12-OZ BEEF SKIRT STEAK
1¼ LB BONELESS, SKINLESS CHICKEN THIGHS
4 PORK LOIN CHOPS, ¾ IN. THICK (ABOUT 1½ LB)
16 CHICKEN TENDERS (ABOUT 1½ LB)
1 LB COD FILLET, ABOUT ¾ IN. THICK

DELI
1 LB GERMAN POTATO SALAD

REFRIGERATED
½ STICK BUTTER
GRATED PARMESAN

FROZEN
1 BAG (12 OZ) MICROWAVE-IN-BAG CUT GREEN BEANS
1¼ CUPS MIXED VEGETABLES

GROCERY
1 JAR (2 OZ) CHOPPED PIMIENTOS
8 OZ WIDE EGG NOODLES
MOJO CRIOLLO SAUCE (WE USED GOYA)
8 FAJITA-SIZE FLOUR TORTILLAS
WORCESTERSHIRE SAUCE
SEASONED DRIED BREAD CRUMBS
¾ CUP PEANUT SATAY SAUCE (WE USED THAI KITCHEN)
DRY RUB BARBECUE SEASONING (WE USED WEBER)
16 SKEWERS (6-IN.)
½ CUP COLA

PANTRY
SALT
PEPPER
OLIVE OIL
CANOLA OIL
NONSTICK SPRAY
CIDER VINEGAR
CORNSTARCH
DIJON MUSTARD
KETCHUP

GROUND CUMIN
DRIED ROSEMARY

Week 3

MAY 15 TO MAY 22

PRODUCE

1 LEMON
1 LIME
3 ONIONS
1 MEDIUM RED ONION
2 HEADS GARLIC (12 CLOVES)
1 SMALL PIECE GINGER
1 LB YUKON GOLD POTATOES
1 LARGE PLUM TOMATO
½ PINT GRAPE TOMATOES
1 SMALL EGGPLANT (8 OZ)
2 SMALL ZUCCHINI (8 OZ)
2 JALAPEÑO PEPPERS
1 BAG (5 OR 6 OZ) BABY SPINACH
16 SCALLIONS
1 BUNCH PARSLEY
1 BUNCH CHIVES
1 BUNCH CILANTRO
1 BUNCH BASIL (OPTIONAL)

BAKERY

24 SMALL DINNER ROLLS

MEAT/POULTRY/FISH

4 THIN-CUT TOP ROUND STEAKS (1 TO 1¼ LB)
3½ LB BONE-IN PORK SHOULDER ROAST
4 LB BONE-IN PORK SHOULDER ROAST
12 OZ CHICKEN BREAST CUTLETS
2½ LB CHICKEN DRUMSTICKS AND THIGHS
4 PIECES 1-IN.-THICK SKINLESS SALMON FILLET (ABOUT 6 OZ EACH)
1 LB PEELED, DEVEINED LARGE SHRIMP

REFRIGERATED

½ STICK BUTTER
MILK
½ CUP SHREDDED PART-SKIM MOZZARELLA
1 TUBE (16–18 OZ) READY-TO-HEAT POLENTA
1 TUB (6–7 OZ) CILANTRO OR BASIL PESTO

GROCERY

1 CAN (14.5 OZ) DICED TOMATOES
1 CAN (14 OZ) DICED TOMATOES WITH ROASTED GARLIC AND ONION
1 CAN (15.25 OZ) WHOLE-KERNEL CORN
1 CAN (14 OZ) MILD RED ENCHILADA SAUCE (OLD EL PASO)
1 CAN (4 OZ) DICED GREEN CHILES
1 CAN (10.75 OZ) CONDENSED CREAM OF POTATO SOUP
1 CUP JARRED ROASTED PEPPERS (PREFERABLY RED AND YELLOW)
1 CUP MARINARA SAUCE
12 OZ ANGEL HAIR PASTA
1 LB CAVATAPPI OR OTHER PASTA
¼ CUP SUN-DRIED TOMATOES
CLASSIC STIR-FRY SAUCE
1 SLOW COOKER LINER (WE USED REYNOLDS)

PANTRY

SALT
PEPPER
OLIVE OIL
OLIVE OIL NONSTICK SPRAY
CIDER VINEGAR
SUGAR
BROWN SUGAR
CRUSHED RED PEPPER
PAPRIKA
DRIED MINCED ONION
GROUND CUMIN
GROUND CARDAMOM
TURMERIC
GROUND CLOVES
SALT-FREE CHILI POWDER
GARLIC POWDER
ALLSPICE (OPTIONAL)

Week 4

MAY 23 TO MAY 31

PRODUCE

2 NAVEL ORANGES
1 LEMON
1 MEDIUM ONION
1 SWEET ONION
1 SMALL RED ONION
1 HEAD GARLIC (5 CLOVES)
1 SMALL PIECE GINGER
2 LARGE SWEET POTATOES
1 PLUM TOMATO
3 MEDIUM CARROTS
1 MEDIUM RED BELL PEPPER
2 MEDIUM YELLOW BELL PEPPERS
3¼ LB ASPARAGUS
1 PKG (8 OZ) SLICED MUSHROOMS
1 HEAD GREEN-LEAF LETTUCE
RADISH SPROUTS
14 SCALLIONS
1 BUNCH PARSLEY (OPTIONAL)
1 BUNCH CILANTRO
FRESH TARRAGON (OR BASIL, CHIVES, PARSLEY OR DILL)

BAKERY

10 SLICES (EACH ¾ IN. THICK) FRENCH BREAD

MEAT/POULTRY/FISH

1½ LB 1-IN.-THICK BONELESS BEEF TOP ROUND STEAK (LONDON BROIL)
12 OZ BEEF TOP ROUND STEAK
8 OZ LEAN GROUND BEEF
1 PORK TENDERLOIN
4 BONELESS, SKINLESS CHICKEN BREASTS (ABOUT 6 OZ EACH)
1 LB LEAN GROUND TURKEY
1 PKG (3½ OZ) FULLY COOKED CHORIZO SAUSAGE
2 LB COD FILLETS (1½ IN. THICK)
1½ LB PEELED, DEVEINED RAW LARGE SHRIMP

REFRIGERATED

1 CONTAINER (6 OZ) REDUCED-FAT SOUR CREAM
½ CUP SHREDDED MOZZARELLA
6 OZ (1½ CUPS) SMOKED GOUDA OR MOZZARELLA
EGGS (8 LARGE)
⅓ CUP ORANGE JUICE

FROZEN

1 BAG (16 OZ) BROCCOLI STIR-FRY MIX (BROCCOLI, CARROTS, ONIONS, RED PEPPERS, CELERY, WATER CHESTNUTS, MUSHROOMS)
2 CUPS CORN KERNELS
6 CUPS COUNTRY-STYLE HASH BROWN POTATOES

GROCERY

1 CAN (14.5 OZ) CHICKEN BROTH
1 CAN (19 OZ) BLACK BEANS
INSTANT BROWN RICE
1 CUP MARINARA SAUCE
2 JARS (7.5 OZ) HOISIN SAUCE
¼ CUP PITTED KALAMATA OLIVES
SEASONED STIR-FRY OIL
STIR-FRY SAUCE
½ CUP CONVERTED WHITE RICE
½ CUP SALSA VERDE (GREEN SALSA)
OLIVE OIL AND VINEGAR DRESSING
½ CUP BOTTLED GREEK VINAIGRETTE DRESSING
GARLIC-FLAVOR NONSTICK SPRAY
HONEY
½ CUP DRY SHERRY OR DRY WHITE WINE

PANTRY

SALT
PEPPER
OLIVE OIL
SUGAR
FLOUR
RICE VINEGAR
SESAME OIL
CRUSHED RED PEPPER
DRIED OREGANO
GROUND CUMIN

BEEF VALENCIA

YIELD
4 servings

ACTIVE
8 minutes

TOTAL
18 minutes

¾ TSP **PEPPER**

¼TSP **SALT**

1 TSP **OIL**

FOUR ¾-IN.-THICK **BONELESS SHELL STEAKS** (ABOUT 6 OZ EACH)

2 **NAVEL ORANGES**, PEEL AND PITH REMOVED, CUT INTO SECTIONS

¾ CUP **GOYA ALCAPARRADO** (MANZANILLA OLIVES, PIMIENTOS AND CAPERS)

SIDE SUGGESTION
Rice

Season steaks with ½ tsp pepper and the salt.

Heat oil in a large nonstick skillet over medium-high heat. Add steaks and cook, turning once, 6 to 7 minutes for medium-rare.

Meanwhile, mix oranges, Alcaparrado and remaining ¼ tsp pepper in medium bowl. Serve steaks topped with mixture.

DIFFERENT TAKES

- Add some sliced red onion and chopped cilantro to orange-olive mixture.
- Rub steak with ground cumin before cooking.
- Use pork chops instead of steak.

PER SERVING
CALORIES 453 **TOTAL FAT** 29G **SATURATED FAT** 10G **CHOLESTEROL** 89MG **SODIUM** 605MG
TOTAL CARBOHYDRATES 10G **DIETARY FIBER** 2G **PROTEIN** 36G

SPRING VEGETABLE & CHICKEN STEW

1 **SLOW COOKER LINER** (WE USED REYNOLDS)

$1\frac{1}{2}$ LB **BONELESS, SKINLESS CHICKEN THIGHS**, CUT IN CHUNKS

2 CUPS **BABY CARROTS**, HALVED LENGTHWISE

1 LARGE **LEEK**, WHITE AND LIGHT GREEN PARTS ONLY, SLICED (2 CUPS)

1 TBSP CHOPPED **FRESH TARRAGON**

1 JAR (12 OZ) **CHICKEN GRAVY**

⅓ CUP **DRY WHITE WINE**

1 TBSP **FLOUR**

½ TSP **SALT**

8 OZ **FRESH ASPARAGUS**, TRIMMED, CUT IN 1- TO 2-IN. LENGTHS

⅓ CUP THAWED **FROZEN PEAS**

YIELD
6 servings

ACTIVE
15 minutes

TOTAL
5 to 8 hours on low

Line a 3-qt or larger slow cooker with liner. Put chicken, carrots, leek and tarragon in slow cooker. Pour in gravy. Put wine, flour and salt in gravy jar; cover and shake to mix. Pour into slow cooker; toss to coat. Cover and cook on low 5 to 8 hours until chicken and vegetables are tender.

Turn to high. Add asparagus; cover and cook on high 10 to 15 minutes until asparagus are crisp-tender. Stir in peas.

PER SERVING
CALORIES 207 **TOTAL FAT** 5G **SATURATED FAT** 1G **CHOLESTEROL** 99MG **SODIUM** 567MG **TOTAL CARBOHYDRATES** 15G **DIETARY FIBER** 2G **PROTEIN** 25G

CHILI BEAN & VEGETABLE WRAPS

YIELD
4 servings

ACTIVE
20 minutes

TOTAL
30 minutes

4 BURRITO-SIZE **99%-FAT-FREE TORTILLAS**

2 TSP **OIL**, PREFERABLY CANOLA

1½ CUPS VERY THIN HALF-SLICES **ONION**

1 LARGE **YELLOW SQUASH** (8 OZ), DICED

1 **RED BELL PEPPER**, CUT IN VERY NARROW STRIPS

2 TSP **CHILI POWDER**

1 BAG (10 OZ) PREWASHED **SPINACH**, COARSE STEMS REMOVED, COARSELY CHOPPED

1 CAN (16 OZ) **BLACK BEANS**, RINSED

2 OZ **PEPPERJACK CHEESE**, SHREDDED (½ CUP)

TOP WITH: **FAT-FREE SOUR CREAM**

SIDE SUGGESTION
Coleslaw

Warm tortillas as package directs.

Heat oil in a large nonstick skillet over medium-high heat. Add onions, squash and bell pepper; sauté 6 minutes or until browned and tender. Stir in chili powder. Cook, stirring, 30 seconds or until fragrant. Add spinach by handfuls, adding more as it cooks down. Stir in beans; heat through.

For each burrito: Place a tortilla on work surface. Spoon ¼ of the filling over bottom third; sprinkle with ¼ of the cheese. Starting at bottom, roll up tightly. Place seam side down on serving platter. Serve with sour cream.

PER SERVING
CALORIES 352 **TOTAL FAT** 8G **SATURATED FAT** 3G **CHOLESTEROL** 15MG **SODIUM** 794MG
TOTAL CARBOHYDRATES 55G **DIETARY FIBER** 7G **PROTEIN** 17G

SALMON WITH CURRY-YOGURT SAUCE

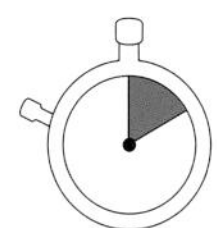

YIELD
4 servings

ACTIVE
10 minutes

TOTAL
15 minutes

4 **SALMON STEAKS OR PIECES OF FILLET** (ABOUT 1 IN. THICK AND 6 OZ EACH)

¼ TSP EACH **SALT** AND **PEPPER**

NONSTICK COOKING SPRAY

1 CUP **LOWFAT PLAIN YOGURT**

2 TBSP EACH CHOPPED **CILANTRO** AND SLICED **SCALLIONS**

1 TBSP EACH **HONEY** AND **CURRY POWDER**

Heat broiler. Line a baking pan with nonstick foil. Place salmon on pan; sprinkle with salt and pepper, and coat with nonstick spray. Broil 8 to 10 minutes or until just cooked through.

Meanwhile, combine remaining ingredients. Serve with salmon.

NOTE Salmon (rich in vitamin D) helps your body absorb the calcium in dairy foods like yogurt.

PER SERVING
CALORIES 338 **TOTAL FAT** 14G **SATURATED FAT** 3G **CHOLESTEROL** 111MG **SODIUM** 274MG **TOTAL CARBOHYDRATES** 10G **DIETARY FIBER** 1G **PROTEIN** 42G

LEMON PORK STIR-FRY

- 1 TBSP **CORNSTARCH**
- ONE 12-OZ **PORK TENDERLOIN**, HALVED LENGTHWISE, CUT CROSSWISE IN 1/4-IN.-THICK SLICES
- 2 TSP **OIL**
- 12 OZ **BABY BOK CHOY**, QUARTERED CROSSWISE
- 1 **BELL PEPPER**, CUT INTO STRIPS
- 1 CUP SHREDDED **CARROTS**
- 2 TBSP EACH **STIR-FRY SAUCE** AND **WATER**
- 1 TSP GRATED **LEMON ZEST**
- 1 TBSP **LEMON JUICE**

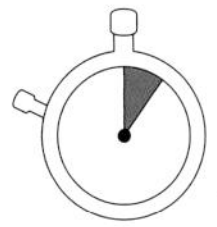

YIELD
4 servings

ACTIVE
6 minutes

TOTAL
15 minutes

Sprinkle cornstarch over pork; toss until coated. Heat 1½ tsp of the oil in a large nonstick skillet. Add pork; stir-fry 3 to 4 minutes until cooked through. Remove.

Heat remaining ½ tsp oil in skillet. Add bok choy, pepper and carrots; stir-fry 4 minutes until crisp-tender.

Add pork and remaining ingredients; toss until hot.

PER SERVING
CALORIES 180 **TOTAL FAT** 7G **SATURATED FAT** 2G **CHOLESTEROL** 54MG **SODIUM** 233MG
TOTAL CARBOHYDRATES 10G **DIETARY FIBER** 3G **PROTEIN** 20G

GREEK CHICKEN SAUTÉ

2 TSP **FLOUR**

¼ TSP EACH **SALT** AND **PEPPER**

4 **BONELESS, SKINLESS CHICKEN BREASTS** (ABOUT 6 OZ EACH)

2 TSP **OLIVE OIL**

2 **CUBANELLE PEPPERS**, SLICED

1 SMALL **SWEET ONION**, SLICED

½ CUP **WATER**

1 CUP **GRAPE TOMATOES**

2 TSP EACH MINCED **GARLIC** AND GRATED **LEMON ZEST**

¼ CUP **CRUMBLED FETA CHEESE**

3 TBSP CHOPPED **DILL**

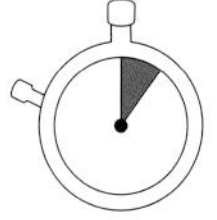

YIELD
4 servings

ACTIVE
6 minutes

TOTAL
17 minutes

Combine flour, salt and pepper; evenly coat chicken.

Heat 1½ tsp oil in a large nonstick skillet. Add chicken; cook, turning once, 8 minutes or until cooked through. Remove.

Heat remaining ½ tsp oil in skillet. Add peppers and onion; sauté 5 minutes or until crisp-tender. Add water, tomatoes, garlic and lemon zest; sauté 2 minutes or until tomatoes soften. Remove from heat; sprinkle with feta and dill. Serve over chicken.

PER SERVING
CALORIES 272 **TOTAL FAT** 7G **SATURATED FAT** 2G **CHOLESTEROL** 107MG **SODIUM** 370MG **TOTAL CARBOHYDRATES** 9G **DIETARY FIBER** 2G **PROTEIN** 42G

PASTA WITH PUMPKIN SAUCE

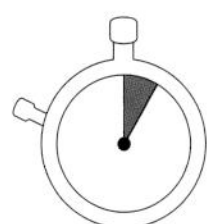

YIELD
6 servings

ACTIVE
5 minutes

TOTAL
20 minutes

1 LB **RADIATORE PASTA**

1½ CUPS **BROCCOLI FLORETS**

8 OZ **TURKEY BREAKFAST SAUSAGE**, REMOVED FROM CASING

1 TSP **PUMPKIN PIE SPICE**

1¼ CUPS **FAT-FREE OR REGULAR HALF-AND-HALF**

1 CUP **CANNED COOKED PUMPKIN**

2 TBSP **BROWN SUGAR**

¼ TSP **SALT**

Cook pasta as package directs, adding broccoli 3 minutes before pasta will be done.

Meanwhile, cook sausage in a large nonstick skillet over medium-high heat, breaking up with spoon, until cooked through, about 6 minutes. Drain fat.

Stir in pumpkin pie spice; cook 1 minute. Stir in half-and-half, pumpkin, sugar and salt. Heat mixture to boiling and cook 1 minute longer.

Drain pasta and broccoli. Return to pot. Add sauce and toss to mix.

PER SERVING
CALORIES 429 **TOTAL FAT** 9G **SATURATED FAT** 2G **CHOLESTEROL** 63MG **SODIUM** 402MG
TOTAL CARBOHYDRATES 70G **DIETARY FIBER** 4G **PROTEIN** 18G

BBQ SKIRT STEAK WITH WARM POTATO SALAD

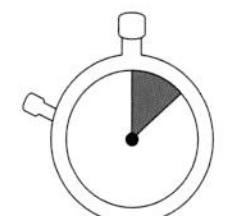

YIELD
4 servings

ACTIVE
8 minutes

TOTAL
10 minutes

2 TSP **OIL**

2 TSP **DRY RUB BARBECUE SEASONING** (WE USED WEBER)

ONE 12-OZ **BEEF SKIRT STEAK**, CUT CROSSWISE INTO 3 PIECES

WARM POTATO SALAD

1 BAG (12 OZ) **MICROWAVE-IN-BAG FROZEN CUT GREEN BEANS** (SUCH AS BIRDS EYE STEAMFRESH)

1 LB **DELI GERMAN POTATO SALAD**

½ SMALL **RED ONION**, THINLY SLICED

1 TBSP **CIDER VINEGAR**

1 TSP **GROUND CUMIN**

Heat oil in large skillet over high heat. Rub barbecue seasoning on steak. Add steak; cook 5 to 6 minutes, turning once, for medium-rare. Let rest 2 minutes before slicing thinly against the grain.

Meanwhile, make **POTATO SALAD**: Steam green beans as package directs. Stir in purchased salad, red onion, vinegar and cumin. Serve with steak.

PER SERVING
CALORIES 353 **TOTAL FAT** 15G **SATURATED FAT** 5G **CHOLESTEROL** 46MG **SODIUM** 744MG **TOTAL CARBOHYDRATES** 31G **DIETARY FIBER** 4G **PROTEIN** 21G

YUCATAN CHICKEN SOFT TACOS

1¼ LB **BONELESS, SKINLESS CHICKEN THIGHS**, VISIBLE FAT TRIMMED

⅓ CUP PLUS 3 TBSP **MOJO CRIOLLO SAUCE** (WE USED GOYA)

3 TSP **OLIVE OIL**

1 **HASS AVOCADO**

½ CUP COARSELY CHOPPED **RED ONION**

½ CUP SLICED **RADISHES**

2 TBSP CHOPPED **CILANTRO**

2 CUPS **LETTUCE**, SHREDDED

8 FAJITA-SIZE **FLOUR TORTILLAS**, WARMED AS PACKAGE DIRECTS

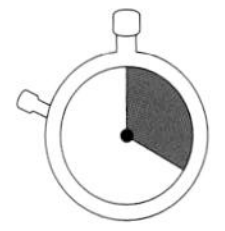

YIELD
4 servings

ACTIVE
20 minutes

TOTAL
50 minutes
(includes 30 minutes marinating)

SIDE SUGGESTION
Sour cream and black beans

Put chicken, ⅓ cup Mojo Criollo sauce and 1 tsp oil in a large plastic ziptop bag. Seal bag; turn to coat and refrigerate 30 minutes or up to 12 hours.

Heat broiler. Line broiler pan with foil; coat rack with nonstick spray. Remove chicken from marinade; place on rack. Drizzle with some of the marinade in bag; reserve the rest.

Broil 15 minutes. Turn and drizzle with reserved marinade; broil until cooked through. Cut in bite-size chunks.

Meanwhile, halve, peel, pit and dice avocado. Toss with onion, radishes, cilantro, remaining 3 Tbsp Mojo Criollo sauce and 2 tsp oil in a bowl.

Put lettuce on top half of tortillas; top with chicken and avocado mixture. Fold bottoms over filling.

PER SERVING
CALORIES 509 **TOTAL FAT** 21G **SATURATED FAT** 4G **CHOLESTEROL** 118MG **SODIUM** 999MG **TOTAL CARBOHYDRATES** 44G **DIETARY FIBER** 4G **PROTEIN** 35G

ROASTED SPAGHETTI SQUASH, TOMATOES & ZUCCHINI

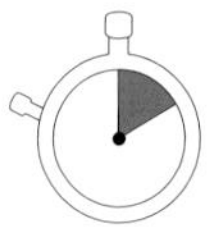

YIELD
4 servings

ACTIVE
10 minutes

TOTAL
55 minutes

1½ PINTS **CHERRY OR GRAPE TOMATOES**

¼ CUP **OLIVE OIL**

2 TSP MINCED **GARLIC**

1 **SPAGHETTI SQUASH**, ABOUT 3½ LB

1 LARGE **ZUCCHINI** (ABOUT 1 LB)

¼ TSP EACH **SALT** AND **PEPPER**

GRATED PARMESAN (OPTIONAL)

Position oven racks to divide oven into thirds. Heat oven to 425°F. Line two 15 x 10 x ½-in. baking pans with nonstick foil.

Halve tomatoes; place tomatoes, 3 Tbsp oil and the garlic in a 13 x 9-in. baking dish. Halve spaghetti squash lengthwise and scoop out seeds. Brush cut surface of squash with a little of the remaining 1 Tbsp oil; place flesh-side down on a foil-lined pan. Quarter zucchini lengthwise and cut into ¾-in. pieces. Place on the other foil-lined pan; toss with remaining oil.

Roast tomatoes and spaghetti squash on top rack 40 minutes until you can easily pierce squash shell. Roast zucchini on bottom rack 30 minutes, tossing once, until tender and slightly browned.

Scrape strands of spaghetti squash into a large bowl. Toss zucchini with roasted tomatoes, salt and pepper; spoon over spaghetti squash. Sprinkle with Parmesan, if desired.

PER SERVING
CALORIES 220 **TOTAL FAT** 14G **SATURATED FAT** 2G **CHOLESTEROL** 0MG **SODIUM** 198MG
TOTAL CARBOHYDRATES 23G **DIETARY FIBER** 6G **PROTEIN** 4G

DIJON-CRUSTED PORK CHOPS

- 4 **PORK LOIN CHOPS**, ¾ IN. THICK (ABOUT 1½ LB)
- 2 TBSP **DIJON MUSTARD**
- ¾ CUP **SEASONED DRIED BREAD CRUMBS**
- 1 TBSP **CANOLA OIL**
- 8 OZ **WIDE EGG NOODLES**
- 1¼ CUPS **FROZEN MIXED VEGETABLES**
- 1 TBSP **BUTTER**
- ¼ TSP EACH **SALT** AND **PEPPER**

YIELD
4 servings

ACTIVE
15 minutes

TOTAL
15 minutes

Heat oven to 350°F. Place a sheet of foil on your kitchen counter. Measure mustard and bread crumbs separately onto foil. Coat pork chops with mustard, then coat with bread crumbs.

Heat oil in a large nonstick skillet over medium-high heat. Add chops and cook 2 to 3 minutes on each side, until bread crumbs are browned. Transfer to a foil-lined baking pan and bake 5 minutes or until cooked through.

Meanwhile, in a large saucepan, heat 4 quarts water to a rapid boil over high heat. Add noodles and cook according to package directions. Add vegetables in the last 5 minutes of cooking. Drain and toss with butter, salt and pepper; serve with pork chops.

PER SERVING
CALORIES 577 **TOTAL FAT** 23G **SATURATED FAT** 8G **CHOLESTEROL** 108MG **SODIUM** 795MG **TOTAL CARBOHYDRATES** 57G **DIETARY FIBER** 4G **PROTEIN** 33G

BAKED COD WITH POTATOES

YIELD
4 servings

ACTIVE
8 minutes

TOTAL
30 minutes

3 TBSP **OLIVE OIL**

1 LB **THIN-SKINNED POTATOES**, SLICED THIN (ABOUT 3 CUPS)

1 MEDIUM-SIZE **ONION**, SLICED THIN

1 JAR (2 OZ) **CHOPPED PIMIENTOS**, DRAINED

½ TSP **DRIED ROSEMARY** LEAVES, CRUMBLED

½ TSP **SALT**

1 LB **COD FILLET**, ABOUT ¾-IN. THICK, CUT IN 4 PIECES

1 TBSP **SEASONED BREAD CRUMBS**

1 TBSP **GRATED PARMESAN**

Place oven rack in lowest position. Heat oven to 450°F.

In a large ovenproof skillet or range-top-to-oven baking dish, heat oil over medium heat. Add potatoes and onion, stirring to coat. Reduce heat to medium-low and cook, stirring occasionally, 10 minutes or until potatoes and onions start to brown and are barely tender. Stir in pimientos, rosemary and salt. Arrange fish over potatoes.

Mix bread crumbs and cheese in a small bowl. Sprinkle over top.

Bake 10 to 12 minutes until fish is opaque at its thickest part when tested with a fork. Serve right away.

NOTE This traditional dish will please just about everyone—especially kids. If cod is unavailable, you can use other lean white fish fillets such as scrod, bass or flounder.

PER SERVING
CALORIES 307 **TOTAL FAT** 12G **SATURATED FAT** 0G **CHOLESTEROL** 50MG **SODIUM** 420MG
TOTAL CARBOHYDRATES 26G **DIETARY FIBER** 0G **PROTEIN** 24G

CHICKEN SATAY SKEWERS

16 **CHICKEN TENDERS** (ABOUT 1½ LB)

16 **SKEWERS** (6 IN.)

¾ CUP **PEANUT SATAY SAUCE** (WE USED THAI KITCHEN)

¼ CUP **LIME JUICE**

1 TSP GRATED **LIME ZEST**

2 TBSP **WATER**

¼ CUP CHOPPED **CILANTRO** *OR* **MINT**

NONSTICK COOKING SPRAY

GARNISH: SMALL **SEEDLESS CUCUMBERS** (OPTIONAL)

YIELD
16 skewers

ACTIVE
15 minutes

TOTAL
20 minutes

Heat stovetop grill pan or broiler. Thread a chicken tender on each skewer.

Mix remaining ingredients in medium bowl. Remove ⅓ cup sauce to small bowl; use to brush both sides of chicken. Reserve remaining sauce for serving. Lightly coat chicken with nonstick spray.

Grill 2 to 3 minutes per side until chicken is cooked through. Garnish with thick slices of small seedless cucumbers, if using. Serve with reserved sauce.

TIP The chicken can be grilled the day before and the remaining sauce refrigerated. Reheat chicken on skewers.

PER SERVING
CALORIES 77 **TOTAL FAT** 3G **SATURATED FAT** 1G **CHOLESTEROL** 24MG **SODIUM** 69MG **TOTAL CARBOHYDRATES** 3G **DIETARY FIBER** 0G **PROTEIN** 9G

BARBECUE BEEF SANDWICHES

1 MEDIUM **ONION**, CHOPPED

3½-LB **BOTTOM ROUND BEEF ROAST**, WELL TRIMMED OF EXCESS FAT

¾ CUP **KETCHUP**

½ CUP **COLA**

1 TBSP EACH **DIJON MUSTARD** AND **WORCESTERSHIRE SAUCE**

3 TBSP **CORNSTARCH**

¼ CUP **WATER**

8 **SANDWICH BUNS**

YIELD
8 servings

ACTIVE
5 minutes

TOTAL
8 to 10 hours on low

Place beef on onion in a 3½-qt or larger slow cooker. Mix ketchup, cola, mustard and Worcestershire sauce in a bowl; pour over beef.

Cover and cook on low 8 to 10 hours. Remove beef to a plate; cover loosely with foil. Increase cooker heat to high. Stir cornstarch and water in a small cup until dissolved. Pour into liquid in cooker; cook 15 to 20 minutes until thickened.

Thinly slice beef, layer on buns and spoon sauce over top.

PER SERVING
CALORIES 462 **TOTAL FAT** 13G **SATURATED FAT** 4G **CHOLESTEROL** 117MG **SODIUM** 692MG
TOTAL CARBOHYDRATES 34G **DIETARY FIBER** 1G **PROTEIN** 48G

GARLIC SHRIMP WITH ANGEL HAIR

12 OZ **ANGEL HAIR PASTA**

2½ TBSP **BUTTER**

2 TBSP **OLIVE OIL**

2 TBSP MINCED **GARLIC**

1 LB **PEELED, DEVEINED LARGE SHRIMP**, THAWED IF FROZEN

1 TBSP GRATED **LEMON ZEST**

¼ TSP EACH **SALT** AND **CRUSHED RED PEPPER**

¼ CUP **LEMON JUICE**

⅓ CUP CHOPPED **PARSLEY**

YIELD
4 servings

ACTIVE
5 minutes

TOTAL
15 minutes

Bring a large pot of lightly salted water to a boil. Add pasta and cook as package directs, reserving about 1 cup of cooking water before draining.

Meanwhile, heat 2 Tbsp of the butter and the oil in a large nonstick skillet over medium-high heat. Add garlic and cook over medium-low heat 30 seconds or until fragrant.

Add shrimp, lemon zest, salt and crushed red pepper; sauté over medium heat 3 to 5 minutes until shrimp is just cooked through.

Stir in lemon juice; remove from heat. Pour over drained pasta; add remaining ½ Tbsp butter, the parsley and about ½ cup of the cooking water (more if desired). Toss to mix and coat.

PER SERVING
CALORIES 586 **TOTAL FAT** 18G **SATURATED FAT** 6G **CHOLESTEROL** 191MG **SODIUM** 455MG **TOTAL CARBOHYDRATES** 66G **DIETARY FIBER** 2G **PROTEIN** 34G

RANCHERO PORK

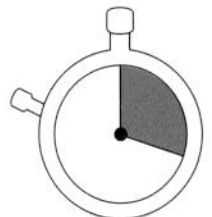

YIELD
8 servings

ACTIVE
18 minutes

TOTAL
8 to 10 hours on low

1 CAN (14 OZ) **MILD RED ENCHILADA SAUCE** (OLD EL PASO)

1 CAN (4 OZ) **DICED GREEN CHILES**

3½ LB **BONE-IN PORK SHOULDER ROAST**, WELL TRIMMED

1 MEDIUM **RED ONION**, SLICED

¼ CUP **FRESH LIME JUICE**

½ CUP CHOPPED **FRESH CILANTRO**

SERVE WITH
Warm corn tortillas

Mix enchilada sauce and chiles in a 4-qt or larger slow cooker. Add pork; spoon sauce over top. Cover and cook on low 8 to 10 hours until pork is very tender.

At least 20 minutes before serving, toss onion slices with lime juice in a medium bowl. Let stand, tossing once or twice, until slightly wilted.

Remove pork to a cutting board. Stir cilantro into mixture in slow cooker. Break pork into bite-size chunks with a wooden spoon and return to cooker; stir to combine.

TO SERVE Spoon pork mixture on warmed tortillas, top with marinated onions, fold and eat.

PER SERVING
CALORIES 268 **TOTAL FAT** 12G **SATURATED FAT** 4G **CHOLESTEROL** 97MG **SODIUM** 607MG
TOTAL CARBOHYDRATES 9G **DIETARY FIBER** 1G **PROTEIN** 29G

EGGPLANT-POLENTA STACKS

1 TBSP PLUS 2 TSP **OLIVE OIL**

1 SMALL **EGGPLANT** (8 OZ), HALVED, SLICED (3 CUPS)

¾ CUP CHOPPED **ONION**

2 SMALL **ZUCCHINI** (8 OZ), SLICED (2 CUPS)

¼ CUP SLICED **SUN-DRIED TOMATOES**

¼ TSP EACH **SALT** AND **PEPPER**

1 TUBE (16 TO 18 OZ) **READY-TO-HEAT POLENTA**, CUT INTO 8 SLICES

1 LARGE **PLUM TOMATO**, CUT INTO 8 SLICES

½ CUP **SHREDDED PART-SKIM MOZZARELLA**

1 CUP **MARINARA SAUCE**, HEATED IN MICROWAVE

GARNISH: CHOPPED **FRESH BASIL** (OPTIONAL)

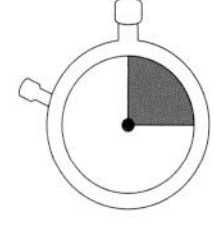

YIELD
4 servings

ACTIVE
15 minutes

TOTAL
30 minutes

Heat 1 Tbsp of the oil in a large, deep nonstick skillet. Add eggplant and onion. Cover and cook over medium-high heat 4 minutes, stirring a few times, until slightly softened.

Add 1 tsp of the remaining oil, the zucchini, sun-dried tomatoes, salt and pepper. Cover and cook 6 to 7 minutes, stirring often, until vegetables are tender. Remove to bowl; wipe or rinse skillet.

Heat remaining 1 tsp oil in skillet. Add polenta; cook 2 minutes over medium-high heat until bottoms are golden.

Off heat, turn polenta and spoon the vegetable mixture onto polenta (it's OK if some falls onto the skillet). Top each with 1 slice of tomato and sprinkle with cheese.

Place skillet over low heat; cover and cook 2 minutes or until cheese melts. Sprinkle with basil, if desired, and serve with sauce.

PER SERVING
CALORIES 282 **TOTAL FAT** 10G **SATURATED FAT** 3G **CHOLESTEROL** 9MG **SODIUM** 948MG **TOTAL CARBOHYDRATES** 39G **DIETARY FIBER** 6G **PROTEIN** 9G

CHICKEN VINDALOO

MARINADE

3 TBSP **CIDER VINEGAR**

2 TBSP **OLIVE OIL**

6 CLOVES **GARLIC**, PEELED

2 **JALAPEÑO PEPPERS**, SEEDED

3 TBSP CHOPPED **GINGER**

2 TSP **GROUND CUMIN**

¾ TSP **GROUND CARDAMOM**

¾ TSP **TURMERIC**

¼ TSP **GROUND CLOVES**

2½ LB **CHICKEN DRUMSTICKS AND THIGHS**, SKIN AND VISIBLE FAT REMOVED

1 TBSP **OLIVE OIL**

2 CUPS CHOPPED **ONIONS**

1 LB **YUKON GOLD POTATOES**, PEELED, CUT IN 1-IN. PIECES

1 CAN (14.5 OZ) **DICED TOMATOES**

2 CUPS **BABY SPINACH**

YIELD
4 servings

ACTIVE
20 minutes

TOTAL
7 hours
(includes marinating)

MARINADE Pulse ingredients in food processor until smooth. Pour into a gallon-size ziptop bag. Add chicken; turn to coat. Refrigerate at least 2 hours or up to 6 hours.

Heat oil in large skillet. Add onions and sauté 8 minutes or until golden. Add chicken, marinade, potatoes and tomatoes. Bring to a simmer, cover and cook 30 minutes or until chicken is cooked through and potatoes are tender.

Remove chicken to a platter. Add spinach to skillet; stir to mix. Cover and cook 1 minute until wilted. Spoon all over chicken.

PER SERVING
CALORIES 454 **TOTAL FAT** 17G **SATURATED FAT** 3G **CHOLESTEROL** 130MG **SODIUM** 373MG
TOTAL CARBOHYDRATES 37G **DIETARY FIBER** 3G **PROTEIN** 38G

BEEF NEGAMAKI

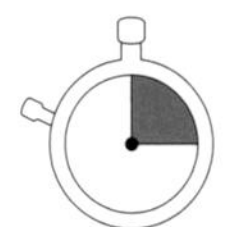

YIELD
4 servings

ACTIVE
15 minutes

TOTAL
50 minutes

12 **SCALLIONS**, ENDS TRIMMED

4 **THIN-CUT TOP ROUND STEAKS** (1 TO 1¼ LB)

¾ CUP **CLASSIC STIR-FRY SAUCE**

3 TBSP **SUGAR**

3 TBSP **WATER**

SIDE SUGGESTION
Rice, edamame

DIFFERENT TAKES

- Substitute thin asparagus spears for the scallions.
- Stir some wasabi into the stir-fry sauce mixture.
- Sprinkle negamaki with toasted sesame seeds before serving.

Microwave scallions in a loosely covered pie plate on high 1 minute to soften.

Place each steak between sheets of plastic wrap. Gently pound until about 8 x 6 in. and ⅛ in. thick. Lay 3 scallions down length of each piece; tightly roll up from a long side. Secure with wooden toothpicks. Put in a large ziptop bag.

Stir sauce, sugar and water in a microwave-safe bowl until sugar dissolves. Add ⅓ cup of mixture to bag; refrigerate 30 minutes or up to 1 hour.

Heat outdoor grill or stovetop grill pan. Grill negamaki 5 minutes, turning to brown on all sides. Discard marinade. Remove picks; trim ends of negamaki, then cut alternately straight across and diagonally in 2-in. lengths.

Microwave sauce in bowl to heat; serve with negamaki.

PER SERVING
CALORIES 313 **TOTAL FAT** 13G **SATURATED FAT** 5G **CHOLESTEROL** 75MG **SODIUM** 920MG **TOTAL CARBOHYDRATES** 27G **DIETARY FIBER** 1G **PROTEIN** 29G

CORN & TOMATO CHOWDER WITH SALMON

1 CAN (10.75 OZ) **CONDENSED CREAM OF POTATO SOUP**

1 SOUP CAN **MILK**

1 CAN (15.25 OZ) **WHOLE-KERNEL CORN**, DRAINED

1 CAN (14 OZ) **DICED TOMATOES WITH ROASTED GARLIC AND ONION**

1 TBSP **OIL**

4 PIECES 1-IN.-THICK **SKINLESS SALMON FILLET** (ABOUT 6 OZ EACH)

1 TSP **SALT**

¼ TSP **PEPPER**

GARNISH: SNIPPED **CHIVES**

YIELD
4 servings

ACTIVE
5 minutes

TOTAL
15 minutes

Combine soup, milk, corn and tomatoes in a medium saucepan. Cook over high heat just until simmering.

Meanwhile, heat oil in a 12-in. nonstick skillet over medium-high heat. Season both sides of salmon with salt and pepper. Add to skillet and cook 2 minutes or until bottom is browned. Turn salmon over; add soup mixture and cook uncovered 10 minutes or until salmon is cooked through.

Using a broad spatula, transfer salmon to soup plates. Add chowder and sprinkle with chives.

PER SERVING
CALORIES 529 **TOTAL FAT** 26G **SATURATED FAT** 6G **CHOLESTEROL** 115MG **SODIUM** 1,899MG
TOTAL CARBOHYDRATES 32G **DIETARY FIBER** 2G **PROTEIN** 40G

SOUTH CAROLINA BBQ PORK SLIDERS

1 **SLOW COOKER LINER** (WE USED REYNOLDS)

¼ CUP PACKED **BROWN SUGAR**

2 TBSP EACH **PAPRIKA** AND **DRIED MINCED ONION**

1½ TSP **SALT-FREE CHILI POWDER**

1½ TSP **SALT**

½ TSP **GARLIC POWDER**

½ TSP **ALLSPICE** (OPTIONAL)

4 LB **BONE-IN PORK SHOULDER ROAST**

¾ CUP **CIDER VINEGAR**

½ CUP SLICED **SCALLIONS**

24 SMALL **DINNER ROLLS**, SPLIT

ACCOMPANIMENT: **HOT PEPPER SAUCE** (OPTIONAL)

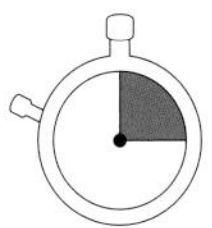

YIELD
8 servings
(3 sliders/serving)

ACTIVE
15 minutes

TOTAL
8 hours

SIDE SUGGESTION
Coleslaw

Line a 4-qt or larger slow cooker with liner. Mix 1 Tbsp of the brown sugar, the paprika, minced onion, chili powder, salt, garlic powder and allspice. Sprinkle 1 Tbsp into bottom of slow cooker. Rub remaining mixture over pork. Add vinegar and remaining brown sugar to slow cooker; stir to mix. Add pork.

Cover and cook on low 8 to 10 hours until pork is fork-tender. Remove pork to cutting board and pull into shreds. Return to slow cooker; add scallions and toss to coat.

Put about ¼ cup onto each roll bottom. Cover with roll tops.

PER SERVING
CALORIES 596 **TOTAL FAT** 26G **SATURATED FAT** 9G **CHOLESTEROL** 110MG **SODIUM** 948MG **TOTAL CARBOHYDRATES** 48G **DIETARY FIBER** 3G **PROTEIN** 39G

PESTO PASTA WITH GRILLED CHICKEN

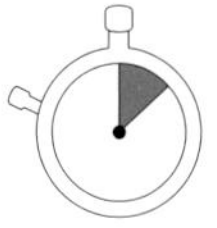

YIELD
6 servings

ACTIVE
8 minutes

TOTAL
20 minutes

- 1 LB **CAVATAPPI OR OTHER PASTA**
- 12 OZ **CHICKEN BREAST CUTLETS**
- **OLIVE OIL COOKING SPRAY**
- ¼ TSP EACH **SALT** AND **PEPPER**
- 1 TUB (6 TO 7 OZ) **CILANTRO OR BASIL PESTO**
- 1 CUP **JARRED ROASTED PEPPERS** (PREFERABLY RED AND YELLOW), DRAINED, CUT IN STRIPS
- 1 CUP HALVED **GRAPE TOMATOES**

Bring a large pot of lightly salted water to a boil. Add pasta and cook as package directs, reserving about 1 cup of cooking water before draining.

Meanwhile, heat stovetop grill pan. Coat chicken with cooking spray and sprinkle with salt and pepper. Grill chicken 4 to 5 minutes, turning once, until cooked through.

Cut chicken into strips. Add to drained pasta along with pesto, peppers, tomatoes and about ½ cup pasta cooking water (or more if desired). Toss to mix and coat.

PER SERVING
CALORIES 507 **TOTAL FAT** 17G **SATURATED FAT** 4G **CHOLESTEROL** 41MG **SODIUM** 543MG
TOTAL CARBOHYDRATES 61G **DIETARY FIBER** 4G **PROTEIN** 27G

ASIAN LETTUCE WRAPS

SAUCE

⅓ CUP **ORANGE JUICE**

1 TBSP EACH **SUGAR** AND **RICE VINEGAR**

¼ TSP EACH **SESAME OIL** AND **CRUSHED RED PEPPER**

WRAPS

½ CUP UNCOOKED **INSTANT BROWN RICE**

8 OZ **LEAN GROUND BEEF**

2 TSP EACH MINCED **GARLIC** AND MINCED **FRESH GINGER**

1 MEDIUM **RED BELL PEPPER**, CUT IN STRIPS

6 **SCALLIONS**, THINLY SLICED (½ CUP)

2 TBSP **HOISIN SAUCE**

8 **GREEN-LEAF LETTUCE LEAVES**, WASHED

GARNISH: **RADISH SPROUTS**

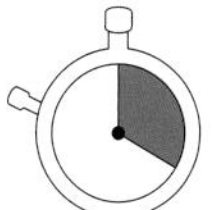

YIELD
4 servings
(2 wraps/serving)

ACTIVE
20 minutes

TOTAL
30 minutes

SIDE SUGGESTION
Carrot-ginger soup

SAUCE Whisk ingredients in small bowl; set aside so flavors blend.

WRAPS Make instant brown rice as package directs, omitting butter.

Meanwhile, cook beef, garlic and ginger in large nonstick skillet over medium-high heat for 3 minutes. Add pepper strips; cook 1 minute more until heated. Remove from heat; stir in scallions and hoisin sauce.

Divide rice, then beef mixture among lettuce leaves. Top with some radish sprouts. Drizzle sauce on top.

PER SERVING
CALORIES 103 **TOTAL FAT** 2G **SATURATED FAT** 1G **CHOLESTEROL** 3MG **SODIUM** 301MG
TOTAL CARBOHYDRATES 19G **DIETARY FIBER** 3G **PROTEIN** 5G

SPRING VEGETABLE FRITTATA

1 CUP **WATER**

3 MEDIUM **CARROTS**, SHREDDED

1 LB **ASPARAGUS**, BOTTOMS TRIMMED (SEE NOTE)

1 TBSP **OIL**, PREFERABLY OLIVE

6 CUPS **FROZEN COUNTRY-STYLE HASH BROWN POTATOES**

1 TSP **SALT**

8 LARGE **EGGS**, BEATEN WITH A FORK

6 OZ (1½ CUPS) **SMOKED GOUDA** *OR* **MOZZARELLA**, SHREDDED

½ CUP SLICED **SCALLIONS**

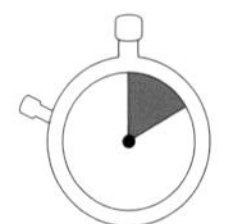

YIELD
6 servings

ACTIVE
10 minutes

TOTAL
34 minutes

NOTE
Hold asparagus with both hands near bottom ends. Bend each spear until it breaks and discard the woody end.

Bring 1 cup water to a boil in a large nonstick skillet. Add carrots and asparagus; reduce heat, cover and simmer 5 to 6 minutes until asparagus are crisp-tender. Drain well; wipe out skillet.

Heat oil in skillet over medium heat. Add potatoes, sprinkle with ½ tsp salt and cook 5 minutes, or until bottoms are lightly browned. Turn with a spatula and press down, pushing some potatoes up the sides of the skillet.

Mix remaining ½ tsp salt with the eggs; pour mixture over potatoes. Top with the carrots and asparagus. Cover and cook over medium-low heat 10 minutes, or until eggs are almost set.

Sprinkle with cheese and scallions, cover and cook 2 to 3 minutes to melt cheese.

PER SERVING
CALORIES 311 **TOTAL FAT** 17G **SATURATED FAT** 7G **CHOLESTEROL** 323MG **SODIUM** 827MG **TOTAL CARBOHYDRATES** 20G **DIETARY FIBER** 3G **PROTEIN** 19G

SPANISH SHRIMP

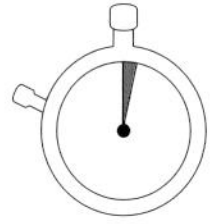

YIELD
6 servings

ACTIVE
2 minutes

TOTAL
7 minutes

1 TSP **OIL**, PREFERABLY OLIVE

1 PKG (3½ OZ) **FULLY COOKED CHORIZO SAUSAGE**, SLICED

1½ LB **PEELED, DEVEINED RAW LARGE SHRIMP**

½ CUP **DRY SHERRY** *OR* **DRY WHITE WINE**

GARNISH: CHOPPED **PARSLEY** (OPTIONAL)

SIDE SUGGESTION
Rice, lemon wedges

Heat oil in a large nonstick skillet over medium-high heat. Add chorizo and sauté 2 minutes until browned.

Add shrimp and sauté 1 to 2 minutes, just until shrimp turn pink.

Add sherry and sauté 1 minute or until shrimp are cooked through. Garnish with parsley, if desired.

PER SERVING
CALORIES 205 **TOTAL FAT** 9G **SATURATED FAT** 3G **CHOLESTEROL** 187MG **SODIUM** 37MG
TOTAL CARBOHYDRATES 2G **DIETARY FIBER** 0G **PROTEIN** 27G

CHICKEN CACCIATORE PARMESAN

2 TBSP **ALL-PURPOSE FLOUR**

4 **BONELESS, SKINLESS CHICKEN BREASTS** (ABOUT 6 OZ EACH)

1 TBSP **OIL**

2 MEDIUM **YELLOW BELL PEPPERS**, CUT IN STRIPS

1 MEDIUM **ONION**, SLICED

1 PKG (8 OZ) **SLICED MUSHROOMS**

1 CUP **JARRED MARINARA SAUCE**

¼ CUP **WATER**

¼ CUP **PITTED KALAMATA OLIVES**

½ CUP **SHREDDED MOZZARELLA**

YIELD
4 servings

ACTIVE
32 minutes

TOTAL
40 minutes

Spread flour on wax paper; dip chicken in flour to coat.

Heat 1½ tsp oil in a 12-in. nonstick skillet over medium high heat. Cook chicken 8 to 10 minutes, turning once, until browned and cooked through; put in an 8 x 8 x 2-in. baking dish.

Heat remaining oil in same skillet over medium-high heat. Add peppers, onion and mushrooms; sauté 12 minutes or until tender.

Off heat, pour sauce into skillet; stir in water and olives. Spoon over chicken in baking dish; sprinkle with cheese. Cover with plastic wrap, then tightly cover with nonstick foil. Freeze up to 3 months.

TO REHEAT Thaw in refrigerator overnight. Heat oven to 350°F. Remove foil and plastic wrap, then re-cover with the nonstick foil. Bake 35 to 40 minutes until sauce bubbles around edges, cheese melts and chicken is heated through.

PER SERVING
CALORIES 359 **TOTAL FAT** 12G **SATURATED FAT** 4G **CHOLESTEROL** 113MG **SODIUM** 469MG **TOTAL CARBOHYDRATES** 15G **DIETARY FIBER** 3G **PROTEIN** 44G

CHINESE PORK ROAST

- 1 JAR (7.5 OZ) **HOISIN SAUCE**
- 2 TBSP EACH **HONEY** AND **RICE VINEGAR**
- 4 **SCALLIONS**, FINELY CHOPPED
- 2 LARGE **SWEET POTATOES**, CUT IN ½-IN. STRIPS
- 1 LB **ASPARAGUS**, TRIMMED
- 3 TSP **OIL**
- ¼ TSP **SALT**
- 1 **PORK TENDERLOIN** (1 LB)

YIELD
4 servings

ACTIVE
15 minutes

TOTAL
40 minutes

Position racks to divide oven in thirds. Heat oven to 500°F. Line 2 rimmed baking pans with nonstick foil.

Whisk ⅓ cup hoisin sauce, the honey, vinegar and scallions in a small bowl until blended; reserve for serving.

Place sweet potatoes on one baking pan, asparagus on the other. Toss potatoes with 2 tsp oil, asparagus with 1 tsp. Sprinkle all with salt; toss.

Move potatoes partially to one side of pan. Place pork on same pan with potatoes; brush with remaining hoisin sauce. Roast pork and potatoes on top rack 15 minutes.

Remove pan from oven, gently toss potatoes and turn pork. Return to oven; roast pork and potatoes on top, asparagus on bottom 10 minutes or until pork registers 155°F on an instant read thermometer. Let pork rest 5 minutes; slice and serve with hoisin-honey sauce.

PER SERVING
CALORIES 304 **TOTAL FAT** 12G **SATURATED FAT** 4G **CHOLESTEROL** 104MG **SODIUM** 810MG
TOTAL CARBOHYDRATES 9G **DIETARY FIBER** 1G **PROTEIN** 37G

ORANGE BEEF & VEGETABLES

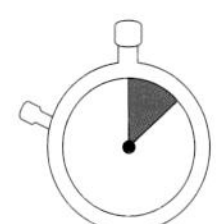

YIELD
4 servings

ACTIVE
8 minutes

TOTAL
16 minutes

1 TBSP **SEASONED STIR-FRY OIL**

12 OZ **BEEF TOP ROUND STEAK**, CUT DIAGONALLY IN THIN SLICES AGAINST THE GRAIN

⅓ CUP **BOTTLED STIR-FRY SAUCE**

1 BAG (16 OZ) **FROZEN BROCCOLI STIR-FRY MIX** (BROCCOLI, CARROTS, ONIONS, RED PEPPERS, CELERY, WATER CHESTNUTS, MUSHROOMS)

2 MEDIUM-SIZE **NAVEL ORANGES**, SCRUBBED (GRATE ZEST FROM ½ AN ORANGE, SQUEEZE JUICE FROM BOTH)

Heat stir-fry oil in a large nonstick skillet over medium-high heat. Add beef in 2 batches and stir-fry 30 to 45 seconds until barely pink. Remove to a bowl with a slotted spoon. Stir in stir-fry sauce.

Put frozen vegetables, grated orange zest and juice in skillet. Cook, stirring, 4 to 5 minutes until vegetables are hot.

Add beef mixture and stir 1 minute until hot.

PER SERVING
CALORIES 262 **TOTAL FAT** 12G **SATURATED FAT** 4G **CHOLESTEROL** 34MG **SODIUM** 824MG **TOTAL CARBOHYDRATES** 18G **DIETARY FIBER** 3G **PROTEIN** 22G

COD & ASPARAGUS WITH TOMATO VINAIGRETTE

2 LB **COD FILLETS** (1½ IN. THICK), CUT IN FIVE PIECES

1 BUNCH (ABOUT 1¼ LB) **ASPARAGUS**, WOODY ENDS SNAPPED OFF

GARLIC-FLAVOR NONSTICK SPRAY

½ TSP EACH **SALT** AND **PEPPER**

1 CUP DICED **PLUM TOMATOES**

¼ CUP **OLIVE OIL AND VINEGAR DRESSING**

2 TBSP CHOPPED **FRESH TARRAGON, BASIL, CHIVES, PARSLEY OR DILL**

10 SLICES (EACH ¾ IN. THICK) **FRENCH BREAD**

YIELD
5 servings

ACTIVE
7 minutes

TOTAL
20 minutes

Heat oven to 500°F. Position racks to divide oven in thirds. Line 2 rimmed baking sheets with nonstick foil.

Place fish on 1 baking sheet; spread asparagus evenly on the other. Coat cod and asparagus with nonstick spray; sprinkle with salt and pepper.

Roast 10 to 12 minutes, switching position of pans halfway through cooking, until cod is just cooked through and asparagus are tender.

Mix remaining ingredients (except bread) in a bowl. Spoon over cod. Serve with bread.

PER SERVING
CALORIES 430 **TOTAL FAT** 7G **SATURATED FAT** 1G **CHOLESTEROL** 69MG **SODIUM** 1,032MG
TOTAL CARBOHYDRATES 50G **DIETARY FIBER** 4G **PROTEIN** 40G

TURKEY CHILI

1 TBSP **OLIVE OIL**

1 LB **LEAN GROUND TURKEY**

1 TBSP MINCED **GARLIC**

2½ TSP **GROUND CUMIN**

½ TSP EACH **SALT** AND **PEPPER**

1 CAN (14.5 OZ) **CHICKEN BROTH**

1 CAN (19 OZ) **BLACK BEANS**, RINSED

2 CUPS **FROZEN CORN KERNELS**

½ CUP UNCOOKED **CONVERTED WHITE RICE**

½ CUP **SALSA VERDE** (GREEN SALSA)

1 CUP CHOPPED **SWEET ONION**

½ CUP CHOPPED **CILANTRO**

TOPPINGS: **REDUCED-FAT SOUR CREAM**, **GREEN SALSA** AND CHOPPED **CILANTRO**

YIELD
4 servings

ACTIVE
12 minutes

TOTAL
50 minutes

Heat oil in a large, deep nonstick skillet over high heat. Add turkey and garlic and cook, stirring to break up meat, 3 to 4 minutes until browned. Add cumin, salt and pepper; cook, stirring, 30 seconds.

Stir in broth, beans, corn, rice and salsa. Bring to a boil, reduce heat, cover and simmer, stirring occasionally, 20 to 25 minutes until rice is tender.

Remove from heat; stir in onion and cilantro. Ladle into bowls and serve with Toppings.

PER SERVING
CALORIES 462 **TOTAL FAT** 14G **SATURATED FAT** 3G **CHOLESTEROL** 83MG **SODIUM** 1,148MG **TOTAL CARBOHYDRATES** 54G **DIETARY FIBER** 7G **PROTEIN** 30G

OREGANO-LEMON MARINATED STEAK

YIELD
4 servings

ACTIVE
24 minutes

TOTAL
1 hour 24 minutes

MARINADE

½ CUP **BOTTLED GREEK VINAIGRETTE DRESSING**

1 TBSP **DRIED OREGANO**

2 TSP FRESHLY GRATED **LEMON ZEST**

1½-LB 1-IN.-THICK **BONELESS BEEF TOP ROUND STEAK** (LONDON BROIL), EXCESS FAT TRIMMED

MARINADE Mix ingredients in a gallon-size ziptop bag. Add steak, press air from bag, seal and turn to distribute marinade. Refrigerate at least 30 minutes or up to 1 hour.

Heat barbecue grill or ridged grill pan. Remove meat from marinade; discard marinade.

Grill 4 to 6 in. from heat source 14 to 16 minutes for medium-rare (145°F on a meat thermometer); 20 to 22 minutes for medium (160°F). Transfer to a cutting board and let rest 10 minutes. Thinly slice steak on a bias, against the grain.

PER SERVING
CALORIES 216 **TOTAL FAT** 9G **SATURATED FAT** 2G **CHOLESTEROL** 81MG **SODIUM** 171MG **TOTAL CARBOHYDRATES** 1G **DIETARY FIBER** 0G **PROTEIN** 31G

JUNE

JUNE SHOPPING LIST

Week 1

JUNE 1 TO JUNE 7

PRODUCE

1 MANGO
3 LEMONS
2 RED ONIONS
3 HEADS GARLIC (13 CLOVES)
1 SMALL PIECE GINGER
7 TOMATOES
1 KIRBY CUCUMBER
2 YELLOW BELL PEPPERS
3 SMALL ZUCCHINI (1 LB)
1 SMALL EGGPLANT (12 OZ)
6 OZ SUGAR SNAP PEAS (1½ CUPS)
1 SEEDLESS CUCUMBER
4 OZ SHIITAKE MUSHROOMS OR 1½ CUPS SLICED WHITE MUSHROOMS
1 HEAD LETTUCE
4 SCALLIONS
FRESH ROSEMARY
1 BUNCH DILL
1 BUNCH BASIL
1 BUNCH PARSLEY
1 BUNCH MINT

BAKERY

5 POCKETLESS PITAS

MEAT/POULTRY/FISH

2 LB BONELESS BEEF CHUCK STEAK, ABOUT 1¼ IN. THICK
ONE 12-OZ PORK TENDERLOIN
4 CHICKEN DRUMSTICKS
4 CHICKEN THIGHS
1 LB BONELESS, SKINLESS CHICKEN THIGHS
12 OZ PEELED EXTRA-JUMBO SHRIMP
12 OZ LARGE SEA SCALLOPS

REFRIGERATED

1 CONTAINER (6 OZ) GREEK YOGURT
1 CONTAINER (15 OZ) FAT-FREE RICOTTA
4 OZ FAT-FREE CREAM CHEESE
1¼ CUPS SHREDDED REDUCED-FAT MOZZARELLA
GRATED PARMESAN

GROCERY

1 CAN (28 OZ) CRUSHED TOMATOES
1 CAN (5 OZ) TUNA IN OLIVE OIL
1 CAN (11 OZ) MANDARIN ORANGES
1 JAR (11.09 OZ) THAI KITCHEN RED CURRY 10-MINUTE SIMMER SAUCE
1 JAR (24 TO 26 OZ) MARINARA SAUCE
1 LB PENNE PASTA
1 PACKAGE (8 OZ) OVEN-READY LASAGNA NOODLES
½ CUP PITTED OLIVES
CAPERS
BULGUR
LIGHT ITALIAN DRESSING
STIR-FRY SAUCE
1 SLOW COOKER LINER (WE USED REYNOLDS)

PANTRY

SALT
PEPPER
OLIVE OIL
NONSTICK SPRAY
DRIED OREGANO
CRUSHED RED PEPPER

Week 2

JUNE 8 TO JUNE 14

PRODUCE

2 LEMONS
1 ONION
2 MEDIUM RED ONIONS
2 HEADS GARLIC (9 CLOVES)
4 SMALL RED POTATOES (1 LB)
3 TOMATOES
1 PT GRAPE TOMATOES
2 CUPS SMALL BROCCOLI FLORETS
1 HEAD LETTUCE
1 BAG (5 OZ) BABY SPINACH
4 CUPS SALAD GREENS
1 BUNCH CILANTRO

BAKERY

3 SLICES WHOLE-GRAIN BREAD
4 HAMBURGER BUNS
2 WHOLE-GRAIN NAAN OR 3 WHOLE-GRAIN POCKETLESS PITAS

MEAT/POULTRY/FISH

1 LB GROUND SIRLOIN
¼ LB GROUND CHUCK
½ LB LEAN GROUND BEEF
4 CHICKEN CUTLETS
1 LB GROUND TURKEY
¾ LB HOT OR SWEET ITALIAN TURKEY SAUSAGE LINKS
1 LB TILAPIA OR CATFISH FILLETS

REFRIGERATED

1 CUP LOWFAT RICOTTA
½ CUP SHREDDED PART-SKIM MOZZARELLA
GRATED PARMESAN
EGGS (3 LARGE)

FROZEN

1 PKG (10 OZ) CHOPPED SPINACH
1 BAG (1 LB) PEPPER STIR-FRY MIX
1 BAG (1 LB) PEPPER STIR-FRY VEGETABLE BLEND (SLICED GREEN, RED AND YELLOW PEPPERS AND ONIONS)

GROCERY

2 CANS (15.5 OZ EACH) BLACK BEANS
3 CANS (15 OZ EACH) CANNELLINI BEANS
1 JAR (26 OZ) MARINARA SAUCE
½ CUP MARINARA SAUCE
1 JAR (8 OZ) ROASTED RED PEPPERS
⅓ CUP PITTED KALAMATA OLIVES
¼ CUP PIMIENTO-STUFFED GREEN OLIVES
MINCED DRIED ONION FLAKES
WORCESTERSHIRE SAUCE
KETCHUP
REDUCED-FAT VINAIGRETTE
PANKO CRISPY BREAD CRUMBS, ITALIAN STYLE (PROGRESSO)

PANTRY

SALT
KOSHER SALT
PEPPER
OLIVE OIL
NONSTICK COOKING SPRAY

DIJON MUSTARD
GARLIC POWDER
GROUND CUMIN
DRIED OREGANO
SMOKED OR REGULAR PAPRIKA

Week 3

JUNE 15 TO JUNE 22

PRODUCE

2 PEACHES
1 ORANGE
1 LARGE LIME
1 LEMON
1 LARGE ONION
1 HEAD GARLIC (4 CLOVES)
1 SMALL PIECE GINGER
3 MEDIUM TOMATOES
2 MEDIUM RED BELL PEPPERS
1 LB BROCCOLINI
1 RED OR GREEN JALAPEÑO PEPPER
1 AVOCADO
1 SEEDLESS CUCUMBER (18 OZ)
1 BUNCH ASPARAGUS
1 PKG (3.5 OZ) SLICED SHIITAKE MUSHROOMS
1 SMALL HEAD (12 OZ) ROMAINE LETTUCE
1 BUNCH WATERCRESS (4 OZ)
4 SCALLIONS
1 BUNCH PARSLEY
2 BUNCHES CILANTRO
1 BUNCH MINT

DELI

8 STRIPS BACON

MEAT/POULTRY/FISH

ONE 1-LB FLANK STEAK (¾ TO 1 IN. THICK)
FOUR ¾-IN.-THICK PORK CHOPS (ABOUT 10 OZ EACH)
4 BONELESS, SKINLESS CHICKEN BREASTS (ABOUT 7 OZ EACH)
8 CHICKEN DRUMSTICKS
8 OZ COOKED TURKEY, TORN IN 1½-IN. PIECES (2 CUPS)
1 LB FROZEN FISH FILLETS OR STEAKS

REFRIGERATED

2 OZ BLUE CHEESE
1 PKG (14 OZ) LOWFAT EXTRA-FIRM TOFU
EGGS (4)

FROZEN

1 CUP SHELLED EDAMAME

GROCERY

1 CAN (14 TO 15 OZ) DICED TOMATOES
1 CAN (11 OZ) VACUUM-PACKED CORN
1 CUP SALSA VERDE (GREEN SALSA)
1 JAR (12 OZ) WHITE CLAM SAUCE
¼ CUP PITTED KALAMATA OR OTHER OLIVES
1 LB LINGUINE PASTA
BARBECUE SAUCE
½ CUP SOUTHWESTERN CHIPOTLE 10-MINUTE MARINADE (MRS. DASH)
BOTTLED DIJON VINAIGRETTE DRESSING
SEASONED RICE VINEGAR
1 PACKAGE (3.5 OZ) PEANUT SAUCE MIX (A TASTE OF THAI)
LITE SOY SAUCE
SESAME SEEDS
¼ CUP ORANGE MARMALADE

PANTRY

SALT
PEPPER
OLIVE OIL
CANOLA OIL
CORNSTARCH
CRUSHED RED PEPPER
GROUND CUMIN
GROUND CINNAMON
CHILI POWDER

Week 4

JUNE 23 TO JUNE 30

PRODUCE

1 ORANGE
2 LIMES
1 ONION
1 HEAD GARLIC (6 CLOVES)
1 SMALL PIECE GINGER
2 MEDIUM POTATOES (1 LB)
1 TOMATO
5 RIPE PLUM TOMATOES
1 CARROT
2 FIRM-RIPE AVOCADOS
2 BAGS (8 OZ EACH) STEAM-IN-BAG SUGAR SNAP PEAS
1 BAG (6 OZ) RADISHES
1 BUNCH ASPARAGUS (ABOUT 1 LB)
1 HEAD ROMAINE LETTUCE
2 BAGS (11.5 OZ EACH) SALSA ENSALADA SUPREME COMPLETE SALAD KIT (FRESH EXPRESS)
2 CUPS SHREDDED CABBAGE
10 SCALLIONS
1 BUNCH CILANTRO
1 BUNCH PARSLEY
1 BUNCH DILL
1 BUNCH BASIL (OPTIONAL)

BAKERY

2 SLICES WHITE SANDWICH BREAD
4 MEDITERRANEAN-STYLE FLATBREADS OR POCKETLESS PITAS

MEAT/POULTRY/FISH

1 LB FLANK STEAK (ABOUT 1 IN. THICK)
ONE 12-OZ FLANK STEAK
1 LB LEAN GROUND BEEF
ONE 12-OZ PORK TENDERLOIN, CUT IN ½-IN.-THICK SLICES
4 BONELESS, SKINLESS CHICKEN BREASTS (ABOUT 5 OZ EACH)
1¼ LB HALIBUT OR MAHI-MAHI FILLETS (ABOUT ¾ IN. THICK)

REFRIGERATED

1 CUP SHREDDED MOZZARELLA
4 OZ FETA CHEESE
GRATED PARMESAN
EGGS (11 LARGE)
1 TUB (10.5 OZ) BUITONI TUSCAN OR CLASSIC BRUSCHETTA

FROZEN

1 BAG (16 OZ) FROZEN STIR-FRY VEGETABLE BLEND

GROCERY

1 CAN (28 OZ) CRUSHED TOMATOES IN PURÉE
1 CAN (15.5 OZ) BLACK BEANS
1 BOTTLE (8 OZ) CREAMY ITALIAN DRESSING
1 JAR (1 LB 8 OZ) MANGO SLICES
1 JAR (9 OZ) SWEET OR HOT MANGO CHUTNEY
12 OZ SPAGHETTI PASTA
1 BOX (7.6 OZ) PLAIN COUSCOUS
OIL AND VINEGAR DRESSING
LITE SOY SAUCE
8 CORN TORTILLAS
SLIVERED ALMONDS

PANTRY

SALT
PEPPER
OLIVE OIL
CHILI POWDER
CRUSHED RED PEPPER (OPTIONAL)

THAI MANGO CHICKEN

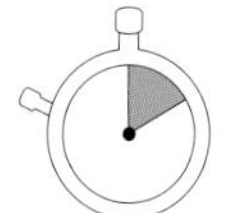

YIELD
4 servings

ACTIVE
10 minutes

TOTAL
20 minutes

1 **MANGO**, PEELED AND CUT INTO ½-IN. CHUNKS

1 JAR (11.09 OZ) **THAI KITCHEN RED CURRY 10-MINUTE SIMMER SAUCE**

1 TSP **OIL**

1 LB **BONELESS, SKINLESS CHICKEN THIGHS**, CUBED

SIDE SUGGESTION
Rice with sliced scallions

Put ½ cup of the mango and the sauce in a food processor or blender and process until smooth.

Heat oil in a large nonstick skillet over medium-high heat. Add chicken and sauté 5 minutes, or until browned.

Add sauce mixture and bring to a simmer. Simmer 3 minutes, or until chicken is cooked through. Stir in remaining mango. Serve in lettuce leaves if desired.

DIFFERENT TAKES

- Sauté a thinly sliced red bell pepper along with the chicken.
- Sprinkle with chopped mint or basil and toasted sliced almonds.
- Use Panang Curry 10-Minute Simmer Sauce instead of Red Curry; sprinkle with chopped peanuts

PER SERVING
CALORIES 228 **TOTAL FAT** 9G **SATURATED FAT** 4G **CHOLESTEROL** 94MG **SODIUM** 688MG **TOTAL CARBOHYDRATES** 13G **DIETARY FIBER** 1G **PROTEIN** 23G

PENNE PUTTANESCA

1 LB **PENNE PASTA**

1 CAN (5 OZ) **TUNA IN OLIVE OIL**

4 CLOVES **GARLIC**, MINCED

1 CAN (28 OZ) **CRUSHED TOMATOES**

½ CUP **PITTED OLIVES**, HALVED

2 TBSP DRAINED **CAPERS**

¼ TSP **CRUSHED RED PEPPER** (OR TO TASTE)

GARNISH: CHOPPED **PARSLEY**

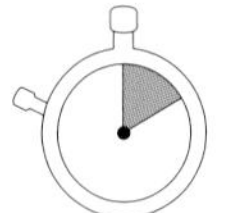

YIELD
6 servings

ACTIVE
10 minutes

TOTAL
25 minutes

SIDE SUGGESTION
Whole-grain Italian bread, baby arugula and grape tomato salad

Cook pasta in lightly salted boiling water as package directs.

Meanwhile, pour 2 tsp oil from tuna into a large nonstick skillet and heat over medium heat. Add garlic and cook 1 minute until fragrant.

Stir in tomatoes, olives, capers and pepper; bring to a simmer. Reduce heat; simmer 5 minutes for flavors to blend. Stir in tuna.

Drain pasta; return to pot. Add sauce and parsley; toss.

PER SERVING
CALORIES 403 **TOTAL FAT** 7G **SATURATED FAT** 1G **CHOLESTEROL** 15MG **SODIUM** 611MG
TOTAL CARBOHYDRATES 66G **DIETARY FIBER** 4G **PROTEIN** 18G

LEMON & MINT SEAFOOD SKEWERS WITH TABBOULEH

1 CUP UNCOOKED **BULGUR**

¼ CUP **LEMON JUICE**

1 TBSP PLUS 1 TSP **OLIVE OIL**

1½ TSP MINCED **GARLIC**

¼ TSP PLUS ⅛ TSP EACH **SALT** AND **PEPPER**

12 OZ PEELED **EXTRA-JUMBO SHRIMP**

12 OZ LARGE **SEA SCALLOPS**

1 CUP CHOPPED **TOMATOES**

1 **KIRBY CUCUMBER**, CHOPPED

¼ CUP EACH CHOPPED **PARSLEY** AND **MINT** AND SLICED **SCALLIONS**

YIELD
4 skewers

ACTIVE
15 minutes

TOTAL
35 minutes

Soak bulgur in a large bowl according to package directions.

About 15 minutes before bulgur will be done, combine 2 Tbsp lemon juice, 1 tsp oil, the garlic and ⅛ tsp each salt and pepper in a ziptop bag. Add shrimp and scallops to bag and marinate 10 minutes. Meanwhile, coat outdoor grill rack with nonstick spray; heat grill.

Thread shrimp and scallops alternately on 8 large metal or wooden skewers. Grill 3 to 4 minutes, turning once, until just barely opaque at centers. Remove to serving plate.

Add remaining 2 Tbsp lemon juice, 1 Tbsp oil and ¼ tsp each salt and pepper to bulgur. Add remaining ingredients and toss to mix. Serve with skewers.

VARIATION Omit scallops and double the amount of shrimp used.

PER SERVING
CALORIES 357 **TOTAL FAT** 7G **SATURATED FAT** 1G **CHOLESTEROL** 157MG **SODIUM** 498MG **TOTAL CARBOHYDRATES** 37G **DIETARY FIBER** 8G **PROTEIN** 1G

PORK STIR-FRY

2 TBSP **OIL**

ONE 12-OZ **PORK TENDERLOIN**, CUT CROSSWISE IN 1/4-IN.-THICK SLICES, THEN CUT IN STRIPS

4 OZ **SHIITAKE MUSHROOMS**, STEMS DISCARDED, SLICED (2 CUPS), *OR* 1 1/2 CUPS SLICED **WHITE MUSHROOMS**

6 OZ **SUGAR SNAP PEAS**, ENDS TRIMMED (1 1/2 CUPS)

2 TSP MINCED **GARLIC**

2 TSP MINCED **GINGER**

1/3 CUP **STIR-FRY SAUCE**

1 CAN (11 OZ) **MANDARIN ORANGES**, DRAINED

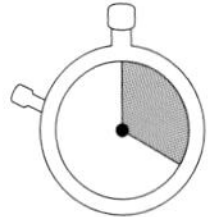

YIELD
6 servings

ACTIVE
20 minutes

TOTAL
30 minutes

SIDE SUGGESTION
Rice with sliced scallions

Heat 1 Tbsp oil in a large nonstick skillet over medium-high heat until very hot but not smoking. Add pork; stir-fry until lightly browned. Remove to a platter.

Heat remaining 1 Tbsp oil in skillet. Add mushrooms; stir-fry until tinged brown. Stir in sugar snap peas and stir-fry 1 minute or until crisp-tender.

Push vegetables to edges of skillet. Put garlic and ginger in middle; cook 30 seconds until fragrant, adding a little more oil if needed.

Add stir-fry sauce and, if needed, a few Tbsp water to thin. Add pork and oranges; stir gently (oranges are delicate) to mix. Heat through.

PER SERVING
CALORIES 255 **TOTAL FAT** 11G **SATURATED FAT** 2G **CHOLESTEROL** 56MG **SODIUM** 521MG
TOTAL CARBOHYDRATES 21G **DIETARY FIBER** 2G **PROTEIN** 21G

BEEF GYROS

1 **SLOW COOKER LINER** (WE USED REYNOLDS)

2 LB **BONELESS BEEF CHUCK STEAK**, ABOUT 1¼ IN. THICK

¼ CUP **OLIVE OIL**

2 TBSP **LEMON JUICE**

1 TBSP MINCED **GARLIC**

1 TSP **DRIED OREGANO**

½ TSP **SALT**

¼ TSP **PEPPER**

YOGURT-DILL SAUCE

1 CUP **GREEK YOGURT**

1 CUP DICED **SEEDLESS CUCUMBER**

1 TBSP SNIPPED **FRESH DILL**

¼ TSP **SALT**

5 **POCKETLESS PITAS**

ACCOMPANIMENTS: **LEAF LETTUCE**, SLICED **TOMATOES** AND **RED ONIONS**

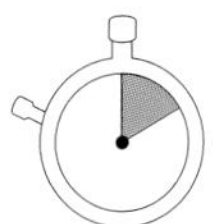

YIELD
5 servings

ACTIVE
10 minutes

TOTAL
6 to 8 hours on low

Line a 3-qt or larger slow cooker with liner; place beef in liner.

Mix oil, lemon juice, garlic, oregano, salt and pepper in a small bowl. Pour over beef, turning to coat. Cover and cook on low 6 to 8 hours until meat is tender.

Meanwhile, make **SAUCE**: Stir ingredients, cover and refrigerate.

Remove beef to cutting board; slice. Return beef to juices in slow cooker to keep warm. Warm pitas as package directs; top with sliced meat. Serve with accompaniments and yogurt sauce.

PER SERVING
CALORIES 722 **TOTAL FAT** 42G **SATURATED FAT** 13G **CHOLESTEROL** 128MG **SODIUM** 818MG **TOTAL CARBOHYDRATES** 38G **DIETARY FIBER** 2G **PROTEIN** 52G

LEMON-ROSEMARY CHICKEN WITH TOMATO BREAD SALAD

MARINADE

2 TBSP CHOPPED **FRESH ROSEMARY**

2 TBSP GRATED **LEMON ZEST**

3 TBSP **LEMON JUICE**

2 TBSP **OLIVE OIL**

2 TSP MINCED **GARLIC**

1 TSP **SALT**

½ TSP FRESHLY GROUND **PEPPER**

4 **CHICKEN DRUMSTICKS**

4 **CHICKEN THIGHS**

TOMATO BREAD SALAD

3 LARGE **TOMATOES**, CUT IN 1-IN. CHUNKS (4 TO 5 CUPS)

1 SMALL **RED ONION**, HALVED AND THINLY SLICED

⅓ CUP **LIGHT ITALIAN DRESSING**

4 LARGE 1-IN.-THICK SLICES **ITALIAN BREAD**

1 CLOVE **GARLIC**, CUT IN HALF

NONSTICK COOKING SPRAY

½ CUP LOOSELY PACKED **BASIL LEAVES**, SLIVERED

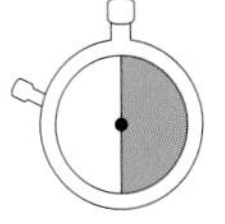

YIELD
5 servings

ACTIVE
30 minutes

TOTAL
1 hour

SIDE SUGGESTION
Grilled zucchini halves

MARINADE Wrap 1 tsp chopped rosemary and 1 tsp grated lemon zest in plastic and keep for garnish. Put remaining rosemary and lemon zest, the lemon juice, olive oil, garlic, salt and pepper in a bowl. Add chicken and turn to coat. Refrigerate 30 minutes or overnight, turning once or twice.

Heat outdoor grill or broiler.

Meanwhile, make the **SALAD**: Toss tomatoes, onion and dressing in a medium bowl. Rub both sides of bread with cut side of garlic clove, then spray with cooking spray; grill 2 minutes per side, or until lightly toasted. When cool enough to handle, cut bread in bite-size chunks. Put basil and bread on top of the tomatoes but don't toss until 10 minutes before serving.

Remove chicken from marinade and place on grill (discard marinade). Cover grill and cook, turning chicken as needed, 30 to 35 minutes until juices run clear when meat is pierced. Sprinkle with reserved lemon zest and rosemary. Serve with the salad.

PER SERVING
CALORIES 521 **TOTAL FAT** 27G **SATURATED FAT** 5G **CHOLESTEROL** 105MG **SODIUM** 829MG
TOTAL CARBOHYDRATES 34G **DIETARY FIBER** 5G **PROTEIN** 36G

GRILLED VEGETABLE LASAGNA

1 PACKAGE (8 OZ) **OVEN-READY LASAGNA NOODLES**

3 SMALL **ZUCCHINI** (1 LB), SLICED LENGTHWISE ½ IN. THICK

1 SMALL **EGGPLANT** (12 OZ), SLICED LENGTHWISE ½ IN. THICK

2 **YELLOW BELL PEPPERS**, QUARTERED, SEEDED

NONSTICK COOKING SPRAY

1 CONTAINER (15 OZ) **FAT-FREE RICOTTA**

4 OZ **FAT-FREE CREAM CHEESE**, SOFTENED

2 TBSP WATER

1 JAR (24 TO 26 OZ) **MARINARA SAUCE**

1¼ CUPS **SHREDDED REDUCED-FAT MOZZARELLA**

2 TBSP GRATED **PARMESAN**

GARNISH: CHOPPED **PARSLEY**

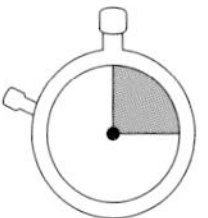

YIELD
4 servings

ACTIVE
15 minutes

TOTAL
15 minutes

NOTE
Colorful grilled vegetables pump up the flavor and nutrition, and we reduced the fat by cutting back on the cheese. (Don't feel like grilling? Try broiling the vegetables instead.)

Put noodles and water to cover in a 13 x 9-in. baking dish. Let soak 15 minutes or until slightly softened and pliable.

Meanwhile, coat vegetables with cooking spray. Grill 8 to 12 minutes, turning as needed, until lightly charred and tender. Remove to a cutting board and cut into bite-size pieces. Toss to mix.

Heat oven to 375°F. Remove noodles to paper towels. Drain water from baking dish and wipe dry. Mix ricotta, cream cheese and 2 Tbsp water in a bowl until well blended.

Spread ½ cup marinara sauce in bottom of baking dish. Lay 3 noodles crosswise on top. Spread noodles with ⅔ cup ricotta mixture. Top with 1 cup vegetables, ⅔ cup sauce, ¼ cup mozzarella and 2 tsp Parmesan. Repeat layers twice.

Top with remaining noodles and sauce (set aside the remaining vegetables and mozzarella). Cover with foil and bake 30 minutes.

Uncover, top with remaining vegetables and cheese, and bake 15 minutes or until noodles are tender when pierced in center and cheese is melted.

PER SERVING
CALORIES 276 **TOTAL FAT** 6G **SATURATED FAT** 2G **CHOLESTEROL** 16MG **SODIUM** 594MG
TOTAL CARBOHYDRATES 38G **DIETARY FIBER** 5G **PROTEIN** 18G

WARM BEAN & SAUSAGE SALAD

¾ LB **HOT OR SWEET ITALIAN TURKEY SAUSAGE LINKS**

½ CUP **WATER**

⅓ CUP **REDUCED-FAT VINAIGRETTE**

1 TBSP **DIJON MUSTARD**

1 MEDIUM **RED ONION**, SLICED

1 JAR (8 OZ) **ROASTED RED PEPPERS**, RINSED AND SLICED

2 CANS (15 OZ EACH) **CANNELLINI BEANS**, RINSED

⅓ CUP **PITTED KALAMATA OLIVES**, HALVED

1 BAG (5 OZ) **BABY SPINACH**

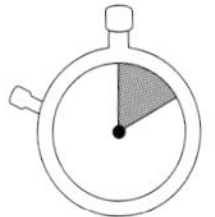

YIELD
4 servings

ACTIVE
10 minutes

TOTAL
25 minutes

SERVING SUGGESTION
Sesame breadsticks

Spray a large nonstick skillet with cooking spray. Cook sausages over medium-high heat 3 minutes or until browned on one side. Turn sausages over, add water and reduce heat to medium. Cover and cook 5 to 7 minutes until sausage is cooked through. Remove to a plate.

While sausage cooks, whisk together vinaigrette and mustard.

Add onion to skillet; cover and cook 3 minutes or until softened. Stir in red peppers, beans, olives and vinaigrette mixture. Heat 2 minutes.

Slice sausages. Divide spinach among 4 plates; spoon bean mixture and then sausages on top.

PER SERVING
CALORIES 384 **TOTAL FAT** 14G **SATURATED FAT** 4G **CHOLESTEROL** 51MG **SODIUM** 1,545MG **TOTAL CARBOHYDRATES** 44G **DIETARY FIBER** 11G **PROTEIN** 24G

MINI MEAT LOAVES

- 3 SLICES **WHOLE-GRAIN BREAD**
- 1 LB **GROUND TURKEY**
- ½ LB **LEAN GROUND BEEF**
- 2 LARGE **EGG WHITES**
- 2 TBSP **MINCED DRIED ONION FLAKES**
- 2 TSP **WORCESTERSHIRE SAUCE**
- ¼ TSP EACH **GARLIC POWDER** AND **SALT**
- 1 PKG (10 OZ) **FROZEN CHOPPED SPINACH**, THAWED AND DRAINED
- 6 TBSP **KETCHUP**

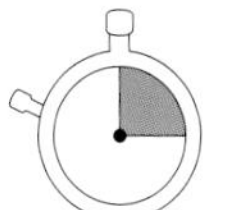

YIELD
6 servings

ACTIVE
15 minutes

TOTAL
35 minutes

SIDE SUGGESTION
Steamed broccoli

Heat oven to 425°F. Line a rimmed baking sheet with nonstick foil.

Tear bread into food processor. Pulse to make coarse crumbs. Add remaining ingredients and 2 Tbsp of the ketchup. Pulse just until blended. Form into 6 loaves (5 x 2½ in. each, about 1 scant cup per loaf) on lined pan.

Evenly spread tops with remaining 4 Tbsp ketchup. Bake 20 minutes until cooked through and instant-read thermometer inserted in center registers 160°F.

PER SERVING
CALORIES 257 **TOTAL FAT** 11G **SATURATED FAT** 3G **CHOLESTEROL** 78MG **SODIUM** 473MG
TOTAL CARBOHYDRATES 13G **DIETARY FIBER** 2G **PROTEIN** 27G

CHICKEN MILANESE

1 LARGE **EGG**, BEATEN

1 CUP **PROGRESSO PANKO CRISPY BREAD CRUMBS, ITALIAN STYLE**

1 TBSP **GRATED PARMESAN**

4 **CHICKEN CUTLETS**

3 TBSP **OLIVE OIL**

2 TBSP **LEMON JUICE**

¼ TSP EACH **SALT** AND **PEPPER**

4 CUPS **SALAD GREENS**

1 CAN (15 OZ) **CANNELLINI BEANS**, RINSED

1 CUP HALVED **GRAPE TOMATOES**

½ CUP SLICED **ONION**

GARNISH: **LEMON WEDGES**

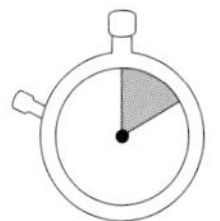

YIELD
4 servings

ACTIVE
10 minutes

TOTAL
15 minutes

SIDE SUGGESTION
Italian bread, steamed green beans

Put egg in a shallow bowl. Mix crumbs and cheese on wax paper. Dip cutlets into egg, then into crumbs to coat.

Heat 1 Tbsp of the oil in a large nonstick skillet. Add cutlets and cook 5 minutes, turning once, until golden and cooked through. Remove.

Whisk remaining 2 Tbsp olive oil, the lemon juice, salt and pepper in a medium bowl. Add remaining ingredients and toss to mix and coat.

Serve cutlets topped with salad mixture. Garnish with lemon wedges.

PER SERVING
CALORIES 418 **TOTAL FAT** 17G **SATURATED FAT** 3G **CHOLESTEROL** 101MG **SODIUM** 592MG **TOTAL CARBOHYDRATES** 39G **DIETARY FIBER** 5G **PROTEIN** 26G

BEST BURGER

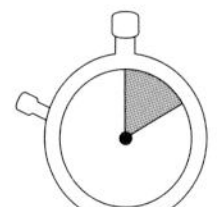

YIELD
4 servings

ACTIVE
10 minutes

TOTAL
20 minutes

1 LB **GROUND SIRLOIN**

¼ LB **GROUND CHUCK**

1 ½ TSP **WORCESTERSHIRE SAUCE**

¼ TSP EACH **KOSHER SALT** AND **PEPPER**

NONSTICK COOKING SPRAY

ACCOMPANIMENTS: **HAMBURGER BUNS**, **LETTUCE**, **TOMATO** AND **RED ONION** SLICES

SIDE SUGGESTION
French fries, coleslaw

Heat outdoor grill or grill pan.

Gently mix ground meats and Worcestershire sauce in a medium bowl with a fork until blended. Shape meat into four patties about 1 in. thick. Sprinkle both sides of patties with salt and pepper.

Coat burgers with nonstick spray. Grill, turning once, 8 to 10 minutes until instant-read thermometer inserted from side to middle registers 160°F. Serve on buns with lettuce, sliced tomato and red onion.

TIP Blending ground sirloin and chuck creates the perfect burger. Sirloin gives delicious flavor and chuck ensures juiciness.

PER SERVING
CALORIES 239 **TOTAL FAT** 12G **SATURATED FAT** 5G **CHOLESTEROL** 72MG **SODIUM** 209MG
TOTAL CARBOHYDRATES 0G **DIETARY FIBER** 0G **PROTEIN** 30G

MEDITERRANEAN FISH STEW

- 2 TSP **OLIVE OIL**
- 4 SMALL **RED POTATOES** (1 LB), SLICED ¼ IN. THICK
- 1 BAG (1 LB) **FROZEN PEPPER STIR-FRY MIX**
- 2 **CLOVES GARLIC**, CHOPPED
- ⅓ CUP **WATER**
- 1 JAR (26 OZ) **MARINARA SAUCE**
- 1 LB **TILAPIA OR CATFISH FILLETS**, CUT INTO 3-IN. PIECES
- ¼ CUP SLICED **PIMIENTO-STUFFED GREEN OLIVES**
- 2 TBSP CHOPPED **CILANTRO**

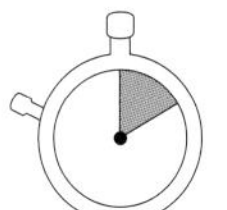

YIELD
4 servings

ACTIVE
10 minutes

TOTAL
25 minutes

SIDE SUGGESTION
French bread, mixed greens salad

Heat oil in a large nonstick skillet over medium-high heat. Spread potatoes in an even layer. Top with frozen peppers; sprinkle with garlic. Cover; cook 5 minutes.

Add water, cover and reduce heat. Simmer 5 minutes or until potatoes are tender, stirring a few times. Add marinara sauce and bring to a boil. Reduce heat; place fish on top. Cover and simmer 4 to 5 minutes until fish is just cooked through. Sprinkle with olives and cilantro.

PER SERVING
CALORIES 359 **TOTAL FAT** 8G **SATURATED FAT** 2G **CHOLESTEROL** 58MG **SODIUM** 980MG **TOTAL CARBOHYDRATES** 42G **DIETARY FIBER** 6G **PROTEIN** 29G

BROCCOLI & TOMATO PIZZAS

- 2 CUPS SMALL **BROCCOLI FLORETS**
- 1½ TSP **OLIVE OIL**
- 1 TBSP MINCED **GARLIC**
- 2 **WHOLE-GRAIN NAAN** *OR* 3 **WHOLE-GRAIN POCKETLESS PITAS**
- ½ CUP **MARINARA SAUCE**
- 1 CUP **LOWFAT RICOTTA**
- 1 CUP QUARTERED **GRAPE OR CHERRY TOMATOES**
- ½ CUP **SHREDDED PART-SKIM MOZZARELLA**

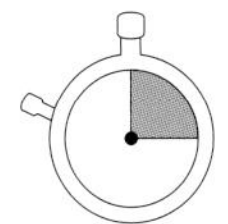

YIELD
4 servings

ACTIVE
15 minutes

TOTAL
35 minutes

SIDE SUGGESTION
Arugula and red onion salad

Heat oven to 475°F. Place a steamer basket in a large skillet. Add water to come up to bottom of basket and bring to a boil over high heat. Add broccoli; cover and simmer 3 minutes or until crisp-tender. Lift basket from skillet; drain water from skillet. Add olive oil and garlic to skillet; add broccoli and toss over medium heat 1 minute or until fragrant.

Place naan or pitas on a baking sheet. Spread each with sauce and top with broccoli, ricotta, tomatoes and mozzarella.

Bake 8 to 10 minutes until cheese melts and bottoms are crisp.

NOTE Broccoli paired with tomatoes provides an antioxidant blast for more cancer-fighting power.

PER SERVING
CALORIES 312 **TOTAL FAT** 12G **SATURATED FAT** 4G **CHOLESTEROL** 26MG **SODIUM** 713MG **TOTAL CARBOHYDRATES** 9G **DIETARY FIBER** 5G **PROTEIN** 18G

CUBAN BEANS

2 TSP **OIL**

4 CLOVES **GARLIC**, MINCED

2 CANS (15.5 OZ EACH) **BLACK BEANS**, RINSED

1 CUP **WATER**

1½ TSP **GROUND CUMIN**

1 TSP **DRIED OREGANO**

1 TSP **SMOKED OR REGULAR PAPRIKA**

¼ TSP **PEPPER**

1 BAG (1 LB) **FROZEN PEPPER STIR-FRY VEGETABLE BLEND** (SLICED GREEN, RED AND YELLOW PEPPERS AND ONIONS)

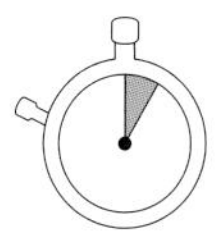

YIELD
4 servings

ACTIVE
5 minutes

TOTAL
15 minutes

SIDE SUGGESTION
Rice, lime wedges

Heat oil in large skillet over medium-high heat. Add garlic; cook 30 seconds.

Stir in remaining ingredients. Bring to simmer, cover and reduce heat. Cook 10 minutes or until vegetables are tender and flavors have blended.

PER SERVING
CALORIES 265 **TOTAL FAT** 3G **SATURATED FAT** 0G **CHOLESTEROL** 0MG **SODIUM** 521MG
TOTAL CARBOHYDRATES 45G **DIETARY FIBER** 17G **PROTEIN** 15G

ORANGE BBQ DRUMSTICKS & BROCCOLINI

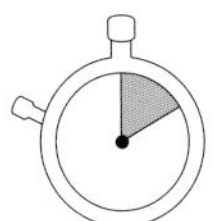

YIELD
4 servings

ACTIVE
10 minutes

TOTAL
35 minutes

- ¾ CUP **BARBECUE SAUCE**
- ¼ CUP **ORANGE MARMALADE**
- 2 TSP **CHILI POWDER**
- 8 **CHICKEN DRUMSTICKS**
- 1 LB **BROCCOLINI**
- ½ CUP **WATER**

SIDE SUGGESTION
Couscous

Heat oven to 450°F. Line a rimmed baking pan with nonstick foil.

Stir together barbecue sauce, orange marmalade and chili powder. Reserve ¼ cup; toss remaining with chicken drumsticks. Place on pan.

Bake 25 minutes or until cooked through. Meanwhile, put broccolini and ½ cup water in glass bowl. Cover; microwave on high until tender. Drizzle chicken with sauce.

PER SERVING
CALORIES 403 **TOTAL FAT** 12G **SATURATED FAT** 3G **CHOLESTEROL** 95MG **SODIUM** 739MG
TOTAL CARBOHYDRATES 41G **DIETARY FIBER** 2G **PROTEIN** 32G

PORK CHOPS WITH PEACH SALSA

½ CUP **SOUTHWESTERN CHIPOTLE 10-MINUTE MARINADE** (MRS. DASH)

FOUR ¾-IN.-THICK **PORK CHOPS** (ABOUT 10 OZ EACH)

PEACH SALSA

2 **PEACHES**, HALVED, PITTED AND DICED

⅓ CUP LOOSELY PACKED **CILANTRO LEAVES**, CHOPPED

GRATED ZEST AND JUICE FROM 1 LARGE **LIME**

1 TBSP FINELY CHOPPED SEEDED **RED OR GREEN JALAPEÑO PEPPER**

¼ TSP **SALT**

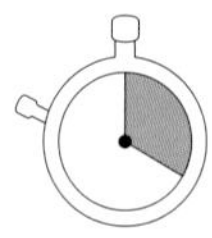

YIELD
4 servings

ACTIVE
20 minutes

TOTAL
2 hours 20 minutes
(includes marinating)

SIDE SUGGESTION
Corn on the cob

Put marinade and pork in a gallon-size ziptop bag, seal bag and turn to coat pork. Refrigerate 2 hours or overnight.

Heat outdoor grill. Meanwhile, make **SALSA**: Mix ingredients in a medium bowl. Cover and refrigerate.

Remove chops from bag; place on grill (discard bag with marinade). Grill, turning as needed to avoid burning, 10 to 12 minutes until cooked through. Serve with the salsa.

PER SERVING
CALORIES 293 **TOTAL FAT** 15G **SATURATED FAT** 4G **CHOLESTEROL** 75MG **SODIUM** 197MG **TOTAL CARBOHYDRATES** 12G **DIETARY FIBER** 1G **PROTEIN** 27G

COBB SALAD

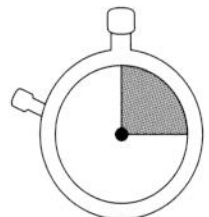

YIELD
6 servings

ACTIVE
15 minutes

TOTAL
15 minutes

1 SMALL HEAD (12 OZ) **ROMAINE LETTUCE**, CHOPPED IN BITE-SIZE PIECES (12 CUPS)

1 BUNCH **WATERCRESS** (4 OZ), TORN INTO SMALL SPRIGS (4 CUPS)

3 MEDIUM-SIZE **RIPE TOMATOES**, CUT IN SMALL PIECES

½ CUP **BOTTLED DIJON VINAIGRETTE DRESSING**

1 CAN (11 OZ) **VACUUM-PACKED CORN**, DRAINED (1½ CUPS)

8 OZ **COOKED TURKEY**, TORN IN 1½-INCH PIECES (2 CUPS)

1 RIPE **AVOCADO**, HALVED, SEEDED AND CUT IN CHUNKS

4 HARD-COOKED **EGGS**, CHOPPED

4 STRIPS **BACON**, FRIED CRISP AND DRAINED ON PAPER TOWELS

2 OZ **BLUE CHEESE**, CRUMBLED (½ CUP)

SIDE SUGGESTION
Whole-grain rolls

Arrange lettuce and watercress on 6 individual plates.

Toss tomatoes with 1 Tbsp of the dressing and toss corn with another Tbsp dressing. Place on lettuce.

Arrange turkey, avocado and eggs on the lettuce. Crumble bacon over turkey and crumble blue cheese over avocado and egg. Serve with remaining dressing.

PER SERVING
CALORIES 253 **TOTAL FAT** 11G **SATURATED FAT** 0G **CHOLESTEROL** 7MG **SODIUM** 643MG
TOTAL CARBOHYDRATES 25G **DIETARY FIBER** 0G **PROTEIN** 15G

LINGUINE CLAMS CASINO

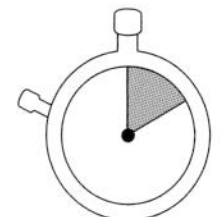

YIELD
6 servings

ACTIVE
10 minutes

TOTAL
25 minutes

1 LB **LINGUINE PASTA**

SAUCE

4 STRIPS **BACON**, CUT CROSSWISE IN THIN STRIPS

1 JAR (12 OZ) **WHITE CLAM SAUCE**

GRATED ZEST OF 1 **LEMON**

¼ TSP **CRUSHED RED PEPPER**

⅔ CUP CHOPPED **FRESH PARSLEY**

SIDE SUGGESTION
Garlic bread, mixed green and cherry tomato salad

Cook pasta in a large pot of lightly salted boiling water as package directs.

Meanwhile, cook bacon in a large, deep skillet until crisp. Remove to paper towel to drain. Drain fat from skillet. Stir in clam sauce, lemon zest and crushed pepper. Cook over low heat until hot.

Add ½ cup pasta cooking water to skillet. Drain pasta; add to skillet with parsley. Toss to mix and coat. Remove to serving plates; sprinkle with bacon.

PER SERVING
CALORIES 376 **TOTAL FAT** 8G **SATURATED FAT** 2G **CHOLESTEROL** 13MG **SODIUM** 658MG **TOTAL CARBOHYDRATES** 59G **DIETARY FIBER** 2G **PROTEIN** 15G

ASIAN PEANUT CHICKEN WITH CUCUMBER SALAD

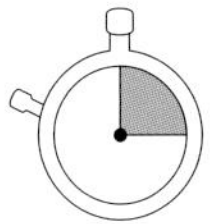

YIELD
4 servings

ACTIVE
15 minutes

TOTAL
25 minutes

1 **SEEDLESS CUCUMBER** (18 OZ)

⅓ CUP **SEASONED RICE VINEGAR**

¼ CUP CHOPPED **MINT**

1 PACKAGE (3.5 OZ) **PEANUT SAUCE MIX** (A TASTE OF THAI), BOTH ENVELOPES

4 **BONELESS, SKINLESS CHICKEN BREASTS** (ABOUT 7 OZ EACH)

1 TBSP **OIL**

1¼ CUPS **WATER**

SIDE SUGGESTION
Jasmine rice

Cut cucumber crosswise in half, then cut each piece lengthwise in half. Place each flat side down and cut into thin lengthwise slices. Toss cucumber, vinegar and mint in a large bowl. Cover and refrigerate until chilled.

Place 1 envelope dry peanut sauce mix on sheet of wax paper; turn chicken breasts in mix to coat.

Heat oil in a large nonstick skillet over medium heat. Add chicken and cook, turning once, 6 minutes or until golden and instant-read thermometer inserted side to center registers 165°F. Remove to a plate; cover slightly to keep warm.

Add water and remaining envelope of peanut sauce mix to skillet. Bring to a boil; cook, stirring, about 3 minutes or until slightly thickened. Serve sauce on the chicken and the cucumber salad alongside.

PER SERVING
CALORIES 331 **TOTAL FAT** 8G **SATURATED FAT** 2G **CHOLESTEROL** 82MG **SODIUM** 1,189MG
TOTAL CARBOHYDRATES 26G **DIETARY FIBER** 3G **PROTEIN** 36G

STEAK VERDE

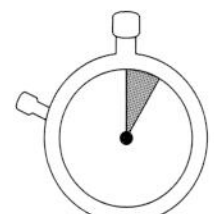

YIELD
4 servings

ACTIVE
5 minutes

TOTAL
20 minutes

ONE 1-LB **FLANK STEAK** (3/4 TO 1 IN. THICK)

1/4 TSP EACH **SALT** AND **PEPPER**

1 CUP **SALSA VERDE** (GREEN SALSA)

1 CUP **CILANTRO LEAVES**

SIDE SUGGESTION
Warm corn or flour tortillas, sliced beefsteak tomato salad

Brush an outdoor grill or stovetop grill pan with oil or coat with nonstick spray; heat.

Season steak with salt and pepper.

Grill steak 9 to 11 minutes, turning once, for medium-rare.

Remove steak to cutting board; let rest 5 minutes. Meanwhile, put salsa and cilantro in a food processor and process until smooth.

Slice steak thinly across the grain and serve with the sauce.

DIFFERENT TAKES

- Rub steak with a little ground cumin before grilling.
- After spooning sauce on steak, scatter diced tomato and avocado on top.
- Good with boneless, skinless, chicken breasts or boneless pork chops instead of steak.

PER SERVING
CALORIES 212 **TOTAL FAT** 9G **SATURATED FAT** 4G **CHOLESTEROL** 47MG **SODIUM** 404MG **TOTAL CARBOHYDRATES** 5G **DIETARY FIBER** 1G **PROTEIN** 25G

ORANGE-SOY TOFU STIR-FRY

¾ CUP **WATER**

1 TSP GRATED **ORANGE ZEST**

¼ CUP **FRESH ORANGE JUICE**

2 TBSP **LITE SOY SAUCE**

1½ TSP **CORNSTARCH**

¼ TSP **CRUSHED RED PEPPER**

2 TSP **CANOLA OIL**

1 PKG (14 OZ) **LOWFAT EXTRA-FIRM TOFU**, PATTED DRY, CUT INTO 1-IN. CUBES

2 TSP EACH MINCED **GARLIC** AND **FRESH GINGER**

1 BUNCH **ASPARAGUS**, CUT IN PIECES

2 MEDIUM **RED BELL PEPPERS**, SLICED

1 CUP **FROZEN SHELLED EDAMAME**

1 PKG (3.5 OZ) **SLICED SHIITAKE MUSHROOMS**

½ CUP SLICED **SCALLIONS**

GARNISH: TOASTED **SESAME SEEDS**

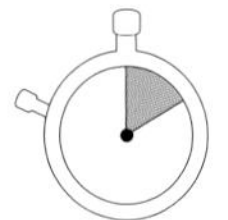

YIELD
4 servings

ACTIVE
10 minutes

TOTAL
25 minutes

SIDE SUGGESTION
Brown rice

Mix water, orange zest, juice, soy sauce, cornstarch and crushed red pepper in a cup.

Heat 1 tsp oil in a large nonstick skillet. Add tofu; cook over high heat 5 minutes, turning often, until golden. Add garlic and ginger. Reduce heat and cook 30 seconds. Remove.

Heat remaining 1 tsp oil in skillet. Add asparagus, peppers, edamame and mushrooms; stir-fry 5 minutes.

Add orange juice mixture and bring to boil. Stir in tofu and scallions; toss. Sprinkle with toasted sesame seeds, if desired.

PER SERVING
CALORIES 295 **TOTAL FAT** 13G **SATURATED FAT** 2G **CHOLESTEROL** 0MG **SODIUM** 306MG
TOTAL CARBOHYDRATES 24G **DIETARY FIBER** 6G **PROTEIN** 23G

MOROCCAN FISH

1 LB **FROZEN FISH FILLETS OR STEAKS**

4 TSP **OLIVE OIL**

¼ TSP **PEPPER**

1 CUP CHOPPED **ONION**

2 TSP MINCED **GARLIC**

½ TSP **GROUND CUMIN**

¼ TSP **GROUND CINNAMON**

1 CAN (14 TO 15 OZ) **DICED TOMATOES**

¼ CUP **PITTED KALAMATA OR OTHER OLIVES**, HALVED

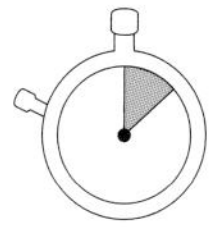

YIELD
4 servings

ACTIVE
8 minutes

TOTAL
20 minutes

SIDE SUGGESTION
Rice and peas

Heat broiler. Line a rimmed baking sheet with nonstick foil.

Place fish on pan and drizzle with 2 tsp of the olive oil. Sprinkle with the pepper. Broil as package directs until fillets are just cooked through.

Meanwhile, heat remaining 2 tsp oil in a large saucepan. Add onion; cover and cook 5 minutes, stirring occasionally, until tender. Add garlic, cumin and cinnamon, and cook, stirring, 1 minute or until fragrant.

Stir in tomatoes and olives, and bring to a simmer. Simmer 3 minutes for flavors to blend.

Spoon about ¼ cup sauce over each serving of fish.

PER SERVING
CALORIES 184 **TOTAL FAT** 7G **SATURATED FAT** 1G **CHOLESTEROL** 43MG **SODIUM** 354MG **TOTAL CARBOHYDRATES** 10G **DIETARY FIBER** 3G **PROTEIN** 19G

CHICKEN SORRENTO

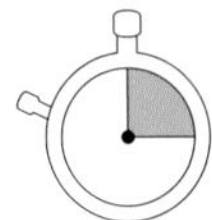

YIELD
4 servings

ACTIVE
15 minutes

TOTAL
15 minutes

4 **BONELESS, SKINLESS CHICKEN BREASTS** (ABOUT 5 OZ EACH)

¼ TSP **SALT**

⅛ TSP **PEPPER**

2 TSP **OLIVE OIL**

1 BOTTLE (8 OZ) **CREAMY ITALIAN DRESSING**

1 BAG (16 OZ) **FROZEN STIR-FRY VEGETABLE BLEND**

Sprinkle chicken with the salt and pepper.

Heat the oil in a large nonstick skillet over medium-high heat. Add chicken; cook 2 minutes on each side, or until golden.

Pour dressing on chicken; turn to coat. Cover, reduce heat and simmer 5 minutes.

Add frozen vegetables, cover and cook 5 minutes or until chicken is cooked through and vegetables are crisp-tender.

PER SERVING
CALORIES 409 **TOTAL FAT** 22G **SATURATED FAT** 3G **CHOLESTEROL** 82MG **SODIUM** 748MG
TOTAL CARBOHYDRATES 15G **DIETARY FIBER** 3G **PROTEIN** 35G

SANTA FE BEEF SALAD

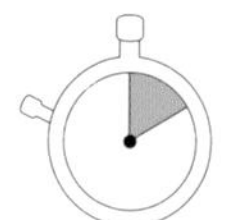

YIELD
4 servings

ACTIVE
10 minutes

TOTAL
30 minutes

2 TSP **OIL**

1 LB **FLANK STEAK** (ABOUT 1 IN. THICK)

¼ TSP EACH **SALT** AND **PEPPER**

2 BAGS (11.5 OZ EACH) **SALSA ENSALADA SUPREME COMPLETE SALAD KIT** (FRESH EXPRESS)

4 RIPE **PLUM TOMATOES**, SLICED

1 CAN (15.5 OZ) **BLACK BEANS**, RINSED

1 FIRM-RIPE **AVOCADO**, PEELED, PITTED AND SLICED

Heat oil in a large nonstick skillet over medium-high heat. Season steak with salt and pepper, place in skillet and cook, turning once, 10 minutes or until an instant-read thermometer inserted from side to center registers 155°F. Remove to a cutting board, cover loosely with foil and let rest 10 minutes. (Temperature will rise to 160°F for medium doneness.)

Remove sour cream dressing, salsa, tortilla strips and cheese from salad bags. Evenly divide lettuce onto four plates. Thinly slice steak diagonally across the grain.

Divide steak, tomatoes, black beans, avocado, cheese and tortilla strips among the plates. Spoon sour cream dressing from one packet and both salsa packets onto salads. (Reserve remaining 1 packet sour cream dressing for another use.)

PER SERVING
CALORIES 412 **TOTAL FAT** 16G **SATURATED FAT** 6G **CHOLESTEROL** 62MG **SODIUM** 545MG
TOTAL CARBOHYDRATES 37G **DIETARY FIBER** 12G **PROTEIN** 35G

MANGO CHUTNEY PORK

1 BOX (7.6 OZ) **PLAIN COUSCOUS**

2 BAGS (8 OZ EACH) **STEAM-IN-BAG SUGAR SNAP PEAS**

2 TSP **OLIVE OIL**

ONE 12-OZ **PORK TENDERLOIN**, CUT IN ½-IN.-THICK SLICES

1 JAR (1 LB 8 OZ) **MANGO SLICES**, DRAINED AND SLICED, 2 CUPS

1 JAR (9 OZ) **SWEET OR HOT MANGO CHUTNEY**

¼ CUP SLICED **SCALLIONS**

¼ CUP TOASTED **SLIVERED ALMONDS**

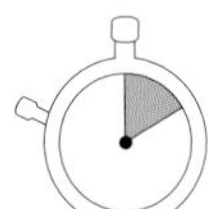

YIELD
4 servings

ACTIVE
10 minutes

TOTAL
10 minutes

Prepare couscous and sugar snap peas as packages direct.

Meanwhile, heat oil in a large skillet over medium-high heat. Add pork and cook 2 minutes per side until lightly browned on the outside but pink in center. Remove to plates; cover loosely with foil to keep warm.

Add mango slices and chutney to skillet; cook, stirring, just until hot. Spoon over pork slices; sprinkle with scallions and almonds. Serve with couscous and sugar snap peas.

PER SERVING
CALORIES 637 **TOTAL FAT** 9G **SATURATED FAT** 1G **CHOLESTEROL** 50MG **SODIUM** 895MG
TOTAL CARBOHYDRATES 109G **DIETARY FIBER** 8G **PROTEIN** 31G

BAJA FISH TACOS

- 2 CUPS SHREDDED **CABBAGE**
- 3 TBSP **LIME JUICE**
- ⅓ CUP CHOPPED **CILANTRO**
- 2 TSP **OLIVE OIL**
- 1 TSP **CHILI POWDER**
- 1¼ LB **HALIBUT OR MAHI-MAHI FILLETS** (ABOUT ¾ IN. THICK)
- 8 **CORN TORTILLAS**, WARMED AS PACKAGE DIRECTS
- 1 **AVOCADO**, DICED
- ¼ CUP SLICED **RADISHES**

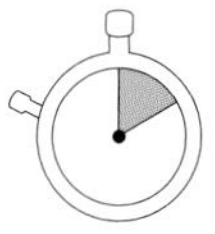

YIELD
4 servings
(2 tacos/serving)

ACTIVE
10 minutes

TOTAL
25 minutes

SIDE SUGGESTION
Black beans with garlic, cumin and cilantro

Toss cabbage and 1 Tbsp of lime juice in a bowl. Mix remaining lime juice, 1 Tbsp of cilantro, the oil and chili powder in a pie plate. Add fish, turn; marinate 10 minutes.

Coat outdoor grill or stovetop grill pan with nonstick spray; heat. Add fish; cook 5 to 7 minutes, turning once, until just cooked through. Remove to plate and break into chunks.

Fill tortillas with cabbage, fish, avocado, radishes and remaining cilantro. Top with salsa as desired.

PER SERVING
CALORIES 382 **TOTAL FAT** 14G **SATURATED FAT** 2G **CHOLESTEROL** 45MG **SODIUM** 183MG **TOTAL CARBOHYDRATES** 31G **DIETARY FIBER** 6G **PROTEIN** 34G

SPAGHETTI & MEATBALLS

MEATBALLS

1 LARGE **EGG**

2 SLICES **WHITE SANDWICH BREAD**, TORN IN SMALL PIECES

1/4 CUP **GRATED PARMESAN**

2 TBSP CHOPPED **FRESH OR DRIED PARSLEY**

1 TSP **SALT**

1/2 TSP **PEPPER**

2 TSP MINCED **GARLIC**

1 LB **LEAN GROUND BEEF**

12 OZ UNCOOKED **SPAGHETTI PASTA**

SAUCE

2 TBSP **OLIVE OIL**

3/4 CUP CHOPPED **ONION**

1 TBSP MINCED **GARLIC**

1 CAN (28 OZ) **CRUSHED TOMATOES IN PURÉE**

1/4 TSP EACH **SALT** AND **PEPPER**

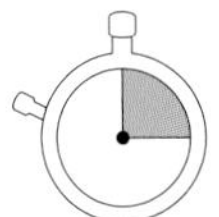

YIELD
4 servings

ACTIVE
15 minutes

TOTAL
35 minutes

SIDE SUGGESTION
Italian bread, mixed baby green salad, grated Parmesan

Heat oven to 425°F. Line a rimmed baking sheet with foil (for easy cleanup). Bring a large pot of lightly salted water to a boil.

Meanwhile, make MEATBALLS: Beat egg with a fork in a medium bowl. Stir in rest of ingredients except beef. Add beef; mix until combined. Form into sixteen 1½-in. balls *(see Tip 1 page 144)*. Place on lined baking sheet. Bake 12 minutes or until cooked through.

SAUCE While meatballs bake, heat oil in a large saucepan over medium heat. Add onion; sauté 5 minutes or until translucent. Add remaining ingredients; bring to a boil, reduce heat and simmer 8 minutes or until slightly thickened.

Meanwhile, add spaghetti to boiling water and cook as package directs. Drain; return to pot. Toss pasta with about ½ the sauce. Stir meatballs into remaining sauce. Spoon on pasta.

PER SERVING
CALORIES 784 **TOTAL FAT** 31G **SATURATED FAT** 10G **CHOLESTEROL** 133MG **SODIUM** 1,288MG
TOTAL CARBOHYDRATES 87G **DIETARY FIBER** 4G **PROTEIN** 38G

GREEK FRITTATA & SALAD

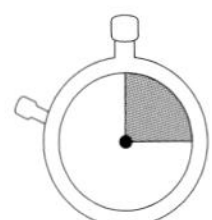

YIELD
5 servings

ACTIVE
15 minutes

TOTAL
30 minutes

2 MEDIUM **POTATOES** (1 LB), PEELED AND CUT IN ½-IN. PIECES

6 LARGE **EGGS**, PLUS WHITES FROM 4 LARGE EGGS

1 TBSP CHOPPED **FRESH DILL**

¼ TSP FRESHLY GROUND **PEPPER**

4 OZ **FETA CHEESE**, CRUMBLED

1 TBSP **OIL**

6 **SCALLIONS**, CHOPPED

6 CUPS TORN **ROMAINE LETTUCE**

1 **TOMATO**, CUT IN WEDGES

1 **CARROT**, SHREDDED

⅓ CUP **OIL AND VINEGAR DRESSING**

Heat broiler. Place potatoes with 2 Tbsp water in a glass pie plate or bowl, cover with plastic wrap and microwave on high 4 minutes or until potatoes are just tender.

Meanwhile, whisk eggs, egg whites, dill and pepper in large bowl until blended. Stir in half the feta.

Heat oil in a 10-in. nonstick skillet over medium heat. Add potatoes; cook 3 minutes until lightly browned. Add scallions; cook 2 minutes until wilted.

Pour egg mixture into skillet and stir gently to distribute evenly. Cook 4 minutes until eggs are set on bottom and sides (eggs will be runny in center). Remove from heat. Sprinkle remaining feta on top.

If skillet handle is not ovenproof, wrap in foil. Broil frittata 4 to 6 in. from heat source 3 minutes or until center is firm. Toss lettuce, tomato and carrot with dressing; serve with frittata.

PER SERVING
CALORIES 340 **TOTAL FAT** 22G **SATURATED FAT** 7G **CHOLESTEROL** 275MG **SODIUM** 388MG
TOTAL CARBOHYDRATES 20G **DIETARY FIBER** 3G **PROTEIN** 17G

ORANGE-SOY BEEF WITH ASPARAGUS

YIELD
4 servings

ACTIVE
5 minutes

TOTAL
23 minutes

1 BUNCH **ASPARAGUS** (ABOUT 1 LB), TRIMMED

ONE 12-OZ **FLANK STEAK**

3 TBSP **LITE SOY SAUCE**

1 TSP GRATED **ORANGE ZEST**

1 TSP **GINGER**

1 TSP MINCED **GARLIC**

¼ TSP **CRUSHED RED PEPPER** (OPTIONAL)

SIDE SUGGESTION
Brown rice with sliced scallions

Coat contact grill with nonstick spray, then heat. Meanwhile, put all ingredients in a gallon ziptop bag and turn to coat.

Place steak on grill; close and grill 6 minutes for medium-rare. Remove to cutting board. Let rest 5 minutes.

Meanwhile, place asparagus on grill; close and grill 5 minutes until crisp-tender. Slice steak thinly across the grain.

PER SERVING
CALORIES 186 **TOTAL FAT** 10G **SATURATED FAT** 4G **CHOLESTEROL** 44MG **SODIUM** 512MG **TOTAL CARBOHYDRATES** 5G **DIETARY FIBER** 1G **PROTEIN** 20G

GRILLED TUSCAN PIZZAS

YIELD
4 servings

ACTIVE
7 minutes

TOTAL
15 minutes

4 **MEDITERRANEAN-STYLE FLATBREADS** *OR* **POCKETLESS PITAS**

2 TSP **OIL**

1 TUB (10.5 OZ) **BUITONI TUSCAN OR CLASSIC BRUSCHETTA**

1 CUP **SHREDDED MOZZARELLA**

GARNISH: **BASIL LEAVES** (OPTIONAL)

SIDE SUGGESTION
Romaine, sweet onion and cucumber salad

Heat outdoor grill. Set up a baking sheet or large tray as a work surface.

Brush flatbreads with oil and place directly on grill. Grill 1½ to 2 minutes until bottoms are lightly charred. Place charred side up on baking sheet. Spread top of each with scant ⅓ cup bruschetta, then top each with ¼ cup mozzarella.

Return pizzas to grill. Close cover and grill 1 to 2 minutes until bottoms are lightly charred and toppings warm. Garnish with torn basil leaves, if desired. Cut in wedges.

DIFFERENT TAKES

- Instead of using bruschetta, spread the flatbreads with prepared pesto.
- Add strips of grilled chicken or shrimp.
- Top with baby arugula leaves and shaved Parmesan.

PER SERVING
CALORIES 337 **TOTAL FAT** 15G **SATURATED FAT** 5G **CHOLESTEROL** 15MG **SODIUM** 698MG
TOTAL CARBOHYDRATES 39G **DIETARY FIBER** 4G **PROTEIN** 12G

JULY

JULY SHOPPING LIST

Week 1
JULY 1 TO JULY 7

PRODUCE
1 FIRM-RIPE MANGO
2 LEMONS
1 LARGE RED ONION
1 VIDALIA ONION
1 HEAD GARLIC (3 CLOVES)
1 LARGE BEEFSTEAK TOMATO
1 LARGE CARROT
2 MEDIUM ZUCCHINI
2 LARGE RED BELL PEPPERS
2 CUPS SMALL BROCCOLI FLORETS
(ABOUT ⅓ OF A LARGE BUNCH)
1 PKG CUBED FRESH BUTTERNUT
SQUASH (1 LB)
1 HEAD LETTUCE
1 BAG (9 OZ) SHREDDED ROMAINE LETTUCE
1 BUNCH PARSLEY

BAKERY
6 WHOLE-WHEAT HAMBURGER BUNS

MEAT/POULTRY/FISH
1 LB LEAN GROUND BEEF
2 LB 90%-LEAN GROUND BEEF
1¼ LB BONELESS,
SKINLESS CHICKEN THIGHS
4 BONELESS, SKINLESS CHICKEN THIGHS
1½ LB CATFISH OR TILAPIA FILLETS
1½ LB SEA SCALLOPS

DELI
6 STRIPS BACON

REFRIGERATED
1 CUP 1% SKIM MILK
½ STICK BUTTER
6 OZ GREEK YOGURT
1 CUP SHREDDED CHEDDAR
6 SLICES (1 OZ EACH) SHARP CHEDDAR
GRATED PARMESAN
EGG (1 LARGE)

FROZEN
1 BAG (10 OZ) GREEN PEAS

GROCERY
3 CANS (14.5 OZ) CHICKEN BROTH
1 CAN (14.5 OZ) DICED TOMATOES
WITH GARLIC AND ONION
1 JAR (12 OZ) MANGO CHUTNEY
CAPERS
12 OZ LINGUINE OR
EGGLESS FETTUCINE PASTA
1 CUP PLAIN COUSCOUS
8 TACO SHELLS
8 SOFT-TACO OR FAJITA-SIZE
FLOUR TORTILLAS
1 PKT (1.25 OZ) TACO SEASONING MIX
1 BOTTLE TACO SAUCE
CHILI SAUCE
LIGHT MAYONNAISE
DILL PICKLE RELISH
WORCESTERSHIRE SAUCE
½ CUP RAISINS
3 JARS (4 OZ EACH) BABY-FOOD
PURÉED CARROTS
2 CUPS PANKO BREAD CRUMBS
6 (10-IN.) BAMBOO SKEWERS

PANTRY
SALT
PEPPER
OLIVE OIL
NONSTICK COOKING SPRAY
CIDER VINEGAR
FLOUR
LIGHT-BROWN SUGAR
CORNSTARCH
GROUND CUMIN
GROUND CINNAMON
SMOKED PAPRIKA
ONION POWDER
CURRY POWDER

Week 2
JULY 8 TO JULY 14

PRODUCE
2 NAVEL ORANGES
1 MEDIUM ONION
1 RED ONION
1 HEAD GARLIC (7 CLOVES)
1 SMALL PIECE FRESH GINGER
1 PT GRAPE TOMATOES
3 CARROTS
4 SMALL ITALIAN EGGPLANTS (7 OZ EACH)
2 MEDIUM BELL PEPPERS
1 JALAPEÑO PEPPER
1 SERRANO CHILE
1 PKG RADISH SPROUTS
14 SCALLIONS
1¼ LB BABY BOK CHOY
1 HEAD BOSTON LETTUCE
2 CUPS BABY SPINACH
1 BUNCH BASIL
1 BUNCH MINT
1 BUNCH PARSLEY (OPTIONAL)
1 BUNCH CILANTRO

MEAT/POULTRY/FISH
ONE 12-OZ BEEF FLANK STEAK
2½-LB BONELESS PORK LOIN ROAST
ONE 8-OZ PORK TENDERLOIN
8 OZ GROUND CHICKEN OR TURKEY
2-LB PIECE SALMON FILLET
(PREFERABLY SOCKEYE OR COHO)

REFRIGERATED
1⅓ CUPS SHREDDED MOZZARELLA
GRATED PARMESAN
1 CONTAINER (5 OZ)
GRATED ROMANO CHEESE
EGG (1 LARGE)
1 LB PIZZA DOUGH

GROCERY
1 CAN (14.5 OZ) DICED TOMATOES
1 CAN (6 OZ) LIGHT TUNA IN OIL
¾ CUP MARINARA OR PIZZA SAUCE
1 JAR (25 OZ) PUTTANESCA PASTA SAUCE
1 LB CELLENTANI OR OTHER PASTA
1 JAR MOJO CRIOLLO MARINADE
REGULAR PEARL BARLEY
KOREAN TERIYAKI STIR-FRY SAUCE
WASABI MAYONNAISE
1 TBSP PICKLED GINGER SLICES
SOY SAUCE
BLACK SESAME SEEDS
DARK SESAME OIL

12 OZ RICE NOODLES
THAI FISH SAUCE
LITE SOY SAUCE
CORNMEAL

PANTRY
SALT
PEPPER
OLIVE OIL
NONSTICK SPRAY
RICE VINEGAR
SUGAR
DRIED OREGANO
CRUSHED RED PEPPER (OPTIONAL)

Week 3

JULY 15 TO JULY 22

PRODUCE
1 LEMON
1 MEDIUM ONION
1 SMALL ONION
2 OR 3 MEDIUM RED ONIONS
1 HEAD GARLIC (7 CLOVES)
2 BAKING POTATOES (ABOUT 1¼ LB)
1 SWEET POTATO (ABOUT 10 OZ)
2 PLUM TOMATOES
1 MEDIUM TOMATO (OPTIONAL)
1 ORANGE BELL PEPPER
1 YELLOW BELL PEPPER
3 BELL PEPPERS
1 ITALIAN FRYING PEPPER
2 POBLANO CHILES
3 MEDIUM ZUCCHINI
1 SPAGHETTI SQUASH (4½ LB)
1 MEDIUM EGGPLANT
1 MEDIUM CUCUMBER
4 SCALLIONS
3 OR 4 ROMAINE HEARTS
1 BUNCH BASIL

BAKERY
2 SLICES WHITE SANDWICH BREAD
4 HAMBURGER BUNS
1 LONG LOAF ITALIAN OR FRENCH BREAD

MEAT/POULTRY/FISH
1 LB 95% LEAN GROUND BEEF
8 CHICKEN DRUMSTICKS (ABOUT 2 LB)
12 OZ LEAN GROUND TURKEY
1 PKG (1¼ LB) ITALIAN TURKEY SAUSAGES
3 LINKS (ABOUT 8 OZ) SWEET OR HOT LEAN ITALIAN TURKEY SAUSAGES
1 LB FRESH ITALIAN CHICKEN OR TURKEY SAUSAGE
4 COD STEAKS (OR HALIBUT STEAKS OR FIRM WHITEFISH FILLETS, SUCH AS RED SNAPPER, TILAPIA OR ORANGE ROUGHY)

DELI
4 OZ FULLY COOKED HAM

REFRIGERATED
¼ CUP FAT-FREE MILK
½ CUP SHREDDED MOZZARELLA
1 CUP SHREDDED CHEDDAR
1 BLOCK PARMESAN
EGGS (2 LARGE)
1 PKG (14 OZ) EXTRA-FIRM TOFU

GROCERY
1 CAN (28 OZ) DICED TOMATOES
1 CAN (14.5 OZ) DICED TOMATOES
1 CAN (14.5 OZ) DICED TOMATOES WITH ONION AND GARLIC
1 CAN (28 OZ) CRUSHED TOMATOES
1 CAN (8 OZ) TOMATO SAUCE
1 CAN (ABOUT 15 OZ) BLACK BEANS
1 CAN (ABOUT 15 OZ) PINTO BEANS
1 CAN (15 TO 16 OZ) CHICKPEAS
1 CAN (11 OZ) VACUUM-PACKED CORN
¼ CUP PIMIENTO-STUFFED OLIVES
CAPERS
¾ CUP BARBECUE SAUCE
¼ CUP BALSAMIC VINAIGRETTE DRESSING
4 BURRITO-SIZE 99% FAT-FREE FLOUR TORTILLAS
CARIBBEAN JERK SEASONING
½ CUP RAISINS (WE PREFER GOLDEN)
1 TBSP DARK RUM (OPTIONAL)

PANTRY
SALT
PEPPER
OLIVE OIL
OLIVE OIL COOKING SPRAY
CIDER VINEGAR
RED-WINE VINEGAR
GROUND CUMIN
GROUND CINNAMON
GROUND CLOVES
DRIED OREGANO
CHILI POWDER

Week 4

JULY 23 TO JULY 31

PRODUCE
2 RIPE MEDIUM PEACHES
3 LARGE NAVEL ORANGES
1 LEMON
2 MEDIUM RED ONIONS
1 HEAD GARLIC (3 CLOVES)
1 PT GRAPE TOMATOES
1 BUNCH BROCCOLI (ABOUT 1¼ LB)
1 RED BELL PEPPER
4 BABY EGGPLANTS (ABOUT 5 OZ EACH)
4 CUPS COLESLAW MIX
4 SCALLIONS
1 BUNCH CILANTRO
1 BUNCH ITALIAN PARSLEY
1 BUNCH BASIL

BAKERY
4 POCKETLESS PITAS

MEAT/POULTRY/FISH
ONE 12-OZ SKIRT STEAK
ONE 12-OZ BEEF TOP ROUND FOR LONDON BROIL
3 LB BABY-BACK RIBS
4 BONELESS, SKINLESS CHICKEN BREASTS (ABOUT 5 OZ EACH)
1 LB CHICKEN TENDERS
1 SALMON FILLET (1½ LB)
1¼ LB LARGE RAW EASY-TO-PEEL CLEANED SHRIMP

REFRIGERATED
1 STICK BUTTER
1 SMALL CONTAINER PART-SKIM RICOTTA
1 BAG SHREDDED PART-SKIM MOZZARELLA
SHREDDED PEPPERJACK CHEESE
GRATED PARMESAN
EGG (1 LARGE)

GROCERY
1 CAN (15 OZ) BLACK BEANS
1 CAN (7 OZ) VACUUM-PACKED CORN
1 CUP MARINARA SAUCE
1 LB LINGUINE PASTA
8 FAJITA-SIZE FLOUR TORTILLAS
NO-SALT-ADDED KETCHUP
COARSE-GRAIN MUSTARD
1 BOTTLE (18 OZ) BARBECUE SAUCE (WE USED CATTLEMAN'S CLASSIC)
WORCESTERSHIRE SAUCE
OLIVE OIL AND VINEGAR DRESSING
STIR-FRY SAUCE
WASABI HORSERADISH MAYONNAISE
SLAW DRESSING
PURE MAPLE SYRUP
30 ROUND BUTTERY CRACKERS

PANTRY
SALT
PEPPER
EXTRA-VIRGIN OLIVE OIL
VEGETABLE OIL
OLIVE-OIL NONSTICK SPRAY
DIJON MUSTARD
BROWN SUGAR
GROUND CUMIN
CRUSHED RED PEPPER
PAPRIKA
INSTANT COFFEE

CHICKEN CURRY SKEWERS

YIELD
6 servings

ACTIVE
12 minutes

TOTAL
1 hour 30 minutes

1 RECIPE VERSATILE MARINADE (SEE RIGHT)

1¼ LB **BONELESS, SKINLESS CHICKEN THIGHS**, CUT IN 1½-IN. PIECES

1 LARGE **RED BELL PEPPER**, CUT IN 1½-IN. PIECES

1 FIRM-RIPE **MANGO**, PEELED AND CUT INTO 1½-IN. PIECES

½ LARGE **RED ONION**, CUT INTO 1½-IN. PIECES

6 (10-IN.) SOAKED **BAMBOO SKEWERS**

1 RECIPE CURRY YOGURT DIP (SEE RIGHT)

SIDE SUGGESTION
Jasmine or basmati rice

Marinate chicken at least 1 hour or overnight.

Position top rack 3 to 4 in. from heat. Heat broiler. Place pieces of chicken, red pepper, mango and red onion on skewers.

Place on broiler pan; broil for 15 minutes, turning every 5 minutes until chicken and vegetables are cooked through and slightly browned. Serve over rice with Curry Yogurt Dip.

VERSATILE MARINADE

¼ cup **olive oil**
¼ cup **lemon or lime juice** *or* **vinegar**
2 tsp minced **garlic**
¼ tsp **salt**
¼ tsp **crushed red pepper** *or* **ground pepper**

Combine ingredients in large ziptop bag; shake to mix. Remove 2 Tbsp marinade to another ziptop bag to toss with veggies before skewering.

Add 1 lb protein to marinade and seal bag. Refrigerate at least 1 hour or overnight.

CURRY YOGURT DIP

½ cup **Greek yogurt**
½ cup **mango chutney**
2 tsp **curry powder**

Combine ingredients in large ziptop bag; shake to mix.

PER SERVING
CALORIES 435 **TOTAL FAT** 18G **SATURATED FAT** 6G **CHOLESTEROL** 98MG **SODIUM** 644MG **TOTAL CARBOHYDRATES** 40G **DIETARY FIBER** 3G **PROTEIN** 29G

SOFT & CRUNCHY BEEF TACOS

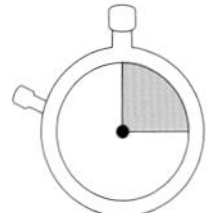

YIELD
4 servings
(2 tacos per serving)

ACTIVE
15 minutes

TOTAL
15 minutes

8 **TACO SHELLS**

8 SOFT-TACO OR FAJITA-SIZE **FLOUR TORTILLAS**

1 CUP **SHREDDED CHEDDAR**

1 LB **LEAN GROUND BEEF**

1 PKT (1.25 OZ) **TACO SEASONING MIX**

¾ CUP **WATER**

1 CUP EACH SHREDDED **ROMAINE LETTUCE** AND **BOTTLED TACO SAUCE**

¼ CUP CHOPPED **RED ONION**

SIDE SUGGESTION
Romaine lettuce, diced avocado and grape tomato salad

Heat oven to 375°F. Put taco shells on a baking sheet; spread flour tortillas on another baking sheet. Sprinkle each tortilla with 1 Tbsp cheese.

Brown ground beef in a large nonstick skillet, breaking up chunks with a spoon. Stir in taco seasoning mix and water. Simmer uncovered, stirring occasionally, 3 minutes or until slightly thickened.

Meanwhile, put baking sheets in oven. Bake 3 minutes, or until cheese melts.

Center a taco shell in each flour tortilla and bring up sides of tortillas. Fill tacos with beef mixture, then shredded lettuce, the rest of the cheese, and the taco sauce and onion.

PER SERVING
CALORIES 808 **TOTAL FAT** 42G **SATURATED FAT** 16G **CHOLESTEROL** 115MG **SODIUM** 1,876MG
TOTAL CARBOHYDRATES 73G **DIETARY FIBER** 4G **PROTEIN** 35G

SCALLOPS WITH LEMON & CAPERS

YIELD
4 servings

ACTIVE
4 minutes

TOTAL
10 minutes

- 1 CUP **CHICKEN BROTH**
- 1 TBSP **CAPERS**
- 1½ TSP **CORNSTARCH**
- 1 TSP MINCED **GARLIC**
- 1 TSP GRATED **LEMON ZEST**
- 2 TBSP **LEMON JUICE**
- ¼ TSP EACH **SALT** AND **PEPPER**
- 3 TSP **BUTTER**
- 1½ LB **SEA SCALLOPS**, PATTED DRY
- 1 TBSP CHOPPED **PARSLEY**

SIDE SUGGESTION
Rice, steamed broccolini

In a 2-cup liquid measure, stir broth, capers, cornstarch, garlic, zest, juice, salt and pepper until cornstarch dissolves.

Melt 2 tsp butter in large nonstick skillet over medium-high heat. When butter just starts to brown, add scallops and cook, turning once, 4 to 5 minutes until golden and cooked through. Remove to a plate.

Add broth mixture to skillet; bring to a boil. Boil 1 minute or until slightly thickened. Remove from heat; stir in remaining butter and parsley. Spoon over scallops.

PER SERVING
CALORIES 192 **TOTAL FAT** 5G **SATURATED FAT** 2G **CHOLESTEROL** 64MG **SODIUM** 765MG **TOTAL CARBOHYDRATES** 6G **DIETARY FIBER** 0G **PROTEIN** 29G

CLASSIC ALL-AMERICAN BACON CHEESEBURGERS

SAUCE

½ CUP **LIGHT MAYONNAISE**

¼ CUP **CHILI SAUCE**

2 TBSP **DILL PICKLE RELISH**

BURGERS

2 LB **90%-LEAN GROUND BEEF**

2 TSP **WORCESTERSHIRE SAUCE**

½ TSP EACH **SALT** AND FRESHLY GROUND **PEPPER**

6 **WHOLE-WHEAT HAMBURGER BUNS**, SPLIT

6 SMALL **LETTUCE LEAVES**

1 LARGE **BEEFSTEAK TOMATO**, CUT IN 6 THIN SLICES

6 THIN SLICES **VIDALIA ONION**

NONSTICK SPRAY

6 SLICES (1 OZ EACH) **SHARP CHEDDAR**

6 STRIPS COOKED **BACON**

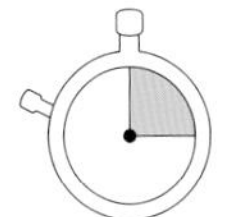

YIELD
6 servings

ACTIVE
15 minutes

TOTAL
30 minutes

SIDE SUGGESTION
Potato salad, corn on the cob

SAUCE Mix ingredients in a bowl.

BURGERS Gently mix ingredients in a large bowl. Shape into six 1-in.-thick burgers.

Heat outdoor grill. Toast buns on grill; remove to a platter. Spread 1 Tbsp sauce on bun tops and bottoms. Top bottoms with lettuce, tomato and onion.

Coat burgers with nonstick spray. Grill, turning once, 10 to 12 minutes, until an instant-read thermometer inserted from side to middle registers 160°F. Top with cheese and bacon; cover grill 45 seconds or until cheese starts to melt. Transfer burgers to buns. Serve remaining sauce on the side.

PER SERVING
CALORIES 605 **TOTAL FAT** 35G **SATURATED FAT** 15G **CHOLESTEROL** 132MG **SODIUM** 939MG
TOTAL CARBOHYDRATES 27G **DIETARY FIBER** 3G **PROTEIN** 44G

PASTA PRIMAVERA

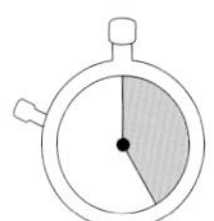

YIELD
5 servings

ACTIVE
25 minutes

TOTAL
55 minutes

12 OZ **LINGUINE** *OR* **EGGLESS FETTUCINE PASTA**

2 CUPS SMALL **BROCCOLI FLORETS** (ABOUT ⅓ OF A LARGE BUNCH)

1 LARGE **CARROT**, DICED (¾ CUP)

2 MEDIUM **ZUCCHINI**, QUARTERED CROSSWISE AND CUT IN THIN STICKS (1½ CUPS)

1 LARGE **RED BELL PEPPER**, QUARTERED AND CUT CROSSWISE IN THIN STRIPS (1¼ CUPS)

½ CUP **FROZEN GREEN PEAS**

SAUCE

2 TBSP **ALL-PURPOSE FLOUR**

1 CUP **CHICKEN BROTH**

1 CUP **1% SKIM MILK**

¼ TSP EACH **SALT** AND **PEPPER**

¼ CUP **GRATED PARMESAN**

SIDE SUGGESTION
Arugula, tomato and red onion salad

NOTE
We substituted 1% milk and flour for the loads of butter and cream that make traditional versions of this sauce so fatty. Even so, you'll be amazed how creamy and satisfying it is.

Cook pasta in a large pot of lightly salted boiling water 5 minutes less than directed on package.

Add broccoli and carrot, and cook, stirring once or twice, 2 minutes. Add remaining vegetables and cook 2 to 3 minutes longer until vegetables and pasta are tender. Drain.

Meanwhile make SAUCE Put flour in a medium saucepan. Slowly whisk in broth and milk until blended. Stir in salt and pepper. Bring to boil over medium-high heat, whisking often. Reduce heat to low and simmer 2 to 3 minutes, stirring constantly, until thickened. Stir in cheese.

Pour over drained vegetables and pasta. Toss to mix and coat.

PER SERVING
CALORIES 355 **TOTAL FAT** 3G **SATURATED FAT** 0G **CHOLESTEROL** 5MG **SODIUM** 680MG **TOTAL CARBOHYDRATES** 65G **DIETARY FIBER** 0G **PROTEIN** 16G

MOROCCAN CHICKEN & COUSCOUS

2 TSP **OLIVE OIL**

4 **BONELESS, SKINLESS CHICKEN THIGHS**, EACH CUT INTO 3 PIECES

¼ TSP **SALT**

1 CAN (14.5 OZ) **CHICKEN BROTH**

1 CAN (14.5 OZ) **DICED TOMATOES WITH GARLIC AND ONION**

1 PKG (ABOUT 1 LB) CUBED **FRESH BUTTERNUT SQUASH**

½ CUP **RAISINS**

2 TSP **GROUND CUMIN**

1 TSP EACH **GROUND CINNAMON** AND **SMOKED PAPRIKA**

1 CUP **PLAIN COUSCOUS**

1 CUP **FROZEN PEAS**

YIELD
5 servings

ACTIVE
5 minutes

TOTAL
30 minutes

Heat oil in a large deep skillet over medium-high heat. Sprinkle chicken with salt and cook 5 minutes, turning once, until browned. Add broth, tomatoes, squash, raisins, cumin, cinnamon and paprika. Bring to a boil; cover and reduce heat. Simmer 15 minutes or until chicken is tender.

Stir in couscous and peas, and bring to a boil. Cover, remove skillet from heat and let stand 5 minutes.

SIDE SUGGESTION
Boston lettuce, orange and toasted almond salad

PER SERVING
CALORIES 347 **TOTAL FAT** 5G **SATURATED FAT** 1G **CHOLESTEROL** 45MG **SODIUM** 752MG
TOTAL CARBOHYDRATES 58G **DIETARY FIBER** 7G **PROTEIN** 20G

PANKO-CRUSTED FISH STICKS

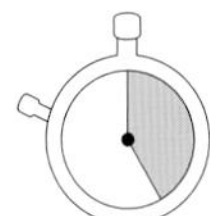

YIELD
4 servings

ACTIVE
25 minutes

TOTAL
40 minutes

CARROT KETCHUP

3 JARS (4 OZ EACH) **BABY-FOOD PURÉED CARROTS**

2 TBSP **LIGHT-BROWN SUGAR**

1 TBSP **CIDER VINEGAR**

¼ TSP **SALT**

1 TBSP **UNSALTED BUTTER**

FISH STICKS

1 LARGE **EGG**

½ TSP EACH **ONION POWDER** AND **SALT**

⅛ TSP **PEPPER**

1½ LB **CATFISH OR TILAPIA FILLETS**

2 CUPS **PANKO BREAD CRUMBS**

NONSTICK COOKING SPRAY

SIDE SUGGESTION
Corn, coleslaw

CARROT KETCHUP Combine puréed carrots, sugar, vinegar and salt in a 1-qt saucepan. Bring to a simmer over medium heat; reduce heat and simmer, uncovered, 15 to 20 minutes until thickened and reduced to about 1 cup. Stir in butter, then remove mixture to a large metal bowl and place in freezer for 10 minutes to quick-chill.

Meanwhile, make FISH STICKS: Heat oven to 450°F. Coat baking sheet with nonstick cooking spray, or line with parchment paper or nonstick foil.

Beat egg, onion powder, salt and pepper in a pie plate or shallow bowl until foamy. Halve fillets lengthwise, then crosswise. Place panko crumbs on a sheet of wax paper.

Dip fish in egg mixture, roll in crumbs to cover and place fish on baking sheet. Coat fish with nonstick cooking spray; bake 12 to 15 minutes until cooked through and browned. Serve with Carrot Ketchup.

PER SERVING
CALORIES 552 **TOTAL FAT** 23G **SATURATED FAT** 5G **CHOLESTEROL** 140MG **SODIUM** 677MG
TOTAL CARBOHYDRATES 51G **DIETARY FIBER** 2G **PROTEIN** 33G

KOREAN BEEF BOK CHOY

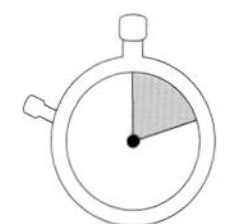

YIELD
4 servings

ACTIVE
12 minutes

TOTAL
12 minutes

ONE 12-OZ **BEEF FLANK STEAK**

4 TSP **OIL**

⅓ CUP **KOREAN TERIYAKI STIR-FRY SAUCE**

1¼ LB **BABY BOK CHOY**, LARGER LEAVES REMOVED AND QUARTERED, CENTERS QUARTERED LENGTHWISE

3 TBSP **WATER**

CRUSHED RED PEPPER (OPTIONAL)

SIDE SUGGESTION
Brown rice with sliced scallions

Cut steak diagonally across the grain in ¼-in.-thick slices.

Heat 1 tsp oil in a large nonstick skillet over medium-high heat until rippling. Add half the meat; stir-fry 30 seconds or until no longer pink. Remove to a bowl. Repeat with another 1 tsp oil and rest of meat. Add to bowl; stir in 2 Tbsp stir-fry sauce.

Add remaining 2 tsp oil to skillet, then bok choy. Stir-fry 30 seconds. Add water; cover and steam 1 minute. Uncover, add remaining sauce and stir-fry 1 minute or until bok choy is crisp-tender. Add meat and juices; stir-fry 30 seconds to heat through. Sprinkle with crushed red pepper, if desired.

PER SERVING
CALORIES 238 **TOTAL FAT** 10G **SATURATED FAT** 4G **CHOLESTEROL** 44MG **SODIUM** 720MG **TOTAL CARBOHYDRATES** 11G **DIETARY FIBER** 1G **PROTEIN** 19G

SOUTH BEACH MOJO PORK

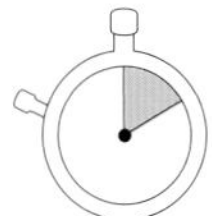

YIELD
6 servings

ACTIVE
10 minutes

TOTAL
10 hours

1 CUP **MOJO CRIOLLO MARINADE** (WE USED GOYA)

1 **JALAPEÑO PEPPER**, SEEDED AND MINCED

1 CLOVE **GARLIC**, MINCED

2½-LB **BONELESS PORK LOIN ROAST**, WELL TRIMMED

2 **NAVEL ORANGES**, PEEL AND WHITE PITH REMOVED, FLESH CUT INTO SECTIONS

½ CUP THINLY SLICED **RED ONION**

¼ CUP CHOPPED **CILANTRO**

SIDE SUGGESTION
Black beans with cumin, garlic and cilantro

Mix ¾ cup of the marinade, the pepper and garlic in a 3½-qt or larger slow cooker. Add pork and turn to coat. (If you have time, cover and place in the refrigerator to let pork marinate for several hours, turning occasionally.)

Cover and cook on low 8 to 10 hours or until pork is tender.

About 10 minutes before serving, combine oranges, onion and remaining ¼ cup marinade in a medium bowl. Leave at room temperature.

Transfer pork to cutting board; slice. Skim fat from top of liquid in slow cooker. Spoon liquid over sliced pork. Stir cilantro into orange mixture; top pork with mixture.

PER SERVING
CALORIES 304 **TOTAL FAT** 12G **SATURATED FAT** 4G **CHOLESTEROL** 104MG **SODIUM** 810MG
TOTAL CARBOHYDRATES 9G **DIETARY FIBER** 1G **PROTEIN** 37G

MEDITERRANEAN STUFFED EGGPLANT

- 4 SMALL **ITALIAN EGGPLANTS** (7 OZ EACH)
- **NONSTICK SPRAY**
- 8 OZ **GROUND CHICKEN OR TURKEY**
- 2 MEDIUM **BELL PEPPERS**, CHOPPED
- 1 MEDIUM **ONION**, CHOPPED
- 2 TSP MINCED **GARLIC**
- 1 CAN (14.5 OZ) **DICED TOMATOES**
- 1 CUP **WATER**
- ½ CUP **REGULAR PEARL BARLEY**
- 2 CUPS **BABY SPINACH**
- 3 TBSP CHOPPED **FRESH BASIL**
- 2 TBSP **GRATED ROMANO CHEESE**

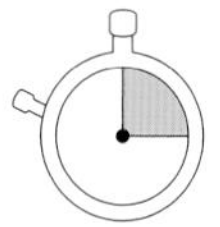

YIELD
4 servings

ACTIVE
15 minutes

TOTAL
40 minutes

SIDE SUGGESTION
Baby spinach, cucumber, tomato and feta salad

Line a rimmed baking sheet with nonstick foil. Halve eggplants lengthwise, then scoop out flesh with spoon, leaving a ½-in.-thick shell. Coat eggplants with nonstick spray; invert on baking sheet. Chop scooped eggplant.

Coat a large nonstick skillet with nonstick spray. Over medium-high heat, cook chicken, peppers, onion, chopped eggplant and garlic 4 minutes. Add tomatoes, water and barley. Reduce heat. Cover; simmer 25 minutes or until barley is tender.

Meanwhile, heat broiler. Broil eggplant shells 12 minutes or until lightly charred and soft, turning once.

Stir spinach and basil into chicken mixture; spoon into eggplant halves. Sprinkle with cheese.

PER SERVING
CALORIES 311 **TOTAL FAT** 10G **SATURATED FAT** 1G **CHOLESTEROL** 3MG **SODIUM** 499MG **TOTAL CARBOHYDRATES** 42G **DIETARY FIBER** 12G **PROTEIN** 17G

FRESH SALMON BURGERS

4 **SCALLIONS**, CUT IN 1-IN. PIECES

1 TBSP **PICKLED GINGER SLICES** (FOUND IN YOUR MARKET'S ASIAN SECTION)

1 TSP **DARK SESAME OIL**

¼ TSP EACH **SALT** AND FRESHLY GROUND **PEPPER**

WHITE FROM 1 LARGE **EGG**

1 TBSP **SOY SAUCE**

2-LB PIECE **SALMON FILLET (PREFERABLY SOCKEYE OR COHO)**, SKIN AND PIN BONES REMOVED, CUT IN 1-IN. CUBES

NONSTICK SPRAY

6 LEAVES **BOSTON LETTUCE**

TOPPINGS: **WASABI MAYONNAISE, PICKLED GINGER SLICES** AND **RADISH SPROUTS**

GARNISH: **BLACK SESAME SEEDS**

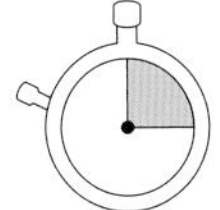

YIELD
6 servings

ACTIVE
15 minutes

TOTAL
24 minutes

SIDE SUGGESTION
Rice, shredded carrot and scallion salad

Heat outdoor grill.

In food processor, pulse scallions, ginger, sesame oil, salt and pepper until finely minced, scraping down sides of processor bowl once or twice. Add egg white and soy sauce; pulse to blend. Add salmon. Pulse just until very finely chopped but not a paste. Shape into 6 burgers, each about ¾ in. thick.

Coat burgers with nonstick spray. Grill, turning once, until done as desired (6 minutes for medium-rare, which is preferred).

Place on lettuce leaves. Top each with wasabi mayonnaise, ginger slices and sprouts; sprinkle with a pinch or two of sesame seeds.

PER SERVING
CALORIES 235 **TOTAL FAT** 10G **SATURATED FAT** 2G **CHOLESTEROL** 83MG **SODIUM** 403MG
TOTAL CARBOHYDRATES 2G **DIETARY FIBER** 0G **PROTEIN** 31G

GRILLED PIZZA

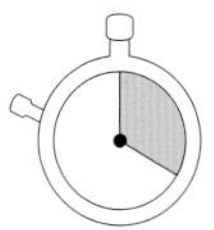

YIELD
4 servings

ACTIVE
20 minutes

TOTAL
30 minutes

2 TBSP **CORNMEAL**

1 LB **PIZZA DOUGH**, AT ROOM TEMPERATURE, QUARTERED

2 TO 3 TBSP **OLIVE OIL**

¾ CUP **MARINARA OR PIZZA SAUCE**

1⅓ CUPS **SHREDDED MOZZARELLA**

8 TSP **GRATED PARMESAN**

1 TSP **DRIED OREGANO**

Heat outdoor gas grill 10 minutes on high heat. After 10 minutes, reduce heat to medium.

Meanwhile, sprinkle 2 tsp cornmeal over each of 2 large baking sheets. To make each pizza, take a quarter of dough and stretch, turning and pulling, until it's about a 7- to 8-in. round or oblong shape and about ⅛-in. thick. (If dough is sticky, flour your hands before stretching.) Brush both sides with olive oil and place on prepared baking sheet. Sprinkle top with ½ tsp cornmeal. Continue with remaining dough and cornmeal to make 4 pizzas.

Lift dough off baking sheets and onto grill. Close cover and grill 3 minutes or until bottoms are firm and have nice grill marks. Using tongs, remove crusts to a baking sheet. Shut off one of the grill burners; close cover.

Spread each crust with 3 Tbsp sauce. Top each with ⅓ cup shredded mozzarella, 2 tsp grated Parmesan and ¼ tsp oregano.

Place pizzas on unlit side of grill so they get indirect heat. Close cover and grill 7 to 10 minutes, rotating pizzas halfway through cooking time, until bottoms are browned and cheese is melted.

PER SERVING
CALORIES 557 **TOTAL FAT** 24G **SATURATED FAT** 7G **CHOLESTEROL** 33MG **SODIUM** 1,117MG **TOTAL CARBOHYDRATES** 64G **DIETARY FIBER** 4G **PROTEIN** 22G

PASTA PUTTANESCA & TUNA

YIELD
6 servings

ACTIVE
5 minutes

TOTAL
25 minutes

1 LB **CELLENTANI OR OTHER PASTA**

1 JAR (25 OZ) **PUTTANESCA PASTA SAUCE**

1 CAN (6 OZ) **LIGHT TUNA IN OIL**, DRAINED

GARNISH: CHOPPED **PARSLEY** (OPTIONAL)

SIDE SUGGESTION
Green salad with shaved Parmesan

Cook pasta in a large pot of lightly salted water as package directs.

Drain pasta in colander. Add pasta sauce and tuna to pasta pot. Bring to a simmer, breaking up tuna with a wooden spoon. Remove from heat.

Add pasta to pot; toss to mix and coat. Transfer to a serving bowl and garnish with chopped parsley if desired.

DIFFERENT TAKES
- Add some crushed red pepper flakes.
- Use canned clams instead of tuna.
- Stir in some chopped fresh basil just before serving.

PER SERVING
CALORIES 369 **TOTAL FAT** 6G **SATURATED FAT** 1G **CHOLESTEROL** 15MG **SODIUM** 786MG
TOTAL CARBOHYDRATES 61G **DIETARY FIBER** 3G **PROTEIN** 17G

SPICY THAI NOODLES WITH PORK & MINT

12 OZ **RICE NOODLES**

¼ CUP **THAI FISH SAUCE**

¼ CUP **RICE VINEGAR**

3 TBSP **SUGAR**

2½ TBSP **OIL**

1½ TBSP **LITE SOY SAUCE**

⅓ CUP **WATER**

ONE 8-OZ **PORK TENDERLOIN**, THINLY SLICED CROSSWISE, SLICES CUT IN HALF

1½ TBSP MINCED **GARLIC**

1½ TBSP GRATED **GINGER**

1 TBSP MINCED SEEDED **SERRANO CHILES**

¾ CUP HALVED **GRAPE TOMATOES**

¾ CUP SHREDDED **CARROTS**

¾ CUP SLICED **SCALLIONS**

¾ CUP SLIVERED **FRESH MINT**

ACCOMPANIMENTS: **LIME** WEDGES, **THAI-STYLE CHILI SAUCE**

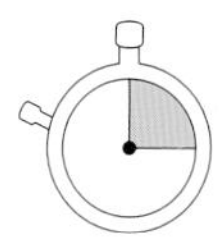

YIELD
4 servings

ACTIVE
15 minutes

TOTAL
25 minutes

SIDE SUGGESTION
Cucumber and red onion salad

Soak noodles in warm water to cover 20 minutes until pliable. Drain.

Meanwhile, in a small bowl mix fish sauce, vinegar, sugar, 1½ Tbsp oil, the soy sauce and water.

Heat 1 tsp oil in a large nonstick skillet over high heat. Add pork; stir-fry 2 minutes until lightly browned and cooked through. Remove to a plate with a slotted spoon.

Heat remaining oil in skillet. Add garlic, ginger and chiles; stir-fry 30 seconds or until fragrant.

Add fish sauce mixture and noodles. Cook, stirring, 2 minutes or until noodles soften and wilt. Remove from heat; add pork, tomatoes, and ½ the carrots, scallions and mint. Toss to mix.

Spoon onto platter; sprinkle with remaining carrots, scallions and mint.

PER SERVING
CALORIES 557 **TOTAL FAT** 13G **SATURATED FAT** 3G **CHOLESTEROL** 37MG **SODIUM** 1,018MG **TOTAL CARBOHYDRATES** 93G **DIETARY FIBER** 3G **PROTEIN** 16G

TURKEY BURGERS WITH CRISPY "FRIES"

OLIVE OIL COOKING SPRAY

2 **BAKING POTATOES** (ABOUT 1¼ LB), SCRUBBED, CUT IN ¾-IN.-THICK WEDGES

1 **SWEET POTATO** (ABOUT 10 OZ), SCRUBBED, CUT IN ¾-IN.-THICK WEDGES

¾ TSP PLUS ½ TSP **SALT**

2 SLICES **WHITE SANDWICH BREAD**

¼ CUP **FAT-FREE MILK**

12 OZ **LEAN GROUND TURKEY**

3 LINKS (ABOUT 8 OZ) **SWEET OR HOT LEAN ITALIAN TURKEY SAUSAGES**, CASINGS REMOVED

¼ TSP **PEPPER**

4 **HAMBURGER BUNS**

SERVE WITH: **LETTUCE**, SLICED **TOMATO** AND **RED ONION** (OPTIONAL)

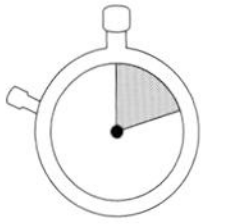

YIELD
4 servings

ACTIVE
12 minutes

TOTAL
42 minutes

SIDE SUGGESTION
Mixed greens salad

Heat oven to 500°F. Position racks to divide oven in thirds. Heat outdoor grill or stovetop grill pan. Coat 2 rimmed baking sheets with cooking spray.

Divide potatoes between baking sheets. Coat with cooking spray; sprinkle with ¾ tsp salt. Toss until evenly coated, then spread in a single layer.

Bake 30 minutes or until tender and golden, switching position of pans and turning potatoes over halfway through baking.

Meanwhile, tear bread in small pieces into a medium bowl. Pour milk over bread; let soak about 1 minute. Add ground turkey, turkey sausage, pepper and remaining ½ tsp salt. Mix with hands until blended. Divide in quarters. With wet hands, shape each portion into a 1-in.-thick patty.

Coat patties with cooking spray and grill 12 to 14 minutes, turning once, until cooked through. Serve in buns (with lettuce, tomato and onion, if desired) with the fries.

PER SERVING
CALORIES 536 **TOTAL FAT** 9G **SATURATED FAT** 2G **CHOLESTEROL** 77MG **SODIUM** 1,444MG
TOTAL CARBOHYDRATES 75G **DIETARY FIBER** 6G **PROTEIN** 37G

PICADILLO BURRITOS

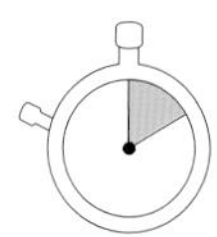

YIELD
4 servings

ACTIVE
10 minutes

TOTAL
20 minutes

1 LB **95%-LEAN GROUND BEEF**

1 CAN (14.5 OZ) **DICED TOMATOES WITH ONION AND GARLIC**

¼ CUP **PIMIENTO-STUFFED OLIVES**, SLICED

1 TBSP **CIDER VINEGAR**

¾ TSP **GROUND CUMIN**

¾ TSP **CINNAMON**

¼ TSP **GROUND CLOVES**

4 BURRITO-SIZE **99%-FAT-FREE FLOUR TORTILLAS**

1 CUP SHREDDED **ROMAINE LETTUCE**

SIDE SUGGESTION
Sliced avocado, sweet onion and beefsteak tomato

Heat a large nonstick skillet over medium-high heat. Crumble in beef and stir 5 minutes or until no longer pink.

Stir in next 6 ingredients, reduce heat and simmer, partially covered, 10 minutes or until most liquid has evaporated.

Heat tortillas as package directs. Top each with ¼ the beef mixture and lettuce, fold in the sides and roll up.

PER SERVING
CALORIES 312 **TOTAL FAT** 7G **SATURATED FAT** 3G **CHOLESTEROL** 70MG **SODIUM** 1,036MG **TOTAL CARBOHYDRATES** 39G **DIETARY FIBER** 12G **PROTEIN** 32G

GRILLED COD WITH CAPONATA

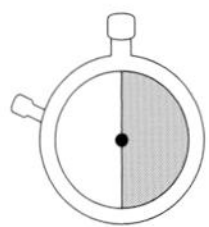

YIELD
4 servings

ACTIVE
30 minutes

TOTAL
1 hour

COD MARINADE

2 TBSP **OLIVE OIL**

2 TBSP **FRESH LEMON JUICE**

1 TSP MINCED **GARLIC**

1 TSP **DRIED OREGANO**

1 TSP **SALT**

4 **COD STEAKS** (SEE NOTE), EACH A SCANT 1 IN. THICK (1¾ LB)

CAPONATA

2 TBSP **OLIVE OIL**

½ CUP CHOPPED **ONION**

1 EACH **ITALIAN FRYING PEPPER** AND **ORANGE AND YELLOW BELL PEPPERS**, CUT IN THIN STRIPS

2 TSP MINCED **GARLIC**

1 MEDIUM **EGGPLANT,** UNPEELED, CUT IN ¾-IN. PIECES

1 CAN (8 OZ) **TOMATO SAUCE**

½ CUP **RAISINS** (WE PREFER GOLDEN)

2 TBSP **RED-WINE VINEGAR**

2 TBSP BOTTLED **CAPERS**, RINSED

MARINADE Mix ingredients in a large ziptop bag. Add cod, seal; turn to coat. Leave at room temperature while preparing caponata.

CAPONATA Heat oil in a large nonstick skillet over medium heat. Add onion and peppers; sauté 2 minutes or until soft. Add garlic; stir 30 seconds or until aromatic. Add eggplant and, stirring often, cook 2 to 3 minutes. Stir in tomato sauce, cover; reduce heat and simmer, stirring twice, 12 minutes, or until eggplant is very tender.

Meanwhile, heat outdoor grill or a stovetop ridged grill pan. Remove fish from bag; discard bag with marinade.

Grill fish 4 to 6 in. from heat source on outdoor grill, 8 to 10 minutes in grill pan, turning once, until opaque at center.

Add raisins, vinegar and capers to caponata. Cover and simmer 5 minutes to develop flavors.

Serve fish with caponata on the side.

SIDE SUGGESTION Orzo, grilled zucchini halves

NOTE Halibut steaks or firm whitefish fillets, such as red snapper, tilapia or orange roughy, can be substituted for the cod.

PER SERVING
CALORIES 369 **TOTAL FAT** 12G **SATURATED FAT** 2G **CHOLESTEROL** 75MG **SODIUM** 927MG **TOTAL CARBOHYDRATES** 34G **DIETARY FIBER** 5G **PROTEIN** 35G

JAMAICAN JERK BBQ CHICKEN

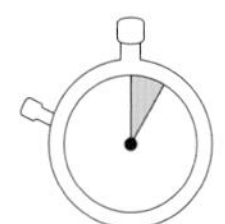

YIELD
4 servings

ACTIVE
5 minutes

TOTAL
8 hours

8 **CHICKEN DRUMSTICKS** (ABOUT 2 LB), SKIN REMOVED

2 TSP **CARIBBEAN JERK SEASONING**

¾ CUP **BARBECUE SAUCE**

1 TBSP **DARK RUM** (OPTIONAL)

¼ CUP SLICED **SCALLIONS**

SIDE SUGGESTION
Cornbread, coleslaw

Rub drumsticks with seasoning. Place in 3½-qt or larger slow cooker. Pour barbecue sauce and rum over chicken. Turn chicken to coat.

Cover and cook on low 6 to 8 hours until chicken is tender. Sprinkle with scallions.

PER SERVING
CALORIES 188 **TOTAL FAT** 5G **SATURATED FAT** 1G **CHOLESTEROL** 98MG **SODIUM** 635MG **TOTAL CARBOHYDRATES** 6G **DIETARY FIBER** 1G **PROTEIN** 27G

SUMMER CHILI

1 TBSP **OIL**

2 **POBLANO CHILES**, SEEDED AND CHOPPED, *OR* 1 CAN (4.5 OZ) **CHOPPED GREEN CHILES**

1 MEDIUM **ONION**, CHOPPED

1 MEDIUM **ZUCCHINI**, DICED

1 TBSP MINCED **GARLIC**

1 CAN (28 OZ) **CRUSHED TOMATOES**

1 CAN (14.5 OZ) **DICED TOMATOES**

1 PKG (14 OZ) **EXTRA-FIRM TOFU**, DRAINED AND CUT IN ½-IN. CUBES

1 CAN EACH (ABOUT 15 OZ) **BLACK BEANS** AND **PINTO BEANS**, RINSED

1 CAN (11 OZ) **VACUUM-PACKED CORN**, **OR 3 EARS FRESH CORN**, KERNELS CUT FROM COBS

3 TBSP **CHILI POWDER**

1 TBSP **GROUND CUMIN**

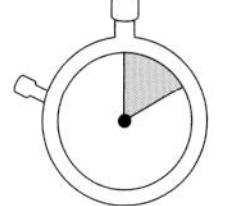

YIELD
6 servings

ACTIVE
10 minutes

TOTAL
40 minutes

SERVE WITH
Baked tortilla chips

Heat oil in a 4-qt pot over medium-high heat.

Add chiles, onion, zucchini and garlic; sauté 4 to 5 minutes until just tender.

Add remaining ingredients; bring to a boil. Reduce heat and simmer, uncovered, 30 minutes to blend flavors.

PER SERVING
CALORIES 284 **TOTAL FAT** 9G **SATURATED FAT** 1G **CHOLESTEROL** 0MG **SODIUM** 747MG
TOTAL CARBOHYDRATES 41G **DIETARY FIBER** 9G **PROTEIN** 17G

SPAGHETTI SQUASH WITH CHUNKY SAUCE

1 **SPAGHETTI SQUASH** (4½ LB)

1 PKG (1¼ LB) **ITALIAN TURKEY SAUSAGES**, REMOVED FROM CASINGS

2 MEDIUM **ZUCCHINI**, QUARTERED LENGTHWISE, CUT CROSSWISE IN ¾-IN.-THICK SLICES

1 SMALL **ONION**, CHOPPED

1 TSP CHOPPED **GARLIC**

1 CAN (28 OZ) **DICED TOMATOES**

¼ CUP **BASIL LEAVES**, THINLY SLICED

½ CUP **GRATED PARMESAN**

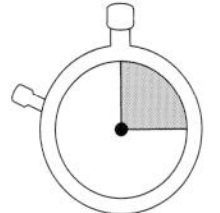

YIELD
6 servings

ACTIVE
15 minutes

TOTAL
30 minutes

Prick squash in a few places. Microwave on high 10 minutes; turn over. Microwave 5 to 10 minutes more until tender when pierced.

Meanwhile, coat a nonstick skillet with nonstick spray. Heat over medium-high heat. Add sausage and cook, breaking up clumps, 5 minutes or until no longer pink.

Add zucchini, onion and garlic; sauté 4 minutes. Add tomatoes, reduce heat and simmer, uncovered, 5 minutes or until hot. Remove from heat; stir in basil.

Cut squash in half. Discard seeds and loosen strands with a fork. Scrape strands into a large bowl; top with the sauce. Top servings with cheese.

PER SERVING
CALORIES 161 **TOTAL FAT** 4G **SATURATED FAT** 2G **CHOLESTEROL** 6MG **SODIUM** 411MG **TOTAL CARBOHYDRATES** 26G **DIETARY FIBER** 6G **PROTEIN** 7G

OPEN-FACE SAUSAGE & PEPPER SANDWICHES

3 **BELL PEPPERS**, CORED AND CUT IN ½-IN.-WIDE STRIPS

2 MEDIUM **RED ONIONS**, CUT IN ½-IN. WEDGES

¼ CUP **BALSAMIC VINAIGRETTE DRESSING**

1 LB **FRESH ITALIAN CHICKEN** OR **TURKEY SAUSAGE**, CUT IN 2-IN. PIECES

1 LONG **LOAF ITALIAN OR FRENCH BREAD**

1 TBSP **OLIVE OIL**

½ TSP **DRIED OREGANO**

½ CUP **SHREDDED MOZZARELLA**

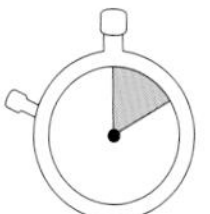

YIELD
4 servings

ACTIVE
10 minutes

TOTAL
25 minutes

Heat oven to 500°F. Line 2 rimmed baking sheets with nonstick foil.

Spread peppers and onions in one pan; drizzle with 3 Tbsp vinaigrette and toss to coat. Place sausage in other pan, drizzle with remaining vinaigrette and toss to coat. Roast 10 minutes or until sausage is cooked through.

Meanwhile, split bread lengthwise, leaving 1 long side attached (like a hinge). Open loaf. Brush cut sides with olive oil, then sprinkle with oregano and cheese.

Remove both pans from oven. Toss peppers and onions and return to oven; place bread cut sides up on oven rack.

Roast 5 minutes or until bread is lightly toasted and vegetables are tender and slightly charred.

Top bread with vegetables and sausage. Cut loaf in quarters. Eat sandwich with fork and knife.

PER SERVING
CALORIES 584 **TOTAL FAT** 26G **SATURATED FAT** 7G **CHOLESTEROL** 72MG **SODIUM** 1,478MG
TOTAL CARBOHYDRATES 59G **DIETARY FIBER** 5G **PROTEIN** 31G

SUPER CHEF'S SALAD

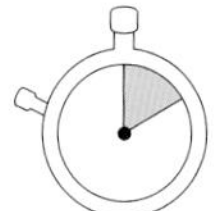

YIELD
4 servings

ACTIVE
10 minutes

TOTAL
15 minutes

2 LARGE **EGGS**

2 **ROMAINE HEARTS**, CUT IN THICK SHREDS

1 CAN (15 TO 16 OZ) **CHICKPEAS**, RINSED AND DRAINED

1 MEDIUM **CUCUMBER**, SLICED

2 **PLUM TOMATOES**, CUT IN WEDGES

1 CUP SHREDDED **CHEDDAR**

4 OZ FULLY COOKED **HAM**, CUT IN STRIPS

SERVE WITH
Warm whole-grain bread or rolls, your favorite dressing

Bring eggs (and water to cover) to a simmer in a small saucepan. Simmer 1 minute. Remove saucepan from heat; cover and let stand 10 minutes. Drain and rinse with cold water. Peel eggs and cut into wedges.

Put romaine in a large salad bowl. Top with eggs and mounds of remaining ingredients.

PER SERVING
CALORIES 336 **TOTAL FAT** 14G **SATURATED FAT** 7G **CHOLESTEROL** 148MG **SODIUM** 728MG **TOTAL CARBOHYDRATES** 31G **DIETARY FIBER** 6G **PROTEIN** 22G

CRISPY PARMESAN CHICKEN TENDERS

YIELD
4 servings

ACTIVE
5 minutes

TOTAL
20 minutes

1 LARGE **EGG**

3 TBSP **BUTTER**, MELTED

30 **ROUND BUTTERY CRACKERS**, CRUSHED (1 CUP)

¼ TSP EACH **PAPRIKA**, **PEPPER** AND **SALT**

3 TBSP **GRATED PARMESAN**

1 LB **CHICKEN TENDERS**

SIDE SUGGESTION
Sautéed grape tomatoes with garlic and fresh basil

Heat oven to 400°F. Line a rimmed baking sheet with foil (for easy cleanup); coat foil with nonstick spray.

Put egg in shallow bowl; beat lightly with a fork. Put melted butter in another shallow bowl. Mix crushed crackers, paprika, pepper and salt on a sheet of wax paper; spread Parmesan on another sheet.

Dip tenders in egg, then cracker mixture to coat, then dip 1 side in melted butter, then Parmesan. Place cheese side up on lined pan.

Bake 12 to 15 minutes or until tenders are golden and cooked through.

PER SERVING
CALORIES 358 **TOTAL FAT** 18G **SATURATED FAT** 8G **CHOLESTEROL** 145MG **SODIUM** 593MG
TOTAL CARBOHYDRATES 15G **DIETARY FIBER** 18G **PROTEIN** 31G

SKIRT STEAK & ONION QUESADILLAS WITH BLACK BEAN SALAD

QUESADILLAS

ONE 12-OZ **SKIRT STEAK**

½ TSP **GROUND CUMIN**

½ TSP **SALT**

½ TSP **PEPPER**

2 MEDIUM **RED ONIONS**, SLICED ¼ IN. THICK

NONSTICK SPRAY

8 FAJITA-SIZE **FLOUR TORTILLAS**

1 CUP **SHREDDED PEPPERJACK CHEESE**

¾ CUP **CILANTRO** SPRIGS

BLACK BEAN SALAD

1 CAN (15 OZ) **BLACK BEANS**, RINSED

1 PT **GRAPE TOMATOES**

1 CAN (7 OZ) **VACUUM-PACKED CORN**

¼ CUP SLICED **SCALLIONS**

¼ CUP **OLIVE OIL AND VINEGAR DRESSING**

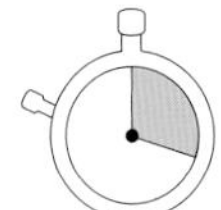

YIELD
4 servings

ACTIVE
18 minutes

TOTAL
35 minutes

QUESADILLAS Heat outdoor grill. Rub steak with cumin, salt and pepper. Coat steak and onions with nonstick spray.

Grill 5 to 6 minutes, turning once, until steak is medium-rare and onions are lightly charred and crisp-tender. Remove to a cutting board; let stand 3 minutes. Leave grill on.

Meanwhile, coat one side of tortillas with nonstick spray. Turn over; sprinkle bottom halves with cheese; top cheese with cilantro.

Slice steak thinly across the grain. Top cheese on tortillas with steak and onions. Fold top half over filling.

Grill 3 minutes, turning once, until lightly charred and cheese melts.

SALAD Mix ingredients. Serve with quesadillas.

PER SERVING
CALORIES 685 **TOTAL FAT** 32G **SATURATED FAT** 11G **CHOLESTEROL** 68MG **SODIUM** 1,408MG
TOTAL CARBOHYDRATES 68G **DIETARY FIBER** 8G **PROTEIN** 34G

SHRIMP WITH CHESAPEAKE DIPPING SAUCE

YIELD
4 servings

ACTIVE
3 minutes

TOTAL
6 minutes

1¼ LB LARGE **RAW EASY-TO-PEEL CLEANED SHRIMP**

¼ CUP **WASABI HORSERADISH MAYONNAISE**

3 TBSP **NO-SALT-ADDED KETCHUP**

SIDE SUGGESTION
New potato salad, corn on the cob

Fill a 2-qt saucepan halfway with water. Lightly salt, and bring to a boil. Add shrimp, reduce heat to medium-low, cover and cook 4 to 5 minutes until shrimp turn pink and are opaque at centers. Drain well.

Meanwhile mix mayonnaise and ketchup in a small bowl as a dipping sauce for the shrimp. Serve with lemon wedges and/or hot pepper sauce, if desired.

PER SERVING
CALORIES 183 **TOTAL FAT** 7G **SATURATED FAT** 1G **CHOLESTEROL** 184MG **SODIUM** 277MG **TOTAL CARBOHYDRATES** 5G **DIETARY FIBER** 0G **PROTEIN** 23G

LINGUINE & GARLIC OIL

1 LB **LINGUINE PASTA**

⅓ CUP **EXTRA-VIRGIN OLIVE OIL**

3 LARGE CLOVES **GARLIC**, FINELY CHOPPED

½ TSP **SALT**

¼ TSP **CRUSHED RED PEPPER**

¼ CUP FINELY CHOPPED **ITALIAN PARSLEY**

1½ TBSP **BUTTER**, SOFTENED

1 TSP FINELY GRATED **LEMON ZEST**

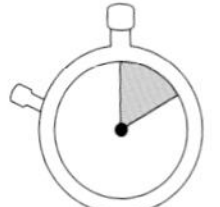

YIELD
6 servings

ACTIVE
10 minutes

TOTAL
25 minutes

SIDE SUGGESTION
Romaine lettuce, roasted pepper, artichoke heart and cannellini beans salad

Cook pasta in a large pot of lightly salted boiling water as package directs.

Meanwhile, gently heat next 4 ingredients in a covered pan over very low heat just until garlic is soft.

Remove ¾ cup pasta cooking water. Drain pasta; transfer to serving bowl. Toss with oil mixture, the water and remaining ingredients.

PER SERVING
CALORIES 416 **TOTAL FAT** 16G **SATURATED FAT** 4G **CHOLESTEROL** 8MG **SODIUM** 487MG
TOTAL CARBOHYDRATES 58G **DIETARY FIBER** 2G **PROTEIN** 10G

CHICKEN BREASTS WITH LEMON & PEPPER

YIELD
4 servings

ACTIVE
5 minutes

TOTAL
17 minutes

4 **BONELESS, SKINLESS CHICKEN-BREASTS** (ABOUT 5 OZ EACH)

½ TSP **SALT**

2 TBSP **BUTTER** *OR* **MARGARINE**

1 TBSP **FRESH LEMON JUICE**

FRESH **COARSELY GROUND PEPPER**

1½ TBSP FINELY CHOPPED **PARSLEY**

SIDE SUGGESTION
Couscous, steamed green beans

Place chicken breasts between 2 sheets of wax paper and gently pound with a meat mallet or bottom of a heavy skillet until about ½ in. thick. Season with salt.

Heat butter in a large, heavy nonstick skillet over medium heat until bubbly and starting to brown. Add chicken and cook about 10 minutes, turning occasionally, or until almost opaque in center and golden on both sides. Remove to serving plates.

Remove skillet from heat and let pan juices cool briefly. Add lemon juice, and stir to loosen brown drippings in bottom of pan. Spoon over chicken, season well with pepper, then sprinkle with parsley.

PROSCIUTTO VARIATION Proceed as directed, until chicken is cooked. Sprinkle chicken with 2 Tbsp freshly grated lemon zest and coarsely ground pepper to taste. Drape each breast half with a very thin slice of prosciutto or other salt-cured ham. Sprinkle with 3 Tbsp finely chopped parsley.

PER SERVING
CALORIES 214 **TOTAL FAT** 9G **SATURATED FAT** 4G **CHOLESTEROL** 106MG **SODIUM** 497MG **TOTAL CARBOHYDRATES** 0G **DIETARY FIBER** 0G **PROTEIN** 30G

STIR-FRIED BEEF WITH BROCCOLI & ORANGES

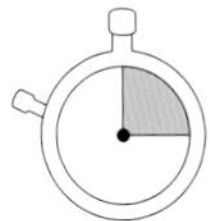

YIELD
4 servings

ACTIVE
15 minutes

TOTAL
33 minutes

1 BUNCH **BROCCOLI** (ABOUT 1¼ LB), STEMS PEELED AND CUT IN ½-IN. PIECES, FLORETS SEPARATED

3 LARGE **NAVEL ORANGES**

3 TSP **VEGETABLE OIL**

12 OZ **BEEF TOP ROUND FOR LONDON BROIL**, SLICED THINLY ON THE DIAGONAL, THEN CUT IN BITE-SIZE STRIPS

½ CUP **BOTTLED STIR-FRY SAUCE**

SIDE SUGGESTION
Brown rice with toasted almonds

Add broccoli to a large pot of lightly salted boiling water. Cook 3 to 5 minutes or until crisp-tender. Drain well.

Squeeze juice from 1 orange into a medium bowl. With a sharp knife, cut peel and white membrane (pith) from remaining 2 oranges. Holding oranges, cut between membranes to release sections. Squeeze juice from membranes into bowl. (You should have ½ cup juice.)

Heat 1 tsp of the oil in a large nonstick skillet over high heat. Add beef in batches and stir-fry until brown, taking care not to crowd skillet and adding remaining oil as needed. Remove beef to a bowl.

Add stir-fry sauce, orange juice and broccoli to skillet. Stir over medium heat 2 to 3 minutes until liquid is slightly reduced and broccoli is hot. Stir in beef and orange sections; cook 1 minute to heat through.

PER SERVING
CALORIES 293 **TOTAL FAT** 12G **SATURATED FAT** 0G **CHOLESTEROL** 52MG **SODIUM** 787MG
TOTAL CARBOHYDRATES 31G **DIETARY FIBER** 0G **PROTEIN** 24G

MUSTARD SALMON

YIELD
5 servings

ACTIVE
5 minutes

TOTAL
15 minutes

1 **SALMON FILLET** (1½ LB), CUT INTO 5 EQUAL PIECES

¼ CUP **COARSE-GRAIN MUSTARD**

2 TBSP **PURE MAPLE SYRUP OR MAPLE-FLAVORED PANCAKE SYRUP**

SIDE SUGGESTION
Steamed new potatoes, sautéed spinach with garlic

Heat oven to 450°F. Line a rimmed baking sheet with foil. Place salmon pieces 1 in. apart, skin side down, on baking sheet.

Stir mustard and maple syrup in small bowl until blended; spoon evenly on salmon.

Bake 10 minutes or until salmon is opaque in center.

PER SERVING
CALORIES 194 **TOTAL FAT** 5G **SATURATED FAT** 1G **CHOLESTEROL** 64MG **SODIUM** 356MG **TOTAL CARBOHYDRATES** 8G **DIETARY FIBER** 0G **PROTEIN** 27G

GRILLED EGGPLANT PARMESAN PIZZAS

4 **BABY EGGPLANTS** (ABOUT 5 OZ EACH), CUT CROSSWISE IN ½-IN.-THICK SLICES

4 **POCKETLESS PITAS**

OLIVE-OIL NONSTICK SPRAY

1 CUP **BOTTLED MARINARA SAUCE**

1 CUP **PART-SKIM RICOTTA**

1 CUP **SHREDDED PART-SKIM MOZZARELLA**

2 TBSP **GRATED PARMESAN**

GARNISH: CHOPPED **FRESH BASIL LEAVES**

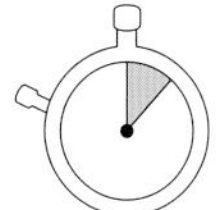

YIELD
4 servings

ACTIVE
7 minutes

TOTAL
23 minutes

SIDE SUGGESTION
Mixed baby greens salad

Heat outdoor grill. Coat eggplant and pitas with nonstick spray.

Grill eggplant 10 minutes or until tender, turning as needed; remove. Grill pitas 1 minute or until bottoms are lightly charred. Remove to a platter; spread grilled sides with the sauce, then top with eggplant, dollops of ricotta, mozzarella and Parmesan.

Return to grill. Cover and grill 1 to 2 minutes until cheeses melt. Remove; cut each in 4 wedges. Garnish with basil.

PER SERVING
CALORIES 427 **TOTAL FAT** 15G **SATURATED FAT** 7G **CHOLESTEROL** 37MG **SODIUM** 976MG
TOTAL CARBOHYDRATES 53G **DIETARY FIBER** 4G **PROTEIN** 23G

BABY-BACK RIBS WITH TEXAS BLACKJACK SAUCE & PEACH COLESLAW

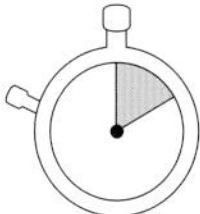

YIELD
4 servings

ACTIVE
10 minutes

TOTAL
1 hour

3 LB **BABY-BACK RIBS**, CUT INTO 4 SECTIONS

1 BOTTLE (18 OZ) **BARBECUE SAUCE** (1½ CUPS; WE USED CATTLEMAN'S CLASSIC)

3 TBSP **BROWN SUGAR**

2 TBSP **INSTANT COFFEE**

2 TBSP **WORCESTERSHIRE SAUCE**

PEACH COLESLAW

¼ CUP **SLAW DRESSING**

1 TBSP **DIJON MUSTARD**

4 CUPS **COLESLAW MIX**

2 RIPE MEDIUM **PEACHES**, CHOPPED

½ CUP CHOPPED **RED BELL PEPPER**

SIDE SUGGESTION
Grilled corn on the cob

Put ribs in large pot with just enough water to cover. Bring to a boil, reduce heat, cover and simmer 45 minutes, or until meat is fork-tender.

Meanwhile, mix barbecue sauce, sugar, coffee and Worcestershire sauce in a small saucepan. Heat over medium heat, stirring until sugar and coffee dissolve. Remove from heat.

COLESLAW Stir dressing and mustard in a large bowl; add coleslaw mix, peaches and red pepper; toss to mix. Refrigerate until serving.

Coat outdoor grill rack with nonstick spray. Heat grill. Place ribs, rounded side down, on rack. Brush with sauce; grill 3 minutes. Turn ribs. Brush with sauce; grill 6 minutes more. Turn ribs again. Brush with sauce; grill another 3 minutes.

Serve with rest of sauce and coleslaw. Ribs and sauce can be prepared one day ahead. Cover and refrigerate until ready to grill.

PER SERVING
CALORIES 880 **TOTAL FAT** 57G **SATURATED FAT** 19G **CHOLESTEROL** 204MG **SODIUM** 1,341MG
TOTAL CARBOHYDRATES 46G **DIETARY FIBER** 2G **PROTEIN** 45G

AUGUST

AUGUST SHOPPING LIST

Week 1
AUGUST 1 TO AUGUST 7

PRODUCE
4 LARGE NAVEL ORANGES
3 LEMONS
2 SMALL RED ONIONS
1 HEAD GARLIC (3 CLOVES)
3 RIPE PLUM TOMATOES
1 LB CARROTS
1 LARGE CUCUMBER
1 LB ZUCCHINI
1 HEAD LETTUCE
1 BAG (5 OR 6 OZ) BABY SPINACH
10 SCALLIONS
1 BUNCH CILANTRO
FRESH OREGANO

BAKERY
4 BURGER BUNS
4 KAISER OR OTHER HARD ROLLS

MEAT/POULTRY/FISH
1½ LB LONDON BROIL (ABOUT 1¼ IN. THICK)
12 OZ PORK CUTLETS
4 BONELESS, SKINLESS CHICKEN BREASTS (ABOUT 6 OZ EACH)
FOUR 3-OZ CHICKEN-BREAST CUTLETS
1¼ LB GROUND TURKEY
FOUR 6-OZ MAHI-MAHI OR HALIBUT FILLETS (ABOUT 1 IN. THICK)

REFRIGERATED
2 STICKS UNSALTED BUTTER
1 CONTAINER (8 OZ) REDUCED-FAT SOUR CREAM
2 OZ CRUMBLED FETA CHEESE
1 BLOCK PARMESAN
EGGS (1 LARGE)
½ CUP BASIL PESTO

GROCERY
1 JAR (16 OZ) SALSA
1 BOX (1 LB) SPAGHETTI
1 BOX (5.7 OZ) MEDITERRANEAN CURRY COUSCOUS
BALSAMIC VINAIGRETTE DRESSING
SEASONED STIR-FRY OIL
1 PACKET (1.13 OZ) MCCORMICK GRILL MATES CHIPOTLE PEPPER MARINADE
KALAMATA OLIVES
SLICED ALMONDS (OPTIONAL)
HONEY
BAKED TORTILLA CHIPS

PANTRY
SALT
PEPPER
OLIVE OIL
NONSTICK COOKING SPRAY
RICE-WINE VINEGAR OR CIDER VINEGAR
DRIED OREGANO
CHILI POWDER
GROUND CUMIN

Week 2
AUGUST 8 TO AUGUST 14

PRODUCE
1 SMALL PINEAPPLE
5 LIMES
4 LEMONS
1 SMALL ONION
1 LARGE SWEET ONION
1 RED ONION
1 SHALLOT
1 HEAD GARLIC (4 CLOVES)
4 LARGE SWEET POTATOES (ABOUT 12 OZ EACH)
5 TOMATOES
8 OZ ASPARAGUS
1 BAG (10 OZ) CUT-UP HEARTS OF ROMAINE LETTUCE, OR 8 CUPS TORN ROMAINE
1 BAG (5 TO 6 OZ) BABY SPINACH
2 SCALLIONS
1 BUNCH CILANTRO
1 BUNCH ITALIAN PARSLEY
FRESH THYME

DELI
ONE 1-LB PRECOOKED HAM STEAK

MEAT/POULTRY/FISH
1 LB SKIRT STEAK
12 OZ THIN-CUT BONELESS PORK CHOPS
6 BONELESS, SKINLESS CHICKEN BREASTS (2¼ LB)
4 BONELESS, SKINLESS CHICKEN BREASTS (ABOUT 6 OZ EACH)
4 TILAPIA FILLETS (6 TO 7 OZ EACH)

REFRIGERATED
1 CUP PLAIN NONFAT OR LOWFAT YOGURT
¾ CUP BASIL PESTO
1 BAG (12 OZ) VEGETABLE MEDLEY (BROCCOLI, BABY CARROTS AND CAULIFLOWER)

GROCERY
1 CAN (8 OZ) PINEAPPLE SLICES
1 CAN (19 OZ) CHICKPEAS
1 JAR (3 OZ) CAPERS
2 TSP JALAPEÑO HOT SAUCE
STIR-FRY SAUCE
1 BOTTLE (8 OZ) LIGHT OIL AND VINEGAR DRESSING
12 OZ RIGATONI
¼ CUP MCCORMICK GRILL MATES MESQUITE SPICE RUB
HONEY

PANTRY
SALT
PEPPER
EXTRA-VIRGIN OLIVE OIL
DIJON MUSTARD
GROUND CUMIN
GROUND CORIANDER
GROUND ALLSPICE
PAPRIKA
CRUSHED RED PEPPER
CAYENNE PEPPER

Week 3
AUGUST 15 TO AUGUST 22

PRODUCE
1 LARGE RIPE NECTARINE

1 SMALL ONION
2 MEDIUM SWEET ONIONS
1 SHALLOT
1 HEAD GARLIC (2 CLOVES)
1 PIECE FRESH GINGER
1 SMALL POTATO
1½ LB RED-SKINNED POTATOES
3 PLUM TOMATOES
2 PT GRAPE OR CHERRY TOMATOES
1 BELL PEPPER
1 CUCUMBER
1 CORN ON THE COB
1 BUNCH ASPARAGUS (ABOUT 1 LB)
1 SMALL HEAD ICEBERG LETTUCE
12 SCALLIONS
1 BAG (5 OZ) BABY ARUGULA
1 BUNCH BASIL
1 BUNCH CILANTRO

BAKERY
BREAD (FOR 1 CUP FRESH BREAD CRUMBS, OPTIONAL)
4 PITA POCKETS
2 SLICES FLATBREAD OR POCKETLESS PITAS

MEAT/POULTRY/FISH
ONE 1½-LB FLANK STEAK
1¼ LB 80%-LEAN GROUND BEEF
4 TRIMMED ¾-IN.-THICK RIB OR LOIN PORK CHOPS (ABOUT 7 OZ EACH)
2 CUPS SHREDDED COOKED CHICKEN
1 LB FLOUNDER OR SOLE FILLETS

DELI
8 SLICES (4 OZ) DELI-THIN SLICED SMOKED TURKEY
1 LB DELI COLESLAW

REFRIGERATED
½ GALLON MILK
½ CUP CRUMBLED RICOTTA SALATA OR FETA
¼ CUP LITE GARLIC AND HERBS SPREADABLE CHEESE
4 SLICES PASTEURIZED PROCESS CHEDDAR (SUCH AS DELI DELUXE)
1 BAG (8 OZ) CLASSIC MELTS 4-CHEESE BLEND (KRAFT)
1 BAG (8 OZ) SHREDDED CHEDDAR
GRATED PARMESAN (OPTIONAL)
EGGS (1 LARGE)

GROCERY
1 CAN (14 OZ) CHICKEN BROTH
1 CAN (15.5 OZ) GREAT NORTHERN BEANS
1 JAR (12 OZ) MEDIUM-HEAT CHIPOTLE SALSA OR REGULAR SALSA
1 JAR (6 OZ) MARINATED ARTICHOKE HEARTS
PITTED KALAMATA OLIVES
½ CUP TARTAR SAUCE
1 LB CAVATAPPI OR OTHER SHORT PASTA
12 OZ WHOLE-WHEAT PENNE PASTA
LIGHT MAYONNAISE
BARBECUE SAUCE
HONEY-DIJON DRESSING
LITE SOY SAUCE
DARK ORIENTAL SESAME OIL
12 TACO SHELLS
1¼ CUPS BAKED POTATO CHIPS

PANTRY
SALT
PEPPER
EXTRA-VIRGIN OLIVE OIL
DIJON MUSTARD
FLOUR
BROWN SUGAR
GROUND CUMIN
CHILI POWDER
ONION POWDER
PAPRIKA

Week 4

AUGUST 23 TO AUGUST 31

PRODUCE
1 NAVEL ORANGE
3 LEMONS
3 LARGE ONIONS
1 MEDIUM ONION
1 RED ONION
2 SHALLOTS
2 HEADS GARLIC (11 CLOVES)
1 PIECE FRESH GINGER
1½ LB ALL-PURPOSE POTATOES
1 LARGE PLUM TOMATO
2 CARROTS
1 YELLOW OR RED BELL PEPPER
2 SMALL BELL PEPPERS
3 CUBANELLE PEPPERS (ITALIAN FRYING PEPPERS)
2 LARGE OR 4 SMALL ZUCCHINI (14 OZ)
1 LB MIXED SUMMER SQUASH (ZUCCHINI, YELLOW SQUASH AND PATTYPAN)
1½ LB ASPARAGUS
4 OZ SNOW PEAS
1 LARGE LEEK
1 LB BOK CHOY
1 BAG (10 OZ) FRESH SPINACH
1 BUNCH SCALLIONS
1 BUNCH FRESH MINT OR PARSLEY
1 BUNCH BASIL
1 BUNCH MINT
1 BUNCH CILANTRO
FRESH THYME OR MARJORAM

BAKERY
4 HAMBURGER ROLLS

MEAT/POULTRY/FISH
ONE 12-OZ BONELESS SIRLOIN STEAK
2 LAMB LEG CENTER STEAKS (ABOUT 12 OZ EACH)
5 CHICKEN THIGHS (1½ LB)
8 OZ SKINLESS SALMON FILLET (¾ TO 1 IN. THICK)
1 LB RAW MEDIUM SHRIMP

DELI
8 OZ CHUNK OF HAM

REFRIGERATED
HEAVY (WHIPPING) CREAM
½ STICK BUTTER
1 CONTAINER (8 OZ) REDUCED-FAT SOUR CREAM
4 OZ ROQUEFORT, GORGONZOLA OR OTHER GOOD-QUALITY BLUE CHEESE
EGGS (9 LARGE)
1 REFRIGERATED PIE CRUST (FROM A 15-OZ BOX OF TWO)
1 BOX (10 OZ) SOY VEGGIE PATTIES

GROCERY
1 CAN (14.5 OZ) REDUCED-SODIUM CHICKEN BROTH
2 CANS (ABOUT 15 OZ EACH) REDUCED-SODIUM BLACK BEANS
1 CAN (15 OZ) YELLOW OR WHITE HOMINY
1 CAN (14.5 OZ) MEXICAN-STYLE DICED TOMATOES
1 CAN (10 OZ) MILD GREEN ENCHILADA SAUCE
1 JAR (2 OZ) SLICED PIMIENTOS
½ CUP PITTED KALAMATA OLIVES
¼ CUP TOMATO SALSA
12 OZ FETTUCCINE PASTA
12 OZ FARFALLE PASTA
LONG-GRAIN RICE
1 BOX (5.6 OZ) TOASTED PINE NUT COUSCOUS
1 BOTTLE BALSAMIC VINAIGRETTE DRESSING
LESS-SODIUM SOY SAUCE (SUCH AS HOUSE OF TSANG)
CHOPPED ALMONDS
1 BAG (5 OZ) POTPOURRI POTATO CHIPS (BY TERRA) OR REGULAR POTATO CHIPS

PANTRY
SALT
PEPPER
OLIVE OIL
EXTRA-VIRGIN OLIVE OIL
CANOLA OIL
RED-WINE VINEGAR
NONSTICK SPRAY
CORNSTARCH
GROUND CUMIN
DRIED OREGANO

GRILLED CHIPOTLE LONDON BROIL

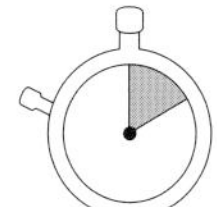

YIELD
6 servings

ACTIVE
10 minutes

TOTAL
4 hours 30 minutes
(includes marinating)

1 PACKET (1.13 OZ) **MCCORMICK GRILL MATES CHIPOTLE PEPPER MARINADE**

1 STICK (½ CUP) **UNSALTED BUTTER**, SOFTENED

¼ CUP **OIL**

¼ CUP **WATER**

1½ LB **LONDON BROIL** (ABOUT 1¼ IN. THICK)

SIDE SUGGESTION
Corn on the cob, sliced beefsteak tomatoes

Mix 2 tsp marinade mix with butter in a medium bowl until thoroughly blended; refrigerate. Or if desired, spoon onto a sheet of wax paper or plastic wrap and roll into a log; refrigerate.

Combine remaining marinade mix, oil and water in a large ziptop bag. Add London broil, turning to coat; marinate in refrigerator at least 4 hours or overnight.

Remove butter from refrigerator. Heat outdoor grill or stovetop grill pan. Remove meat from marinade. Grill 2 to 3 minutes per side for medium-rare. Serve with seasoned butter.

DIFFERENT TAKES

- Add chopped cilantro to butter with marinade mix.
- Add 1 tsp grated lime zest to butter mixture; add 2 Tbsp lime juice to the marinade.
- Use a packet of McCormick Peppercorn & Garlic Marinade instead. Prepare as above, adding 2 Tbsp balsamic vinegar to marinade.

PER SERVING
CALORIES 326 **TOTAL FAT** 25G **SATURATED FAT** 13G **CHOLESTEROL** 79MG **SODIUM** 396MG **TOTAL CARBOHYDRATES** 1G **DIETARY FIBER** 0G **PROTEIN** 24G

SPAGHETTI WITH SHAVED VEGGIES

- 1 LB **ZUCCHINI**, ENDS TRIMMED
- 1 LB **CARROTS**, PEELED
- 1 BOX (1 LB) **SPAGHETTI PASTA**
- 5 TBSP **UNSALTED BUTTER**, CUT UP
- 2 CLOVES **GARLIC**, MINCED
- 1 TBSP GRATED **LEMON ZEST**
- 1 TBSP **LEMON JUICE**
- ½ TSP **SALT**
- ¼ TSP FRESHLY GROUND **PEPPER**
- SHAVED **PARMESAN**

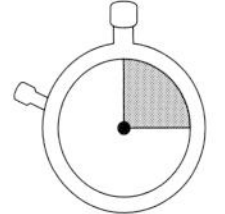

YIELD
5 servings

ACTIVE
15 minutes

TOTAL
25 minutes

SIDE SUGGESTION
Mixed greens salad

Bring a 5- to 6-qt pot of salted water to a boil. Meanwhile, if zucchini are long, halve crosswise. Using a vegetable peeler, shave zucchini and carrots into ribbons.

Cook pasta until al dente as package directs. Add zucchini and carrot shavings to the pasta pot. Cook 1 minute or until vegetables are just tender. Remove and reserve 1 cup pasta cooking water, then drain pasta mixture.

Meanwhile, melt butter in same pot used to cook pasta. Add garlic; cook 30 seconds. Remove from heat.

Return pasta and vegetables to pot. Add lemon zest and juice, salt and pepper; toss. Add enough reserved pasta water to create a thin sauce. Top with Parmesan.

PER SERVING
CALORIES 488 **TOTAL FAT** 13G **SATURATED FAT** 8G **CHOLESTEROL** 31MG **SODIUM** 399MG
TOTAL CARBOHYDRATES 79G **DIETARY FIBER** 6G **PROTEIN** 16G

ORANGE CHICKEN WITH WILTED SPINACH SALAD

4 LARGE **NAVEL ORANGES**

¼ CUP **OLIVE OIL**

2 TBSP **RICE-WINE VINEGAR** *OR* **CIDER VINEGAR**

1 TBSP **HONEY**

¼ TSP EACH **SALT** AND **PEPPER**

4 **BONELESS, SKINLESS CHICKEN BREASTS** (ABOUT 6 OZ EACH)

1 SMALL **RED ONION**, HALVED AND SLICED

1 BAG (5 OR 6 OZ) **BABY SPINACH**

GARNISH: TOASTED **SLICED ALMONDS** (OPTIONAL)

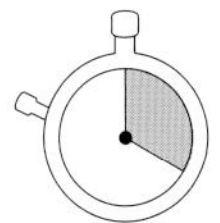

YIELD
4 servings

ACTIVE
20 minutes

TOTAL
35 minutes

Squeeze juice from 1 orange (you should have ½ cup). Whisk orange juice, 3 Tbsp oil, vinegar, honey, salt and pepper in small bowl. Place 5 Tbsp juice mixture into a large ziptop bag. Add chicken, seal bag and marinate at room temperature 15 minutes or in refrigerator 2 hours.

Meanwhile, remove peel and white pith from remaining 3 oranges. Cut into segments; place in medium bowl.

Heat stovetop grill pan over medium heat. Remove chicken from marinade; discard bag and marinade. Grill chicken 4 to 5 minutes per side until cooked through; remove to plate and cover to keep warm.

Heat remaining 1 Tbsp oil in a medium skillet over medium-high heat. Sauté onion 1 minute, add remaining juice mixture and cook 1 minute more. Remove skillet from heat; add orange segments.

Place spinach in a large bowl; toss with half the orange mixture. Evenly divide spinach onto serving plates; place a chicken breast on top of each. Spoon remaining orange mixture on top; sprinkle with almonds, if desired.

NOTE The oranges enhance the iron absorption from spinach.

PER SERVING
CALORIES 404 **TOTAL FAT** 13G **SATURATED FAT** 3G **CHOLESTEROL** 70MG **SODIUM** 297MG
TOTAL CARBOHYDRATES 26G **DIETARY FIBER** 5G **PROTEIN** 37G

GREEK LEMON & OREGANO MAHI-MAHI

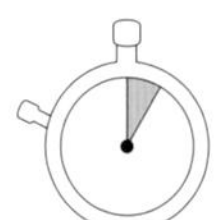

YIELD
4 servings

ACTIVE
5 minutes

TOTAL
23 minutes

1/4 CUP **LEMON JUICE**

1 1/2 TBSP **OLIVE OIL**

1/2 TSP **DRIED OREGANO**

1/4 TSP EACH **SALT** AND **PEPPER**

FOUR 6-OZ **MAHI-MAHI OR HALIBUT FILLETS** (ABOUT 1 IN. THICK)

FOUR 1/4-IN.-THICK SLICES **RED ONION**

NONSTICK COOKING SPRAY

GARNISH: GRILLED **LEMON WEDGES OR SLICES, KALAMATA OLIVES, FRESH OREGANO**

SIDE SUGGESTION
Orzo, sautéed spinach

Mix lemon juice, oil, oregano, salt and pepper in a pie plate or shallow bowl. Remove and reserve 1 Tbsp. Add fish to pie plate and turn to coat. Marinate 10 minutes.

Meanwhile, heat outdoor grill or stovetop grill pan. Coat onion with cooking spray. Grill 5 minutes, or until lightly charred and tender, turning once. Remove.

Grill fish 8 to 10 minutes, turning once, until just cooked through. Remove to serving platter and drizzle with reserved lemon juice mixture. Scatter onions on top. Garnish with lemon, olives and oregano.

PER SERVING
CALORIES 205 **TOTAL FAT** 6G **SATURATED FAT** 1G **CHOLESTEROL** 124MG **SODIUM** 296MG **TOTAL CARBOHYDRATES** 4G **DIETARY FIBER** 1G **PROTEIN** 32G

TEX-MEX TURKEY BURGERS

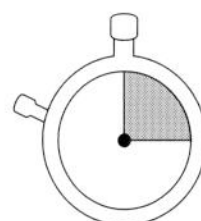

YIELD
4 servings

ACTIVE
15 minutes

TOTAL
30 minutes

1¼ LB **GROUND TURKEY**

¾ CUP CRUSHED **BAKED TORTILLA CHIPS**

¼ CUP SLICED **SCALLIONS**

½ CUP **WATER**

1 LARGE **EGG**

1 TSP MINCED **GARLIC**

1 TSP **CHILI POWDER**

1 TSP **GROUND CUMIN**

¼ TSP **SALT**

2 TSP **OIL**

4 **BURGER BUNS**

4 **LETTUCE LEAVES**

TOPPINGS: **SALSA** AND **REDUCED-FAT SOUR CREAM**

SIDE SUGGESTION
Baked tortilla chips, sliced avocados on lettuce

Mix turkey, chips, scallions, water, the egg, garlic, chili powder, cumin and salt in a large bowl until very well blended. Shape into 4 burgers.

Heat oil in a large nonstick skillet over medium heat. Fry burgers 12 to 15 minutes, turning occasionally, until no longer pink at center and internal temperature registers at least 165°F on a meat thermometer inserted from side to middle.

Serve on buns with lettuce. Top with salsa and sour cream.

PER SERVING
CALORIES 434 **TOTAL FAT** 18G **SATURATED FAT** 1G **CHOLESTEROL** 157MG **SODIUM** 632MG
TOTAL CARBOHYDRATES 36G **DIETARY FIBER** 2G **PROTEIN** 32G

CURRIED COUSCOUS WITH PORK

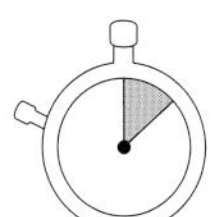

YIELD
4 servings

ACTIVE
8 minutes

TOTAL
16 minutes

1 TBSP BOTTLED **SEASONED STIR-FRY OIL**

12 OZ **PORK CUTLETS**, CUT DIAGONALLY IN ¾-IN.-WIDE STRIPS

1 LARGE **CUCUMBER**, HALVED, SEEDED AND SLICED (2½ CUPS)

1⅓ CUPS **WATER**

1 BOX (5.7 OZ) **MEDITERRANEAN CURRY COUSCOUS** (WITH SPICE PACKET)

¼ CUP FINELY CHOPPED **FRESH CILANTRO**

Heat stir-fry oil in a large nonstick skillet over medium-high heat. Add pork in 2 batches and stir-fry each batch 30 to 45 seconds until no longer pink. Remove to a bowl with a slotted spoon.

Add cucumber to skillet and stir-fry 45 seconds to 1 minute until crisp-tender. Add to bowl with pork; stir to mix. Cover loosely to keep warm.

Put the water and contents of spice packet (omit any olive oil or butter called for on packet) into same skillet. Bring to a boil, reduce heat to low, cover and simmer 2 minutes. Stir in couscous, cover, remove from heat and let stand 5 minutes. Fluff couscous lightly with fork.

Spoon pork and cucumber in center of serving platter. Surround with couscous and sprinkle with cilantro.

NOTE If your skillet has no lid, use a baking sheet or pizza pan as a cover.

PER SERVING
CALORIES 291 **TOTAL FAT** 9G **SATURATED FAT** 0G **CHOLESTEROL** 58MG **SODIUM** 379MG **TOTAL CARBOHYDRATES** 32G **DIETARY FIBER** 0G **PROTEIN** 23G

PESTO CHICKEN SANDWICHES WITH TOMATO-FETA SALAD

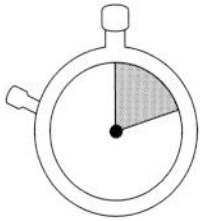

YIELD
4 servings

ACTIVE
12 minutes

TOTAL
12 minutes

3 RIPE **PLUM (ROMA) TOMATOES**, SLICED

½ CUP **CRUMBLED FETA CHEESE** (2 OZ)

⅓ CUP BOTTLED **BALSAMIC VINAIGRETTE DRESSING**

⅓ CUP SLICED **SCALLIONS**

FOUR 3-OZ **CHICKEN-BREAST CUTLETS**

½ CUP PURCHASED **REFRIGERATED BASIL PESTO**

4 **KAISER OR OTHER HARD ROLLS**, SPLIT

Heat barbecue grill (see Tip). Meanwhile, put tomatoes, cheese, dressing and scallions in a bowl and toss to mix. Set aside.

Brush cutlets lightly with 1 Tbsp pesto. Grill 3 to 4 minutes, turning once, until cooked through.

Spread rolls with remaining pesto. Place a cutlet on bottom of each. Top with tomato-feta salad; drizzle with dressing left in bowl. Cover with roll tops.

TIP If you don't have a grill but want your food to look and taste grilled, use a ridged grill pan. Most have a baked-on black finish that resists sticking and, when heated, leaves "grill" marks. The ridges also keep foods above any fat that may drip off. When the grill pan is hot, lightly coat it with oil before adding food. Stovetop grilling can be smoky, so turn on your stove's hood fan. You can make this sandwich lowfat by opting for reduced-fat feta cheese, vinaigrette salad dressing and basil pesto.

PER SERVING
CALORIES 521 **TOTAL FAT** 28G **SATURATED FAT** 6G **CHOLESTEROL** 67MG **SODIUM** 978MG
TOTAL CARBOHYDRATES 37G **DIETARY FIBER** 2G **PROTEIN** 31G

HAM WITH HAWAIIAN SALSA & SWEET POTATOES

SALSA

¼ **FRESH PINEAPPLE**, CORED AND FINELY DICED

½ **RED ONION**, FINELY DICED

2 TBSP CHOPPED **CILANTRO**

2 TSP FRESHLY GRATED **LIME ZEST**

1 TBSP **FRESH LIME JUICE**

¼ TSP **CRUSHED RED PEPPER**

¼ TSP **SALT**

SWEET POTATOES

2 TBSP **OIL**

½ TSP **SALT**

¼ TSP FRESHLY GROUND **PEPPER**

2 LARGE **SWEET POTATOES** (ABOUT 12 OZ EACH), EACH CUT IN 8 LONG WEDGES

HAM

1½ TSP **HONEY**

ONE 1-LB **PRECOOKED HAM STEAK**

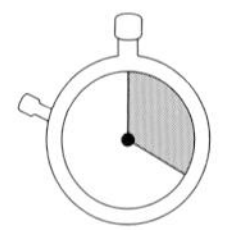

YIELD
4 servings

ACTIVE
20 minutes

TOTAL
50 minutes

SALSA Gently mix ingredients in a serving bowl.

Heat outdoor grill.

SWEET POTATOES Mix oil, salt and pepper in a large bowl. Add potatoes; stir to coat. Grill 30 minutes, turning wedges occasionally, until slightly charred and tender when pierced.

HAM Mix honey with 1 tsp water. Brush on ham. About 3 minutes before potatoes are done, add ham to grill. Grill, turning once, until hot and marked with grill lines. Serve with the salsa and sweet potatoes.

NOTE Grilling times given are approximate. If using a gas grill, bear in mind that when cooking food with the lid closed, even a quick peek can cool the grill enough to require an increase in cooking time.

PER SERVING
CALORIES 416 **TOTAL FAT** 18G **SATURATED FAT** 4G **CHOLESTEROL** 58MG **SODIUM** 1,797MG **TOTAL CARBOHYDRATES** 44G **DIETARY FIBER** 5G **PROTEIN** 20G

RIGATONI WITH PESTO & CHICKPEAS

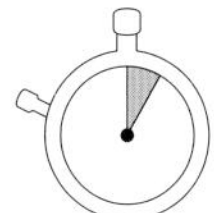

YIELD
4 servings

ACTIVE
5 minutes

TOTAL
20 minutes

12 OZ **RIGATONI**

1 CAN (19 OZ) **CHICKPEAS**, RINSED

¾ CUP **PREPARED BASIL PESTO**

GARNISH: **DICED TOMATOES** AND **ITALIAN PARSLEY**, CUT IN NARROW STRIPS

Bring a large pot of lightly salted water to a boil. Add pasta and cook as package directs, reserving ½ cup cooking water.

Meanwhile, process ¾ cup chickpeas and the pesto in a food processor until smooth, scraping down sides as needed. Slowly pour reserved ½ cup pasta cooking water through feed tube; process until creamy.

Set a colander in kitchen sink; put the remaining chickpeas in the colander and drain the pasta. Return pasta and chickpeas to pot. Add pesto mixture and toss to mix and coat. Serve immediately, topping with tomatoes and parsley.

PER SERVING
CALORIES 639 **TOTAL FAT** 26G **SATURATED FAT** 4G **CHOLESTEROL** 7MG **SODIUM** 484MG
TOTAL CARBOHYDRATES 81G **DIETARY FIBER** 6G **PROTEIN** 20G

YOGURT-GRILLED CHICKEN

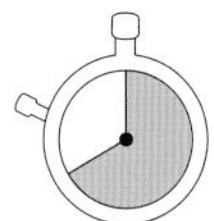

YIELD
6 servings

ACTIVE
40 minutes

TOTAL
47 minutes

YOGURT MARINADE

1 TSP **GROUND CUMIN**

½ TSP EACH **GROUND CORIANDER** AND **GROUND RED PEPPER** (CAYENNE)

⅛ TSP **GROUND ALLSPICE**

1 CUP **PLAIN NONFAT** OR **LOW-FAT YOGURT**

½ TSP FRESHLY GRATED **LEMON ZEST**

2 TBSP **FRESH LEMON JUICE**

2 TSP MINCED **GARLIC**

½ TSP **SALT**

6 **BONELESS**, **SKINLESS CHICKEN BREASTS** (2¼ LB)

SIDE SUGGESTION
Grilled sliced eggplant, rice pilaf

Put cumin, coriander, red pepper and allspice in a small saucepan. Stir over low heat 1 to 2 minutes until fragrant. (Take care not to burn spices.) Scrape into a medium bowl and stir in remaining marinade ingredients until blended.

Add chicken and gently stir to coat. Let stand at room temperature 30 minutes, or cover and refrigerate overnight.

Heat grill or broiler.

Remove chicken from marinade; discard marinade. Grill or broil 3 inches from heat source 3 to 4 minutes. Turn chicken over and broil 3 minutes longer or until opaque in middle. Serve hot or at room temperature.

PER SERVING
CALORIES 207 **TOTAL FAT** 2G **SATURATED FAT** 0G **CHOLESTEROL** 99MG **SODIUM** 271MG **TOTAL CARBOHYDRATES** 3G **DIETARY FIBER** 0G **PROTEIN** 41G

TILAPIA & VEGETABLE PACKETS

4 CUPS **BABY SPINACH**

4 **TILAPIA FILLETS** (6 TO 7 OZ EACH)

8 TSP **EXTRA-VIRGIN OLIVE OIL**

8 OZ THIN **ASPARAGUS**, TRIMMED AND CUT INTO LENGTHS ABOUT 2 IN. LONG

4 TSP EACH **CAPERS** AND MINCED **SHALLOTS**

2 TSP **FRESH THYME LEAVES**

1 TSP **SALT**

½ TSP **PEPPER**

8 TO 12 THIN SLICES **LEMON**

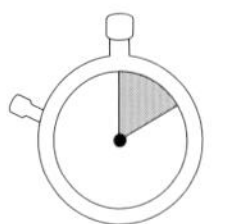

YIELD
4 servings

ACTIVE
10 minutes

TOTAL
25 minutes

SERVE WITH
French bread

Place oven rack in center of oven. Heat oven to 425°F.

Place 1 cup spinach in center of a piece of parchment paper or nonstick foil (about 16 in. long). Top with a tilapia fillet. Brush fish with 1 tsp of the olive oil. Scatter ½ cup of the asparagus on and around fish. Scatter 1 tsp each of the shallots and capers, and ½ tsp of the thyme over top. Drizzle with another tsp of the oil; sprinkle with ¼ tsp of the salt and ⅛ tsp of the pepper. Top fish with 2 or 3 slices of the lemon.

Bring long ends of paper together and fold down 3 times to make a seam. Place on a rimmed baking pan and tuck ends underneath. Repeat with remaining ingredients to make 4 packets.

Bake 15 minutes or until packets are puffed. Open 1 packet to test doneness. If fish isn't opaque at center, reseal packet and return to oven. Check again after 5 minutes.

PER SERVING
CALORIES 284 **TOTAL FAT** 13G **SATURATED FAT** 2G **CHOLESTEROL** 92MG **SODIUM** 802MG
TOTAL CARBOHYDRATES 6G **DIETARY FIBER** 2G **PROTEIN** 39G

CHIMICHURRI STEAK

1½ LB **SWEET POTATOES**, PEELED AND CUT INTO ¾-IN. PIECES

2 TBSP **LIGHT OIL AND VINEGAR DRESSING**

1 TBSP **DIJON MUSTARD**

2 **SCALLIONS**, CHOPPED

1 LB **SKIRT STEAK**, CUT IN 4 EQUAL PIECES

½ TSP EACH **PAPRIKA** AND **SALT**

1 CLOVE **GARLIC**

½ BUNCH **CILANTRO** (ABOUT 1 CUP PACKED CILANTRO)

3 TBSP **OLIVE OIL**

2 TBSP **LIME JUICE**

½ TSP **CRUSHED RED PEPPER**

YIELD
4 servings

ACTIVE
8 minutes

TOTAL
18 minutes

Steam potatoes 10 minutes or until tender; rinse under cold water and toss with dressing, mustard and scallions. Chill or serve at room temperature.

Heat grill or stovetop grill pan. Rub steaks with paprika and salt. Grill 2 to 3 minutes on each side for medium-rare. Remove to plate; let stand.

Pulse garlic and cilantro in food processor until finely chopped. Remove to bowl; stir in olive oil, lime juice and crushed red pepper. Spoon onto steak.

PER SERVING
CALORIES 400 **TOTAL FAT** 22G **SATURATED FAT** 6G **CHOLESTEROL** 51MG **SODIUM** 566MG **TOTAL CARBOHYDRATES** 27G **DIETARY FIBER** 4G **PROTEIN** 24G

PORK-VEGETABLE STIR-FRY

12 OZ THIN-CUT BONELESS **PORK CHOPS**, CUT IN NARROW STRIPS

½ CUP **STIR-FRY SAUCE**

1 TBSP **OIL**

1 BAG (12 OZ) **REFRIGERATED VEGETABLE MEDLEY** (BROCCOLI, BABY CARROTS AND CAULIFLOWER), BROCCOLI AND CAULIFLOWER CUT IN SMALL PIECES, CARROTS CUT LENGTHWISE IN THIN STRIPS, OR 12 OZ SIMILAR VEGETABLE MIXTURE

1 CAN (8 OZ) **PINEAPPLE SLICES**, DRAINED, JUICE RESERVED, SLICES CUT IN WEDGES

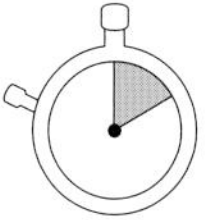

YIELD
4 servings

ACTIVE
10 minutes

TOTAL
20 minutes

SIDE SUGGESTION
Quick-cooking brown rice

Toss pork with 2 Tbsp stir-fry sauce.

Heat 1½ tsp oil in a large, deep nonstick skillet or a wok over medium-high heat until hot but not smoking. Add pork and stir-fry 2 minutes or just until lightly browned. Remove to a plate. (If pan has a crusty residue, wipe clean with a paper towel.)

Heat remaining 1½ tsp oil in skillet. Add vegetables; stir-fry 3 minutes. Stir in pineapple juice and remaining stir-fry sauce. Bring to a boil, reduce heat and simmer, stirring often, 3 minutes or until vegetables are crisp-tender and sauce thickens slightly. Add pork and pineapple; heat through.

PER SERVING
CALORIES 295 **TOTAL FAT** 14G **SATURATED FAT** 4G **CHOLESTEROL** 57MG **SODIUM** 797MG
TOTAL CARBOHYDRATES 28G **DIETARY FIBER** 2G **PROTEIN** 21G

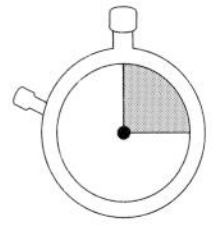

YIELD
4 servings

ACTIVE
15 minutes

TOTAL
1 hour

SIZZLING CHICKEN FAJITA SALAD

DRESSING & MARINADE

1 BOTTLE (8 OZ) **OIL AND VINEGAR DRESSING**

¼ CUP **MCCORMICK GRILL MATES MESQUITE SPICE RUB**

2 TSP **JALAPEÑO HOT SAUCE**

4 **BONELESS, SKINLESS CHICKEN BREASTS** (ABOUT 6 OZ EACH)

PICO DE GALLO

1 LB **PLUM TOMATOES**, SEEDED AND CHOPPED

1 SMALL **ONION**, CHOPPED

¼ CUP CHOPPED **CILANTRO**

2 TBSP **FRESH LIME JUICE**

1 TSP CHOPPED **GARLIC**

¼ TSP **SALT**

1 LARGE **SWEET ONION**, CUT IN ½-IN.-THICK SLICES

1 BAG (10 OZ) **CUT-UP HEARTS OF ROMAINE LETTUCE** *OR* 8 CUPS **TORN ROMAINE**

DRESSING & MARINADE Whisk ingredients in a bowl until blended. Reserve ⅓ cup to dress the salad. Put chicken breasts and ½ cup Marinade in a large ziptop bag. Refrigerate about 45 minutes.

PICO DE GALLO Combine ingredients in a bowl. Cover; leave at room temperature.

Heat outdoor grill or a large stovetop grill pan.

Brush the onion slices with remaining Dressing.

Remove chicken from marinade; discard bag with marinade. Grill chicken and onion 5 minutes on each side, or until chicken is cooked through and onion is tender. Transfer chicken and onion to a cutting board.

Toss lettuce with reserved Dressing. Divide among 4 serving plates. Cut chicken in strips, onion slices in half. Serve on salad along with Pico de Gallo and accompaniments.

ACCOMPANIMENTS Sliced tomatoes, guacamole, sour cream and shredded Cheddar.

PER SERVING
CALORIES 502 **TOTAL FAT** 25G **SATURATED FAT** 4G **CHOLESTEROL** 99MG **SODIUM** 1570MG **TOTAL CARBOHYDRATES** 23G **DIETARY FIBER** 4G **PROTEIN** 43G

PITA BURGERS WITH GARDEN RELISH

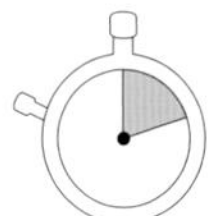

YIELD
4 servings

ACTIVE
12 minutes

TOTAL
22 minutes

RELISH

½ CUP FRESH OR CANNED **CORN KERNELS**

¼ CUP EACH DICED **BELL PEPPER** AND **CUCUMBER**

2 TBSP EACH SLICED **SCALLIONS**, CHOPPED **CILANTRO** AND **HONEY-DIJON DRESSING**

1¼ LB **80%-LEAN GROUND BEEF**

1 TSP EACH **GROUND CUMIN** AND **CHILI POWDER**

½ TSP **SALT**

4 **SLICES PASTEURIZED PROCESS CHEDDAR** (SUCH AS DELI DELUXE)

4 **PITA POCKETS**, CUT IN HALF

SIDE SUGGESTION
Potato salad

Heat outdoor grill or stovetop grill pan.

RELISH Mix ingredients in a small bowl.

Using your hands or a wooden spoon, gently but thoroughly mix beef, cumin, chili powder and salt in a bowl until blended. Form into four ¾-in.-thick patties. Gently flatten centers slightly, leaving a higher edge.

Grill 5 minutes; turn burgers and top with cheese. Grill 5 minutes more or just until cooked through. Cut each in half crosswise. Place in pitas and add relish.

PER SERVING
CALORIES 606 **TOTAL FAT** 32G **SATURATED FAT** 13G **CHOLESTEROL** 114MG **SODIUM** 1,155MG
TOTAL CARBOHYDRATES 39G **DIETARY FIBER** 2G **PROTEIN** 37G

MACARONI & CHEESE

YIELD
6 servings

ACTIVE
5 minutes

TOTAL
20 minutes

1 LB UNCOOKED **CAVATAPPI** OR OTHER SHORT PASTA

1 TSP **OIL**

1 SMALL **ONION**, FINELY CHOPPED

3 TBSP **FLOUR**

½ TSP EACH **SALT**, **ONION POWDER** AND **PAPRIKA**

2½ CUPS **MILK**

1 TBSP **DIJON MUSTARD**

1 BAG (8 OZ) **CLASSIC MELTS 4-CHEESE BLEND** (KRAFT)

1 CUP **FRESH BREAD CRUMBS** (OPTIONAL)

2 TBSP **GRATED PARMESAN** (OPTIONAL)

GARNISH: SLICED **SCALLIONS** AND **PAPRIKA**

Cook pasta as package directs. For crumb-topped, grease a shallow 2-qt baking dish.

While pasta cooks, heat oil in medium saucepan over medium heat. Sauté onion 3 minutes or until translucent. Stir in flour, salt, onion powder and paprika; whisk in milk until blended. Bring to a boil over medium-high heat, whisking often. Reduce heat and simmer 2 minutes or until slightly thickened.

Over low heat, whisk in mustard and then cheese until melted and smooth.

Drain pasta; return to pot, add sauce and toss to coat. Serve immediately.

If making crumb-topped, transfer to the baking dish, sprinkle with bread crumbs and Parmesan and broil 2 to 3 minutes until crumbs are toasted. Garnish with scallions and paprika.

PER SERVING
CALORIES 524 **TOTAL FAT** 16G **SATURATED FAT** 9G **CHOLESTEROL** 56MG **SODIUM** 886MG
TOTAL CARBOHYDRATES 71G **DIETARY FIBER** 2G **PROTEIN** 21G

ASPARAGUS SOUP WITH TURKEY & TOMATO TARTS

SOUP

1 CAN (14 OZ) **CHICKEN BROTH**

1 CUP COARSELY CHOPPED **SWEET ONION**

1 SMALL **POTATO**, PEELED, CUT IN 1-IN. CHUNKS

½ CUP **WATER**

¼ TSP EACH **SALT** AND **PEPPER**

1 BUNCH **ASPARAGUS** (ABOUT 1 LB), TOUGH ENDS TRIMMED, SPEARS CUT IN QUARTERS

TARTS

2 SLICES **FLATBREAD** OR **POCKETLESS PITAS**

¼ CUP **LITE GARLIC AND HERBS SPREADABLE CHEESE**

8 SLICES (4 OZ) **DELI-THIN SLICED SMOKED TURKEY**

3 **PLUM TOMATOES**, SLICED

¼ CUP EACH THINLY SLICED **SWEET ONION** AND **BASIL LEAVES**

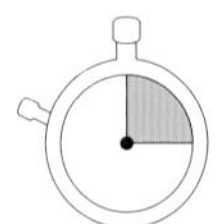

YIELD
4 servings

ACTIVE
15 minutes

TOTAL
30 minutes

Heat oven to 425°F.

SOUP Bring all ingredients except asparagus to a boil in a medium saucepan. Reduce heat; cover and simmer 10 minutes, or until potato is almost tender. Add asparagus; cook 5 minutes or until asparagus and potato are tender. Set aside 10 minutes to cool slightly.

Meanwhile, make TARTS: Place flatbreads on a baking sheet. Bake 7 minutes or until slightly crisp. Remove from oven; spread each with 2 Tbsp cheese spread. Top each with 4 slices turkey, folded to fit, and ½ the sliced tomato, onion and basil. Cut each into 4 wedges.

Purée soup in blender until smooth. Accompany each serving with 2 tart wedges.

The soup can be made up to 3 days ahead. Reheat, or serve chilled.

PER SERVING
CALORIES 264 **TOTAL FAT** 7G **SATURATED FAT** 2G **CHOLESTEROL** 20MG **SODIUM** 996MG **TOTAL CARBOHYDRATES** 35G **DIETARY FIBER** 3G **PROTEIN** 17G

CRUNCHY FISH STICKS & SMASHED POTATOES

1½ LB **RED-SKINNED POTATOES**, SCRUBBED AND CUT IN 1-IN. CHUNKS

1 CUP (4 OZ) **SHREDDED CHEDDAR**

½ CUP **MILK**

¼ CUP THINLY SLICED **SCALLIONS**

¼ TSP **SALT**

¼ TSP **PEPPER**

1 LARGE **EGG**

1 LB **FLOUNDER OR SOLE FILLETS**, CUT IN 1-IN.-WIDE STRIPS

1¼ CUPS CRUSHED **BAKED POTATO CHIPS**

¾ TSP **PAPRIKA**

¾ TSP **SALT**

½ CUP **TARTAR SAUCE**

¾ CUP **GRAPE OR CHERRY TOMATOES**, CUT UP

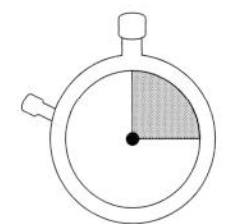

YIELD
4 servings

ACTIVE
15 minutes

TOTAL
35 minutes

SIDE SUGGESTION
Sautéed sugar snap peas

Heat oven to 450°F. Set a wire rack on a foil-lined (for easy cleanup) rimmed baking sheet; coat rack with nonstick spray.

Cook potatoes in lightly salted boiling water 10 to 15 minutes until tender. Drain; return to pot and mash with a potato masher. Add cheese; stir until melted. Add milk, scallions, salt and pepper; stir to blend. Cover to keep hot.

While potatoes cook, beat egg in a bowl until foamy. Add fish strips; toss to coat. In another bowl, mix crushed chips, paprika and salt. Put a few fish strips at a time into chip mixture. Using a fork, toss strips to coat. Place on prepared rack.

Bake 10 minutes, or until coating is crisp and fish is cooked through. With a broad spatula, transfer fish to a platter.

Mix tartar sauce and tomatoes. Serve with the fish.

PER SERVING
CALORIES 643 **TOTAL FAT** 32G **SATURATED FAT** 10G **CHOLESTEROL** 153MG **SODIUM** 1,254MG
TOTAL CARBOHYDRATES 52G **DIETARY FIBER** 5G **PROTEIN** 37G

BBQ PORK CHOPS WITH NECTARINE SLAW

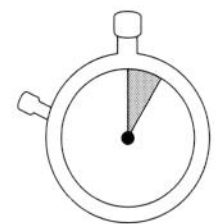

YIELD
4 servings

ACTIVE
5 minutes

TOTAL
25 minutes

1 LB **DELI COLESLAW**

1 LARGE RIPE **NECTARINE**, SLICED

4 TRIMMED ¾-IN.-THICK **RIB OR LOIN PORK CHOPS** (ABOUT 7 OZ EACH)

¼ TSP EACH **SALT** AND **PEPPER**

½ CUP PLUS 2 TBSP **BARBECUE SAUCE**

1 CAN (15.5 OZ) **GREAT NORTHERN BEANS**, DRAINED

2 TBSP **WATER**

Toss coleslaw with nectarine slices; cover and refrigerate.

Heat outdoor grill or grill pan. Season pork with salt and pepper; grill pork, turning once, 10 minutes or until an instant-read thermometer inserted from side to center registers 155°F. Brush chops with 2 Tbsp barbecue sauce; let pork rest 5 minutes.

Meanwhile, warm beans, remaining ½ cup barbecue sauce and water in small saucepan on stovetop.

Serve chops with beans and slaw.

PER SERVING
CALORIES 470 **TOTAL FAT** 9G **SATURATED FAT** 3G **CHOLESTEROL** 87MG **SODIUM** 1,001MG **TOTAL CARBOHYDRATES** 61G **DIETARY FIBER** 8G **PROTEIN** 38G

CHICKEN TACOS

SAUCE

⅓ CUP **LIGHT MAYONNAISE**

1 TSP **GROUND CUMIN**

2 TBSP **MEDIUM-HEAT CHIPOTLE SALSA** OR REGULAR SALSA

2 CUPS SHREDDED **COOKED CHICKEN**

½ CUP **MEDIUM-HEAT CHIPOTLE SALSA OR REGULAR SALSA**

12 **TACO SHELLS**

½ SMALL HEAD **ICEBERG LETTUCE**, CORED AND SHREDDED

4 OZ (1 CUP) **SHREDDED CHEDDAR** OR **MONTEREY JACK CHEESE**

1 CUP **CILANTRO LEAVES**

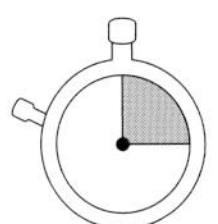

YIELD
4 servings
(makes 12 tacos)

ACTIVE
15 minutes

TOTAL
15 minutes

SIDE SUGGESTION
Mexican rice mix with chopped cilantro

SAUCE Mix mayonnaise, cumin and salsa in a small bowl.

Combine chicken and ½ cup salsa in a microwave-safe bowl. Microwave on high, stirring once, until hot, about 1½ minutes.

Fill taco shells with chicken mixture, lettuce, cheese and cilantro; drizzle with Sauce.

PER SERVING
CALORIES 517 **TOTAL FAT** 29G **SATURATED FAT** 10G **CHOLESTEROL** 99MG **SODIUM** 966MG **TOTAL CARBOHYDRATES** 36G **DIETARY FIBER** 4G **PROTEIN** 31G

MEDITERRANEAN PASTA WITH TOMATOES & ARUGULA

- 12 OZ **WHOLE-WHEAT PENNE PASTA**
- 2 TBSP **EXTRA-VIRGIN OLIVE OIL**
- ½ CUP CHOPPED **SHALLOTS**
- 1 PINT **CHERRY OR GRAPE TOMATOES**, HALVED
- 1 JAR (6 OZ) **MARINATED ARTICHOKE HEARTS**, DRAINED AND QUARTERED
- ¼ CUP **PITTED KALAMATA OLIVES**, HALVED
- ½ TSP **SALT**
- ¼ TSP **PEPPER**
- 4 CUPS **BABY ARUGULA**
- ½ CUP CRUMBLED **RICOTTA SALATA OR FETA**

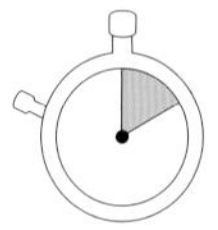

YIELD
4 servings

ACTIVE
10 minutes

TOTAL
25 minutes

SERVE WITH
Whole-grain Italian bread

Bring a 5- to 6-qt pot of salted water to a boil. Add pasta and cook as package directs, removing and reserving ¾ cup pasta cooking water. Drain.

Meanwhile, heat oil in a 12-in. nonstick skillet. Add shallots and cook 5 minutes. Add tomatoes; toss until soft, about 1 minute.

Remove pan from heat. Add artichoke hearts, olives, salt and pepper to skillet; toss. Stir in drained pasta, arugula and reserved pasta water; toss. Sprinkle servings with ricotta salata.

PER SERVING
CALORIES 519 **TOTAL FAT** 19G **SATURATED FAT** 5G **CHOLESTEROL** 19MG **SODIUM** 885MG **TOTAL CARBOHYDRATES** 75G **DIETARY FIBER** 10G **PROTEIN** 16G

ASIAN GRILLED FLANK STEAK

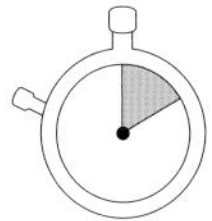

YIELD
4 servings

ACTIVE
10 minutes

TOTAL
30 minutes

- ½ CUP **LITE SOY SAUCE**
- 3 TBSP PACKED **BROWN SUGAR**
- 2 TBSP GRATED **FRESH GINGER**
- 2 CLOVES **GARLIC**, MINCED
- 2 TSP **DARK ORIENTAL SESAME OIL**
- ¼ TSP FRESHLY GROUND **PEPPER**
- 1½-LB **FLANK STEAK**

SIDE SUGGESTION
Grilled pepper halves and whole scallions, brown rice

Heat outdoor grill or ridged grill pan.

Mix all ingredients except steak in a gallon-size ziptop food bag. Add steak, seal bag and turn to coat. Marinate at room temperature at least 5 minutes or refrigerate up to 1 day.

Remove steak; reserve marinade. Grill, turning once, 14 to 16 minutes for medium-rare. Remove to a cutting board; let rest 5 minutes.

Meanwhile, bring reserved marinade to a boil in a saucepan or in a microwave-safe bowl. Boil 1 minute.

Slice steak thinly against the grain; serve with the marinade.

PER SERVING
CALORIES 365 **TOTAL FAT** 18G **SATURATED FAT** 7G **CHOLESTEROL** 85MG **SODIUM** 1,306MG
TOTAL CARBOHYDRATES 14G **DIETARY FIBER** 0G **PROTEIN** 35G

VEGGIE BURGERS WITH ZUCCHINI

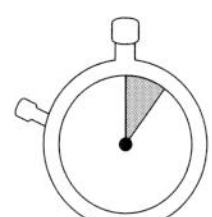

YIELD
4 servings

ACTIVE
6 minutes

TOTAL
26 minutes

2 LARGE **ZUCCHINI** OR 4 SMALL (14 OZ), CUT DIAGONALLY IN ½-IN.-THICK SLICES

NONSTICK SPRAY

½ TSP EACH **SALT** AND **PEPPER**

1 BOX (10 OZ) **SOY VEGGIE PATTIES**

4 **HAMBURGER ROLLS**

¼ CUP BOTTLED **TOMATO SALSA**

1 BAG (5 OZ) **POTPOURRI POTATO CHIPS** (BY TERRA) OR REGULAR POTATO CHIPS

SIDE SUGGESTION
Cucumber and cherry tomato salad

Remove broiler pan with rack from oven. Heat broiler.

Place zucchini slices in a single layer on broiler rack. Coat both sides with nonstick spray; sprinkle with salt and pepper.

Broil 4 in. from heat source 4 to 5 minutes per side until charred and tender. Remove to a plate.

Place burgers on rack and broil as package directs (don't overcook or burgers will be tough).

Place rolls, cut side up, on rack. Broil briefly to toast.

Top bottom of each roll with a burger, zucchini and salsa. Cover with roll top. Serve with potato chips.

PER SERVING
CALORIES 435 **TOTAL FAT** 15G **SATURATED FAT** 3G **CHOLESTEROL** 0MG **SODIUM** 1,067MG **TOTAL CARBOHYDRATES** 53G **DIETARY FIBER** 10G **PROTEIN** 21G

CUBAN BLACK BEANS & RICE

1 CUP **LONG-GRAIN RICE**

1½ TSP **OLIVE OIL**

1¼ CUPS CHOPPED **ONIONS**

2 **CUBANELLE PEPPERS** (ITALIAN FRYING PEPPERS), DICED

4 OZ **HAM** (PIECE FROM DELI), DICED

1 TBSP MINCED **GARLIC**

1 TSP EACH **GROUND CUMIN** AND **DRIED OREGANO**

2 CANS (ABOUT 15 OZ EACH) **REDUCED-SODIUM BLACK BEANS**, UNDRAINED

½ CUP **WATER**

2 TSP **RED-WINE VINEGAR**

½ CUP CHOPPED **CILANTRO**

GARNISH: **LIME WEDGES**, DICED **RED ONION**

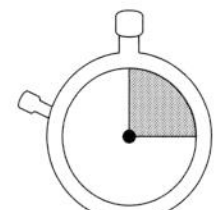

YIELD
4 servings

ACTIVE
15 minutes

TOTAL
35 minutes

SERVE WITH
Hot pepper sauce

Bring 2 cups water to a boil in a small saucepan. Add rice and cook as package directs.

Meanwhile, heat oil in a large nonstick skillet over medium-high heat. Add onions and peppers; cook, stirring, until tender, about 7 minutes. Add ham; cook 2 minutes or until browned.

Add garlic, cumin and oregano; cook, stirring, until fragrant, about 30 seconds.

Stir in beans and their liquid and water; bring to a simmer. Reduce heat to low and simmer for flavors to blend, about 5 minutes. Remove from heat; stir in vinegar and cilantro. Garnish with lime and diced onion.

PER SERVING
CALORIES 398 **TOTAL FAT** 4G **SATURATED FAT** 1G **CHOLESTEROL** 11MG **SODIUM** 747MG
TOTAL CARBOHYDRATES 79G **DIETARY FIBER** 13G **PROTEIN** 18G

SLOW COOKER CHICKEN POSOLE

1 CAN (15 OZ) **YELLOW OR WHITE HOMINY**, DRAINED

1 CAN (14.5 OZ) **MEXICAN-STYLE DICED TOMATOES**

1 CAN (10 OZ) **MILD GREEN ENCHILADA SAUCE**

2 **CARROTS**, DICED

1 MEDIUM **ONION**, CHOPPED

3 CLOVES **GARLIC**, MINCED

2 TSP **GROUND CUMIN**

5 **CHICKEN THIGHS** (1½ LB), SKIN REMOVED

CHOPPED **CILANTRO** (OPTIONAL)

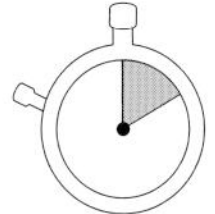

YIELD
4 servings

ACTIVE
10 minutes

TOTAL
3 to 3 hours 30 minutes on high

SERVE WITH
Lime wedges and warm corn tortilla chips

Combine hominy, tomatoes, enchilada sauce, carrots, onion, garlic and cumin in a 4-qt slow cooker. Add chicken and stir to combine. Cover and cook on high 3 to 3½ hours until chicken is cooked through and vegetables tender. Skim and discard any fat from the surface.

Remove chicken; pull meat off bones into large shreds. Stir back into slow cooker. Stir in cilantro, if using.

PER SERVING
CALORIES 262 **TOTAL FAT** 7G **SATURATED FAT** 1G **CHOLESTEROL** 80MG **SODIUM** 1,083MG **TOTAL CARBOHYDRATES** 26G **DIETARY FIBER** 5G **PROTEIN** 22G

SHRIMP LIMONE WITH PASTA & ASPARAGUS

- 12 OZ **FETTUCCINE PASTA**
- 2 **LEMONS**
- 4 TSP **OLIVE OIL**
- 1 LB **RAW MEDIUM SHRIMP**, PEELED AND DEVEINED
- 1 LARGE **ONION**, THINLY SLICED
- 1½ LB **ASPARAGUS**, WOODY ENDS SNAPPED OFF, SPEARS CUT IN 1½-IN. PIECES
- 2 TSP MINCED **GARLIC**
- ½ TSP **PEPPER**
- ¼ TSP **SALT**
- ¾ CUP **HEAVY (WHIPPING) CREAM**
- 1 CUP **BASIL LEAVES**, CUT IN STRIPS
- ½ CUP **PITTED KALAMATA OLIVES**

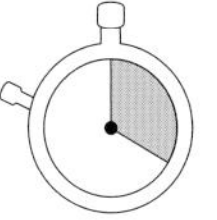

YIELD
4 servings

ACTIVE
20 minutes

TOTAL
32 minutes

Boil pasta as package directs. Remove and reserve ⅓ cup pasta water. Drain pasta; put in a serving bowl.

Meanwhile, grate 2 tsp lemon zest and squeeze 3 Tbsp juice from lemons.

Heat 2 tsp oil in a large nonstick skillet. Add shrimp and sauté 2 to 3 minutes until just cooked. Transfer to a plate.

Heat remaining 2 tsp oil in skillet. Add onion; sauté until translucent. Add asparagus, garlic, pepper and salt. Sauté 2 to 3 minutes until asparagus are crisp-tender. Stir in cream, lemon zest and juice, basil and olives; bring to a boil. Pour over pasta. Add reserved cooking water; toss to mix and coat.

PER SERVING
CALORIES 721 **TOTAL FAT** 29G **SATURATED FAT** 12G **CHOLESTEROL** 201MG **SODIUM** 902MG
TOTAL CARBOHYDRATES 81G **DIETARY FIBER** 6G **PROTEIN** 36G

SPANISH TORTILLA

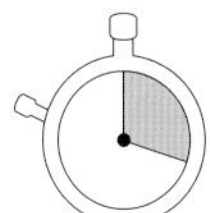

YIELD
4 servings

ACTIVE
18 minutes

TOTAL
40 minutes

1 TBSP **OIL**

1½ LB **ALL-PURPOSE POTATOES**, PEELED AND DICED

1 LARGE **ONION**, CHOPPED

1 LARGE **CUBANELLE PEPPER**, CHOPPED

4 OZ CHUNK OF **HAM**, CHOPPED

½ TSP **DRIED OREGANO** *OR* **ITALIAN SEASONING**

¼ TSP EACH **SALT** AND **PEPPER**

8 LARGE **EGGS**

SERVE WITH: **SALSA**

SIDE SUGGESTION
Mixed baby greens salad

Heat oven to 350°F. Heat oil in a 10-in. ovenproof nonstick skillet over medium heat. Add potatoes and onion; sauté 5 minutes until potatoes are just tender.

Add chopped pepper and ham, oregano, salt and pepper; cook 3 minutes until pepper is just tender.

Whisk eggs in a medium bowl. Pour into skillet, shaking pan a bit to distribute evenly.

Bake 15 to 20 minutes until center is set. Let stand 2 minutes. Run spatula around edge of skillet and under tortilla. Place serving platter over skillet and invert. Serve with salsa.

PER SERVING
CALORIES 369 **TOTAL FAT** 15G **SATURATED FAT** 4G **CHOLESTEROL** 434MG **SODIUM** 601MG
TOTAL CARBOHYDRATES 40G **DIETARY FIBER** 4G **PROTEIN** 20G

BEEF STIR-FRY

2 TBSP **CORNSTARCH**

ONE 12-OZ **BONELESS SIRLOIN STEAK**, CUT IN NARROW STRIPS

4 TSP **CANOLA OIL**

2 SMALL **BELL PEPPERS**, CUT IN ½-IN. STRIPS

1 LB **BOK CHOY**, STALKS AND LEAVES CUT IN HALF LENGTHWISE, THEN CROSSWISE IN 1-IN. PIECES, STALKS AND LEAVES SEPARATED

4 OZ **SNOW PEAS**

1½ TBSP MINCED **FRESH GINGER**

2 TSP MINCED **GARLIC**

1 TSP GRATED **ORANGE ZEST**

½ CUP **ORANGE JUICE**

1 TBSP PLUS 1 TSP **LESS-SODIUM SOY SAUCE** (SUCH AS HOUSE OF TSANG)

GARNISH: CHOPPED TOASTED **ALMONDS**, SHREDDED **CARROTS** AND SLICED **SCALLIONS**

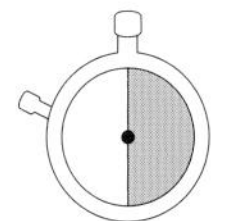

YIELD
4 servings

ACTIVE
30 minutes

TOTAL
45 minutes

SIDE SUGGESTION
Rice with sliced scallions

Put cornstarch in a plastic food bag, add beef, seal and shake to coat.

Heat 2 tsp oil in a large nonstick skillet over medium-high heat. Add beef; stir-fry 3 minutes or until cooked through. Remove to a plate.

Heat remaining oil in skillet; add peppers and bok choy stalks. Stir-fry 5 minutes or until almost crisp-tender.

Add bok choy leaves and snow peas; stir-fry 2 minutes. Push vegetables to edge of skillet; put ginger and garlic in middle. Cook 30 seconds until fragrant. Add beef, orange zest and juice, and soy sauce. Stir to combine with vegetables until simmering. Transfer to serving plates or bowls and sprinkle with the garnishes.

PER SERVING
CALORIES 296 **TOTAL FAT** 17G **SATURATED FAT** 5G **CHOLESTEROL** 57MG **SODIUM** 321MG **TOTAL CARBOHYDRATES** 15G **DIETARY FIBER** 2G **PROTEIN** 20G

BALSAMIC LAMB STEAKS WITH SPINACH & COUSCOUS

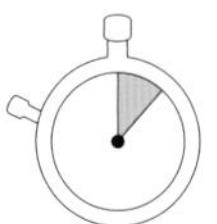

YIELD
4 servings

ACTIVE
7 minutes

TOTAL
22 minutes

⅓ CUP **BOTTLED BALSAMIC VINAIGRETTE DRESSING**

2 **LAMB LEG CENTER STEAKS** (ABOUT 12 OZ EACH)

2 TSP **OLIVE OIL**

1 BOX (5.6 OZ) **TOASTED PINE NUT COUSCOUS**

1 JAR (2 OZ) **SLICED PIMIENTOS**

2 TBSP CHOPPED **FRESH MINT OR PARSLEY**

1 BAG (10 OZ) **FRESH SPINACH**

¼ CUP SLICED **SCALLIONS**

Put dressing in a shallow dish, add lamb steaks and turn to coat. Let marinate at room temperature 5 minutes.

While lamb marinates, bring 1¼ cups water, the oil and spice packet from couscous mix to a boil in a medium saucepan. Remove from heat, add couscous, cover and let stand 5 minutes or until water is absorbed.

Meanwhile, heat a large nonstick skillet over medium heat. Add lamb, increase heat to medium-high and cook 5 minutes, turning steaks once, until browned and slightly pink at center. Remove to a cutting board.

Fluff couscous with a fork; stir in pimientos and chopped mint. Cover until serving.

Add spinach to skillet (in batches if necessary); toss over high heat 2 minutes or until wilted and tender.

Slice lamb and sprinkle with scallions. Serve with the couscous and spinach.

PER SERVING
CALORIES 443 **TOTAL FAT** 10G **SATURATED FAT** 3G **CHOLESTEROL** 135MG **SODIUM** 1,462MG **TOTAL CARBOHYDRATES** 57G **DIETARY FIBER** 4G **PROTEIN** 29G

RUSTIC SUMMER SQUASH TART

1 TBSP **EXTRA-VIRGIN OLIVE OIL**

1 LB **MIXED SUMMER SQUASH** (ZUCCHINI, YELLOW SQUASH AND PATTYPAN), CUT IN ¼-IN. ROUNDS

2 **SHALLOTS**, THINLY SLICED

2 TSP CHOPPED **FRESH THYME** *OR* **MARJORAM**, PLUS SPRIGS FOR GARNISH

1 TSP CHOPPED **GARLIC**

FRESHLY GROUND **PEPPER**

1 **REFRIGERATED PIE CRUST** (FROM A 15-OZ BOX OF TWO)

4 OZ **ROQUEFORT, GORGONZOLA OR OTHER GOOD-QUALITY BLUE CHEESE**

1 ROASTED **YELLOW OR RED PEPPER** (FRESHLY ROASTED OR FROM A JAR), CUT IN STRIPS

1 LARGE **PLUM TOMATO**, SLICED, SEEDS REMOVED

1 LARGE **EGG**, BEATEN

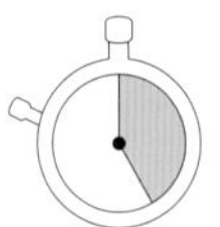

YIELD
12 servings

ACTIVE
25 minutes

TOTAL
1 hour 5 minutes

Heat oil in a large nonstick skillet over medium heat. Add squash and shallots and cook, turning pieces as they start to color, 7 minutes or until crisp-tender. Remove from heat; stir in thyme, garlic and pepper to taste. Cool to room temperature.

Heat oven to 400°F. Line a baking sheet with parchment paper; unroll or unfold pie crust on the parchment. With a rolling pin, roll crust to a 13-in. round. Crumble ½ the cheese over crust to within 2 in. of edge. Arrange squash mixture, pepper strips and tomato slices on cheese; fold edge of the crust over filling and brush crust with egg.

Bake 35 to 40 minutes until pastry is golden. Slide tart, still on parchment, onto a wire rack. Crumble remaining cheese over top. Let cool before serving.

PER SERVING
CALORIES 144 **TOTAL FAT** 9G **SATURATED FAT** 4G **CHOLESTEROL** 29MG **SODIUM** 263MG **TOTAL CARBOHYDRATES** 12G **DIETARY FIBER** 1G **PROTEIN** 3G

FARFALLE WITH SALMON & MINT

12 OZ **FARFALLE PASTA**

1 TBSP **BUTTER**

1 LARGE **LEEK**, WHITE AND LIGHT GREEN PART ONLY, HALVED LENGTHWISE, THINLY SLICED CROSSWISE (2 CUPS; SEE NOTE)

1¼ CUP **REDUCED-SODIUM CHICKEN BROTH**

¼ TSP EACH **SALT** AND **PEPPER**

8 OZ SKINLESS **SALMON FILLET** (¾ TO 1 IN. THICK)

2 TSP GRATED **LEMON ZEST**

½ CUP **REDUCED-FAT SOUR CREAM**

½ CUP SLICED **MINT**

YIELD
4 servings

ACTIVE
7 minutes

TOTAL
20 minutes

NOTE
Leeks are naturally sandy, so clean well before using. Soak leek slices in a bowl of water. Agitate to release sand; rinse and drain.

Bring a 5- to 6-qt pot of salted water to a boil. Add pasta and cook as package directs. Drain.

Meanwhile, melt butter in a 12-in. nonstick skillet over medium heat. Add leek, ½ cup broth, and the salt and pepper; simmer and cook 1 minute.

Place salmon on leeks; cover. Cook over medium heat 5 minutes or until leeks are tender and salmon is cooked.

Remove salmon to a plate. Add remaining ¾ cup broth and the lemon zest to skillet; bring to a simmer.

Break up salmon. Place in pasta pot along with drained pasta, leek mixture, sour cream and mint. Toss to mix.

PER SERVING
CALORIES 506 **TOTAL FAT** 12G **SATURATED FAT** 5G **CHOLESTEROL** 50MG **SODIUM** 515MG
TOTAL CARBOHYDRATES 73G **DIETARY FIBER** 4G **PROTEIN** 26G

SEPTEMBER

- *Check recipe page 323 for ingredients you need for the coating of your choice for Oven-Fried Drumsticks.*

SEPTEMBER SHOPPING LIST

Week 1

SEPTEMBER 1 TO SEPTEMBER 7

PRODUCE

1 NAVEL ORANGE
2 ONIONS
1 LARGE RED ONION
1 MEDIUM SWEET ONION
1 HEAD GARLIC (4 CLOVES)
1 BAG (20 OZ) RED POTATO WEDGES
2 LARGE RIPE TOMATOES
1 LARGE BEEFSTEAK TOMATO
2 MEDIUM CARROTS
2 BELL PEPPERS
6 PORTOBELLO MUSHROOMS (4 TO 5 OZ EACH)
2 BAGS (6 OZ EACH) BABY SPINACH TRIO (BABY SPINACH, ARUGULA AND CARROTS) OR 2 BAGS (6 OZ EACH) BABY SPINACH
1 BUNCH CILANTRO
1 BUNCH PARSLEY
1 BUNCH BASIL

BAKERY

½ A 1-LB LOAF FRENCH BREAD
1 LOAF CIABATTA BREAD OR SIX 4-IN.-SQUARE PIECES HERBED FOCACCIA BREAD

MEAT/POULTRY/FISH

12-OZ ¾-IN.-THICK SIRLOIN STEAK
4 BONE-IN CHICKEN BREASTS (ABOUT 2¾ LB) OR 8 CHICKEN DRUMSTICKS (ABOUT 2½ LB)
8 CHICKEN DRUMSTICKS (3½ LB)
1¼ LB GROUND TURKEY
1 LB ITALIAN SAUSAGES

REFRIGERATED

1 BAG (8 OZ) SHREDDED CHEDDAR
12 OZ FONTINA CHEESE
1 CONTAINER (5 OZ) BLUE CHEESE
GRATED PARMESAN
EGG (1 LARGE)
1 TUBE (13.8 OZ) PIZZA CRUST

GROCERY

1 CAN (8 OZ) TOMATO SAUCE
1 CAN (10 OZ) MILD ENCHILADA SAUCE
1 JAR (24 TO 26 OZ) MARINARA SAUCE
1 LB PAPPARDELLE PASTA
BARBECUE SAUCE (WE USED SWEET BABY RAY'S HONEY CHIPOTLE)
OLIVE OIL AND VINEGAR DRESSING
⅓ CUP PITTED KALAMATA OLIVES
ORANGE MARMALADE
GARLIC-FLAVOR COOKING SPRAY
½ CUP DRY WHITE WINE (OPTIONAL)

PANTRY

SALT
PEPPER
OLIVE OIL
EXTRA-VIRGIN OLIVE OIL
NONSTICK SPRAY
BALSAMIC VINEGAR
SALT-FREE CHILI POWDER
GROUND CUMIN
DRIED ROSEMARY

Week 2

SEPTEMBER 8 TO SEPTEMBER 14

PRODUCE

1 FIRM-RIPE MANGO
4 CLEMENTINES
1 NAVEL ORANGE (OR 2 CLEMENTINES)
2 LIMES
1 LEMON
1 LARGE ONION
1 MEDIUM RED ONION
2 SMALL RED ONIONS
1 SMALL SWEET ONION
4 HEADS GARLIC (18 CLOVES)
2 LB (ABOUT 5 MEDIUM) ALL-PURPOSE POTATOES
3 SMALL SWEET POTATOES
3 PLUM TOMATOES
2 SMALL CARROTS
1 RED BELL PEPPER
1 BELL PEPPER
2 MEDIUM POBLANO PEPPERS
2 MEDIUM ZUCCHINI (1 LB)
1 MEDIUM EGGPLANT (1 LB)
LETTUCE (OPTIONAL)
8 CUPS SALAD GREENS
1 BAG (6 OZ) BABY SPINACH
1 BUNCH CILANTRO
1 BUNCH FRESH MINT

BAKERY

1 BAG POCKETLESS PITAS

MEAT/POULTRY/FISH

1 LB LEAN GROUND BEEF
ONE 1-LB PORK TENDERLOIN
1 CUT-UP WHOLE CHICKEN (ABOUT 4 LB)
1 PKG (24 OZ) APPETIZER-SIZE COOKED TURKEY MEATBALLS
FOUR 5-OZ SALMON FILLETS
1 LB THAWED FROZEN OR FRESH COD OR SCROD FILLETS

FROZEN

1 BAG (10 OZ) CORN NIBLETS

REFRIGERATED

1 CONTAINER (6 OZ) PLAIN GREEK YOGURT
SOUR CREAM (OPTIONAL)
1 CUP DICED FRESH MOZZARELLA
SHREDDED CHEESE (OPTIONAL)
EGG (1 LARGE)

GROCERY

1 CAN (14.5 OZ) REDUCED-SODIUM CHICKEN BROTH
1 CAN (14 OZ) DICED TOMATOES
2 CANS (8 OZ) TOMATO SAUCE
1 CAN (15 OZ) RED KIDNEY BEANS
1 CAN (15 OZ) BLACK BEANS
1 CAN (15 OZ) CHICKPEAS
1 JAR (16 OZ) SMOOTH CHIPOTLE OR ROJA SALSA (WE USED OLD EL PASO)
1½ CUPS MARINARA SAUCE
12 OZ BOW-TIES (FARFALLE) PASTA
ASIAN GINGER SALAD DRESSING
GROUND CHIPOTLE CHILE PEPPER
PLAIN DRY BREAD CRUMBS
2 TBSP COCOA CHILI SPICE BLEND OR UNSWEETENED COCOA

1 SLOW COOKER LINER (WE USED REYNOLDS)
UNSALTED TOASTED ALMONDS
TOASTED PUMPKIN SEEDS (OPTIONAL)

PANTRY
SALT
PEPPER
OLIVE OIL
NONSTICK SPRAY
BALSAMIC VINEGAR
BROWN SUGAR
GROUND CUMIN
GROUND CINNAMON
GARLIC POWDER
SALT-FREE CHILI POWDER
DRIED OREGANO
DRIED THYME
DRIED MINCED ONION
FENNEL SEEDS (OPTIONAL)

Week 3

SEPTEMBER 15 TO SEPTEMBER 22

PRODUCE
1 LARGE ONION
2 MEDIUM ONIONS
1 SMALL ONION
1 LARGE SWEET ONION
1 MEDIUM VIDALIA OR SWEET ONION
1 HEAD GARLIC (8 CLOVES)
1 SMALL PIECE FRESH GINGER
12 OZ YUKON GOLD POTATOES
3 BELL PEPPERS
1 ZUCCHINI
6 OZ CRIMINI OR WHITE MUSHROOMS
2 BAGS (5 TO 6 OZ EACH) BABY SPINACH
8 SCALLIONS
1 BUNCH CILANTRO
1 BUNCH CELERY
1 BUNCH BASIL

MEAT/POULTRY/FISH
2 BONELESS SHELL STEAKS (ABOUT 12 OZ EACH)
12 OZ TERIYAKI-MARINATED PORK OR BEEF TENDERLOIN
12 OZ LEAN GROUND PORK
4 CHICKEN CUTLETS (8 OZ)
8 CHICKEN DRUMSTICKS (2¼ LB)
2 EACH CHICKEN DRUMSTICKS AND THIGHS (1¼ LB)
8 OZ GROUND TURKEY BREAST
1 LB SPICY ITALIAN SAUSAGES
8 OZ RAW LARGE PEELED SHRIMP

DELI
4 OZ ANDOUILLE OR OTHER SMOKED SAUSAGE

FROZEN
1 BAG (16 OZ) FROZEN STIR-FRY VEGETABLES
1 BAG (16 OZ) FROZEN ASIAN STIR-FRY VEGETABLES
1 BAG (16 OZ) CUT OKRA

REFRIGERATED
1½ CUPS SKIM MILK
1 CONTAINER (8 OZ) HEAVY CREAM
1 CONTAINER (15 OZ) PART-SKIM RICOTTA
GRATED PARMESAN
EGG (1 LARGE)

GROCERY
2 CANS (14.5 OZ) FAT-FREE CHICKEN BROTH
1 CAN (14.5 OZ) REDUCED-SODIUM CHICKEN BROTH
2 CANS (28 OZ EACH) CRUSHED TOMATOES
1 CAN (6 OZ) TOMATO PASTE
1 CAN (10 OZ) MILD ENCHILADA SAUCE
1 CAN (13.5 OZ) COCONUT MILK (NOT CREAM OF COCONUT)
8 OZ ANGEL-HAIR PASTA
1 LB GEMELLI PASTA
1 BOX (16 OZ) CURLY-EDGE LASAGNA
WHITE RICE
KOREAN TERIYAKI STIR-FRY SAUCE (SUCH AS HOUSE OF TSANG)
1 PKG (1.25 OZ) HUNTER SAUCE BLEND
LITE SOY SAUCE
CHILI GARLIC SAUCE
1 BAG (9 OZ) UNSALTED TORTILLA CHIPS

PANTRY
SALT
PEPPER
OLIVE OIL
CORNSTARCH
FLOUR
GROUND CUMIN
GROUND NUTMEG
CURRY POWDER
CAJUN SEASONING
DRIED OREGANO
DRIED THYME

Week 4

SEPTEMBER 23 TO SEPTEMBER 30

PRODUCE
2 LEMONS
3 MEDIUM ONIONS
1 MEDIUM RED ONION
2 HEADS GARLIC (9 CLOVES)
1 MEDIUM TOMATO
1 BELL PEPPER
1 MEDIUM ZUCCHINI (ABOUT 6 OZ)
2 LB ASPARAGUS
1 PKG (12 OZ) MICROWAVE-IN-BAG BROCCOLI RABE OR 16-OZ MICROWAVE-IN-BAG BROCCOLI
3 SCALLIONS
1 BUNCH CILANTRO
1 BUNCH MINT

MEAT/POULTRY/FISH
2 LB LEAN GROUND BEEF
2 LB MEAT LOAF MIXTURE (BEEF, PORK AND VEAL)
4 BONELESS PORK CHOPS (ABOUT 5 OZ EACH)
ONE 3- TO 3½-LB CHICKEN
20 CHICKEN TENDERLOINS (TENDERS) OR 4 BONELESS, SKINLESS CHICKEN BREASTS (ABOUT 5 OZ EACH)
2 TURKEY THIGHS (1 LB EACH)

REFRIGERATED
½ CUP MILK
1 STICK BUTTER
1 CONTAINER (16 OZ) REDUCED-FAT SOUR CREAM
½ CUP SHREDDED PART-SKIM MOZZARELLA
3 OZ CRUMBLED FETA CHEESE
2 CUPS SHREDDED MONTEREY JACK
EGGS (3 LARGE)
1 PKG (16 OZ) BUITONI REFRIGERATED MOZZARELLA & HERB DOUBLE-STUFFED RAVIOLI
1 PKG (10 OZ) FULLY BAKED PIZZA CRUST (ABOUT 12 IN. DIAMETER)

GROCERY
1 CAN (15.5 OZ) CANNELLINI BEANS
1 CAN (16 OZ) CHICKPEAS
1 CAN (11 OZ) WHOLE-KERNEL CORN
1 CAN (4.5 OZ) CHOPPED GREEN CHILES
1 JAR (16 OZ) MEDIUM GREEN TOMATILLO SALSA
1 CUP (8 OZ) TOMATO SAUCE
2 CUPS MARINARA OR ALFREDO SAUCE
KETCHUP
WORCESTERSHIRE SAUCE
1 BOX SALTINE CRACKERS
PLAIN DRIED BREAD CRUMBS
PEACH OR APRICOT JAM
¾ CUP APRICOT PRESERVES

PANTRY
SALT
PEPPER
OLIVE OIL
VEGETABLE OIL
CIDER VINEGAR
DISTILLED WHITE VINEGAR
DIJON MUSTARD
SUGAR
BROWN SUGAR
GROUND CINNAMON
GROUND CUMIN
CURRY POWDER
DRIED THYME
DRIED TARRAGON

ITALIAN STEAK & BREAD SALAD

ONE 12-OZ ¾-IN.-THICK **SIRLOIN STEAK**

½ A 1-LB LOAF **FRENCH BREAD**, SPLIT

GARLIC-FLAVOR COOKING SPRAY

½ TSP **SALT**

½ TSP **PEPPER**

2 CUPS RIPE **TOMATO** CHUNKS

2 BAGS (6 OZ EACH) **BABY SPINACH TRIO** (BABY SPINACH, ARUGULA AND CARROTS), *OR* 2 BAGS (6 OZ EACH) BABY SPINACH

½ CUP SLICED **ONION**

½ CUP CRUMBLED **BLUE CHEESE**

½ CUP **OLIVE OIL AND VINEGAR DRESSING**

YIELD
4 servings

ACTIVE
7 minutes

TOTAL
15 minutes

SIDE SUGGESTION
Grilled corn on the cob

Heat outdoor grill or stovetop ridged grill pan. Coat steak and cut surfaces of bread with garlic spray; sprinkle with salt and pepper.

Grill steak, turning once, 6 minutes, or until an instant-read thermometer inserted from side to middle registers 155°F. Remove to a cutting board, cover loosely with foil and let rest. (Temperature of steak will continue to rise to 160°F for medium doneness.)

Meanwhile, grill bread, cut sides down, 2 minutes, or until lightly toasted.

Cut bread in chunks; thinly slice steak. Combine in a bowl with remaining ingredients; toss to mix.

PER SERVING
CALORIES 564 **TOTAL FAT** 32G **SATURATED FAT** 10G **CHOLESTEROL** 64MG **SODIUM** 1,120MG **TOTAL CARBOHYDRATES** 41G **DIETARY FIBER** 4G **PROTEIN** 28G

CHILI-ORANGE CHICKEN

¾ CUP **MILD ENCHILADA SAUCE**

¼ CUP **BARBECUE SAUCE** (WE USED SWEET BABY RAY'S HONEY CHIPOTLE)

1 TBSP **SALT-FREE CHILI POWDER**

1 TSP **GROUND CUMIN**

4 **BONE-IN CHICKEN BREASTS** (ABOUT 2¾ LB), SKIN REMOVED, *OR* 8 **CHICKEN DRUMSTICKS** (ABOUT 2½ LB), SKIN REMOVED

3 TBSP **ORANGE MARMALADE**

½ CUP CHOPPED **CILANTRO**

2 TSP GRATED **ORANGE ZEST**

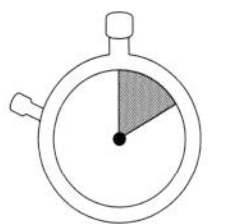

YIELD
4 servings

ACTIVE
10 minutes

TOTAL
3 to 4 hours on high *or* 5 to 7 hours on low

SIDE SUGGESTION
Rice

Mix enchilada sauce and barbecue sauce in a 6-qt or larger slow cooker.

Mix chili powder and cumin in a small cup. Rub all over chicken. Put chicken in slow cooker and turn to coat with sauce.

Cover and cook on high 3 to 4 hours or on low 5 to 7 hours until chicken is cooked through.

Turn off cooker. Remove chicken to a serving platter. Stir marmalade into sauce until blended. Stir in cilantro and orange zest, then pour over chicken.

TIP Want to spice things up? Add ¼ tsp or more crushed chipotle chile pepper to the enchilada and barbecue sauce mix.

PER SERVING
CALORIES 318 **TOTAL FAT** 6G **SATURATED FAT** 1G **CHOLESTEROL** 130MG **SODIUM** 698MG
TOTAL CARBOHYDRATES 20G **DIETARY FIBER** 1G **PROTEIN** 44G

GRILLED SWEET ONION & CHEDDAR PIZZA

YIELD
6 servings

ACTIVE
6 minutes

TOTAL
25 minutes

1 TUBE (13.8 OZ) **REFRIGERATED PIZZA CRUST**

1 MEDIUM, **SWEET ONION**, SLICED ½ IN. THICK

NONSTICK SPRAY

1 CAN (8 OZ) **TOMATO SAUCE**

1¼ CUPS **SHREDDED CHEDDAR**

GARNISH: CHOPPED **PARSLEY**

SIDE SUGGESTION
Sliced beefsteak tomatoes on lettuce

Heat outdoor grill. Line a baking sheet with nonstick foil. Unroll dough on foil; press into a 16 x 10-in. rectangle. Coat dough and onion with nonstick spray.

Grill onion 10 minutes, turning slices as needed, until tender. Remove; cut bite-size. Invert dough on grill; peel off foil. Grill 1 minute until bottom is lightly browned. Turn crust over and spread with sauce; top with onion and cheese. Cover and grill 2 minutes until cheese melts; remove. Sprinkle with parsley; cut in 12 pieces.

PER SERVING
CALORIES 273 **TOTAL FAT** 10G **SATURATED FAT** 5G **CHOLESTEROL** 25MG **SODIUM** 1,013MG **TOTAL CARBOHYDRATES** 34G **DIETARY FIBER** 2G **PROTEIN** 13G

ROASTED SAUSAGES, PEPPERS & POTATOES

YIELD
6 servings

ACTIVE
5 minutes

TOTAL
25 minutes

- 1 LB **ITALIAN SAUSAGES**
- 2 **BELL PEPPERS**, CUT IN 1-IN. STRIPS
- 1 BAG (20 OZ) **RED POTATO WEDGES**
- 1 TBSP **OLIVE OIL**
- 1 TSP CHOPPED **GARLIC**
- 1/4 TSP EACH **SALT** AND **PEPPER**
- 1/3 CUP **PITTED KALAMATA OLIVES**
- GARNISH: CHOPPED **PARSLEY**

Position racks to divide oven into thirds. Heat oven to 500°F. Line 2 large rimmed baking sheets with foil (for easy cleanup).

Divide sausages, peppers and potatoes between pans; toss with oil, garlic, salt and pepper.

Roast 10 minutes. Toss; switch position of pans. Roast 10 more minutes until sausages are cooked.

Cut sausages into slices; toss with potatoes, peppers and olives. Sprinkle with parsley.

PER SERVING
CALORIES 319 **TOTAL FAT** 20G **SATURATED FAT** 7G **CHOLESTEROL** 51MG **SODIUM** 869MG
TOTAL CARBOHYDRATES 16G **DIETARY FIBER** 4G **PROTEIN** 14G

PAPPARDELLE WITH TURKEY RAGU

- 1 LB **PAPPARDELLE PASTA**
- 2 MEDIUM **CARROTS**, HALVED
- 1 MEDIUM **ONION**, QUARTERED
- 2 CLOVES **GARLIC**, PEELED
- 2 TSP **OLIVE OIL**
- 1¼ LB **GROUND TURKEY**
- ½ TSP CRUSHED **ROSEMARY**
- ¼ TSP **PEPPER**
- ½ CUP **DRY WHITE WINE** (OPTIONAL)
- 1 JAR (24 TO 26 OZ) **MARINARA SAUCE**

SERVE WITH: **GRATED PARMESAN**

YIELD
6 servings

ACTIVE
4 minutes

TOTAL
15 minutes

SIDE SUGGESTION
Baby arugula, sliced red onion and cucumber salad

Bring a large pot of lightly salted water to a boil. Add pasta and cook as package directs.

Meanwhile, put carrots, onion and garlic in a food processor; pulse until finely chopped. Heat oil in large nonstick skillet over medium-high heat. Sauté chopped vegetables 4 minutes or until tender.

Add turkey, rosemary and pepper; cook, breaking up clumps, 4 minutes or until no longer pink. Add wine, if desired; simmer, uncovered, 1 minute.

Stir in marinara sauce, reduce heat and simmer, covered, 2 minutes to blend flavors. Toss with drained pasta. Serve with grated Parmesan.

PER SERVING
CALORIES 562 **TOTAL FAT** 14G **SATURATED FAT** 3G **CHOLESTEROL** 77MG **SODIUM** 661MG **TOTAL CARBOHYDRATES** 78G **DIETARY FIBER** 7G **PROTEIN** 29G

STUFFED PORTOBELLO "BURGERS"

6 **PORTOBELLO MUSHROOMS** (4 TO 5 OZ EACH), STEMS REMOVED, CAPS WIPED WITH A DAMP PAPER TOWEL

SIX ¼-IN.-THICK SLICES FROM 1 LARGE **RED ONION** (SLICES SLIGHTLY SMALLER THAN MUSHROOM CAPS)

6 TBSP EXTRA-VIRGIN **OLIVE OIL**, PLUS EXTRA FOR DRIZZLING

1 LOAF **CIABATTA BREAD**, HALVED HORIZONTALLY AND CUT IN 6 PIECES, *OR* SIX 4-IN.-SQUARE PIECES **HERBED FOCACCIA BREAD**

2 TBSP **BALSAMIC VINEGAR**

1 CLOVE **GARLIC**, CRUSHED THROUGH A PRESS

½ TSP EACH **SALT** AND FRESHLY GROUND **PEPPER**

12 OZ **FONTINA CHEESE**, CUT IN 6 SLICES

18 LARGE LEAVES **FRESH BASIL**, PLUS EXTRA FOR GARNISH

6 THICK SLICES **BEEFSTEAK TOMATO**

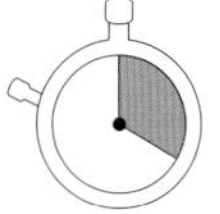

YIELD
6 servings

ACTIVE
20 minutes

TOTAL
35 minutes

SIDE SUGGESTION
Marinated green bean salad

TO SERVE
Place a mushroom "burger" on each piece of grilled bread. Cut a few basil leaves in thin strips and sprinkle on burgers for garnish.

Heat outdoor grill. Brush mushrooms and onion slices with 3 Tbsp oil. Grill onion and mushrooms, gill sides down, 12 minutes, turning after 6 minutes, or until onion and mushrooms are crisp-tender.

Meanwhile, brush cut sides of bread with 2 Tbsp oil. Grill, cut sides down, 2 minutes or just until lightly toasted. Transfer to a platter; cover with foil to keep warm.

Mix remaining 1 Tbsp oil, the vinegar, garlic, and ¼ tsp each salt and pepper. Using a spatula, place an onion slice in the cavity of each mushroom and brush with vinegar mixture. Top each with cheese, 3 basil leaves and a tomato slice. Drizzle tomatoes with oil, if desired, and sprinkle with remaining salt and pepper.

Cover grill and cook 2 to 3 minutes or until cheese is melty and soft.

PER SERVING
CALORIES 516 **TOTAL FAT** 32G **SATURATED FAT** 13G **CHOLESTEROL** 65MG **SODIUM** 1,027MG **TOTAL CARBOHYDRATES** 43G **DIETARY FIBER** 3G **PROTEIN** 22G

OVEN-FRIED DRUMSTICKS

DRUMSTICKS

8 **CHICKEN DRUMSTICKS** (3½ LB)

1 LARGE **EGG**

YOUR CHOICE OF **CRUNCHY COATING**, RIGHT

NONSTICK SPRAY

CRUNCHY COATING

ITALIAN: 1 CUP **WHEAT GERM**, ⅓ CUP **GRATED PARMESAN**, ¼ TSP EACH **GARLIC SALT** AND **PEPPER**

HONEY-MUSTARD: 3 CUPS **HONEY-MUSTARD PRETZEL PIECES**, ¼ TSP **PEPPER**

MEXICAN: 3 CUPS **TORTILLA CHIPS**, 2 TSP EACH **CHILI POWDER** AND **GROUND CUMIN**

KRISPIE RANCH: 1½ CUPS **CRISP RICE CEREAL** (RICE KRISPIES), 1 ENVELOPE **RANCH DRESSING MIX**

CHEESY: 3 CUPS **CHEESE CRACKERS**, 1 TSP **ONION POWDER**, ¼ TSP **PEPPER**

HERB: 1½ CUPS **HERB STUFFING MIX**, 1 TSP EACH **ONION POWDER** AND **PAPRIKA**

CURRY: 3 CUPS **FRENCH FRIED ONION RINGS**, 2 TSP **CURRY POWDER**

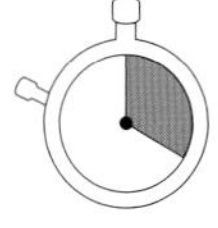

YIELD
4 servings

ACTIVE
20 minutes

TOTAL
50 minutes

SIDE SUGGESTION
Baked potato wedges, mixed greens salad

Heat oven to 400°F. Line a jelly-roll pan or shallow roasting pan with foil. Coat with nonstick cooking spray.

Skin chicken by grasping skin with paper towels and pulling off.

In a pie plate or shallow bowl, slightly beat egg. Coat a few drumsticks at a time in egg.

Place desired Crunchy Coating in plastic food bag. If using tortilla chips, stuffing mix, french fried onions, cheese crackers or honey-mustard pretzels, close bag and crush with a rolling pin. Put 1 or 2 drumsticks in the bag at a time and shake to coat chicken evenly.

Place on prepared pan; lightly coat drumsticks with cooking spray. (If using fried onions or honey-mustard pretzels, do not spray.) Bake 30 to 35 minutes until chicken is cooked through and coating is browned.

PER SERVING
NOT AVAILABLE DUE TO THE VARIOUS OPTIONS.

MEATBALL SOUVLAKI

YOGURT SAUCE

1 CUP **PLAIN GREEK YOGURT**

⅓ CUP CHOPPED **FRESH MINT**

¼ CUP **WATER**

¼ TSP EACH **GROUND CUMIN**, **GARLIC POWDER** AND **SALT**

MEATBALLS

⅓ CUP **PLAIN DRY BREAD CRUMBS**

1 LARGE **EGG**

⅓ CUP **WATER**

1 TBSP **DRIED MINCED ONION**

1 TSP **GROUND CUMIN**

¼ TSP EACH **GARLIC POWDER**, **SALT** AND **PEPPER**

1 LB **LEAN GROUND BEEF**

1 LB MEDIUM **ZUCCHINI**, CUT INTO ½-IN. ROUNDS

1 MEDIUM **RED ONION**, CUT INTO ½-IN.-THICK WEDGES

2 TSP **OLIVE OIL**

3 **PLUM TOMATOES**, CUT INTO 4 WEDGES

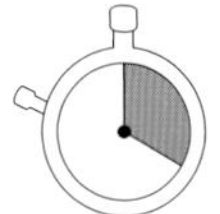

YIELD
4 servings

ACTIVE
20 minutes

TOTAL
45 minutes

SIDE SUGGESTION
Warmed pocketless pitas, lettuce

Position racks to divide oven in thirds. Heat oven to 500°F. Line 2 rimmed baking pans with nonstick foil.

YOGURT SAUCE Mix all sauce ingredients in medium bowl, cover and refrigerate until ready to serve with meatballs.

MEATBALLS Stir bread crumbs, egg, water, minced onion, cumin, garlic powder, salt and pepper until blended. Add beef; stir with fork until thoroughly blended. Roll rounded Tbsps into balls; place on a lined baking pan.

Put zucchini and red onion on other lined baking pan; toss with oil. Place vegetables on top rack, meatballs on bottom. Roast 20 minutes.

Remove pans from oven, turn browned vegetables over, then push to one side and add tomatoes; turn meatballs. Roast meatballs and vegetables 5 minutes more or until zucchini is tender; toss together.

Serve on pitas with lettuce if desired. Top with the yogurt sauce.

PER SERVING
CALORIES 363 **TOTAL FAT** 19G **SATURATED FAT** 9G **CHOLESTEROL** 132MG **SODIUM** 450MG **TOTAL CARBOHYDRATES** 17G **DIETARY FIBER** 3G **PROTEIN** 31G

GLAZED SALMON ON GREENS & ORANGE SALAD

FOUR 5-OZ **SALMON FILLETS**

⅓ CUP **ASIAN GINGER SALAD DRESSING**

2 TBSP **CLEMENTINE OR ORANGE JUICE**

½ CUP THINLY SLICED **RED ONION**

8 CUPS **SALAD GREENS** (WE USED ARUGULA, MIZUNA AND FRISÉE)

4 **CLEMENTINES**, PEELED AND SLICED

⅓ CUP CHOPPED **UNSALTED TOASTED ALMONDS**

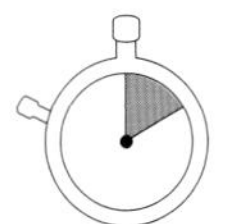

YIELD
4 servings

ACTIVE
10 minutes

TOTAL
30 minutes

SERVE WITH
Sesame breadsticks

Place salmon skin-side down on foil-lined rimmed baking sheet. Spoon on or brush salmon with 2 Tbsp of the dressing. Let stand 15 minutes.

Put remaining dressing and the juice in a large bowl; add onions and toss to coat. Heat broiler.

Broil salmon 8 to 10 minutes or until just cooked through.

Add salad greens and clementines to bowl with onions; toss to mix and coat. Arrange salad on serving plates. Garnish with chopped almonds.

PER SERVING
CALORIES 406 **TOTAL FAT** 21G **SATURATED FAT** 2G **CHOLESTEROL** 90MG **SODIUM** 245MG
TOTAL CARBOHYDRATES 18G **DIETARY FIBER** 4G **PROTEIN** 37G

CHIPOTLE PORK WITH MANGO RELISH & CUMIN SWEET POTATOES

ONE 1-LB **PORK TENDERLOIN**

3 SMALL **SWEET POTATOES**, CUT IN ½-IN. WEDGES

2 TSP **BROWN SUGAR**

1 TSP EACH **GROUND CHIPOTLE CHILE PEPPER** AND **GROUND CUMIN**

½ TSP **GROUND CINNAMON**

¼ TSP EACH **GARLIC POWDER** AND **SALT**

NONSTICK SPRAY

MANGO RELISH

1 FIRM-RIPE **MANGO**, PITTED, PEELED AND CHOPPED

¼ CUP EACH CHOPPED **RED BELL PEPPER** AND MINCED **RED ONION**

2 TBSP EACH **LIME JUICE** AND CHOPPED **CILANTRO**

SERVE WITH: **LIME WEDGES**

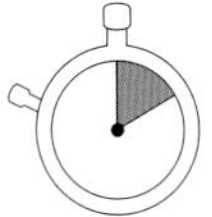

YIELD
4 servings

ACTIVE
10 minutes

TOTAL
30 minutes

Position racks to divide oven in thirds. Heat oven to 500°F. Line 2 rimmed baking sheets with nonstick foil.

Place pork on 1 baking sheet, sweet potatoes on the other. Mix brown sugar, chile powder, ½ tsp cumin, cinnamon, garlic powder and salt; rub over tenderloin.

Coat potatoes with nonstick spray; toss with remaining ½ tsp cumin. Roast potatoes on bottom rack and pork on top rack 10 minutes.

Remove pans from oven; gently toss potatoes and turn pork. Roast 8 to 10 minutes more until an instant-read thermometer inserted in center of pork reads 155°F and potatoes are tender.

Place pork on cutting board; let rest while making relish.

MANGO RELISH Mix all relish ingredients in bowl. Slice pork, top with relish and serve with potatoes. Squeeze lime wedges on potatoes.

PER SERVING
CALORIES 284 **TOTAL FAT** 5G **SATURATED FAT** 2G **CHOLESTEROL** 67MG **SODIUM** 215MG
TOTAL CARBOHYDRATES 34G **DIETARY FIBER** 4G **PROTEIN** 26G

BOW-TIES MARINARA WITH MEATBALLS

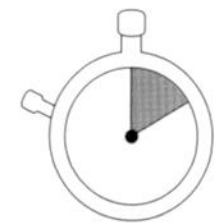

YIELD
4 servings

ACTIVE
10 minutes

TOTAL
20 minutes

- 12 OZ **BOW-TIES (FARFALLE) PASTA**
- 1 BAG (6 OZ) **BABY SPINACH**
- 1½ CUPS **MARINARA SAUCE**
- 2 TBSP **BALSAMIC VINEGAR**
- 1 PKG (24 OZ) **APPETIZER-SIZE COOKED TURKEY MEATBALLS**
- 1 CUP DICED **FRESH MOZZARELLA**

Cook pasta in a large pot of lightly salted boiling water as package directs, stirring in baby spinach just before pasta is done.

Meanwhile, heat the marinara sauce, balsamic vinegar and turkey meatballs in a medium saucepan over medium heat, stirring occasionally, until hot.

Drain pasta and spinach, return to pot and add marinara mixture. Toss with fresh mozzarella.

PER SERVING
CALORIES 821 **TOTAL FAT** 28G **SATURATED FAT** 9G **CHOLESTEROL** 152MG **SODIUM** 1,649MG **TOTAL CARBOHYDRATES** 84G **DIETARY FIBER** 9G **PROTEIN** 52G

ROASTED GREEK CHICKEN & VEGETABLES

1 CUT-UP **WHOLE CHICKEN** (ABOUT 4 LB), BREASTS CUT IN HALF IF LARGE

1 MEDIUM **EGGPLANT** (1 LB), CUT IN 1½-IN. CHUNKS

1 **BELL PEPPER**, CUT IN 1 ½-IN PIECES

12 UNPEELED WHOLE CLOVES **GARLIC**

2 TSP **OIL**

ZEST AND JUICE OF 1 **LEMON**

1 TSP EACH **SALT**, **PEPPER** AND **DRIED OREGANO**

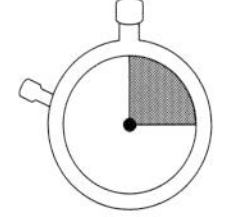

YIELD
5 servings

ACTIVE
15 minutes

TOTAL
45 minutes

SIDE SUGGESTION
Orzo

Heat oven to 450°F. Line 2 rimmed baking sheets with nonstick foil.

Put chicken on 1 side of each pan; put vegetables and garlic on the other side. Drizzle vegetables with oil. Sprinkle chicken and vegetables with lemon zest and juice, and the salt, pepper and oregano; toss to coat.

Roast side by side on middle oven rack, turning chicken and vegetables once, 25 to 30 minutes until chicken is cooked through and vegetables are tender.

PER SERVING
CALORIES 428 **TOTAL FAT** 26G **SATURATED FAT** 7G **CHOLESTEROL** 111MG **SODIUM** 571MG
TOTAL CARBOHYDRATES 13G **DIETARY FIBER** 3G **PROTEIN** 35G

MARVELOUS MEATLESS CHILI

1 **SLOW COOKER LINER** (WE USED REYNOLDS)

1 SMALL **SWEET ONION**, FINELY CHOPPED

2 MEDIUM **POBLANO PEPPERS**, CHOPPED

1 TBSP MINCED **GARLIC** (3 CLOVES)

1 CAN (15 OZ) **RED KIDNEY BEANS**, RINSED

1 CAN (15 OZ) **BLACK BEANS**, RINSED

1 CAN (15 OZ) **CHICKPEAS**, RINSED

1 CUP **FROZEN CORN NIBLETS**

1 JAR (16 OZ) **SMOOTH CHIPOTLE OR ROJA SALSA** (WE USED OLD EL PASO)

1 CAN (8 OZ) **TOMATO SAUCE**

¾ CUP **WATER**

2 TBSP **COCOA CHILI SPICE BLEND** (WE USED MCCORMICK) *OR* **UNSWEETENED COCOA**

2 TBSP **SALT-FREE CHILI POWDER**

2 TSP **GROUND CUMIN**

⅓ CUP CHOPPED **CILANTRO**

SERVE WITH: **SOUR CREAM**, **SHREDDED CHEESE**, TOASTED **PUMPKIN SEEDS**

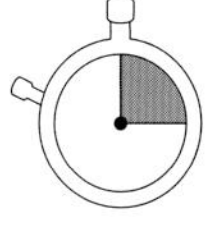

YIELD
6 servings
(makes 7 cups)

ACTIVE
15 minutes

TOTAL
6 to 8 hours on low

SIDE SUGGESTION
Sliced avocados on lettuce

Line a 3-qt or larger slow cooker with liner. Mix all ingredients except cilantro in slow cooker. Cover and cook on low 6 to 8 hours until vegetables are tender and flavors are blended.

Stir in cilantro. Top with sour cream, cheese and/or toasted pumpkin seeds.

PER SERVING
CALORIES 323 **TOTAL FAT** 3G **SATURATED FAT** 0G **CHOLESTEROL** 0MG **SODIUM** 942MG **TOTAL CARBOHYDRATES** 62G **DIETARY FIBER** 18G **PROTEIN** 16G

FISH & POTATO STEW

- 2 TSP **OLIVE OIL**
- 1½ CUPS EACH CHOPPED **ONIONS** AND THINLY SLICED **CARROTS**
- 3 LARGE CLOVES **GARLIC**, MINCED
- 1 TSP **FENNEL SEEDS** (OPTIONAL)
- ½ TSP EACH **DRIED THYME**, **SALT** AND **PEPPER**
- 2¼ CUPS **WATER**
- 1 CAN (14.5 OZ) **REDUCED-SODIUM CHICKEN BROTH**
- 2 LB (ABOUT 5 MEDIUM) **ALL-PURPOSE POTATOES**, PEELED AND CUT INTO 1-IN. CHUNKS
- 1 CAN (14 OZ) **DICED TOMATOES**
- 1 CAN (8 OZ) **TOMATO SAUCE**
- 1 LB THAWED **FROZEN OR FRESH COD OR SCROD FILLETS**, CUT IN 1-IN. CHUNKS

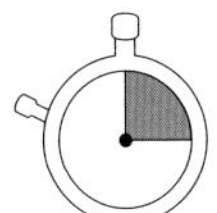

YIELD
6 servings

ACTIVE
15 minutes

TOTAL
45 minutes

SERVE WITH
French bread.

Heat oil in a 4- to 5-qt pot over medium heat. Add onions and carrots; cook, stirring often, 5 minutes or until onions are translucent. Stir in garlic, fennel seeds, thyme, salt and pepper; cook, stirring, 1 minute or until fragrant.

Stir in water, broth and potatoes; bring to a boil. Reduce heat, cover and simmer 10 minutes or until potatoes are tender.

Stir in tomatoes and tomato sauce; bring to a simmer. Stir in fish. Cover and simmer 5 minutes, or until fish is opaque at center.

PER SERVING
CALORIES 253 **TOTAL FAT** 2G **SATURATED FAT** 0G **CHOLESTEROL** 33MG **SODIUM** 697MG
TOTAL CARBOHYDRATES 41G **DIETARY FIBER** 6G **PROTEIN** 18G

STIR-FRY PORK & VEGETABLES WITH SCALLION RICE

YIELD
4 servings

ACTIVE
5 minutes

TOTAL
17 minutes

2 CUPS UNCOOKED **5-MINUTE WHITE RICE**

⅓ CUP SLICED **SCALLIONS**

1 TBSP **OIL**

12 OZ **TERIYAKI-MARINATED PORK OR BEEF TENDERLOIN**, CUT CROSSWISE IN ¼-IN.-THICK SLICES (SEE NOTE)

½ CUP **KOREAN TERIYAKI STIR-FRY SAUCE** (SUCH AS HOUSE OF TSANG)

1 BAG (16 OZ) **FROZEN STIR-FRY VEGETABLES**

¼ CUP **WATER**

1 TBSP GRATED **FRESH GINGER** (OPTIONAL)

Cook rice in water as package directs for 4 servings. Stir in scallions.

Meanwhile, heat oil in a large nonstick skillet over medium-high heat. Add pork and stir-fry 3 to 4 minutes until lightly browned and cooked through. Remove to a bowl; stir in 1 Tbsp stir-fry sauce.

To skillet, add frozen vegetables, remaining stir-fry sauce, the water and ginger, if using. Stirring often, bring to a boil. Reduce heat, cover and simmer 2 to 3 minutes until vegetables are crisp-tender. Stir in pork; serve over the rice.

NOTE Look for vacuum-packed ready-to-cook marinated meats in the refrigerated meat section of your market.

PER SERVING
CALORIES 459 **TOTAL FAT** 8G **SATURATED FAT** 2G **CHOLESTEROL** 38MG **SODIUM** 1,447MG **TOTAL CARBOHYDRATES** 65G **DIETARY FIBER** 3G **PROTEIN** 21G

STEAK & ONIONS WITH HUNTER SAUCE

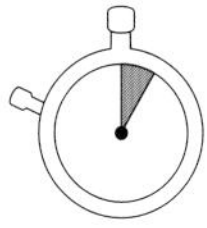

YIELD
4 servings

ACTIVE
5 minutes

TOTAL
25 minutes

2 TSP **OIL**

1 LARGE **SWEET ONION**, SLICED

2 **BONELESS SHELL STEAKS** (ABOUT 12 OZ EACH), CUT IN HALF

¼ TSP EACH **SALT** AND **PEPPER**

1 PKG (1.25 OZ) **HUNTER SAUCE BLEND**

1 CUP **WATER**

SIDE SUGGESTION
Mashed potatoes

Heat oil in a large nonstick skillet over medium-high heat. Add onion; cover and cook, stirring often, 7 to 9 minutes until lightly browned and tender.

Meanwhile, heat another medium or large nonstick skillet over medium-high heat. Sprinkle steaks with salt and pepper. Add to skillet and cook, turning once, 8 minutes for medium-rare. Remove to serving plates.

Add sauce blend and water to skillet. Whisk over medium heat to combine. Bring to a boil, scraping up browned bits on bottom of pan. Boil 1 minute until thickened. Serve steaks topped with onion and sauce.

DIFFERENT TAKES

- Stir balsamic vinegar, to taste, into the prepared sauce.
- Sauté sliced mushrooms along with the onion.
- Slice steak and serve on toasted garlic bread, topped with the onion and sauce.

PER SERVING
CALORIES 480 **TOTAL FAT** 31G **SATURATED FAT** 12G **CHOLESTEROL** 114MG **SODIUM** 584MG
TOTAL CARBOHYDRATES 13G **DIETARY FIBER** 1G **PROTEIN** 34G

BRAZILIAN CHICKEN CURRY

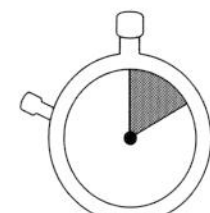

YIELD
4 servings

ACTIVE
10 minutes

TOTAL
4 to 5 hours on high *or* 6 to 8 hours on low

- ¾ CUP **COCONUT MILK** (NOT CREAM OF COCONUT)
- 2 TBSP **TOMATO PASTE**
- 1 TBSP EACH MINCED **GARLIC** AND **FRESH GINGER**
- ½ TSP **SALT**
- ¼ TSP FRESHLY GROUND **PEPPER**
- 1 MEDIUM **VIDALIA OR SWEET ONION**, THINLY SLICED
- 2 **BELL PEPPERS**, CUT INTO 1-IN. STRIPS AND HALVED CROSSWISE
- 12 OZ **YUKON GOLD POTATOES**, CUT INTO 1-IN. PIECES
- 4 TSP **CURRY POWDER**
- 8 **CHICKEN DRUMSTICKS**, SKIN REMOVED (2¼ LB)
- 3 TBSP CHOPPED **FRESH CILANTRO**

SERVE WITH
French bread

Mix coconut milk, tomato paste, garlic, ginger, salt and pepper in a 6-qt slow cooker. Add onion, peppers and potatoes; mix well until vegetables are evenly coated.

Rub curry powder all over chicken. Place chicken on top of vegetables in slow cooker.

Cover and cook on high 4 to 5 hours or on low 6 to 8 hours until chicken is cooked through and vegetables are tender. Sprinkle with chopped cilantro.

PER SERVING
CALORIES 393 **TOTAL FAT** 15G **SATURATED FAT** 9G **CHOLESTEROL** 110MG **SODIUM** 497MG **TOTAL CARBOHYDRATES** 30G **DIETARY FIBER** 5G **PROTEIN** 34G

GEMELLI WITH SPICY SAUSAGE & SPINACH

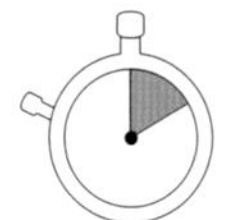

YIELD
6 servings

ACTIVE
10 minutes

TOTAL
15 minutes

1 LB **GEMELLI PASTA**

1 TBSP **OLIVE OIL**

1 SMALL **ONION**, CHOPPED

1 LB **SPICY ITALIAN SAUSAGES**, CASINGS REMOVED

1 CUP **REDUCED-SODIUM CHICKEN BROTH**

½ CUP **HEAVY CREAM**

¼ TSP **GROUND NUTMEG**

2 BAGS (5 TO 6 OZ EACH) **BABY SPINACH**

GRATED PARMESAN

Bring a 5- to 6-qt pot of salted water to a boil. Add pasta; cook as package directs.

Meanwhile, heat oil in a 10- to 12-in. nonstick skillet over medium-high heat. Add onion; sauté 2 minutes or until just beginning to brown. Add sausage and cook, crumbling with a spoon, until browned, about 4 minutes.

Stir in chicken broth, stirring to dissolve any browned bits. Stir in cream and nutmeg; simmer 1 minute. Remove from heat.

Place spinach in colander; drain pasta over the spinach (spinach will wilt). Return pasta and spinach to pot; toss with sausage mixture. Serve with grated Parmesan.

PER SERVING
CALORIES 655 **TOTAL FAT** 34G **SATURATED FAT** 14G **CHOLESTEROL** 85MG **SODIUM** 826MG **TOTAL CARBOHYDRATES** 65G **DIETARY FIBER** 5G **PROTEIN** 23G

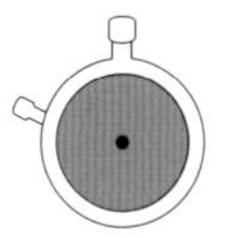

YIELD
12 servings

ACTIVE
1 hour

TOTAL
2 hours 10 minutes

GUILT-FREE LASAGNA

MEAT SAUCE

1 MEDIUM **ONION**, PEELED AND QUARTERED

2 MEDIUM CLOVES **GARLIC**

6 OZ **CRIMINI MUSHROOMS** *OR* **WHITE MUSHROOMS**, STEMS TRIMMED

8 OZ **GROUND TURKEY BREAST**

2 CANS (28 OZ EACH) **CRUSHED TOMATOES**

1 CUP **WATER**

1 TSP **SALT**

¾ TSP **PEPPER**, OR MORE TO TASTE

WHITE SAUCE

1 TBSP **CORNSTARCH**

1 TBSP **FLOUR**

¼ TSP **SALT**

¼ TSP **PEPPER**

1½ CUPS **SKIM MILK**

½ CUP PACKED **FRESH BASIL LEAVES**, CHOPPED

¼ CUP **GRATED PARMESAN**, PLUS MORE FOR SERVING

1 BOX (16 OZ) **CURLY-EDGE LASAGNA NOODLES**, COOKED AND DRAINED ACCORDING TO PACKAGE

1 CONTAINER (15 OZ) **PART-SKIM RICOTTA**

SIDE SUGGESTION
Steamed broccoli

TIP
Can be assembled and baked up to 2 days before serving. Refrigerate tightly covered. To serve, bake, covered, in a 350°F oven 45 minutes or until lasagna is hot in the center.

MEAT SAUCE Place onion and garlic in food processor and pulse until coarsely chopped. Add mushrooms and pulse until onions and mushrooms are very finely chopped. Heat a 3-qt-deep nonstick skillet or Dutch oven over medium heat 1 minute. Add chopped ingredients and cook, stirring occasionally, 5 minutes or until nearly dry and browned. Add ground turkey and, breaking up chunks with a wooden spoon, cook until no longer pink. Stir in tomatoes, water, salt and pepper. Bring to a boil, reduce heat, cover and simmer, stirring occasionally, 45 minutes or until slightly thickened. Remove from heat.

Meanwhile make **WHITE SAUCE**: In a small skillet, whisk cornstarch, flour, salt and pepper to mix. Gradually whisk in milk until blended. Bring to a boil over medium heat and, whisking often, boil gently until smooth and creamy, about 3 minutes. Remove from heat and stir in basil and Parmesan.

Heat oven to 400°F. Lightly coat a 13 x 9-in. baking dish with nonstick cooking spray.

Assemble lasagna (see Note): Place 1 cup meat sauce in baking dish and tilt to cover bottom. Top with 3 noodles, 2 cups meat sauce, then another 3 noodles. Drop spoonfuls ricotta cheese over the top, using all the cheese. Pour on all the White Sauce, top with 3 more noodles, 1½ cups meat sauce, another 3 noodles, another 1½ cups meat sauce, and 3 more noodles, then 1 more cup meat sauce. Reserve remaining sauce (about 2 cups).

Coat a large sheet of foil with nonstick cooking spray. Cover baking dish tightly with foil, sprayed side down.

Bake 50 minutes or until noodles are tender and lasagna is hot in center. Let cool 10 minutes before serving. Meanwhile, heat reserved meat sauce. Serve at the table along with grated Parmesan.

NOTE This recipe uses 15 noodles. If the brand you use has more, cook them all and use the extra to fill spaces in the noodle layers.

PER SERVING
CALORIES 274 **TOTAL FAT** 4G **SATURATED FAT** 0G **CHOLESTEROL** 25MG **SODIUM** 549MG **TOTAL CARBOHYDRATES** 41G **DIETARY FIBER** 0G **PROTEIN** 17G

ASIAN-INSPIRED NOODLES

3 CUPS EACH CANNED FAT-FREE **CHICKEN BROTH** AND **WATER**

1 BAG (16 OZ) **FROZEN ASIAN STIR-FRY VEGETABLES**

1 TBSP **OIL**

4 **CHICKEN CUTLETS** (8 OZ)

1/8 TSP EACH **SALT** AND **PEPPER**

1 MEDIUM **ONION**

1 TSP MINCED **GARLIC**

8 OZ **ANGEL-HAIR PASTA**, BROKEN IN HALF

2 TBSP EACH **LITE SOY SAUCE** AND CHOPPED **CILANTRO**

1 TO 2 TBSP **CHILI GARLIC SAUCE** (SEE NOTE)

GARNISH: **CILANTRO SPRIGS**

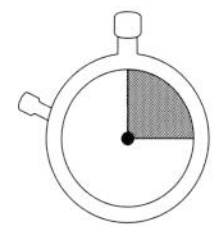

YIELD
4 servings

ACTIVE
15 minutes

TOTAL
15 minutes

NOTE
Chili garlic sauce is spicy hot, so add it cautiously. Look for it in the Asian food section of your supermarket.

Microwave broth and water in a microwave-safe measuring until hot. Microwave vegetables as package directs.

Meanwhile, heat oil in a heavy 5-qt pot over medium-high heat. Season chicken with salt and pepper, add to pot and cook 4 to 6 minutes, turning once, until lightly browned and cooked through.

While chicken cooks, thinly slice onion. Transfer chicken to a cutting board. Add onion to pot; sauté 3 minutes or until golden. Add garlic; cook 30 seconds or until fragrant. Add broth and water; bring to a boil. Add pasta; cook as package directs.

Meanwhile, thinly slice chicken. Add to pot along with the vegetables, soy sauce, cilantro and chili garlic sauce. Ladle into 4 large soup bowls. Garnish with cilantro.

PER SERVING
CALORIES 382 **TOTAL FAT** 5G **SATURATED FAT** 1G **CHOLESTEROL** 33MG **SODIUM** 920MG **TOTAL CARBOHYDRATES** 57G **DIETARY FIBER** 5G **PROTEIN** 25G

PORK ALBONDIGAS

- 12 OZ **LEAN GROUND PORK**
- ½ CUP GRATED, UNPEELED **ZUCCHINI**
- ½ CUP CRUSHED **UNSALTED TORTILLA CHIPS**
- ¼ CUP SLICED **SCALLIONS**
- 2 TBSP CHOPPED **CILANTRO** *OR* **MINT**
- 1 LARGE **EGG**
- 1½ TSP MINCED **GARLIC**
- ½ TSP **SALT**
- ½ TSP **GROUND CUMIN**
- ½ TSP **DRIED OREGANO**
- 1 CAN (10 OZ) **MILD ENCHILADA SAUCE**
- ½ CUP **WATER**

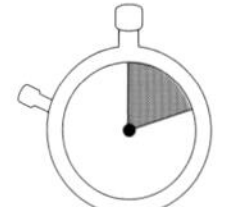

YIELD
4 servings

ACTIVE
12 minutes

TOTAL
22 minutes

SIDE SUGGESTION
Rice

In large bowl, using hands or a wooden spoon, mix all ingredients except enchilada sauce until blended. With moistened hands, roll into twenty 1½-in. meatballs.

Coat a large nonstick skillet with nonstick spray. Heat over medium heat, add meatballs, increase heat to medium-high and cook, turning, 5 minutes, or until brown on all sides.

Add enchilada sauce and water to skillet. Bring to a boil, reduce heat, cover and simmer, stirring occasionally, 5 minutes, or until meatballs are cooked through.

PER SERVING
CALORIES 330 **TOTAL FAT** 24G **SATURATED FAT** 7G **CHOLESTEROL** 114MG **SODIUM** 618MG
TOTAL CARBOHYDRATES 11G **DIETARY FIBER** 1G **PROTEIN** 17G

CAJUN CHICKEN & SHRIMP

2 EACH **CHICKEN DRUMSTICKS** AND **THIGHS** (1¼ LB), SKIN REMOVED, IF DESIRED

1 LARGE **ONION**, SLICED

1 LARGE **BELL PEPPER**, CUT IN THIN STRIPS

4 OZ **ANDOUILLE** OR OTHER SMOKED SAUSAGE, SLICED ¼ IN. THICK

½ CUP SLICED **CELERY**

2 CUPS **WATER**

1 CUP **UNCOOKED RICE**

¼ TSP EACH **CAJUN SEASONING**, **DRIED THYME**, **SALT**

8 OZ RAW LARGE PEELED **SHRIMP**

1 CUP **FROZEN CUT OKRA**

YIELD
4 servings

ACTIVE
10 minutes

TOTAL
40 minutes

SIDE SUGGESTION
Mixed greens salad

Coat a large nonstick skillet with nonstick spray. Heat over medium-high heat. Add chicken and cook, turning once, 5 minutes until browned.

Add onion, pepper, sausage and celery; sauté 3 minutes until sausage is browned. Stir in water, rice and seasonings; bring to a boil.

Cover and simmer 15 minutes or until chicken and rice are almost tender. Stir in shrimp and okra; cover and, stirring once or twice, cook 5 minutes or until chicken and shrimp are cooked through and rice and okra are tender.

PER SERVING
CALORIES 415 **TOTAL FAT** 9G **SATURATED FAT** 3G **CHOLESTEROL** 154MG **SODIUM** 559MG **TOTAL CARBOHYDRATES** 47G **DIETARY FIBER** 4G **PROTEIN** 34G

THE BEST MEAT LOAF

¾ CUP **KETCHUP**

2 LARGE **EGGS**

½ CUP **MILK**

2 TBSP **WORCESTERSHIRE SAUCE**

1 TSP **SALT**

¼ TSP **PEPPER**

2 LB **MEAT LOAF MIXTURE** (BEEF, PORK AND VEAL)

½ CUP CHOPPED **SCALLION**

½ CUP **BELL PEPPER**

1 CUP CRUSHED **SALTINE CRACKERS** (24 CRACKERS)

1 TBSP MINCED **GARLIC**

1 TBSP PACKED **BROWN SUGAR**

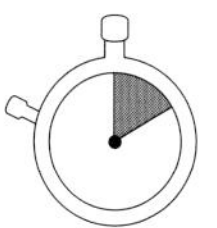

YIELD
6 servings

ACTIVE
10 minutes

TOTAL
1 hour

SIDE SUGGESTION
Mashed potatoes, peas and carrots

Heat oven to 425°F. Line a rimmed baking sheet with nonstick foil.

Whisk ½ cup ketchup with the next 5 ingredients in a large bowl.

Add meat loaf mixture, scallion, bell pepper, saltines and garlic. Mix well with hands or with a wooden spoon.

Place on baking sheet and pat into an 11 x 5-in. oval loaf. Mix remaining ¼ cup ketchup and the brown sugar; spread over loaf.

Bake 50 minutes, or until a meat thermometer inserted in center registers 160°F. Let rest 5 minutes before slicing. Leftovers are great served cold with mustard or horseradish sauce.

PER SERVING
CALORIES 499 **TOTAL FAT** 31G **SATURATED FAT** 12G **CHOLESTEROL** 194MG **SODIUM** 1,094MG
TOTAL CARBOHYDRATES 22G **DIETARY FIBER** 1G **PROTEIN** 31G

PORK CHOPS WITH SWEET MUSTARD SAUCE

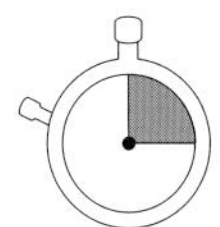

YIELD
4 servings

ACTIVE
15 minutes

TOTAL
15 minutes

¼ CUP **CIDER VINEGAR**

¼ MEDIUM **RED ONION**, THINLY SLICED, PLUS ⅓ CUP FINELY CHOPPED

1 TBSP **OLIVE OIL**

4 **BONELESS PORK CHOPS** (ABOUT 5 OZ EACH), TRIMMED OF EXCESS FAT

1 TSP **SALT**

¼ TSP **PEPPER**

⅓ CUP **REDUCED-FAT SOUR CREAM**

¼ CUP **DIJON MUSTARD**

2½ TBSP **PEACH OR APRICOT JAM**

SIDE SUGGESTION
Mashed potatoes, steamed broccoli florets

Pour vinegar over onion slices in a shallow dish. Marinate at least 10 minutes or until ready to serve.

Meanwhile, heat oil in a large nonstick skillet over medium-high heat. Season pork with salt and pepper on both sides. Add to skillet and cook, turning once, 7 to 8 minutes until browned and cooked through.

While pork cooks, mix sour cream, mustard, jam and chopped onion until blended. Serve on the pork; top with the pickled onions.

PER SERVING
CALORIES 313 **TOTAL FAT** 13G **SATURATED FAT** 4G **CHOLESTEROL** 97MG **SODIUM** 1,001MG
TOTAL CARBOHYDRATES 12G **DIETARY FIBER** 1G **PROTEIN** 32G

MOROCCAN BEEF SAUTÉ

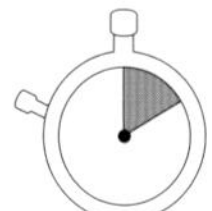

YIELD
6 servings

ACTIVE
10 minutes

TOTAL
30 minutes

1 LB **LEAN GROUND BEEF**

1 MEDIUM **ZUCCHINI** (ABOUT 6 OZ), QUARTERED LENGTHWISE, THEN THINLY SLICED CROSSWISE (ABOUT 1¾ CUPS)

1 MEDIUM **ONION**, PEELED AND QUARTERED

2 CLOVES **GARLIC**

2 TBSP EACH **VEGETABLE OIL** AND **DISTILLED WHITE VINEGAR**

2 TSP **CURRY POWDER**

1 TSP EACH **GROUND CINNAMON, SALT** AND **SUGAR**

½ TSP **PEPPER**

1½ CUPS **WATER**

1 MEDIUM **TOMATO**, CUT IN ½-IN. PIECES

1 CAN (16 OZ) **CHICKPEAS**, DRAINED

⅓ CUP LIGHTLY PACKED **CILANTRO**, CHOPPED

SIDE SUGGESTION
Couscous with sliced almonds and cilantro

Cook ground beef in a large nonstick skillet over medium-high heat, breaking up chunks with a wooden spoon, 5 minutes or until no longer pink. Remove with a slotted spoon to a bowl.

Add zucchini to skillet and stir until lightly browned, about 3 minutes. Meanwhile, put onion and garlic in a food processor and pulse until very finely chopped. Add oil, vinegar, curry powder, cinnamon, salt, sugar and pepper; process until a paste. Add onion mixture and beef to zucchini. Stir until boiling.

Stir in water and simmer until slightly thickened, about 5 minutes. Stir in tomato and chickpeas and heat through. Remove from heat and stir in cilantro.

PER SERVING
CALORIES 267 **TOTAL FAT** 13G **SATURATED FAT** 3G **CHOLESTEROL** 49MG **SODIUM** 576MG
TOTAL CARBOHYDRATES 17G **DIETARY FIBER** 5G **PROTEIN** 20G

ROAST CHICKEN WITH ASPARAGUS

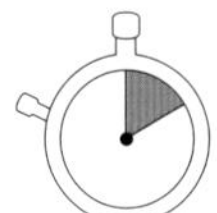

YIELD
6 servings

ACTIVE
10 minutes

TOTAL
1 hour

ONE 3- TO 3½-LB **CHICKEN**

2 TBSP EACH MELTED **BUTTER** AND **FRESH LEMON JUICE** (SAVE LEMON RINDS)

1 TSP **DRIED THYME**

½ TSP EACH **SALT**, **DRIED TARRAGON** AND FRESHLY GROUND **PEPPER**

2 LB **ASPARAGUS**, TOUGH ENDS SNAPPED OFF

LEMON WEDGES

SIDE SUGGESTION
Roasted new potatoes

Heat oven to 475°F. Line a rimmed baking sheet with nonstick foil.

Place chicken, breast side down, on baking sheet. Drizzle with 1 Tbsp each butter and lemon juice. Sprinkle with ½ the thyme, salt, tarragon and pepper. Put lemon rinds in body cavity. Tie legs together with kitchen twine.

Roast chicken 20 minutes. Reduce temperature to 400°F. Turn chicken breast side up, drizzle with remaining butter and lemon juice, and sprinkle with remaining thyme, salt, tarragon and pepper. Roast 30 minutes more.

Place asparagus around chicken, turning to coat with pan juices. Roast 10 to 15 minutes until an instant-read thermometer inserted in thickest part of thigh, not touching bone, registers 170°F and asparagus are crisp-tender. Let stand 10 minutes before carving.

Skim fat off pan juices. Serve juices with the chicken and lemon wedges with the asparagus.

PER SERVING
CALORIES 361 **TOTAL FAT** 23G **SATURATED FAT** 8G **CHOLESTEROL** 109MG **SODIUM** 324MG
TOTAL CARBOHYDRATES 5G **DIETARY FIBER** 1G **PROTEIN** 33G

SKILLET RAVIOLI WITH BROCCOLI RABE

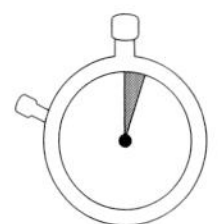

YIELD
4 servings

ACTIVE
3 minutes

TOTAL
17 minutes

1 PKG (16 OZ) **BUITONI REFRIGERATED MOZZARELLA & HERB DOUBLE-STUFFED RAVIOLI**

1 PKG (12 OZ) **MICROWAVE-IN-BAG BROCCOLI RABE**, *OR* 16-OZ **MICROWAVE-IN-BAG BROCCOLI**

2 CUPS **MARINARA OR ALFREDO SAUCE**

½ CUP **SHREDDED PART-SKIM MOZZARELLA**

SIDE SUGGESTION
Romaine, cannellini bean and red onion salad

Fill a large skillet halfway with water. Cover; bring to a boil. Add ravioli; boil 8 minutes, or until tender. Meanwhile, cook broccoli rabe as package directs.

Drain ravioli; return to skillet. Gently stir in sauce and broccoli rabe; cook until hot. Sprinkle with cheese, cover and cook 1 minute until cheese melts.

PER SERVING
CALORIES 478 **TOTAL FAT** 18G **SATURATED FAT** 7G **CHOLESTEROL** 77MG **SODIUM** 1,434MG **TOTAL CARBOHYDRATES** 60G **DIETARY FIBER** 5G **PROTEIN** 23G

HOMEMADE TAKEOUT CHICKEN FINGERS

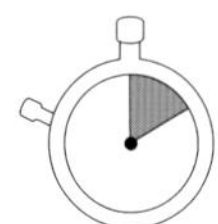

YIELD
4 servings
(20 chicken tenders)

ACTIVE
10 minutes

TOTAL
20 minutes

¾ CUP **PLAIN DRIED BREAD CRUMBS**

1¼ TSP **SALT**

½ TSP **PEPPER**

½ TSP **DRIED THYME**

1 LARGE **EGG**

20 **CHICKEN TENDERLOINS** (TENDERS), THAWED IF FROZEN, *OR* 4 **BONELESS, SKINLESS CHICKEN-BREASTS** (ABOUT 5 OZ EACH), EACH BREAST HALF CUT IN 5 LONG STRIPS

DIPPING SAUCE

¾ CUP **APRICOT PRESERVES**

⅓ CUP **REDUCED-FAT SOUR CREAM**

SIDE SUGGESTION
Rice, steamed broccoli

Heat oven to 450°F. Lightly coat a baking sheet with nonstick cooking spray.

In a large plastic food bag, mix bread crumbs, salt, pepper and thyme. Beat egg with a fork in a medium bowl. Add chicken and stir to coat. Remove 3 strips at a time, let excess egg drip off, then place in bag with crumb mixture. Close top and shake until chicken is well coated. Arrange on prepared baking sheet. Repeat with remaining chicken.

Bake 10 minutes, turning once, until lightly golden and meat is opaque throughout. Remove with tongs to a rack and let cool.

Mix **DIPPING SAUCE** ingredients and spoon into small jars or containers with tight-fitting lids. Pack chicken fingers in plastic containers. Refrigerate until ready to go, then pack in a cooler.

PER SERVING
CALORIES 436 **TOTAL FAT** 7G **SATURATED FAT** 0G **CHOLESTEROL** 142MG **SODIUM** 999MG
TOTAL CARBOHYDRATES 55G **DIETARY FIBER** 0G **PROTEIN** 39G

GREEK-STYLE PIZZA

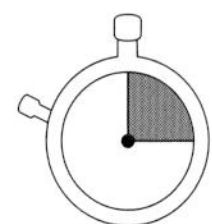

YIELD
4 servings

ACTIVE
15 minutes

TOTAL
34 minutes

- 1 TSP **OLIVE OIL**
- 1/3 CUP FINELY CHOPPED **ONION**
- 2 TSP MINCED **GARLIC**
- 1 1/2 TSP **GROUND CUMIN**
- 1 LB **LEAN GROUND BEEF**
- 1 CUP (8 OZ) **TOMATO SAUCE**
- 1/4 TSP EACH **SALT** AND FRESHLY GROUND **PEPPER**
- 1/4 CUP PACKED **FRESH MINT LEAVES**, CUT IN SHREDS
- 1 PACKAGED **FULLY BAKED PIZZA CRUST**, ABOUT 12 IN. IN DIAMETER (SEE NOTE)
- 3/4 CUP (3 OZ) CRUMBLED **FETA CHEESE**

SIDE SUGGESTION
Lettuce, sliced cucumber and roasted pepper salad

NOTE
This recipe calls for a fully baked pizza crust, sometimes called Italian bread shell. Buy a thin or a thick one.

Heat oven to 450°F. Heat oil in a large nonstick skillet. Add onion and garlic and cook over medium heat until tender, about 2 minutes. Stir in cumin and cook 30 seconds or until fragrant.

Increase heat to medium-high, add beef and cook, breaking up clumps, 3 minutes or until no longer pink. Drain off fat. Stir in tomato sauce, salt and pepper. Cook 2 minutes or until heated through. Remove skillet from heat and stir in half the mint.

Place pizza crust on a large baking sheet. Top with beef mixture and sprinkle with feta. Bake 8 to 10 minutes until crust is hot. Sprinkle with the remaining mint. Serve immediately.

PER SERVING
CALORIES 619 **TOTAL FAT** 30G **SATURATED FAT** 0G **CHOLESTEROL** 88MG **SODIUM** 985MG **TOTAL CARBOHYDRATES** 56G **DIETARY FIBER** 0G **PROTEIN** 26G

GREEN TURKEY CHILI

1 MEDIUM **ONION**, CHOPPED

2 **TURKEY THIGHS** (1 LB EACH), SKIN REMOVED

1 CAN (15.5 OZ) **CANNELLINI BEANS**, RINSED

1 CAN (11 OZ) **WHOLE-KERNEL CORN**, DRAINED

1½ CUPS MEDIUM **GREEN TOMATILLO SALSA**

1 CAN (4.5 OZ) **CHOPPED GREEN CHILES**

2 TSP MINCED **GARLIC**

1½ TSP **GROUND CUMIN**

½ TSP **SALT**

⅓ CUP CHOPPED **CILANTRO**

TOPPINGS: **SOUR CREAM, SHREDDED MONTEREY JACK CHEESE**

YIELD
4 servings

ACTIVE
5 minutes

TOTAL
8 to 10 hours on low

SIDE SUGGESTION
Shredded romaine, diced avocado and tomato salad

Put turkey thighs on top of onion in a 3½-qt or larger slow cooker. Add beans and corn. Mix salsa, chiles, garlic, cumin and salt in a medium bowl; pour over top.

Cover and cook on low 8 to 10 hours until meat is tender. Remove turkey to a cutting board. Cut bite-size; discard bones.

Return meat to cooker; stir in cilantro. Serve with toppings.

PER SERVING
CALORIES 323 **TOTAL FAT** 7G **SATURATED FAT** 2G **CHOLESTEROL** 97MG **SODIUM** 373MG
TOTAL CARBOHYDRATES 34G **DIETARY FIBER** 7G **PROTEIN** 34G

OCTOBER

OCTOBER SHOPPING LIST

Week 1

OCTOBER 1 TO OCTOBER 7

PRODUCE

1 EMPIRE, FUJI OR BRAEBURN APPLE
1 LEMON
2 LARGE ONIONS
4 HEADS GARLIC (3 WHOLE HEADS PLUS 5 CLOVES)
1 LARGE BAKING POTATO
1 MEDIUM BAKING POTATO
1 CARROT
2 BELL PEPPERS
1 SMALL EGGPLANT (ABOUT 12 OZ)
1 MEDIUM ZUCCHINI (ABOUT 6 OZ)
2 LARGE YELLOW SQUASH OR ZUCCHINI (ABOUT 14 OZ EACH)
6 OZ GREEN BEANS
1 LB BROCCOLI RABE
1 PKG (8 OZ) SLICED MUSHROOMS
1 CELERY STALK
FRESH THYME
FRESH ROSEMARY

BAKERY

8 SLICES FIRM WHITE BREAD

MEAT/POULTRY/FISH

4-LB BONE-IN PORK LOIN ROAST
4 BONELESS, SKINLESS CHICKEN BREASTS (ABOUT 6 OZ EACH)
1 LB BONELESS, SKINLESS CHICKEN THIGHS,
1 LB TURKEY TENDERLOINS
1 LB HOT ITALIAN SAUSAGE
FOUR 1-IN.-THICK SALMON STEAKS (ABOUT 7 OZ EACH)

FROZEN

1 CUP CUT GREEN BEANS

REFRIGERATED

½ CUP SHREDDED REDUCED-FAT CHEDDAR
⅓ CUP REFRIGERATED BASIL PESTO
APPLE CIDER

GROCERY

1 CARTON (32 OZ) CHICKEN BROTH
1 CAN (14.5 OZ) CHICKEN BROTH
1 CAN (28 OZ) DICED TOMATOES IN JUICE
1 CAN (16 OZ) CANNELLINI BEANS
1 CAN (8 OZ) WHOLE-BERRY CRANBERRY SAUCE
1 JAR (12 OZ) ONION GRAVY
12 OZ TOMATO SAUCE
12 OZ MINI RIGATONI PASTA
POULTRY SEASONING
¼ CUP DRY WHITE WINE

PANTRY

SALT
PEPPER
OLIVE OIL
CANOLA OIL
FLOUR
LIGHT BROWN SUGAR
DIJON MUSTARD
SEASONED DRIED BREAD CRUMBS

Week 2

OCTOBER 8 TO OCTOBER 14

PRODUCE

2 GALA APPLES
1 LIME
2 ONIONS
1 LARGE SWEET ONION
5 MEDIUM YUKON GOLD POTATOES
2 LARGE RUSSET POTATOES
8 VERY SMALL RED POTATOES
2½ LB SWEET POTATOES
4 CARROTS
1 PKG BABY CARROTS
4 LARGE BELL PEPPERS
2 LEEKS
1 BUNCH CILANTRO
1 BUNCH CHIVES OR PARSLEY
1 BUNCH BASIL (OPTIONAL)

MEAT/POULTRY/FISH

8 OZ LEAN GROUND BEEF
1 PORK TENDERLOIN (ABOUT 1 LB)
4 BONELESS, SKINLESS CHICKEN BREASTS (ABOUT 7 OZ EACH)
1 TURKEY OR BEEF KIELBASA (14 OZ)
1¼ LB FLOUNDER, TILAPIA OR CATFISH FILLETS
2 LB MUSSELS

FROZEN

2 BOXES (10 OZ EACH) CHOPPED SPINACH

REFRIGERATED

1 CONTAINER (8 OZ) REDUCED-FAT SOUR CREAM
½ CUP PART-SKIM MOZZARELLA
1½ CUPS SHREDDED MONTEREY JACK CHEESE
¼ CUP MEXICAN BLEND SHREDDED CHEESE
EGG (1 LARGE)

GROCERY

1 CAN (14.5 OZ) CHICKEN BROTH
1 CAN (14.5 OZ) DICED TOMATOES WITH GARLIC
1 CAN (10.75 OZ) CONDENSED CREAM OF CELERY SOUP
1 CAN (11 OZ) WHOLE-KERNEL CORN
1 JAR (25 OZ) FRA DIAVOLO SAUCE OR OTHER SPICY MARINARA
1 CUP SALSA
CAPERS
12 OZ LINGUINE
ORZO PASTA
LIGHT MAYONNAISE
LOW-SODIUM OLD BAY SEASONING (MCCORMICK)
1½ CUPS PANKO BREAD CRUMBS

PANTRY

SALT
PEPPER
VEGETABLE OIL
NONSTICK SPRAY
FLOUR
HONEY-DIJON MUSTARD
COUNTRY-STYLE DIJON MUSTARD
DRIED THYME
DRIED OREGANO
GROUND NUTMEG
FENNEL SEEDS

Week 3
OCTOBER 15 TO OCTOBER 22

PRODUCE
1 LEMON
1 LIME
1 LARGE ONION
3 MEDIUM ONIONS
1 MEDIUM RED ONION
1 SMALL RED ONION
1 HEAD GARLIC (1 CLOVE)
1 SMALL PIECE FRESH GINGER
6 SMALL RED POTATOES
1 PLUM TOMATO
2 LARGE CARROTS
3 SMALL PARSNIPS
1 SMALL RUTABAGA
2 SMALL RED BELL PEPPERS
1 JALAPEÑO PEPPER
2 AVOCADOS
6 OZ SNOW PEAS
1 HEAD LETTUCE
1 BUNCH SCALLIONS
1 BUNCH CILANTRO

BAKERY
BREAD (FOR ½ CUP COARSE FRESH BREAD CRUMBS)

MEAT/POULTRY/FISH
1½-LB BONELESS SIRLOIN STEAK
2 LB CUBED BEEF STEW MEAT
1 ROASTING CHICKEN (5½ LB)
4 BONELESS, SKINLESS CHICKEN BREASTS (1¼ LB)
2 CUPS COOKED CHICKEN
2 TURKEY THIGHS (ABOUT 2 LB)
4 CATFISH FILLETS (6 TO 8 OZ EACH)

FROZEN
1 BAG (10 OZ) CUT BELL PEPPERS (MIXED RED AND GREEN)

REFRIGERATED
3 CUPS 1% LOWFAT MILK
½ CUP REDUCED-FAT SOUR CREAM
1 CONTAINER (32 OZ) PLAIN LOWFAT YOGURT
2 OZ ⅓-LESS-FAT CREAM CHEESE (NEUFCHÂTEL)
4 OZ SHREDDED REDUCED-FAT EXTRA-SHARP CHEDDAR
4 OZ SHREDDED PART-SKIM MOZZARELLA
GRATED ROMANO CHEESE
1 CONTAINER (16 OZ) FRESH SALSA
1 BAG (1 LB 4 OZ) DICED POTATOES AND ONIONS
HORSERADISH

GROCERY
1 CAN (14.5 OZ) CHUNKY PASTA-STYLE TOMATOES
1 CAN (15 OZ) BLACK BEANS
1 CAN (8.75 OZ) WHOLE-KERNEL CORN
1 CAN (16 OZ) WHOLE CRANBERRY SAUCE
8 OZ CURLY OR REGULAR ELBOW MACARONI
½ CUP ORANGE MARMALADE
½ CUP SALT-FREE SOUTHWESTERN CHIPOTLE MARINADE
½ CUP TERIYAKI SAUCE
FAT-FREE RED-WINE VINAIGRETTE
8 FAT-FREE FAJITA-SIZE FLOUR TORTILLAS
1 CUP PECANS
1 SLOW COOKER LINER (WE USED REYNOLDS)

PANTRY
SALT
PEPPER
HONEY MUSTARD
SUGAR
CORNSTARCH
CHILI POWDER
GROUND CUMIN
DRIED THYME

Week 4
OCTOBER 23 TO OCTOBER 31

PRODUCE
3 LARGE ONIONS
1 SMALL RED ONION
1 HEAD GARLIC (6 CLOVES)
1 SMALL PIECE FRESH GINGER
1 LB RED-SKINNED POTATOES
2 SMALL TOMATOES
1 MEDIUM CARROT
1½ LB BUTTERNUT SQUASH (OR 3½ CUPS FROZEN BUTTERNUT SQUASH CHUNKS)
1 RED BELL PEPPER
1 SEEDLESS CUCUMBER
2 HEADS OR TWO 10-OZ BAGS CHOPPED ROMAINE LETTUCE
1 BAG (6 OZ) BABY SPINACH
8 SCALLIONS
1 BUNCH CILANTRO
1 BUNCH PARSLEY
FRESH DILL

MEAT/POULTRY/FISH
ONE 1¼-LB BONELESS PORK BUTT (SHOULDER)
4 CHICKEN THIGHS (1¼ LB)
1 LB CHICKEN TENDERS
4 CENTER-CUT PIECES SALMON FILLET (5 TO 6 OZ EACH)
1 PACKAGE (14 OZ) SEAPAK TILAPIA TENDERS
1 LB FROZEN PEELED MEDIUM SHRIMP

FROZEN
1 BOX (10 OZ) CHOPPED SPINACH

REFRIGERATED
4½ CUPS MILK
1 STICK BUTTER
¾ CUP REDUCED-FAT SOUR CREAM
2 OZ REDUCED-FAT CREAM CHEESE
1 CONTAINER (15 OZ) PART-SKIM RICOTTA
⅓ CUP SHREDDED JACK CHEESE
2 (1 OZ EACH) MOZZARELLA STRING CHEESE
6 OZ FETA CHEESE
5 OZ GORGONZOLA CHEESE
5 OZ FONTINA CHEESE
GRATED PARMESAN
EGG (1 LARGE)

GROCERY
2 CANS (14.5 OZ) CHICKEN BROTH
1 CAN (14.5 OZ) DICED TOMATOES
1 CAN (14 OZ) CRUSHED TOMATOES IN PURÉE
1 JAR (4 OZ) CHOPPED PIMIENTOS
1 JAR (14 OZ) MEATLESS SPAGHETTI SAUCE
⅓ CUP PIZZA SAUCE
1½ CUPS JARRED MILD GREEN SALSA
1 LB MINI PENNE PASTA
TWELVE 6 X 3-IN. STRIPS NO-BOIL LASAGNA NOODLES
2 CUPS 5-MINUTE RICE
1 PACKET BEEFY-ONION SOUP MIX (FROM A 2.2-OZ BOX)
1 PKT ONION SOUP MIX (FROM A 2-OZ BOX)
SOY SAUCE
CREAMY MUSTARD SPREAD (SUCH AS DIJONNAISE)
½ CUP RED CURRANT JELLY
DICED OLIVES (BLACK OR KALAMATA) GREEK SALAD DRESSING
BLACK OLIVES
1 PKG (10 OZ) PREBAKED MINI 8-IN. PIZZA CRUSTS
5 CORN TORTILLAS
PLAIN DRY BREAD CRUMBS

PANTRY
SALT
PEPPER
OIL
FLOUR
GROUND CUMIN
DRIED OREGANO
SWEET PAPRIKA
SESAME SEEDS
CARAWAY SEEDS

APPLE-STUFFED CHICKEN

1 **EMPIRE, FUJI OR BRAEBURN APPLE**, CORED AND FINELY DICED

½ CUP **SHREDDED REDUCED-FAT CHEDDAR**

2 TBSP **SEASONED DRIED BREAD CRUMBS**

1½ TSP CHOPPED **FRESH THYME**, PLUS 3 LARGE SPRIGS

1 TBSP **LEMON JUICE**

½ TSP EACH **SALT** AND FRESHLY GROUND **PEPPER**, MIXED

4 **SKINLESS, BONELESS CHICKEN BREASTS** (ABOUT 6 OZ EACH)

¼ CUP **ALL-PURPOSE FLOUR**, FOR DREDGING

2 TSP **CANOLA OIL**

¾ CUP **APPLE CIDER**

½ CUP **CHICKEN BROTH**

2 TSP **DIJON MUSTARD**

YIELD
6 servings

ACTIVE
20 minutes

TOTAL
40 minutes

SIDE SUGGESTION
Brown rice, steamed green beans

Coat 12 wooden toothpicks with nonstick spray. In a small bowl, mix apple, cheese, bread crumbs, chopped thyme, lemon juice and half the salt mixture. On a cutting board, lightly press each chicken breast flat with one hand; using a sharp knife, carefully cut into side of breast to form a deep horizontal pocket (do not pierce top, bottom or far side of breast).

Divide the apple mixture into 4 portions and stuff into chicken pockets. With the prepared toothpicks, pin closed. Sprinkle the remaining salt mixture over breasts. Dredge chicken in flour to lightly coat; tap off excess flour. (At this point, chicken can be refrigerated, covered, up to 6 hours.)

Heat oil in a large nonstick skillet over medium-high heat. Add chicken and brown 3 minutes per side. Pour ½ cup of the apple cider and the broth into skillet; add thyme sprigs. Bring mixture to a boil; reduce heat to low, cover and simmer 5 to 7 minutes until chicken is cooked through and stuffing registers 165°F on an instant-read thermometer.

Remove chicken to a serving plate; cover with foil to keep warm. Whisk mustard and remaining ¼ cup cider into juices in skillet; boil mixture 3 minutes on high until reduced and slightly thickened. Spoon sauce over chicken and serve.

PER SERVING
CALORIES 342 **TOTAL FAT** 8G **SATURATED FAT** 3G **CHOLESTEROL** 109MG **SODIUM** 693MG
TOTAL CARBOHYDRATES 20G **DIETARY FIBER** 2G **PROTEIN** 45G

PASTA WITH BROCCOLI RABE & SAUSAGE

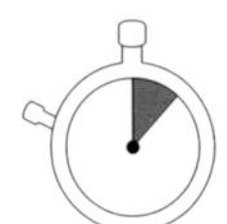

YIELD
4 servings

ACTIVE
7 minutes

TOTAL
30 minutes

12 OZ **MINI RIGATONI PASTA**

1 LB **BROCCOLI RABE**, ENDS TRIMMED, STACKED AND CUT IN 1-IN.-WIDE STRIPS

1 LB **HOT ITALIAN SAUSAGE**, CASING(S) REMOVED

Bring a large pot of lightly salted water to a boil. Add pasta and cook as package directs, adding broccoli rabe 3 minutes before pasta will be done. Reserve 1 cup cooking water. Drain pasta and broccoli rabe; return to pot.

While pasta cooks, heat a large nonstick skillet over medium-high heat. Add sausage and cook, breaking up large chunks, 5 to 7 minutes until browned and cooked through. Add reserved water.

Cook, stirring, 1 minute to loosen brown bits on bottom of pan. Pour over pasta mixture in pot; cook, stirring, 1 minute to heat and mix.

PER SERVING
CALORIES 724 **TOTAL FAT** 37G **SATURATED FAT** 13G **CHOLESTEROL** 86MG **SODIUM** 1,239MG **TOTAL CARBOHYDRATES** 67G **DIETARY FIBER** 2G **PROTEIN** 29G

GARLIC & ROSEMARY ROAST PORK

YIELD
8 servings

ACTIVE
5 minutes

TOTAL
1 hour 30 minutes

4 CLOVES **GARLIC**, MINCED, PLUS
3 WHOLE HEADS **GARLIC**

2 TBSP CHOPPED **FRESH ROSEMARY**

1 TSP **SALT**

½ TSP **PEPPER**

ONE 4-LB **BONE-IN PORK LOIN ROAST**

1 TBSP **OIL**

SIDE SUGGESTION
Roasted new potatoes and baby carrots

Heat oven to 375°F. Mix minced garlic, rosemary, salt and pepper in a small bowl; rub all over pork.

Put meat, bone side down, in a large roasting pan. Cut about ¼ in. off tops of heads of garlic; place heads around pork. Drizzle garlic with oil, rolling heads in oil to coat.

Roast, uncovered, 1¼ hours or until an instant-read thermometer inserted in thickest part of roast (not touching bone) registers 155°F. Let rest 15 minutes (temperature of meat will rise to 160°F). Carve and serve with cloves of roasted garlic to squeeze from skins onto pork.

DIFFERENT TAKES

- Spread pork with Dijon mustard, then with the garlic-rosemary mixture.
- Arrange small new potatoes around the pork before roasting.
- Squeeze roasted garlic into mashed potatoes or toss with cooked vegetables.

PER SERVING
CALORIES 338 **TOTAL FAT** 19G **SATURATED FAT** 7G **CHOLESTEROL** 99MG **SODIUM** 326MG
TOTAL CARBOHYDRATES 5G **DIETARY FIBER** 0G **PROTEIN** 34G

ITALIAN VEGETABLE STEW

YIELD
10 cups

ACTIVE
15 minutes

TOTAL
4 hours on high
or 8 hours on low

6 OZ **GREEN BEANS**, TRIMMED AND CUT IN HALF (1¾ CUP)

1½ CUPS SLICED **ONIONS**

2 TSP MINCED **GARLIC**

1 SMALL **EGGPLANT** (ABOUT 12 OZ), CUT IN 1-IN. CHUNKS

2 LARGE **YELLOW SQUASH** *OR* **ZUCCHINI** (ABOUT 14 OZ EACH), CUT IN 1-IN. CHUNKS

2 **BELL PEPPERS**, CORED, SEEDED AND CUT IN NARROW STRIPS

1 LARGE **BAKING POTATO**, PEELED AND CUT IN ½-IN. CHUNKS

1½ CUPS (12 OZ) **TOMATO SAUCE**

¼ CUP **OLIVE OIL**

1 TSP **SALT**

Put green beans, onions and garlic in a 4-qt or larger slow cooker. Mix all of the remaining ingredients in a bowl. Add to slow cooker.

Cover and cook on low 8 hours or on high 4 hours, until vegetables are tender.

PER CUP
CALORIES 135 **TOTAL FAT** 6G **SATURATED FAT** 0G **CHOLESTEROL** 0MG **SODIUM** 433MG
TOTAL CARBOHYDRATES 20G **DIETARY FIBER** 0G **PROTEIN** 3G

HOT TURKEY SANDWICH

2 TBSP **ALL-PURPOSE FLOUR**

1 TSP **POULTRY SEASONING**

⅛ TSP EACH **SALT** AND FRESHLY GROUND **PEPPER**

1 LB **TURKEY TENDERLOINS**, CUT IN ⅓-IN.-THICK SLICES

2 TSP **OIL**

1 PKG (8 OZ) **SLICED MUSHROOMS**

1 JAR (12 OZ) **ONION GRAVY**

¼ CUP **DRY WHITE WINE**

8 SLICES **FIRM WHITE BREAD**

1 CAN (8 OZ) **WHOLE-BERRY CRANBERRY SAUCE**

YIELD
4 servings

ACTIVE
12 minutes

TOTAL
12 minutes

SIDE SUGGESTION
Baby spinach and sliced pear salad

Mix flour, poultry seasoning, salt and pepper in a plastic food bag. Add turkey slices and shake to coat.

Heat oil in a nonstick skillet over medium-high heat. Add turkey; cook, turning once, 5 minutes or until cooked through. Remove to plate and cover to keep warm.

Add sliced mushrooms to pan. Sauté 3 minutes or until mushrooms start to brown. Add onion gravy and dry white wine; boil 1 minute. Remove from heat.

Spread bread with whole-berry cranberry sauce. Top with turkey and gravy.

PER SERVING
CALORIES 449 **TOTAL FAT** 8G **SATURATED FAT** 2G **CHOLESTEROL** 68MG **SODIUM** 932MG
TOTAL CARBOHYDRATES 57G **DIETARY FIBER** 3G **PROTEIN** 35G

MUSTARD-GLAZED SALMON STEAKS

YIELD
4 servings

ACTIVE
3 minutes

TOTAL
17 minutes

FOUR 1-IN.-THICK **SALMON STEAKS** (ABOUT 7 OZ EACH)

¼ CUP EACH **LIGHT BROWN SUGAR** AND **DIJON MUSTARD**

SIDE SUGGESTION
Couscous, steamed broccoli

Heat oven to 425°F. Line a rimmed baking sheet with nonstick foil. Place salmon steaks on top.

Whisk brown sugar and mustard in small bowl until blended. Evenly divide on top of each salmon steak, spreading to cover.

Bake 15 minutes or until cooked through. Broil, 4 in. from top, 2 minutes or until top is golden.

PER SERVING
CALORIES 352 **TOTAL FAT** 14G **SATURATED FAT** 2G **CHOLESTEROL** 109MG **SODIUM** 178MG **TOTAL CARBOHYDRATES** 15G **DIETARY FIBER** 0G **PROTEIN** 40G

CHICKEN MINESTRONE WITH PESTO

1 CAN (28 OZ) **DICED TOMATOES IN JUICE**, UNDRAINED

4 CUPS **CHICKEN BROTH**

1 LB **BONELESS, SKINLESS CHICKEN THIGHS**, CUT IN 1-IN. CHUNKS

1 MEDIUM **BAKING POTATO**, PEELED AND DICED

½ CUP EACH CHOPPED **ONION**, **CARROT** AND **CELERY**

¼ TSP **PEPPER**

1 CAN (16 OZ) **CANNELLINI BEANS**, RINSED

1 MEDIUM **ZUCCHINI** (ABOUT 6 OZ), DICED

1 CUP **FROZEN CUT GREEN BEANS**, THAWED

⅓ CUP **PREPARED REFRIGERATED BASIL PESTO**

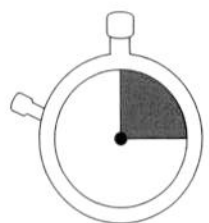

YIELD
6 servings

ACTIVE
15 minutes

TOTAL
7 to 9 hours on low

SERVE WITH
Italian bread

Mix all ingredients except the cannellini beans, zucchini, green beans and basil pesto in a 4-qt or larger slow cooker.

Cover and cook on low 7 to 9 hours until chicken is cooked through and vegetables are tender.

Stir in cannellini beans, zucchini and green beans. Cover and cook on high 15 minutes, or until zucchini is tender.

Spoon into bowls; top servings with pesto.

PER SERVING
CALORIES 289 **TOTAL FAT** 9G **SATURATED FAT** 2G **CHOLESTEROL** 67MG **SODIUM** 827MG
TOTAL CARBOHYDRATES 27G **DIETARY FIBER** 6G **PROTEIN** 25G

BRAISED PORK & APPLE STEW

- 2 TSP **VEGETABLE OIL**
- 1 **PORK TENDERLOIN** (ABOUT 1 LB), CUT INTO 1½-IN. CHUNKS
- ¼ TSP EACH **SALT** AND FRESHLY GROUND **BLACK PEPPER**
- 1 TBSP **ALL-PURPOSE FLOUR**
- 1 CAN (14.5 OZ) **CHICKEN BROTH**
- 2 **GALA APPLES**, CORED AND EACH CUT INTO 8 WEDGES
- 8 VERY SMALL **RED POTATOES**, HALVED
- 1 CUP **BABY CARROTS**
- ½ TSP **DRIED THYME**
- 3 TBSP **HONEY-DIJON MUSTARD**

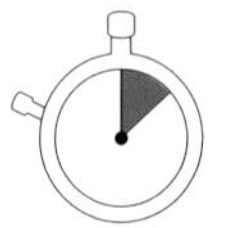

YIELD
4 servings

ACTIVE
8 minutes

TOTAL
30 minutes

Heat oil in 5- to 6-qt pot over medium-high heat. While oil heats, sprinkle pork with salt and pepper, and coat with flour. Cook pork 4 minutes until browned, turning once; remove to a plate.

Add broth, apples, potatoes, carrots and thyme to pot and bring to a boil. Cover, reduce heat and simmer 12 minutes, or until potatoes are tender. Stir in pork and mustard.

Cover and simmer 4 to 5 minutes, until pork is just cooked through.

PER SERVING
CALORIES 364 **TOTAL FAT** 7G **SATURATED FAT** 2G **CHOLESTEROL** 74MG **SODIUM** 555MG
TOTAL CARBOHYDRATES 47G **DIETARY FIBER** 5G **PROTEIN** 29G

ITALIAN ORZO & BEEF STUFFED PEPPERS

4 LARGE **BELL PEPPERS**, HALVED LENGTHWISE THROUGH STEM, SEEDED

NONSTICK SPRAY

½ CUP **ORZO PASTA**

8 OZ **LEAN GROUND BEEF**

1 CUP CHOPPED **ONION**

2 TSP EACH **FENNEL SEEDS** AND **OREGANO**

1 CAN (14.5 OZ) **DICED TOMATOES WITH GARLIC**

½ CUP DICED **PART-SKIM MOZZARELLA**

GARNISH: CHOPPED **BASIL** (OPTIONAL)

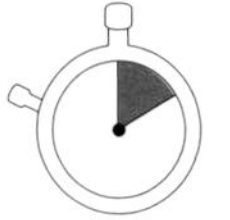

YIELD
4 servings

ACTIVE
10 minutes

TOTAL
35 minutes

SIDE SUGGESTION
Mixed greens salad

Heat broiler. Line a rimmed baking sheet with nonstick foil. Put peppers cut side down in pan; coat peppers with nonstick spray.

Broil 12 minutes, turning once, until lightly charred and tender. Reduce oven temperature to 400°F.

Meanwhile, bring a medium pot of lightly salted water to a boil. Add orzo and cook as package directs; drain.

While pasta cooks, coat a large nonstick skillet with nonstick spray; heat over medium heat. Add beef, onion, fennel seeds and oregano. Cook 6 minutes, breaking up meat with a wooden spoon, until beef is browned and onions are tender. Remove from heat.

Add orzo, tomatoes with their juices, and mozzarella to skillet; toss to mix, then fill peppers. Bake 5 minutes or until cheese melts. Sprinkle with basil, if desired.

PER SERVING
CALORIES 328 **TOTAL FAT** 11G **SATURATED FAT** 5G **CHOLESTEROL** 46MG **SODIUM** 437MG
TOTAL CARBOHYDRATES 36G **DIETARY FIBER** 6G **PROTEIN** 22G

ENGLISH OVEN-FRIED FISH 'N' CHIPS

LIME TARTAR SAUCE

½ CUP **LIGHT MAYONNAISE**

1 TSP GRATED **LIME ZEST**

2 TBSP **LIME JUICE**

1 TBSP **CAPERS**, CHOPPED

FISH 'N' CHIPS

2 LARGE **RUSSET POTATOES**, CUT IN ½-IN. SPEARS

NONSTICK COOKING SPRAY

¼ TSP EACH **SALT** AND **PEPPER**

1 LARGE **EGG**

1 TSP **LOW-SODIUM OLD BAY SEASONING** (MCCORMICK)

1½ CUPS **PANKO BREAD CRUMBS**

1¼ LB **FLOUNDER, TILAPIA OR CATFISH FILLETS**, HALVED LENGTHWISE

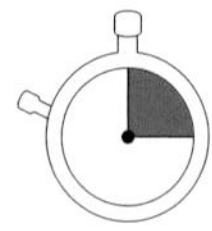

YIELD
4 servings

ACTIVE
15 minutes

TOTAL
45 minutes

SIDE SUGGESTION
Peas

Heat oven to 450°F. Line 2 rimmed baking sheets with foil; coat with nonstick spray.

SAUCE Stir ingredients in small bowl, cover and refrigerate.

FISH 'N' CHIPS Place potatoes on a baking sheet, coat with nonstick spray, sprinkle with salt and pepper, and toss. Bake 30 minutes, turning after 15 minutes.

Meanwhile, beat egg and Old Bay Seasoning in pie plate or shallow bowl with fork until foamy. Place panko crumbs on a sheet of wax paper.

Dip fish in egg mixture, roll in crumbs to cover and place on second baking sheet. Coat fish with nonstick spray and bake 12 minutes or until fish is cooked through and browned. Serve with Lime Tartar Sauce and potatoes.

PER SERVING
CALORIES 492 **TOTAL FAT** 16G **SATURATED FAT** 3G **CHOLESTEROL** 63MG **SODIUM** 625MG **TOTAL CARBOHYDRATES** 55G **DIETARY FIBER** 4G **PROTEIN** 31G

SWEET POTATO LASAGNA

YIELD
6 servings

ACTIVE
25 minutes

TOTAL
1 hour 50 minutes

1 CAN (10.75 OZ) **CONDENSED CREAM OF CELERY SOUP**

½ CUP **REDUCED-FAT SOUR CREAM**

¼ CUP THINLY CUT **ONION**

2 BOXES (10 OZ EACH) **FROZEN CHOPPED SPINACH**, THAWED AND SQUEEZED DRY

¼ TSP **GROUND NUTMEG**

2½ LB **SWEET POTATOES**, PEELED AND THINLY SLICED

1½ CUPS **SHREDDED MONTEREY JACK CHEESE**

Heat oven to 350°F. Coat a shallow 2-qt baking dish with nonstick cooking spray.

Mix soup, sour cream and onion in a large bowl. In a medium bowl, mix spinach, nutmeg and ¾ cup soup mixture. Add potatoes to large bowl and toss to coat.

Layer ½ the potatoes over bottom of prepared baking dish. Sprinkle with ⅓ the cheese, and top with the spinach mixture, ½ the remaining cheese and all the remaining potatoes. Cover dish tightly with foil.

Bake 1 hour 20 minutes or until potatoes are tender when pierced through the foil. Uncover and sprinkle with remaining cheese. Bake 5 minutes to melt cheese.

PER SERVING
CALORIES 341 **TOTAL FAT** 14G **SATURATED FAT** 7G **CHOLESTEROL** 43MG **SODIUM** 633MG
TOTAL CARBOHYDRATES 42G **DIETARY FIBER** 6G **PROTEIN** 13G

CHEESY SALSA CHICKEN

2 TBSP **ALL-PURPOSE FLOUR**

¼ TSP EACH **SALT** AND **GROUND PEPPER**

4 **BONELESS, SKINLESS CHICKEN BREASTS** (ABOUT 7 OZ EACH)

2 TSP **OIL**

1 CUP **SALSA**

½ CUP DRAINED **CANNED CORN**

¼ CUP **MEXICAN BLEND SHREDDED CHEESE**

GARNISH: CHOPPED **CILANTRO**

YIELD
4 servings

ACTIVE
2 minutes

TOTAL
10 minutes

SIDE SUGGESTION
White rice

Mix flour, salt and pepper on a sheet of wax paper. Add chicken; turn to coat. Shake off excess.

Heat oil in a large nonstick skillet over medium-high heat. Add chicken and cook 6 minutes, turning once, until golden and instant-read thermometer inserted side to center registers 165°F.

Top breasts with salsa, corn and cheese. Cover and cook over low heat 1 minute or until cheese melts. Sprinkle with cilantro.

CHICKEN PICCATA VARIATION
Cook chicken breasts as directed above and remove to dinner plates or platter. Add ½ cup chicken broth, ¼ cup water and 2 thinly sliced large garlic cloves to skillet; bring to a boil. Reduce heat and simmer 1 minute or until garlic is tender. Stir in 2 Tbsp lemon juice and 1 tsp capers; remove from heat. Stir in 1 Tbsp butter until melted, then 2 Tbsp snipped chives. Spoon over chicken.

PER SERVING
CALORIES 285 **TOTAL FAT** 8G **SATURATED FAT** 3G **CHOLESTEROL** 123MG **SODIUM** 383MG **TOTAL CARBOHYDRATES** 4G **DIETARY FIBER** 0G **PROTEIN** 47G

MUSSELS FRA DIAVOLO

YIELD
4 servings

ACTIVE
5 minutes

TOTAL
15 minutes

12 OZ **LINGUINE PASTA**

1 JAR (25 OZ) **FRA DIAVOLO SAUCE OR OTHER SPICY MARINARA**

2 LB SCRUBBED **MUSSELS**, BEARDS REMOVED

GARNISH: CHOPPED **CHIVES OR PARSLEY**

Cook linguine as package directs in large pot of salted boiling water.

Meanwhile, heat sauce over medium-high heat in large straight-sided skillet until simmering. Add mussels; cook, covered, 8 minutes or until mussels are opened. Discard any mussels that don't open.

Drain linguine, spoon mussels with sauce on top and sprinkle with chives.

DIFFERENT TAKES

- Substitute 1 lb peeled large shrimp for the mussels.
- Add ⅓ cup white wine when heating the sauce.
- Serve mussels over soft polenta instead of pasta.

PER SERVING
CALORIES 452 **TOTAL FAT** 7G **SATURATED FAT** 1G **CHOLESTEROL** 14MG **SODIUM** 957MG
TOTAL CARBOHYDRATES 79G **DIETARY FIBER** 7G **PROTEIN** 18G

DOUBLE ONION, KIELBASA & POTATO ROAST WITH MUSTARD SAUCE

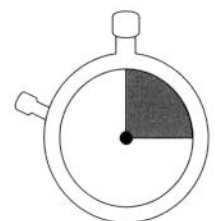

YIELD
4 servings

ACTIVE
15 minutes

TOTAL
30 minutes

MUSTARD SAUCE

½ CUP **REDUCED-FAT SOUR CREAM**

2 TBSP **COUNTRY-STYLE DIJON MUSTARD**

1 TBSP **WATER**

2 **LEEKS**, CHOPPED

1 LARGE **SWEET ONION**, CUT INTO ½-IN.-THICK WEDGES

4 TSP **OIL**

4 **CARROTS**, CUT IN 1½-IN. PIECES

5 MEDIUM **YUKON GOLD POTATOES**, CUT LENGTHWISE IN QUARTERS, THEN HALVED CROSSWISE

¼ TSP EACH **SALT** AND **PEPPER**

1 **TURKEY OR BEEF KIELBASA** (14 OZ), CUT IN 2-IN. PIECES, THEN HALVED LENGTHWISE

Position racks to divide oven in thirds. Heat oven to 500°F. Line 2 rimmed baking pans with nonstick foil.

MUSTARD SAUCE Combine sauce ingredients; chill.

Toss leeks and onion with 2 tsp oil on one baking pan. Toss carrots and potatoes on other pan with remaining 2 tsp oil. Sprinkle all with salt and pepper.

Place onions on top rack, carrots and potatoes on bottom. Roast 15 minutes.

Remove pans from oven; toss. Add kielbasa to carrots and potatoes. Return to oven; roast 15 minutes more or until vegetables are tender. Toss kielbasa with vegetables; pass sauce.

PER SERVING
CALORIES 484 **TOTAL FAT** 26G **SATURATED FAT** 9G **CHOLESTEROL** 81MG **SODIUM** 1,593MG
TOTAL CARBOHYDRATES 45G **DIETARY FIBER** 5G **PROTEIN** 18G

SIRLOIN STEAK WITH GOLDEN ONIONS

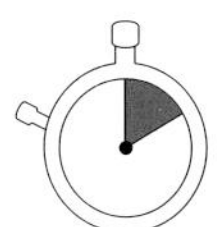

YIELD
5 servings

ACTIVE
10 minutes

TOTAL
25 minutes

STEAK & ONIONS

1½-LB **BONELESS SIRLOIN STEAK**, FAT TRIMMED

½ TSP EACH **SALT** AND **PEPPER**

3 MEDIUM **ONIONS**, SLICED ¼ IN. THICK

HORSERADISH SAUCE

½ CUP **REDUCED-FAT SOUR CREAM**

2 TBSP EACH **PREPARED HORSERADISH** AND SLICED **SCALLIONS**

¼ TSP EACH **PEPPER** AND **SUGAR**

STEAK & ONIONS Coat a large nonstick skillet with nonstick spray; heat on medium-high. Sprinkle steak with salt and pepper. Add to skillet. Scatter onions around steak.

Cook over medium-high heat, turning steak once and stirring onions often, 12 minutes, or until steak is medium-rare and onions are golden and tender. (For more well-done meat, cook steak longer and remove onions first.) Transfer steak to cutting board; let stand 5 minutes.

HORSERADISH SAUCE Meanwhile, stir sauce ingredients in a small bowl to combine.

Slice steak thinly against the grain. Serve steak and onions with the Horseradish Sauce.

PER SERVING
CALORIES 265 **TOTAL FAT** 12G **SATURATED FAT** 5G **CHOLESTEROL** 93MG **SODIUM** 332MG
TOTAL CARBOHYDRATES 9G **DIETARY FIBER** 1G **PROTEIN** 29G

CRANBERRY-CHIPOTLE TURKEY

YIELD
4 servings

ACTIVE
10 minutes

TOTAL
8 to 10 hours on low

1 LARGE **ONION**, THINLY SLICED

2 **TURKEY THIGHS** (ABOUT 2 LB), SKIN AND EXCESS FAT REMOVED

1 CAN (16 OZ) **WHOLE CRANBERRY SAUCE**

½ CUP **SALT-FREE SOUTHWESTERN CHIPOTLE MARINADE** (WE USED MRS. DASH)

SIDE SUGGESTION
Mashed sweet potatoes, broccoli spears

Place onion, then turkey thighs in a 3½-qt or larger slow cooker.

Stir ½ cup cranberry sauce and ¼ cup chipotle marinade in small bowl until blended. Spoon over thighs to coat.

Cover and cook on low 8 to 10 hours until turkey is tender. Remove turkey thighs to cutting board. Cut meat in large pieces from both sides of each thigh bone and slice.

Remove onion from cooking liquid with slotted spoon; discard cooking liquid. Microwave remaining cranberry sauce and chipotle marinade about 2 minutes until melted. Stir in onion and spoon over turkey.

PER SERVING
CALORIES 415 **TOTAL FAT** 11G **SATURATED FAT** 3G **CHOLESTEROL** 108MG **SODIUM** 145MG
TOTAL CARBOHYDRATES 41G **DIETARY FIBER** 2G **PROTEIN** 37G

OVEN-ROASTED CHICKEN & ROOT VEGETABLES

1 **ROASTING CHICKEN** (5½ LB), GIBLETS RESERVED FOR ANOTHER USE

½ TSP EACH **SALT**, **PEPPER** AND **DRIED THYME**

6 SMALL **RED POTATOES**, HALVED

½ SMALL **RUTABAGA**, PEELED AND CUT IN 1½-IN. CHUNKS

1 MEDIUM **RED ONION**, CUT IN 12 WEDGES

2 LARGE **CARROTS**, CUT IN 2-IN. LENGTHS, THICKER PARTS HALVED LENGTHWISE

3 SMALL **PARSNIPS**, PEELED AND CUT IN 2-IN. LENGTHS, THICKER PARTS HALVED LENGTHWISE

YIELD
6 servings

ACTIVE
20 minutes

TOTAL
1 hour 30 minutes

SIDE SUGGESTION
Baby greens salad

Heat oven to 400°F. Line a large roasting pan with nonstick foil. Place chicken on foil and sprinkle with half the salt, pepper and thyme.

Roast chicken 25 minutes. Add vegetables to pan (if there's not enough room in pan, place on a nonstick foil-lined rimmed baking sheet). Sprinkle with remaining salt, pepper and thyme, and toss to coat with drippings.

Roast 35 to 45 minutes longer, tossing vegetables once or twice, until vegetables are tender and a meat thermometer inserted in the thickest part of the thigh, not touching bone, registers 170°F.

Remove chicken to a cutting board; let rest 5 minutes before carving. Arrange on platter with vegetables.

PER SERVING
CALORIES 642 **TOTAL FAT** 31G **SATURATED FAT** 9G **CHOLESTEROL** 152MG **SODIUM** 377MG **TOTAL CARBOHYDRATES** 38G **DIETARY FIBER** 5G **PROTEIN** 51G

MACARONI & CHEESE

8 OZ **CURLY OR REGULAR ELBOW MACARONI**

3 CUPS **1% LOWFAT MILK**

2 TBSP **CORNSTARCH**

2 OZ **⅓-LESS-FAT CREAM CHEESE (NEUFCHÂTEL)**, CUT IN SMALL PIECES, AT ROOM TEMPERATURE

½ TSP EACH **SALT** AND **PEPPER**

1 CUP (4 OZ) **SHREDDED REDUCED-FAT EXTRA-SHARP CHEDDAR**

¼ CUP **GRATED ROMANO CHEESE**

½ CUP **COARSE FRESH BREAD CRUMBS**

1 **PLUM TOMATO**, THINLY SLICED

YIELD
4 servings

ACTIVE
15 minutes

TOTAL
1 hour

SIDE SUGGESTION
Butter lettuce and grape tomato salad

Cook macaroni as package directs 8 minutes, or just until firm-tender. Drain in a colander.

In same pot, whisk ½ cup milk and the cornstarch until smooth. Heat remaining 2½ cups milk in microwave or saucepan until very hot. Add to pot and stir over medium heat until sauce comes to a simmer. Simmer, stirring constantly, 1 minute or until slightly thickened. Remove pot from heat. Add cream cheese, salt and pepper; whisk until cheese melts and sauce is smooth.

Heat oven to 375°F. Grease a shallow 2-qt baking dish.

Toss ¼ cup Cheddar, 2 Tbsp Romano cheese and the bread crumbs in a small bowl until blended.

Stir pasta and remaining Cheddar and Romano cheeses into sauce until blended. Transfer to prepared baking dish. Top with tomato slices; sprinkle with bread crumb mixture.

Bake 20 to 25 minutes until bubbly and brown on top.

PER SERVING
CALORIES 455 **TOTAL FAT** 12G **SATURATED FAT** 8G **CHOLESTEROL** 43MG **SODIUM** 757MG
TOTAL CARBOHYDRATES 58G **DIETARY FIBER** 2G **PROTEIN** 26G

CHINESE ORANGE BEEF

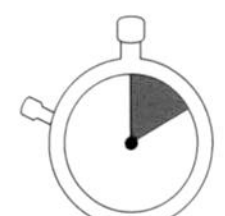

YIELD
5 servings

ACTIVE
10 minutes

TOTAL
8 to 10 hours on low

1 **SLOW COOKER LINER** (WE USED REYNOLDS)

2 LB CUBED **BEEF STEW MEAT**

½ CUP **TERIYAKI SAUCE**

½ CUP **ORANGE MARMALADE**

1 TSP EACH MINCED **GARLIC** AND **FRESH GINGER**

1 **RED BELL PEPPER**, CUT IN ½-IN.-THICK STRIPS

6 OZ **SNOW PEAS**, STRINGS REMOVED

4 **SCALLIONS**, THINLY SLICED

Line a 3-qt or larger slow cooker with liner. Add beef, teriyaki sauce, orange marmalade, garlic and ginger to slow cooker. Cover and cook on low 8 to 10 hours until beef is tender.

Turn to high. Stir in pepper strips and snow peas; cover and cook on high 10 minutes until vegetables are crisp-tender. Top with scallions.

PER SERVING
CALORIES 572 **TOTAL FAT** 33G **SATURATED FAT** 13G **CHOLESTEROL** 120MG **SODIUM** 1,110MG **TOTAL CARBOHYDRATES** 30G **DIETARY FIBER** 2G **PROTEIN** 38G

CHICKEN & POTATO PIZZAIOLA

YIELD
4 servings

ACTIVE
5 minutes

TOTAL
30 minutes

1 BAG (10 OZ) **FROZEN CUT BELL PEPPERS** (MIXED RED AND GREEN)

1 BAG (1 LB 4 OZ) **REFRIGERATED DICED POTATOES AND ONIONS**

4 **SKINLESS, BONELESS CHICKEN BREASTS** (1¼ LB)

1 CAN (14.5 OZ) **CHUNKY PASTA-STYLE TOMATOES**

1 CUP **SHREDDED PART-SKIM MOZZARELLA** (4 OZ)

SIDE SUGGESTION
Romaine lettuce and red onion salad

Heat a large nonstick skillet over medium-high heat. Add peppers and stir 2 minutes or until thawed.

Stir in potatoes and onions. Cook 2 minutes, turning occasionally with a plastic spatula. If mixture sticks, stir in 1 to 2 Tbsp water.

Arrange chicken on top. Spoon tomatoes on chicken, letting juices run over potatoes. Cover, reduce heat to low and simmer 20 minutes or until chicken is opaque at center.

Sprinkle with cheese, remove from heat and cover until cheese melts.

PER SERVING
CALORIES 394 **TOTAL FAT** 6G **SATURATED FAT** 0G **CHOLESTEROL** 99MG **SODIUM** 984MG **TOTAL CARBOHYDRATES** 38G **DIETARY FIBER** 0G **PROTEIN** 44G

SOFT CHICKEN TACOS & BEAN SALAD

PICKLED ONIONS

1 SMALL **RED ONION**, HALVED, THINLY SLICED

2 TBSP **FRESH LEMON JUICE**

¼ TSP **SALT**

BLACK BEAN SALAD

1 CAN (15 OZ) **BLACK BEANS**, RINSED

1 SMALL **RED BELL PEPPER**, CHOPPED

1 CAN (8.75 OZ) **WHOLE-KERNEL CORN,** DRAINED

2 **SCALLIONS**, FINELY CHOPPED

1 **JALAPEÑO PEPPER**, SEEDED, MINCED

2 TBSP FAT-FREE **RED-WINE VINAIGRETTE**

¾ CUP LOOSELY PACKED **CILANTRO**, CHOPPED

TACOS

2 CUPS COOKED **CHICKEN**, SHREDDED

2 TBSP FRESH **LIME JUICE**

½ TSP **CHILI POWDER**

½ TSP EACH GROUND **CUMIN** AND **SALT**

8 FAT-FREE FAJITA-SIZE **FLOUR TORTILLAS**

TOPPINGS: SHREDDED **LETTUCE**, **PURCHASED FRESH SALSA**, SLICED **AVOCADO** AND **PLAIN LOWFAT YOGURT**

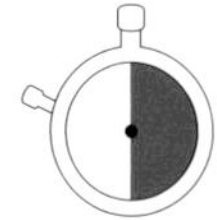

YIELD
4 servings

ACTIVE
30 minutes

TOTAL
90 minutes
(includes chilling)

PICKLED ONIONS Soak onion in a bowl of ice water at least 30 minutes. Drain, then pat dry with paper towels. Dry bowl, return onion and toss with lemon juice and salt. Cover and refrigerate at least 1 hour.

BLACK BEAN SALAD Mix ingredients in a bowl. Refrigerate, covered, at least 1 hour.

TACOS Combine chicken, lime juice, chili powder, cumin and salt in a bowl. Warm tortillas; spoon on chicken mixture, pickled onions and Toppings. Roll up and eat out of hand. Serve with the bean salad.

PER SERVING
CALORIES 439 **TOTAL FAT** 1G **SATURATED FAT** 1G **CHOLESTEROL** 62MG **SODIUM** 1,314MG
TOTAL CARBOHYDRATES 61G **DIETARY FIBER** 10G **PROTEIN** 34G

PECAN-CRUSTED CATFISH

YIELD
4 servings

ACTIVE
7 minutes

TOTAL
21 minutes

1 CUP **PECANS**

2 TBSP **HONEY MUSTARD**

2 TSP **WATER**

4 **CATFISH FILLETS** (6 TO 8 OZ EACH)

SIDE SUGGESTION
Roasted sweet potato wedges; sautéed turnip greens or kale

Heat oven to 450°F. Line a rimmed baking pan with nonstick foil.

Finely chop pecans by hand or in food processor. Spread on a sheet of wax paper. Put honey mustard in small cup; stir in water. Brush one side of fillets with mustard mixture, then press into chopped pecans. Place on baking pan.

Bake 10 to 14 minutes until pecans are lightly toasted and fish is just cooked through.

DIFFERENT TAKES
- Stir a few drops of hot sauce into the mustard mixture.
- Use walnuts instead of pecans.
- Use tilapia fillets instead of catfish.

PER SERVING
CALORIES 425 **TOTAL FAT** 31G **SATURATED FAT** 4G **CHOLESTEROL** 100MG **SODIUM** 188MG **TOTAL CARBOHYDRATES** 7G **DIETARY FIBER** 3G **PROTEIN** 32G

THREE-CHEESE MACARONI WITH SPINACH

YIELD
12 servings

ACTIVE
25 minutes

TOTAL
55 minutes

½ STICK (4 TBSP) **BUTTER**, PLUS EXTRA FOR BAKING DISH

1 CUP CHOPPED **ONION**

⅓ CUP **ALL-PURPOSE FLOUR**

4½ CUPS **MILK**

¼ TSP **SALT**

¼ TSP **PEPPER**

5 OZ **GORGONZOLA CHEESE**, BROKEN IN CHUNKS

5 OZ **FONTINA CHEESE**, RIND REMOVED, CUT IN CHUNKS

1 CUP **GRATED PARMESAN**

1 LB **MINI PENNE PASTA**

1 BAG (6 OZ) **BABY SPINACH**

2 TBSP **PLAIN DRY BREAD CRUMBS**

GARNISH: CHOPPED **PARSLEY**

Bring a large pot of lightly salted water to a boil. Heat oven to 375°F. Butter a shallow 3-qt baking dish or casserole.

Melt butter in a large saucepan over medium heat. Add onion and sauté 5 minutes or until slightly softened but not browned. Whisk in flour; cook 2 minutes or until blended. Slowly whisk in milk. Cook, whisking constantly, until mixture bubbles and thickens. Remove from heat; stir in salt, pepper, then Gorgonzola, fontina and ¾ cup Parmesan. Stir until cheese melts and sauce is smooth; set aside.

Stir pasta into boiling water. When water returns to a boil, cook 2 minutes less than time suggested on package. Drain well. Return pasta to pot, add spinach and cheese sauce and toss until spinach is wilted and pasta is evenly coated. Pour into prepared baking dish.

Mix rest of Parmesan with bread crumbs; sprinkle over top.

Bake about 30 minutes until browned on top. Cool 5 minutes before serving. Garnish with parsley.

PER SERVING
CALORIES 380 **TOTAL FAT** 17G **SATURATED FAT** 11G **CHOLESTEROL** 53MG **SODIUM** 685MG **TOTAL CARBOHYDRATES** 39G **DIETARY FIBER** 2G **PROTEIN** 17G

PORK GOULASH

ONE $1\frac{1}{4}$-LB **BONELESS PORK BUTT (SHOULDER)**, CUT IN 1-IN. CHUNKS

1 CAN (14 OZ) **CRUSHED TOMATOES IN PURÉE**

1 PACKET **BEEFY-ONION SOUP MIX** (FROM A 2.2-OZ BOX)

2 TBSP **SWEET PAPRIKA**

2 TSP MINCED **GARLIC**

1 TSP **CARAWAY SEEDS**

$\frac{3}{4}$ CUP **REDUCED-FAT SOUR CREAM**

3 TBSP SNIPPED **FRESH DILL**

YIELD
6 servings

ACTIVE
5 minutes

TOTAL
7 to 9 hours on low

SIDE SUGGESTION
Egg noodles, peas

Mix all ingredients except sour cream and dill in a 3-qt or larger slow cooker.

Cover and cook on low 7 to 9 hours until pork is tender.

Stir in sour cream and dill.

SLOW COOKER TIP Heat settings can vary from brand to brand, so check for doneness after the shortest cooking time given.

PER SERVING
CALORIES 300 **TOTAL FAT** 20G **SATURATED FAT** 7G **CHOLESTEROL** 77MG **SODIUM** 614MG **TOTAL CARBOHYDRATES** 11G **DIETARY FIBER** 1G **PROTEIN** 20G

VEGETABLE CANNELLONI

FILLING

1 PACKAGE (10 OZ) **FROZEN CHOPPED SPINACH**, THAWED AND SQUEEZED DRY

1 JAR (4 OZ) **CHOPPED PIMIENTOS**, DRAINED

1 MEDIUM **CARROT**, PEELED AND SHREDDED

1 CONTAINER (15 OZ) **PART-SKIM RICOTTA**

2 TBSP **FINELY GRATED PARMESAN**

¼ TSP **SALT**

¼ TSP **PEPPER**

NOODLES

TWELVE 6 X 3-IN. STRIPS **NO-BOIL LASAGNA NOODLES**

1 JAR (14 OZ) **MEATLESS TOMATO SAUCE** (1¾ CUPS)

¼ CUP **WATER**

YIELD
6 servings

ACTIVE
15 minutes

TOTAL
40 minutes

SIDE SUGGESTION
Baby lettuce and cucumber salad

Mix Filling ingredients in a medium bowl until blended.

Pour 4 cups water into an 8-in. square microwave-safe baking dish. Microwave on high until steaming hot, about 5 minutes.

Add 2 strips of noodles. Cook on high 1 minute to soften. Remove noodles to work surface with ridges going from left to right. Place ¼ cup filling toward far edge of each. Starting at far end, roll up noodles, enclosing filling.

Repeat with remaining noodles.

Pour hot water from dish. Add ¼ cup tomato sauce and tilt to coat bottom. Arrange rolls on sauce in 2 even rows. Add ¼ cup water to remaining tomato sauce and pour evenly over rolls.

Cover dish with plastic wrap and poke 2 holes in wrap for venting. Microwave on high 20 minutes (rotating dish ½ turn once after 10 minutes if there's no turntable) until pasta is tender and filling is hot. Let stand about 5 minutes before serving.

PER SERVING
CALORIES 282 **TOTAL FAT** 6G **SATURATED FAT** 0G **CHOLESTEROL** 23MG **SODIUM** 654MG
TOTAL CARBOHYDRATES 39G **DIETARY FIBER** 0G **PROTEIN** 17G

CHICKEN & SQUASH STEW

1 CUP PACKED **FRESH CILANTRO**, FINELY CHOPPED

1 TSP EACH **GROUND CUMIN** AND **DRIED OREGANO**

1/4 TSP EACH **SALT** AND **PEPPER**

NONSTICK SPRAY

4 **CHICKEN THIGHS** (1 1/4 LB), SKIN AND EXCESS FAT REMOVED

1 1/3 CUPS COARSELY CHOPPED **ONION**

4 LARGE CLOVES **GARLIC**, CHOPPED

1 CAN (14.5 OZ) **DICED TOMATOES**

1 CUP **CHICKEN BROTH**

1 1/2 LB **BUTTERNUT SQUASH**, PEELED, SEEDED AND CUT IN 1-IN. CHUNKS, *OR* 3 1/2 CUPS **FROZEN BUTTERNUT SQUASH CHUNKS**

YIELD
4 servings

ACTIVE
35 minutes

TOTAL
1 hour

Mix cilantro, cumin, oregano, salt and pepper in a medium bowl. Add chicken; toss to coat, pressing mixture to adhere if necessary.

Coat a large nonstick skillet with nonstick spray. Heat over medium heat, add chicken and onions, and cook, turning chicken once, 4 to 5 minutes until browned.

Add remaining ingredients (except frozen squash, if using instead of fresh). Bring to a boil, reduce heat, cover and simmer about 25 minutes, adding frozen squash for last 10 minutes, until chicken is cooked through and squash is tender.

PER SERVING
CALORIES 193 **TOTAL FAT** 3G **SATURATED FAT** 1G **CHOLESTEROL** 51MG **SODIUM** 530MG **TOTAL CARBOHYDRATES** 28G **DIETARY FIBER** 5G **PROTEIN** 16G

GREEK TILAPIA TENDERS SALAD

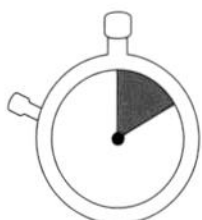

YIELD
3 servings

ACTIVE
10 minutes

TOTAL
18 minutes

1 PACKAGE (14 OZ) **SEAPAK TILAPIA TENDERS**

2 HEADS OR TWO 10-OZ BAGS OF CHOPPED **ROMAINE LETTUCE**

2 SMALL **TOMATOES**, DICED

1 **SEEDLESS CUCUMBER**, SLICED

½ CUP **RED ONION**, DICED

¼ CUP DICED **OLIVES (BLACK OR KALAMATA)**

2 TBSP **PREPARED GREEK SALAD DRESSING**

1 PACKAGE (6 OZ) **FETA CHEESE**

Heat oven to 425°F.

Place the frozen tilapia tenders on a baking sheet and bake according to the package instructions.

Assemble salads in three bowls—chopped romaine, diced tomatoes, sliced cucumber, diced onion, olives and salad dressing.

Cut fully cooked tilapia tenders into bite size pieces and place over salads.

Sprinkle with feta cheese.

PER SERVING
CALORIES 676 **TOTAL FAT** 43G **SATURATED FAT** 13G **CHOLESTEROL** 80MG **SODIUM** 1,673MG
TOTAL CARBOHYDRATES 69G **DIETARY FIBER** 7G **PROTEIN** 29G

SKILLET ENCHILADAS SUIZAS

YIELD
4 servings

ACTIVE
3 minutes

TOTAL
8 minutes

1½ CUPS **BOTTLED MILD GREEN SALSA**

½ CUP **WATER**

5 **CORN TORTILLAS**, TORN IN QUARTERS

1 LB **FROZEN PEELED MEDIUM SHRIMP**, THAWED

2 OZ **REDUCED-FAT CREAM CHEESE**, SOFTENED

⅓ CUP EACH SHREDDED **JACK CHEESE** AND CHOPPED **CILANTRO**

SIDE SUGGESTION
Rice

Bring first 3 ingredients to a simmer in large nonstick skillet. Cover and simmer 1 minute.

Add shrimp, cover and cook 1 minute. Over low heat, stir in cream cheese until melted. Sprinkle with remaining ingredients, cover and cook 1 minute until cheese melts

PER SERVING
CALORIES 275 **TOTAL FAT** 9G **SATURATED FAT** 4G **CHOLESTEROL** 192MG **SODIUM** 929MG **TOTAL CARBOHYDRATES** 22G **DIETARY FIBER** 2G **PROTEIN** 29G

SESAME CHICKEN FINGERS WITH DIPPING SAUCE & ONION RICE

RICE

2 CUPS **WATER**

1 PKT **ONION SOUP MIX** (FROM A 2-OZ BOX)

2 TSP **BUTTER** *OR* **MARGARINE**

2 CUPS UNCOOKED **5-MINUTE RICE**

2 TBSP SLICED **SCALLIONS**

CHICKEN

½ CUP **SESAME SEEDS**

1 LARGE **EGG** WHITE

1 LB **CHICKEN TENDERS**

1 TBSP **OIL**

DIPPING SAUCE

½ CUP **RED CURRANT JELLY**, MELTED

3 TBSP **SOY SAUCE**

1 TSP GRATED **FRESH GINGER**

YIELD
4 servings

ACTIVE
10 minutes

TOTAL
10 minutes

RICE Bring water, soup mix and butter to a boil in a medium skillet. Stir in rice and scallions, remove from heat, cover and let stand 5 minutes or until liquid is absorbed and rice is tender.

CHICKEN Meanwhile, spread sesame seeds on wax paper. Beat egg white in a shallow bowl with a fork. Coat tenders with egg white, then seeds.

Heat oil in a large nonstick skillet. Add tenders and cook over medium heat 2 minutes per side or until golden and cooked through.

DIPPING SAUCE Whisk ingredients in a medium bowl until smooth. Spoon into small bowls.

Serve chicken with the sauce; serve rice on the side.

PER SERVING
CALORIES 591 **TOTAL FAT** 16G **SATURATED FAT** 3G **CHOLESTEROL** 71MG **SODIUM** 1,515MG
TOTAL CARBOHYDRATES 76G **DIETARY FIBER** 3G **PROTEIN** 35G

SALMON-POTATO SKILLET

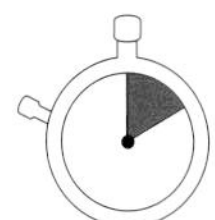

YIELD
4 servings

ACTIVE
10 minutes

TOTAL
25 minutes

1 CAN (14.5 OZ) **CHICKEN BROTH**

½ CUP **WATER**

1 LB **RED-SKINNED POTATOES**

1 **RED BELL PEPPER**

4 **CENTER-CUT PIECES SALMON FILLET** (5 TO 6 OZ EACH)

⅓ CUP EACH THINLY SLICED WHITE AND GREEN PART OF **SCALLIONS** (KEEP SEPARATE)

2 TBSP **CREAMY MUSTARD SPREAD** (SUCH AS DIJONNAISE)

Bring broth and water to a boil in a large, deep nonstick skillet with a lid.

Meanwhile, scrub and thinly slice potatoes. Add to broth; return to a gentle boil and cook 10 minutes.

While potatoes cook, halve, core and thinly slice red pepper. Place salmon on potatoes; top with pepper strips and white part of scallion. Bring to a simmer; cover and cook 10 minutes or until salmon is cooked through and potatoes are tender. Remove skillet from heat.

Using a slotted spoon, transfer salmon, vegetables and potatoes to dinner plates. Add mustard and green part of scallion to liquid in skillet; stir until blended. Spoon over salmon.

PER SERVING
CALORIES 407 **TOTAL FAT** 19G **SATURATED FAT** 3G **CHOLESTEROL** 92MG **SODIUM** 584MG **TOTAL CARBOHYDRATES** 25G **DIETARY FIBER** 3G **PROTEIN** 34G

SPIDERWEB PIZZAS

YIELD
2 servings

ACTIVE
5 minutes

TOTAL
10 minutes

1 PKG (10 OZ) **PREBAKED MINI 8-IN PIZZA CRUSTS** (WE USED BOBOLI)

⅓ CUP **PIZZA SAUCE**

2 PKGS (1 OZ EACH) **MOZZARELLA STRING CHEESE**

3 LARGE **PITTED BLACK OLIVES**

SIDE SUGGESTION
Spinach salad

Heat oven to 450°F. Place crusts on a baking sheet; top with sauce. Pull cheese into thin strips; place on pizzas in the shape of a web.

Bake pizzas for 8 to 10 minutes until cheese melts. Cool 3 minutes.

Cut off one end of 2 olives for spider heads. Halve remaining olives lengthwise. Use one half for body; cut remaining pieces into strips for legs. Assemble spider on each pizza.

PER SERVING
CALORIES 534 **TOTAL FAT** 16G **SATURATED FAT** 8G **CHOLESTEROL** 16MG **SODIUM** 1,198MG
TOTAL CARBOHYDRATES 75G **DIETARY FIBER** 4G **PROTEIN** 24G

NOVEMBER

NOVEMBER SHOPPING LIST

Week 1

NOVEMBER 1 TO NOVEMBER 7

PRODUCE

1 PEAR
1 LEMON
1 LIME
5 MEDIUM ONIONS
2 HEADS GARLIC (10 CLOVES)
1½ LB NEW POTATOES
1 MEDIUM SWEET POTATO (10 TO 12 OZ)
2 LARGE TOMATOES
4 PLUM TOMATOES
1 PT GRAPE TOMATOES
6 MEDIUM CARROTS
1 MEDIUM PARSNIP
2 CUBANELLE PEPPERS
1 LARGE EGGPLANT (1¼ LB)
1 LEEK
1 BUNCH WATERCRESS
1 BUNCH BASIL
1 BUNCH CILANTRO
FRESH CHIVES
FRESH OREGANO

MEAT/POULTRY/FISH

4½-LB TOP ROUND BONELESS BEEF ROAST
1¼ LB LEAN GROUND BEEF
1 BONELESS LEG OF LAMB (4 TO 6 LB)
4 BONELESS, SKINLESS CHICKEN BREASTS
2 LB BONELESS, SKINLESS CHICKEN THIGHS
1 LB MEDIUM-SIZE SHRIMP

FROZEN

1 BAG (16 TO 20 OZ) MIXED VEGETABLES

REFRIGERATED

1 CONTAINER (16 OZ) REDUCED-FAT SOUR CREAM
½ CUP RICOTTA
2 OZ FETA CHEESE

GROCERY

2 CANS (14.5 OZ) CHICKEN BROTH
1 CAN (14.5 OZ) BEEF BROTH
1 CAN (28 OZ) DICED ROASTED TOMATOES
1 CAN (15.5 OZ) CANNELLINI BEANS
1 CAN (15 OZ) WHOLE-KERNEL CORN
1 JAR (16 OZ) SALSA VERDE (GREEN SALSA)
3 TBSP TOMATO PASTE
12 OZ RIGATONI PASTA
1 BOX (13.75 OZ) INSTANT MASHED POTATO FLAKES
1 ENVELOPE (1.25 OZ) HUNTER SAUCE MIX (WE USED MCCORMICK)
½ CUP RAISINS OR SLICED DATES
¼ CUP TOASTED PINE NUTS
⅓ CUP DRY RED WINE OR BEEF BROTH

PANTRY

SALT
PEPPER
OLIVE OIL
GRAINY DIJON MUSTARD
FLOUR
GROUND CUMIN
GROUND CINNAMON
GROUND GINGER
GROUND CORIANDER
DRIED THYME
DRIED ROSEMARY

Week 2

NOVEMBER 8 TO NOVEMBER 14

PRODUCE

2 LIMES
2 MEDIUM ONIONS
1 SMALL ONION
1 HEAD GARLIC (4 CLOVES)
3 LARGE RIPE TOMATOES
4 CARROTS
1 SMALL BUTTERNUT SQUASH
1 RED BELL PEPPER
2 CUBANELLE PEPPERS
1 SMALL RIPE AVOCADO
4 OZ MUSHROOMS
1 HEAD ROMAINE LETTUCE
4 SCALLIONS
1 BUNCH BASIL
1 BUNCH MINT
1 BUNCH PARSLEY
1 BUNCH CILANTRO (OPTIONAL)

BAKERY

4 CRUSTY ROLLS
6 SANDWICH-SIZE PITA POCKETS

MEAT/POULTRY/FISH

FOUR ½-IN.-THICK BLADE STEAKS (ABOUT 1¼ LB)
8 THIN PORK-LOIN CUTLETS (12 OZ)
1 LB CHICKEN TENDERS
4 EACH CHICKEN DRUMSTICKS AND THIGHS, (2¼ LB)
FOUR ¾-IN.-THICK PIECES COD FILLET (ABOUT 6 OZ EACH)
1½ LB SEA SCALLOPS

REFRIGERATED

HEAVY (WHIPPING) CREAM
8 OZ SHREDDED MOZZARELLA
GRATED PARMESAN
⅓ CUP PESTO

GROCERY

1 CAN (28 OZ) DICED TOMATOES
1 CAN (14.5 OZ) DICED TOMATOES IN JUICE
1 CAN (14.5 OZ) DICED TOMATOES (PREFERABLY FIRE-ROASTED) WITH GREEN CHILES
1 CAN (15 OZ) CHICKPEAS
1 CAN (14 OZ) LIGHT COCONUT MILK
⅓ CUP PIMIENTO-STUFFED GREEN OLIVES
CAPERS
GREEN CURRY PASTE
¼ CUP REDUCED-FAT MAYONNAISE
FISH SAUCE
ONE 16-OZ BOX RICE NOODLES
PICKLED JALAPEÑO PEPPERS
YELLOW CORNMEAL
⅓ CUP RAISINS
ALMONDS (OPTIONAL)

PANTRY

SALT
PEPPER
OLIVE OIL
FLOUR

GROUND CUMIN
GROUND CINNAMON
GROUND GINGER
CHILI POWDER
CAYENNE PEPPER
DRIED OREGANO

Week 3

NOVEMBER 15 TO NOVEMBER 22

PRODUCE
1 LIME
1 LARGE ONION
1 MEDIUM ONION
1 SMALL ONION
2 SHALLOTS
1 HEAD GARLIC (6 CLOVES)
1 PIECE GINGER
1 LARGE TOMATO
2 PLUM TOMATOES
2 RED BELL PEPPERS
2 BELL PEPPERS (ANY COLOR)
1 LARGE ZUCCHINI
1 MEDIUM ZUCCHINI
1 LARGE HEAD CAULIFLOWER
2 PKG (3.5 OZ EACH) SHIITAKE MUSHROOMS
1 FIRM-RIPE AVOCADO
1 SMALL HEAD LETTUCE
1 BAG (12 OZ) BROCCOLI SLAW
8 SCALLIONS
1 BUNCH CILANTRO
FRESH TARRAGON (OR DRIED)

MEAT/POULTRY/FISH
4 FULLY COOKED SPICY BEEF SAUSAGES (FROM A 14-OZ PKG)
1½-LB BONELESS PORK LOIN ROAST
4 BONELESS, SKINLESS CHICKEN BREASTS (6 OZ EACH)
4 EACH CHICKEN DRUMSTICKS AND THIGHS (ABOUT 2½ LB)
1 LB 97%-LEAN GROUND TURKEY
1½ LB TILAPIA FILLETS

FROZEN
½ CUP PEAS

REFRIGERATED
¼ CUP MILK
½ CUP HEAVY CREAM
1 CONTAINER (8 OZ) REDUCED-FAT SOUR CREAM
1 CUP SHREDDED MEXICAN OR TACO CHEESE BLEND
4 OZ FAT-FREE CREAM CHEESE

GROCERY
1 CAN (14 OZ) VEGETABLE BROTH
1 CAN (13.5 OZ) LITE COCONUT MILK (NOT CREAM OF COCONUT)
1 CAN (11 OZ) MEXICAN-STYLE CORN
1 BAG (16 OZ) RED LENTILS
1 JAR (16 OZ) THICK & CHUNKY SALSA
2 CUPS MARINARA SAUCE
1 CUP PICO DE GALLO
1 BOX (14.5 OZ) PENNE RIGATE
2 CUPS INSTANT BROWN RICE
1 BOX (8 OZ) RED BEANS AND RICE MIX
2 TBSP JAMAICAN JERK SEASONING (SUCH AS WALKERSWOOD)
HOISIN SAUCE
12 SMALL FLOUR TORTILLAS
1 PKG (1.25 OZ) LOW-SODIUM TACO SEASONING MIX
BAKED TORTILLA CHIPS
YELLOW CORNMEAL
TARRAGON VINEGAR
¼ CUP VODKA

PANTRY
SALT
PEPPER
OLIVE OIL
RICE-WINE VINEGAR
DIJON MUSTARD
FLOUR
SUGAR
CHILI POWDER
RED CURRY POWDER
GROUND CUMIN

Week 4

NOVEMBER 23 TO NOVEMBER 30

PRODUCE
1 SMALL FRESH PINEAPPLE
2 ONIONS
1 LARGE ONION
1 MEDIUM RED ONION
1 HEAD GARLIC (6 CLOVES)
2 LARGE SWEET POTATOES
1 TOMATO
1 PT GRAPE TOMATOES
1 CARROT
4 BELL PEPPERS (ANY COLOR)
1 RED BELL PEPPER
1 MEDIUM ZUCCHINI
2 CELERY STICKS
1 LARGE ZUCCHINI
1 PACKAGE (8 OZ) SLICED MUSHROOMS
3 SCALLIONS
2 BUNCHES CILANTRO
1 BUNCH PARSLEY (OPTIONAL)
FRESH THYME
FRESH ROSEMARY (OR DRIED)

BAKERY
4 SANDWICH ROLLS

DELI
1 STRIP BACON

FROZEN
1 CUP CORN

MEAT/POULTRY/FISH
ONE 3½-LB ROLLED AND TIED BONELESS BEEF CHUCK ROAST
8 OZ LEAN GROUND BEEF
1 PORK TENDERLOIN (ABOUT 12 OZ)
4 BONELESS, SKINLESS CHICKEN BREASTS (5 TO 6 OZ EACH)
1 WHOLE TURKEY (12 TO 14 LB), FRESH OR THAWED FROZEN
8 OZ DICED COOKED TURKEY BREAST
FOUR 6- TO 8-OZ SALMON STEAKS OR FILLETS

REFRIGERATED
½ STICK BUTTER
1 CONTAINER (6 OZ) REDUCED-FAT SOUR CREAM
6 OZ REDUCED-FAT SWISS CHEESE
1 BAG (8 OZ) REDUCED-FAT SHREDDED CHEDDAR
GRATED PARMESAN

GROCERY
1 CAN (14.5 OZ) CHICKEN BROTH
1 CAN (28 OZ) WHOLE TOMATOES IN JUICE
1 CAN (28 OZ) CRUSHED TOMATOES
1 CAN (15.5 OZ) LOW-SODIUM BLACK BEANS
1 CAN (15 OZ) 100% PURE PUMPKIN
1 JAR (7 OZ) ROASTED RED PEPPERS
1 JAR (7 OZ) ROASTED RED PEPPERS
1¼ CUPS SALSA VERDE (GREEN SALSA)
BARBECUE SAUCE
LOWFAT MAYONNAISE
BOTTLED ITALIAN DRESSING
8 CORN TORTILLAS
CORNMEAL
BULGUR
1 CUP DRY RED WINE (OR 1 TBSP RED-WINE VINEGAR)
½ CUP DRY WHITE WINE (OPTIONAL)

PANTRY
SALT
PEPPER
OLIVE OIL
SALT-FREE CHILI POWDER
GROUND CUMIN
DRIED THYME

RIGATONI ALLA NORMA

YIELD
4 servings

ACTIVE
8 minutes

TOTAL
18 minutes

12 OZ **RIGATONI PASTA**

2 TBSP **OLIVE OIL**

1 MEDIUM **ONION**, SLICED

4 CLOVES **GARLIC**, SLICED

1 LARGE **EGGPLANT** (1¼ LB), CUT INTO ¾-IN. CHUNKS

¼ TSP EACH **SALT** AND **PEPPER**

1 CAN (28 OZ) **DICED ROASTED TOMATOES**

½ CUP TORN **FRESH BASIL LEAVES**, PLUS MORE FOR GARNISH

½ CUP **RICOTTA**

SIDE SUGGESTION
Baby arugula salad

Bring a large pot of lightly salted water to a boil. Add pasta and cook as package directs.

Meanwhile, heat oil in a large nonstick skillet over medium-high heat. Add onion and garlic; sauté 2 minutes. Add eggplant, salt and pepper; cook 5 minutes or until eggplant starts to brown.

Add tomatoes and their juices, cover and cook 3 minutes or until eggplant is tender. Add to drained pasta along with basil. Top each serving with a couple Tbsp of ricotta; garnish with more basil.

PER SERVING
CALORIES 543 **TOTAL FAT** 12G **SATURATED FAT** 4G **CHOLESTEROL** 16MG **SODIUM** 669MG
TOTAL CARBOHYDRATES 90G **DIETARY FIBER** 8G **PROTEIN** 18G

SHEPHERD'S PIE

1 BOX **INSTANT MASHED POTATO FLAKES**

1 MEDIUM **SWEET POTATO** (10 TO 12 OZ), PEELED AND DICED

¼ TSP **PEPPER**

1¼ LB **LEAN GROUND BEEF**

1 MEDIUM **ONION**, CHOPPED

1 TSP **DRIED THYME**

1 ENVELOPE (1.25 OZ) **HUNTER SAUCE MIX** (WE USED MCCORMICK)

3 TBSP **TOMATO PASTE**

1½ CUPS **WATER**

1 BAG (16 TO 20 OZ) **FROZEN MIXED VEGETABLES** (4 CUPS)

YIELD
8 servings

ACTIVE
15 minutes

TOTAL
45 minutes

Heat oven to 400°F. Prepare instant potatoes for 4 servings as package directs, adding diced sweet potatoes to water in step 1. Bring to a boil and simmer, covered, 5 minutes or until sweet potatoes are soft. Remove from heat (do not drain). Mash sweet potatoes in saucepan, then continue as package directs. Stir in pepper.

Meanwhile, cook ground beef and onion in a large skillet over medium-high heat, stirring, 5 minutes or until beef is no longer pink. Stir in thyme, sauce mix, tomato paste and water until well mixed. Bring to a boil, stir in frozen vegetables and remove skillet from heat.

Spoon meat and vegetable mixture into a 2-qt shallow baking dish. Spread mashed potatoes on top to within 1 in. from edges of dish. Bake, uncovered, 20 minutes or until mixture is bubbly and heated through. If desired, place casserole under broiler until potatoes are slightly browned.

PER SERVING
CALORIES 267 **TOTAL FAT** 7G **SATURATED FAT** 3G **CHOLESTEROL** 46MG **SODIUM** 305MG
TOTAL CARBOHYDRATES 30G **DIETARY FIBER** 4G **PROTEIN** 18G

SHRIMP WITH POTATOES & FETA

YIELD
4 servings

ACTIVE
20 minutes

TOTAL
47 minutes

1½ LB **NEW POTATOES**, CUT IN ½-IN.-THICK SLICES

½ CUP **WATER**

4 TSP **OLIVE OIL**, PREFERABLY EXTRA-VIRGIN

1 TBSP CHOPPED **FRESH OREGANO** *OR* ¾ TEASPOON **DRIED**

¼ TSP FRESHLY GRATED **LEMON ZEST**

½ TSP EACH **SALT** AND FRESHLY GROUND **PEPPER**

4 **PLUM TOMATOES**, SLICED

1 TSP MINCED **GARLIC**

1 LB MEDIUM-SIZE **SHRIMP**, SHELLED AND DEVEINED

2 OZ **FETA CHEESE**, CRUMBLED (½ CUP)

Put potatoes and water in a 13 x 9-in. glass baking dish. To cook potatoes in microwave: Cover with vented plastic wrap and microwave on high 6 minutes. Stir, cover and microwave 6 minutes longer or until potatoes are just tender. To cook in conventional oven: Cover with foil and bake in a 350°F oven 40 minutes or until just tender.

Drain potatoes, then return to baking dish. Add 2 tsp of the oil, the oregano, lemon zest and ¼ tsp each of the salt and pepper and stir to mix.

Heat oven to 400°F. Toss tomatoes, garlic, remaining 2 tsp oil and remaining ¼ tsp each salt and pepper in a medium bowl. Spoon over potato mixture, then arrange shrimp on top.

Bake 15 minutes. Remove from oven and sprinkle with feta.

PER SERVING
CALORIES 324 **TOTAL FAT** 10G **SATURATED FAT** 0G **CHOLESTEROL** 152MG **SODIUM** 585MG
TOTAL CARBOHYDRATES 34G **DIETARY FIBER** 0G **PROTEIN** 24G

GREEN CHILI

YIELD
6 servings
(makes 8 cups)

ACTIVE
10 minutes

TOTAL
5 o 6 hours on high *or*
8 to 9 hours on low

1 JAR (16 OZ) **SALSA VERDE** (GREEN SALSA, 1¾ CUP)

2 LB **BONELESS, SKINLESS CHICKEN THIGHS**, CUT INTO 1 ½-IN. PIECES

1 CAN (15 OZ) **WHOLE-KERNEL CORN**, DRAINED

1 CAN (15.5 OZ) **CANNELLINI BEANS**, RINSED

2 **CUBANELLE PEPPERS**, CHOPPED

1 MEDIUM **ONION**, FINELY CHOPPED

1 TBSP MINCED **GARLIC**

2 TSP **GROUND CUMIN**

½ TSP **SALT**

½ CUP CHOPPED **CILANTRO**

SERVE WITH: **LIME WEDGES, SOUR CREAM**

Mix all ingredients except cilantro in a 3½-qt or larger slow cooker.

Cover and cook on high 5 to 6 hours or on low 8 to 9 hours until chicken is cooked through.

Stir in cilantro; serve with lime wedges and sour cream.

DIFFERENT TAKES

- Use 2 large turkey thighs instead of chicken thighs. Remove the skin and cook as above; shred the meat and serve in warmed flour or corn tortillas.
- Substitute a 2-lb pork shoulder roast for the chicken. Cook 6 to 7 hours on high or 9 to 10 hours on low. Shred or cut meat into bite-size pieces.
- Instead of canned corn, add a 15- or 16-oz can black beans, rinsed and well drained, or a 15- or 16-oz can hominy (which will thicken and bulk up the chili).

PER SERVING
CALORIES 322 **TOTAL FAT** 7G **SATURATED FAT** 2G **CHOLESTEROL** 125MG **SODIUM** 825MG
TOTAL CARBOHYDRATES 29G **DIETARY FIBER** 5G **PROTEIN** 35G

SWEET & SPICY LAMB TAGINE

1 TSP EACH **GROUND CUMIN, CINNAMON, GINGER** AND **CORIANDER**

2 TBSP **OLIVE OIL**

1 **BONELESS LEG OF LAMB** (4 TO 6 LB), TRIMMED OF FAT AND CUT INTO BITE-SIZE PIECES

SALT AND FRESHLY GROUND **PEPPER**, TO TASTE

1½ CUPS **CHICKEN BROTH**

2 LARGE **TOMATOES**, PEELED, SEEDED AND COARSELY CHOPPED

1 MEDIUM **ONION**, CHOPPED

1 **LEEK**, WHITE PART ONLY, CLEANED AND SLICED

2 MEDIUM **CARROTS**, PEELED AND CHOPPED

1 **PEAR**, PEELED AND DICED

½ CUP **RAISINS** *OR* **SLICED DATES**

¼ CUP **TOASTED PINE NUTS**

YIELD
6 servings

ACTIVE
35 minutes

TOTAL
4 to 5 hours on high *or* 8 to 10 hours on low

SIDE SUGGESTION
Couscous

Combine cumin, cinnamon, ginger and coriander, and divide mixture in half.

In a large nonstick skillet, heat 1 Tbsp of the oil over high heat; add lamb, half the spice mixture and salt and pepper to taste. Brown the lamb well on all sides, then transfer it to the slow cooker, draining any fat from the skillet.

Heat remaining oil and spice mixture in the same skillet over medium heat until aromatic, about 20 to 30 seconds. Add to slow cooker. Add the chicken broth, tomatoes, onion, leek, carrots, pear and raisins; stir well.

Cover and cook on high 4 to 5 hours, or on low 8 to 10 hours, until lamb is tender. Sprinkle with pine nuts.

PER SERVING
CALORIES 679 **TOTAL FAT** 28G **SATURATED FAT** 8G **CHOLESTEROL** 246MG **SODIUM** 765MG
TOTAL CARBOHYDRATES 25G **DIETARY FIBER** 4G **PROTEIN** 80G

MUSTARD CHICKEN ON GREENS

½ CUP **ALL-PURPOSE FLOUR**

4 **BONELESS, SKINLESS CHICKEN BREASTS**

3 TSP **OLIVE OIL**

1 PINT **GRAPE TOMATOES**

½ TSP MINCED **GARLIC**

¾ CUP **CHICKEN BROTH**

3 TBSP EACH **GRAINY DIJON MUSTARD** AND **REDUCED-FAT SOUR CREAM**

1 TBSP SNIPPED **CHIVES**

1 BUNCH **WATERCRESS**

YIELD
4 servings

ACTIVE
10 minutes

TOTAL
15 minutes

Put flour in large plastic bag, add chicken and shake to coat.

Heat 1 tsp oil in large nonstick skillet over medium-high heat. Sauté grape tomatoes about 3 minutes or until some begin to soften. Add garlic; cook 30 seconds. Remove to plate.

Heat remaining 2 tsp oil in same skillet. Cook chicken about 5 minutes each side, or until instant-read thermometer inserted from side to middle registers 160°F. Remove to plate; cover.

Add broth to skillet, stirring to dissolve browned bits. Whisk in mustard and sour cream. Simmer until slightly thickened; add chives.

Place chicken on watercress; spoon mustard sauce on top. Serve with tomatoes.

PER SERVING
CALORIES 215 **TOTAL FAT** 6G **SATURATED FAT** 2G **CHOLESTEROL** 70MG **SODIUM** 451MG **TOTAL CARBOHYDRATES** 9G **DIETARY FIBER** 1G **PROTEIN** 29G

HERB-COATED ROAST BEEF WITH VEGETABLES & GRAVY

YIELD
9 servings

ACTIVE
15 minutes

TOTAL
1 hour 50 minutes

- 1 TBSP MINCED **GARLIC**
- 2 TSP **DRIED THYME**
- 2 TSP CRUSHED **DRIED ROSEMARY**
- 1 TSP **SALT**
- ½ TSP **PEPPER**
- 4½-LB **TOP ROUND BONELESS BEEF ROAST**
- 4 TBSP **DIJON MUSTARD**
- 1 TBSP **OIL**
- 1½ LB **CARROTS**, CUT IN THIRDS, THEN IN ½-IN.-WIDE STICKS
- 8 OZ **PARSNIPS**, CUT IN THIRDS, THEN IN ½-IN.-WIDE STICKS
- 1 MEDIUM **ONION**, CUT IN ½-IN. WEDGES
- 1 CAN (14½ OZ) **BEEF BROTH**
- 2 TBSP **FLOUR**
- ⅓ CUP **DRY RED WINE OR BEEF BROTH**

Adjust oven racks so one is in middle and other in lowest position. Heat oven to 425°F. Set a wire rack into a shallow roasting pan (not disposable foil). Line a rimmed baking sheet with nonstick foil. Mix garlic, thyme, rosemary, salt and pepper in a small bowl.

Place roast on rack in roasting pan. Brush with 3 Tbsp mustard and sprinkle with 3 Tbsp herb mixture, patting it on the mustard.

Add remaining 1 Tbsp mustard and the oil to remaining herb mixture; toss with carrots, parsnips and onion. Spread on baking sheet.

Roast the beef on upper rack 20 minutes. Reduce oven temperature to 325°F. Place vegetables on lower rack. Roast meat and vegetables 1¼ hours or until a meat thermometer inserted in center of roast registers 140°F for medium-rare. Remove roast to carving board, tent with foil and let rest 20 minutes (temperature will rise to about 145°F for medium-rare). While roast rests, continue roasting vegetables until tender.

Meanwhile, stir broth into flour in a bowl until blended. Place roasting pan over medium-high heat; add wine and stir to scrape up any brown bits on bottom. Add broth to roasting pan. Stirring with a whisk, bring to a boil, reduce heat and simmer 1 minute or until thickened. Serve roast with vegetables and gravy.

PER SERVING
CALORIES 498 **TOTAL FAT** 23G **SATURATED FAT** 9G **CHOLESTEROL** 138MG **SODIUM** 647MG **TOTAL CARBOHYDRATES** 16G **DIETARY FIBER** 4G **PROTEIN** 50G

PITA PIZZAS

YIELD
6 servings

ACTIVE
10 minutes

TOTAL
20 minutes

6 **SANDWICH-SIZE PITA POCKETS**

8 OZ **SHREDDED MOZZARELLA** (2 CUPS)

1 TSP **DRIED OREGANO**

2 TBSP **OLIVE OIL**

½ TSP **PEPPER**

2 CUPS DICED **TOMATOES**

½ CUP **FRESH BASIL LEAVES**, STACKED, ROLLED UP, THEN CUT CROSSWISE IN NARROW STRIPS

Heat oven to 450°F. Place pitas on a large baking sheet.

Top with cheese and oregano, equally divided. Bake until cheese is bubbly, about 10 minutes.

Add oil and pepper to tomatoes and toss gently to mix and coat. Serve tomatoes and basil in separate bowls to spoon on hot pitas.

PER SERVING
CALORIES 328 **TOTAL FAT** 14G **SATURATED FAT** 0G **CHOLESTEROL** 29MG **SODIUM** 469MG
TOTAL CARBOHYDRATES 38G **DIETARY FIBER** 0G **PROTEIN** 14G

THAI NOODLE BOWL

4 **SCALLIONS**

½ **RED BELL PEPPER**

1 LB **CHICKEN TENDERS**

1 CAN (14 OZ) **LIGHT COCONUT MILK**

½ CUP **WATER**

1 TBSP EACH **GREEN CURRY PASTE** AND **FISH SAUCE** (SEE NOTE)

½ A 16-OZ BOX **RICE NOODLES**
2 TSP **OIL**

2 CUPS SHREDDED **CARROTS**

⅓ CUP **MINT LEAVES**

LIME WEDGES

YIELD
4 servings

ACTIVE
10 minutes

TOTAL
15 minutes

NOTE
Green curry paste and fish sauce (nam pla) can be found in your supermarket's Asian food section.

Bring 4 cups water to a boil in a 12-in. deep-sided skillet. Meanwhile, slice scallions and red pepper. Cut each chicken tender crosswise in thirds.

Whisk coconut milk, ½ cup water, curry paste and fish sauce in bowl until blended.

Add noodles to boiling water; cook as package directs.

Meanwhile, heat oil in a large nonstick skillet over medium-high heat. Sauté chicken, red pepper and carrots 5 minutes or until cooked through. Add coconut milk mixture; simmer 2 minutes and remove from heat.

Add scallions and mint leaves. Drain noodles. Spoon some noodles into each bowl; ladle chicken mixture with broth on top. Serve with lime wedges.

PER SERVING
CALORIES 483 **TOTAL FAT** 13G **SATURATED FAT** 6G **CHOLESTEROL** 66MG **SODIUM** 594MG
TOTAL CARBOHYDRATES 58G **DIETARY FIBER** 4G **PROTEIN** 30G

SCALLOPS WITH CREAMY PESTO

YIELD
4 servings

ACTIVE
5 minutes

TOTAL
10 minutes

1½ TSP **OIL**

1½ LB **SEA SCALLOPS**, PATTED DRY

⅓ CUP **REFRIGERATED PREPARED PESTO**

2 TBSP **HEAVY (WHIPPING) CREAM**

Heat oil in a large nonstick skillet over medium-high heat. Add scallops and cook 4 minutes, turning once, until golden and just barely opaque at centers. Remove to a plate. Off heat, add pesto and cream to skillet; stir to blend.

Spoon pesto-cream sauce onto serving plates and top with scallops.

PER SERVING
CALORIES 268 **TOTAL FAT** 12G **SATURATED FAT** 4G **CHOLESTEROL** 73MG **SODIUM** 452MG
TOTAL CARBOHYDRATES 7G **DIETARY FIBER** 1G **PROTEIN** 31G

SKILLET CHICKEN & CHICKPEAS

- 2 TSP **OIL**
- 1 MEDIUM **ONION**, SLICED
- 2 CLOVES **GARLIC**, MINCED
- 1½ TSP **GROUND CUMIN**
- ½ TSP EACH **GROUND CINNAMON**, **GINGER** AND **SALT**
- ¼ TSP **PEPPER**
- 1 CAN (28 OZ) **DICED TOMATOES**
- 4 EACH **CHICKEN DRUMSTICKS** AND **THIGHS**, SKINNED (2¼ LB)
- 1 CAN (15 OZ) **CHICKPEAS**, RINSED
- 1 SMALL **BUTTERNUT SQUASH**, PEELED, SEEDED AND CUBED (3 CUPS)
- ⅓ CUP **RAISINS**
- GARNISH: CHOPPED **CILANTRO**, TOASTED **ALMONDS** (OPTIONAL)

YIELD
4 servings

ACTIVE
15 minutes

TOTAL
45 minutes

SIDE SUGGESTION
Couscous

Heat oil in a large nonstick skillet over medium-high heat. Sauté onion 2 minutes. Add garlic and spices; cook 30 seconds until fragrant.

Stir in tomatoes and their juices until blended. Add chicken and chickpeas. Bring to a boil; cover, reduce heat and simmer 15 minutes.

Add butternut squash and raisins; simmer, covered, 10 to 15 minutes more until squash is tender and chicken is cooked through. If desired, garnish with cilantro and almonds.

PER SERVING
CALORIES 460 **TOTAL FAT** 9G **SATURATED FAT** 2G **CHOLESTEROL** 116MG **SODIUM** 889MG **TOTAL CARBOHYDRATES** 58G **DIETARY FIBER** 12G **PROTEIN** 38G

PORK CUTLET SANDWICHES

YIELD
4 servings

ACTIVE
15 minutes

TOTAL
18 minutes

8 THIN **PORK-LOIN CUTLETS** (12 OZ)

¼ TSP EACH **GROUND CUMIN, CHILI POWDER, SALT, BLACK PEPPER** AND **GROUND RED PEPPER** (CAYENNE)

¼ CUP **REDUCED-FAT MAYONNAISE**

1 TBSP MINCED **PICKLED JALAPEÑO PEPPER**

½ TSP FRESHLY GRATED **LIME ZEST**

1 TBSP **OLIVE OIL**

4 **CRUSTY ROLLS**, SPLIT IN HALF

4 LEAVES **ROMAINE LETTUCE**

1 LARGE RIPE **TOMATO**, THINLY SLICED

1 SMALL RIPE **AVOCADO**, HALVED, SEEDED, PEELED AND SLICED

Place cutlets between sheets of plastic wrap. With a meat mallet or bottom of a heavy skillet, pound to about ⅛ in. thick. In a small bowl mix cumin, chili powder, salt and peppers. Sprinkle mixture over both sides of cutlets.

In same bowl, mix mayonnaise, jalapeño and lime zest.

Heat ½ Tbsp of the oil in a large nonstick skillet over medium-high heat. Add 4 of the cutlets and cook 1 minute, turning once, until browned and just cooked through. Remove to a plate. Repeat with remaining oil and cutlets.

Spread bottom of rolls with mayonnaise mixture. Top with lettuce, pork cutlet, sliced tomato and avocado. Replace roll tops.

PER SERVING
CALORIES 479 **TOTAL FAT** 26G **SATURATED FAT** 0G **CHOLESTEROL** 57MG **SODIUM** 657MG
TOTAL CARBOHYDRATES 38G **DIETARY FIBER** 0G **PROTEIN** 24G

ITALIAN STEAK & PEPPERS WITH CREAMY POLENTA

- ¾ CUP **YELLOW CORNMEAL**
- 2¾ CUPS **WATER**
- ¾ TSP **SALT**
- FOUR ½-IN.-THICK **BLADE STEAKS** (ABOUT 1¼ LB)
- ½ TSP **PEPPER**
- 4 TSP **OIL**
- 1 SMALL **ONION**, SLICED
- 2 **CUBANELLE PEPPERS** (ABOUT 8 OZ), CHOPPED
- 4 OZ **MUSHROOMS**, QUARTERED
- 1 CLOVE **GARLIC**, MINCED
- 1 CAN (14.5 OZ) **DICED TOMATOES IN JUICE**
- ¼ CUP **GRATED PARMESAN**

YIELD
4 servings

ACTIVE
20 minutes

TOTAL
25 minutes

Mix cornmeal, 2½ cups water and ¼ tsp salt in a 2-qt glass bowl. Cover with plastic wrap; microwave on high 12 to 14 minutes, whisking every 3 minutes, until thick.

Sprinkle ¼ tsp each salt and pepper on both sides of steaks.

Heat 2 tsp oil in large skillet over medium-high heat. Cook steaks 2 to 3 minutes per side until browned and cooked to medium. Remove to platter; loosely cover with foil.

Heat remaining 2 tsp oil in same skillet. Sauté onion, peppers and mushrooms about 4 minutes. Add garlic and cook 1 minute more.

Stir in tomatoes and their juices, ¼ cup water, and remaining ¼ tsp each salt and pepper. Simmer, covered, 5 minutes. Whisk Parmesan into polenta. Spoon vegetables and sauce on steak; serve with polenta.

PER SERVING
CALORIES 472 **TOTAL FAT** 22G **SATURATED FAT** 8G **CHOLESTEROL** 88MG **SODIUM** 896MG **TOTAL CARBOHYDRATES** 34G **DIETARY FIBER** 3G **PROTEIN** 34G

COD VERACRUZ-STYLE

2 TBSP **FLOUR**

¼ TSP **SALT**

¼ TSP **PEPPER**

FOUR ¾-IN.-THICK PIECES **COD FILLET** (ABOUT 6 OZ EACH)

1½ TBSP **OLIVE OIL** (PREFERABLY EXTRA-VIRGIN)

1 MEDIUM **ONION**, THINLY SLICED

1 TSP MINCED **GARLIC**

1 CAN (14.5 OZ) **DICED TOMATOES (PREFERABLY FIRE-ROASTED) WITH GREEN CHILES**

½ CUP **WATER**

⅓ CUP **PIMIENTO-STUFFED GREEN OLIVES**, HALVED

1 TBSP **CAPERS**, RINSED

½ TSP **DRIED OREGANO**

GARNISH: CHOPPED **PARSLEY**

YIELD
4 servings

ACTIVE
10 minutes

TOTAL
24 minutes

SIDE SUGGESTION
Boiled or steamed new potatoes

Mix flour, salt and pepper on sheet of wax paper; add fish and turn to coat.

Heat 1 Tbsp oil in a large nonstick skillet. Add cod and cook over medium-high heat, turning once, 5 to 7 minutes until golden and just cooked through. Remove to a platter; cover to keep warm.

Heat remaining ½ Tbsp oil in skillet. Add onion and sauté over medium-high heat 3 minutes or until golden. Add garlic; cook 1 minute until fragrant. Stir in remaining ingredients, bring to a boil, reduce heat and simmer 2 minutes to develop flavors. Spoon over fish. Garnish with chopped parsley.

PER SERVING
CALORIES 247 **TOTAL FAT** 8G **SATURATED FAT** 8G **CHOLESTEROL** 73MG **SODIUM** 1,000MG
TOTAL CARBOHYDRATES 11G **DIETARY FIBER** 3G **PROTEIN** 32G

CURRIED RED LENTILS

- 1 TBSP **OIL**
- 1 MEDIUM **ONION**, CHOPPED
- 2 TSP CHOPPED **GARLIC**
- 2 TSP **RED CURRY POWDER**
- 1 CAN (14 OZ) **VEGETABLE BROTH**
- 1 CAN (13.5 OZ) **LITE COCONUT MILK** (NOT CREAM OF COCONUT)
- ½ CUP **WATER**
- 1 BAG (16 OZ) **RED LENTILS**, PICKED OVER AND RINSED
- 3 CUPS **FRESH CAULIFLOWER FLORETS**
- 1 **RED BELL PEPPER**, SEEDED AND COARSELY CHOPPED
- 1 MEDIUM **ZUCCHINI**, CUT IN ¾-IN. PIECES
- ¼ CUP CHOPPED **FRESH CILANTRO**

YIELD
5 servings

ACTIVE
20 minutes

TOTAL
about 35 minutes

Heat oil in a large pot over medium heat. Add onion; sauté 4 minutes or until translucent. Add garlic and curry powder; cook 1 minute.

Stir broth, coconut milk and water into saucepan. Bring to a boil. Add lentils, cauliflower, pepper and zucchini. Cover and reduce heat.

Return to a simmer, cover and cook, stirring once, 10 to 12 minutes until lentils and vegetables are just tender. Stir in cilantro.

PER SERVING
CALORIES 424 **TOTAL FAT** 8G **SATURATED FAT** 3G **CHOLESTEROL** 0MG **SODIUM** 125MG
TOTAL CARBOHYDRATES 65G **DIETARY FIBER** 39G **PROTEIN** 29G

JERK CHICKEN WITH VEGETABLES

YIELD
4 servings

ACTIVE
13 minutes

TOTAL
30 minutes

2 TBSP **JAMAICAN JERK SEASONING** (SUCH AS WALKERSWOOD, SEE NOTE)

1 TBSP PLUS 1½ TSP **OIL**

4 **BONELESS, SKINLESS, CHICKEN BREASTS** (6 OZ EACH)

1 SMALL **ONION**, CUT IN THIN WEDGES

1 LARGE **RED BELL PEPPER**, CUT IN ¼-IN.-WIDE STRIPS

1 LARGE **ZUCCHINI**, CUT LENGTHWISE IN 2 X ¼-IN. STICKS

¼ TSP **SALT**

GARNISH: **LIME WEDGES**

Mix jerk seasoning and 1 Tbsp oil in a sturdy ziptop bag. Add chicken; turn to coat. Heat a stovetop ridged grill pan over medium heat or heat oven broiler.

Remove chicken from bag. Grill 4 to 5 minutes on each side until chicken is cooked through. Remove to cutting board and let rest 5 minutes.

Meanwhile, heat remaining 1½ tsp oil in a large nonstick skillet over medium-high heat. Add onion and red pepper; sauté 4 minutes until almost crisp-tender. Add zucchini; sauté vegetables 3 minutes. Season with salt.

Slice the chicken, serve with the vegetables and garnish with lime wedges.

NOTE Jerk is a spicy (often very spicy) seasoning blend widely used in the Caribbean. Look for paste jerk seasoning in the barbecue or hot sauce section of your market.

PER SERVING
CALORIES 261 **TOTAL FAT** 7G **SATURATED FAT** 1G **CHOLESTEROL** 99MG **SODIUM** 897MG
TOTAL CARBOHYDRATES 6G **DIETARY FIBER** 1G **PROTEIN** 40G

PORK & MUSHROOM MOO SHU

YIELD
6 servings

ACTIVE
10 minutes

TOTAL
4 to 6 hours on high
or 6 to 9 hours on low

1½-LB **BONELESS PORK LOIN ROAST**, FAT TRIMMED, QUARTERED

2 PACKAGES (3.5 OZ EACH) **SHIITAKE MUSHROOMS**, STEMS REMOVED, CAPS SLICED

¾ CUP **HOISIN SAUCE**

2 TBSP **WATER**

2 TSP FRESHLY GRATED **GINGER**

1 BAG (12 OZ) **BROCCOLI SLAW**

½ CUP SLICED **SCALLIONS**

3 TBSP **RICE-WINE VINEGAR**

1 TBSP **SUGAR**

¼ TSP **SALT**

12 SMALL **FLOUR TORTILLAS**, WARMED

Put pork, mushrooms, ½ cup of the hoisin sauce, water and ginger in a 4-qt or larger slow cooker. Turn pork to coat.

Cover and cook on high 4 to 6 hours or on low 6 to 9 hours until pork is tender.

Turn off cooker. Remove pork to a cutting board and, using 2 forks, pull meat into shreds. Return pork to cooker; stir in remaining ¼ cup hoisin sauce.

Toss broccoli slaw, scallions, vinegar, sugar and salt in a bowl to mix.

Fill each tortilla with ⅓ cup each broccoli slaw and pork mixture. Roll up.

PER SERVING
CALORIES 428 **TOTAL FAT** 12G **SATURATED FAT** 3G **CHOLESTEROL** 59MG **SODIUM** 986MG
TOTAL CARBOHYDRATES 50G **DIETARY FIBER** 5G **PROTEIN** 30G

CRISPY TILAPIA WITH AVOCADO PICO DE GALLO

YIELD
4 servings

ACTIVE
12 minutes

TOTAL
12 minutes

1 FIRM-RIPE **AVOCADO**

1 CUP **PICO DE GALLO**

¼ CUP CHOPPED **CILANTRO**

½ CUP **YELLOW CORNMEAL**

½ TSP EACH **CHILI POWDER**, **GROUND CUMIN** AND **SALT**

¼ CUP **MILK**

1½ LB **TILAPIA FILLETS**

3 TBSP **OIL**

SIDE SUGGESTION
Corn on the cob

Coarsely chop avocado. Stir into pico de gallo with chopped cilantro; set aside.

Mix cornmeal, chili powder, ground cumin and salt on a sheet of wax paper. Place milk in a shallow bowl or pie plate. Dip tilapia fillets into milk, then cornmeal mixture to coat.

Heat oil in a large nonstick skillet over medium heat. Cook tilapia 2 to 3 minutes per side. Top with avocado mixture.

PER SERVING
CALORIES 370 **TOTAL FAT** 14G **SATURATED FAT** 2G **CHOLESTEROL** 87MG **SODIUM** 694MG **TOTAL CARBOHYDRATES** 26G **DIETARY FIBER** 3G **PROTEIN** 37G

TURKEY TACO SKILLET

1 LB **97%-LEAN GROUND TURKEY**

1 PKG (1.25 OZ) **LOW-SODIUM TACO SEASONING MIX**

2 CUPS **WATER**

1 JAR (16 OZ) **THICK & CHUNKY SALSA**

1 CAN (11 OZ) **MEXICAN-STYLE CORN**

2 CUPS **INSTANT BROWN RICE**

1 CUP **SHREDDED MEXICAN OR TACO CHEESE BLEND**

2 CUPS SHREDDED **LETTUCE**

1 LARGE **TOMATO**, CHOPPED

½ CUP **REDUCED-FAT SOUR CREAM**

SERVE WITH: **BAKED TORTILLA CHIPS**

YIELD
6 servings

ACTIVE
5 minutes

TOTAL
26 minutes

Cook turkey in a large nonstick skillet over high heat, stirring to break up meat, 5 minutes or until browned. Stir in seasoning mix, water, salsa and corn; bring to a boil. Stir in rice. Cover and remove from heat; let stand 12 to 15 minutes until liquid is absorbed. Sprinkle with cheese; cover and let stand 1 to 2 minutes to melt cheese.

On plates, top rice mixture with lettuce, tomato and sour cream. Serve with tortilla chips.

PER SERVING
CALORIES 381 **TOTAL FAT** 14G **SATURATED FAT** 6G **CHOLESTEROL** 71MG **SODIUM** 1,255MG
TOTAL CARBOHYDRATES 40G **DIETARY FIBER** 3G **PROTEIN** 30G

CAJUN SAUSAGE & RICE

YIELD
4 servings

ACTIVE
10 minutes

TOTAL
20 minutes

1 BOX (8 OZ) **RED BEANS AND RICE MIX**

1 TSP **OLIVE OIL**

2 **BELL PEPPERS**, CUT BITE-SIZE

4 **FULLY COOKED SPICY BEEF SAUSAGES** (FROM A 14-OZ PKG), SLICED

SLICED **SCALLIONS** (OPTIONAL)

Bring 3½ cups water to a boil in a large saucepan. Add rice mix, reduce heat, cover and simmer 10 minutes.

Meanwhile, heat the oil in a large nonstick skillet over medium-high heat. Add peppers; sauté 5 minutes or until lightly charred in a few places. Add sausage; sauté 3 minutes or until lightly browned.

Place mixture on rice (don't stir), cover and simmer 10 minutes until rice is tender. Stir to mix; sprinkle with scallions, if desired.

PER SERVING
CALORIES 471 **TOTAL FAT** 25G **SATURATED FAT** 11G **CHOLESTEROL** 60MG **SODIUM** 1,629MG
TOTAL CARBOHYDRATES 47G **DIETARY FIBER** 5G **PROTEIN** 17G

TARRAGON CHICKEN

4 EACH **CHICKEN DRUMSTICKS** AND **THIGHS** (ABOUT 2½ LB)

1 LARGE **ONION**, VERY THINLY SLICED

4 CLOVES **GARLIC**, PEELED AND THINLY SLICED

2 **PLUM TOMATOES**, DICED

⅓ CUP **TARRAGON VINEGAR**

1½ TBSP CHOPPED **FRESH TARRAGON** *OR* 2 TSP **DRIED**

1 TBSP **DIJON MUSTARD**

¾ TSP **SALT**

½ TSP **PEPPER**

½ CUP **HEAVY CREAM**

2 TBSP **ALL-PURPOSE FLOUR**

YIELD
4 servings

ACTIVE
20 minutes

TOTAL
7 hours on low, plus 45 minutes

Remove skin from chicken by grasping it with paper towels and pulling it off.

Mix all ingredients except heavy cream and flour in a 4½-qt or larger slow cooker.

Cover and cook on low 7 hours until chicken is cooked through and onions are soft.

Whisk heavy cream and flour in a small bowl until smooth. Stir in some hot liquid from cooker, then stir the mixture into cooker. Turn setting to high; cover and cook 25 minutes until liquid thickens.

PER SERVING
CALORIES 544 **TOTAL FAT** 36G **SATURATED FAT** 14G **CHOLESTEROL** 213MG **SODIUM** 706MG
TOTAL CARBOHYDRATES 12G **DIETARY FIBER** 1G **PROTEIN** 40G

PENNE ALLA VODKA

YIELD
6 servings

ACTIVE
5 minutes

TOTAL
20 minutes

1 BOX (14.5 OZ) **PENNE RIGATE PASTA**

½ CUP **FROZEN PEAS**

1½ TSP **OLIVE OIL**

⅓ CUP CHOPPED **SHALLOTS**

¼ CUP **VODKA**

2 CUPS **MARINARA SAUCE**

4 OZ **FAT-FREE CREAM CHEESE**, BROKEN INTO CHUNKS

Cook pasta in large pot of salted boiling water as box directs. Add peas just before draining pasta.

Meanwhile, heat olive oil in a medium saucepan. Add shallots; cover and cook over medium heat 3 minutes.

Add vodka; boil until evaporated, about 2 minutes. Stir in marinara sauce; simmer 2 minutes to blend flavors.

Stir in cream cheese and cook, stirring, until melted.

Drain pasta and peas. Return to pot; add sauce and gently toss to combine.

PER SERVING
CALORIES 341 **TOTAL FAT** 5G **SATURATED FAT** 1G **CHOLESTEROL** 3MG **SODIUM** 557MG
TOTAL CARBOHYDRATES 68G **DIETARY FIBER** 10G **PROTEIN** 12G

THE ULTIMATE POT ROAST

ONE $3\frac{1}{2}$-LB **ROLLED AND TIED BONELESS BEEF CHUCK ROAST**

1 TSP **SALT**

1 TSP **PEPPER**

1 TBSP **OLIVE OIL**

1 STRIP **BACON**, CUT IN SMALL PIECES

$1\frac{1}{2}$ CUPS CHOPPED **ONIONS**

$\frac{3}{4}$ CUP FINELY CHOPPED **CARROT**

$\frac{3}{4}$ CUP FINELY CHOPPED **CELERY**

1 TBSP MINCED **GARLIC**

1 CAN (28 OZ) **WHOLE TOMATOES IN JUICE**

1 CUP **DRY RED WINE** *OR* 1 CUP WATER PLUS 1 TBSP RED-WINE VINEGAR

$\frac{1}{4}$ TSP **DRIED THYME**

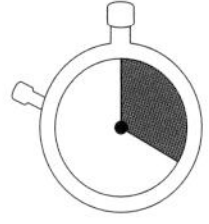

YIELD
8 servings

ACTIVE
20 minutes

TOTAL
3 hours 30 minutes

SIDE SUGGESTION
Egg noodles

Sprinkle meat all over with salt and pepper. Heat oil in a large Dutch oven over medium-high heat. Add meat and brown on all sides. Remove meat and discard oil.

Add bacon to pot and cook 2 minutes to render some fat. Add onions, carrot and celery and cook, stirring often, until slightly softened, about 5 minutes. Stir in garlic and cook 1 minute. Add tomatoes and their juice, the wine and thyme, and bring to a boil, breaking tomatoes into large chunks with a wooden spoon. Return meat to pot.

Cover and cook over low heat 3 hours or until meat is very tender, turning meat 3 or 4 times.

Remove meat to a cutting board and let stand 10 minutes.

Meanwhile, increase heat and cook sauce about 5 minutes until slightly thickened. Cut meat in thin slices; serve with the sauce.

PER SERVING
CALORIES 570 **TOTAL FAT** 43G **SATURATED FAT** 0G **CHOLESTEROL** 145MG **SODIUM** 605MG **TOTAL CARBOHYDRATES** 9G **DIETARY FIBER** 0G **PROTEIN** 36G

PORK WITH PINEAPPLE BBQ SALSA & SWEET POTATOES

YIELD
4 servings

ACTIVE
7 minutes

TOTAL
32 minutes

1 **PORK TENDERLOIN** (ABOUT 12 OZ)

2 LARGE **SWEET POTATOES**, CUT IN ½-IN. WEDGES

⅓ CUP **BARBECUE SAUCE**

¼ CUP CHOPPED **CILANTRO**

2 TSP **OIL**

½ TSP **CHILI POWDER**

1½ CUPS DICED FRESH OR CANNED **PINEAPPLE**

3 TBSP CHOPPED **RED ONION**

Position racks to divide oven in thirds. Heat oven to 500°F. Line 2 rimmed baking sheets with nonstick foil.

Place pork on 1 baking sheet, sweet potatoes on the other. Mix 3 Tbsp of the barbecue sauce with 1 Tbsp of the cilantro; brush on pork. Drizzle potatoes with oil; sprinkle with chili powder. Toss to coat; spread evenly.

Roast pans 10 minutes; remove from oven. Gently toss sweet potatoes and turn pork. Return to oven; roast potatoes 8 minutes or until tender, pork 15 minutes or until medium.

Remove pork to cutting board; let rest while combining pineapple, onion, and remaining cilantro and barbecue sauce in a bowl. Slice pork; top with the pineapple salsa. Serve with the sweet potatoes.

PER SERVING
CALORIES 258 **TOTAL FAT** 6G **SATURATED FAT** 1G **CHOLESTEROL** 47MG **SODIUM** 301MG
TOTAL CARBOHYDRATES 33G **DIETARY FIBER** 4G **PROTEIN** 19G

ROAST TURKEY

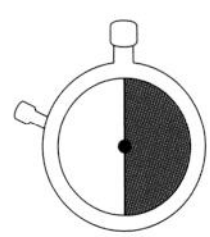

YIELD
8 servings
(with leftovers)

ACTIVE
30 minutes

TOTAL
4 hours 30 minutes

1 **WHOLE TURKEY** (12 TO 14 LB), FRESH OR THAWED FROZEN

1 TBSP **BUTTER**, MELTED

½ TSP EACH **SALT** AND **PEPPER**

⅓ CUP CHOPPED **PARSLEY** (OPTIONAL)

1 CUP **CHICKEN BROTH**

GARNISH: **FRESH HERBS**

SIDE SUGGESTION
Steamed green beans, mashed sweet potatoes

Heat oven to 325°F. Remove giblets, neck and any fat from turkey body and neck cavities. Discard fat. Dry turkey inside and out with paper towels.

Tie or clamp legs together. Twist wing tips under back. Brush skin with butter; sprinkle with salt, pepper and chopped parsley, if desired.

Place breast side up on a rack in a shallow roasting pan. Insert a standard meat thermometer (if not using an instant-read) into center of a thigh next to body (not touching bone). Add broth to pan.

Roast 3 to 3¾ hours, basting every 30 minutes with pan juices, adding more broth or water if pan seems dry. If breast gets too brown, cover it loosely with foil.

About 2 hours before turkey should be done, untie legs so heat can penetrate body cavity.

About 1¼ hours before turkey should be done, start checking for doneness. When thermometer inserted in thigh registers 180°F, remove turkey to a large serving platter or carving board. Let rest at least 30 minutes before serving for juicier meat and easier carving.

PLAN AHEAD Plan to have the turkey done about 1 hour before the rest of the meal. The turkey will stay hot for at least 1 hour, covered with foil.

PER 4-OZ SERVING
CALORIES 191 **TOTAL FAT** 5G **SATURATED FAT** 2G **CHOLESTEROL** 87MG **SODIUM** 84MG
TOTAL CARBOHYDRATES 0G **DIETARY FIBER** 0G **PROTEIN** 33G

TURKEY ENCHILADAS SUIZAS

8 **CORN TORTILLAS**, STACKED AND WRAPPED IN FOIL

1¼ CUPS **SALSA VERDE** (GREEN SALSA)

½ CUP **REDUCED-FAT SOUR CREAM**

¼ CUP CHOPPED **CILANTRO**

1½ CUPS (8 OZ) DICED **COOKED TURKEY BREAST**

6 OZ **REDUCED-FAT SWISS CHEESE**, SHREDDED (1½ CUPS)

1 JAR (7 OZ) **ROASTED RED PEPPERS**, SLICED

GARNISH: DICED **TOMATO** AND SLICED **SCALLION**

YIELD
4 servings

ACTIVE
15 minutes

TOTAL
40 minutes

Place tortillas in oven. Heat to 425°F.

Mix salsa, sour cream and cilantro in a medium bowl. Spread ½ cup over bottom of a shallow 2- to 2½-qt baking dish. In another bowl, combine turkey, 1 cup cheese and the roasted peppers. Remove tortillas from oven.

Spoon scant ½ cup turkey mixture down center of each tortilla. Roll up; place seam side down in baking dish. Pour remaining salsa mixture over top.

Cover with foil and bake 15 minutes or until bubbly. Uncover; sprinkle with remaining cheese and bake 10 minutes or until cheese has melted.

PER SERVING
CALORIES 399 **TOTAL FAT** 15G **SATURATED FAT** 9G **CHOLESTEROL** 89MG **SODIUM** 479MG
TOTAL CARBOHYDRATES 34G **DIETARY FIBER** 3G **PROTEIN** 33G

ROASTED SALMON & GRAPE TOMATOES

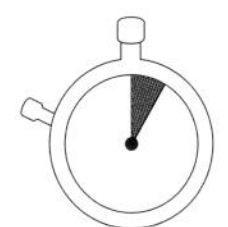

YIELD
4 servings

ACTIVE
5 minutes

TOTAL
27 minutes

1 PT **GRAPE TOMATOES**

1½ TBSP CHOPPED **FRESH THYME**

2 TSP **OLIVE OIL**

¼ TSP EACH **SALT** AND **PEPPER**

FOUR 6- TO 8-OZ **SALMON STEAKS OR FILLETS**

Heat oven to 425°F. Line a rimmed baking pan with nonstick foil.

Toss tomatoes, 1 Tbsp of the thyme, the olive oil, and ⅛ tsp each salt and pepper on baking pan. Roast 10 minutes.

Remove from oven. Push tomato mixture to one side of pan. Add salmon to other side. Sprinkle salmon with the remaining ⅛ tsp each salt and pepper and the remaining ½ Tbsp thyme. Roast 10 minutes or until salmon is just cooked through and tomatoes are tender.

To serve, spoon tomatoes and juices over salmon.

PER SERVING
CALORIES 316 **TOTAL FAT** 15G **SATURATED FAT** 2G **CHOLESTEROL** 109MG **SODIUM** 237MG **TOTAL CARBOHYDRATES** 3G **DIETARY FIBER** 1G **PROTEIN** 41G

BEEF & VEGETABLES ON POLENTA

- 3 CUPS **WATER**
- 3/4 CUP **CORNMEAL**
- 1/2 TSP **SALT**
- 1 1/2 TSP **OLIVE OIL**
- 1 LARGE **ZUCCHINI**, QUARTERED LENGTHWISE, SLICED
- 1 PACKAGE (8 OZ) SLICED **MUSHROOMS**
- 8 OZ **LEAN GROUND BEEF**
- 1/2 CUP **DRY WHITE WINE** (OPTIONAL)
- 1 TSP **CHOPPED FRESH** (OR 1/2 TSP DRIED) **ROSEMARY**
- 1 TSP MINCED **GARLIC**
- 1 JAR (25 TO 26 OZ) **MARINARA SAUCE**
- 1/3 CUP **GRATED PARMESAN**

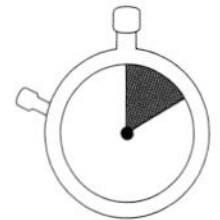

YIELD
4 servings

ACTIVE
10 minutes

TOTAL
23 minutes

Mix water, cornmeal and salt in a 2-qt microwave-safe bowl. Cover with vented plastic wrap and microwave on high, whisking twice, until thick and smooth (about 10 minutes).

Meanwhile, heat oil in a large nonstick skillet over medium-high heat. Sauté zucchini and mushrooms 5 minutes, stirring often, until tender. Transfer to a serving bowl.

Add beef to skillet; cook, breaking up with a wooden spoon, until browned, about 3 minutes. Stir in wine (if using), rosemary and garlic; cook 1 minute. Stir in marinara and bring to a simmer.

Add zucchini and mushroom mixture; heat through. Stir Parmesan into polenta. Spoon polenta onto plates and top with sauce.

PER SERVING
CALORIES 440 **TOTAL FAT** 15G **SATURATED FAT** 5G **CHOLESTEROL** 46MG **SODIUM** 1,192MG
TOTAL CARBOHYDRATES 54G **DIETARY FIBER** 7G **PROTEIN** 22G

VEGGIE CHILI

5½ CUPS **WATER**

¾ CUP **BULGUR**

2 TSP **OLIVE OIL**

1 CUP EACH CHOPPED **ONION** AND **RED BELL PEPPER**

2 TBSP **SALT-FREE CHILI POWDER**

2 TSP EACH MINCED **GARLIC** AND **GROUND CUMIN**

1 CAN (28 OZ) **CRUSHED TOMATOES**

1 CAN (15 OZ) **100% PURE PUMPKIN**

1 MEDIUM **ZUCCHINI**, DICED

1 CUP **FROZEN CORN**

1 CAN (15.5 OZ) **LOW-SODIUM BLACK BEANS**, RINSED

½ CUP CHOPPED **CILANTRO**

ACCOMPANIMENTS: **REDUCED-FAT SHREDDED CHEDDAR, REDUCED-FAT SOUR CREAM**

YIELD
6 servings

ACTIVE
10 minutes

TOTAL
25 minutes

Put 3 cups of the water and the bulgur in a medium microwave-safe bowl. Cover and microwave on high until bulgur is tender, about 15 minutes.

Meanwhile, heat oil in a large nonstick skillet. Add onion and pepper; sauté 5 minutes. Add chili powder, garlic and cumin; sauté until fragrant.

Add remaining 2½ cups water, the tomatoes, pumpkin, zucchini and corn; bring to a boil over medium-high heat. Reduce heat and simmer 10 minutes, stirring occasionally, until vegetables are tender.

Stir in beans and bulgur; heat through. Remove from heat and stir in cilantro. Serve with accompaniments.

PER SERVING
CALORIES 266 **TOTAL FAT** 3G **SATURATED FAT** 1G **CHOLESTEROL** 0MG **SODIUM** 249MG
TOTAL CARBOHYDRATES 52G **DIETARY FIBER** 14G **PROTEIN** 12G

BROILED CHICKEN & PEPPER SANDWICHES

YIELD
4 servings

ACTIVE
8 minutes

TOTAL
36 minutes

4 **BELL PEPPERS** (ANY COLOR), HALVED AND SEEDED

4 **BONELESS, SKINLESS CHICKEN BREASTS** (5 TO 6 OZ EACH)

¼ CUP **BOTTLED ITALIAN DRESSING**

4 **SANDWICH ROLLS**

½ CUP **LOWFAT MAYONNAISE**

Heat broiler. Line broiler pan with foil for easy cleanup. Place pepper halves on broiler-pan rack, cut sides down. Broil 4 to 5 in. from heat source 12 to 15 minutes until skins are mostly charred. Remove peppers to a saucepan and cover.

Brush smooth sides of chicken breasts with some dressing. Place smooth side down on same broiler-pan rack; brush top of breasts with some dressing.

Broil 6 to 7 minutes. Turn chicken over, brush with some dressing and broil 5 to 6 minutes longer until chicken is opaque in center.

Meanwhile, pull charred skin from peppers. Cut each pepper half into 4 strips. Cut chicken into ¼-in.-wide strips. In a bowl, toss pepper and chicken strips with remaining dressing. Cut rolls in half and toast, if desired. Spread cut surfaces with mayonnaise. Top bottoms with pepper and chicken mixture, dividing evenly. Replace roll tops.

PER SERVING
CALORIES 480 **TOTAL FAT** 15G **SATURATED FAT** 0G **CHOLESTEROL** 91MG **SODIUM** 794MG
TOTAL CARBOHYDRATES 43G **DIETARY FIBER** 0G **PROTEIN** 42G

DECEMBER

DECEMBER SHOPPING LIST

Week 1
DECEMBER 1 TO DECEMBER 7

PRODUCE
2 LARGE ONIONS
2 MEDIUM ONIONS
1 HEAD GARLIC (6 CLOVES)
2 LB RED POTATOES
2 PLUM TOMATOES
1 PT CHERRY OR GRAPE TOMATOES
4 CARROTS
1 RED BELL PEPPER
3 CELERY STICKS
1 HEAD ROMAINE LETTUCE
1 LB FRESH KALE
3 SCALLIONS
FRESH CHIVES OR SCALLIONS
1 BUNCH PARSLEY

BAKERY
4 SLICES FIRM WHITE BREAD

DELI
5 STRIPS THIN-SLICED BACON
5 SLICES TURKEY BACON

MEAT/POULTRY/FISH
ONE 4-LB EYE-ROUND BEEF ROAST
1½ LB LEAN GROUND BEEF
1½ LB LEAN GROUND PORK
4 BONELESS, SKINLESS CHICKEN BREASTS (ABOUT 5 OZ EACH)
8 CHICKEN DRUMSTICKS (2¼ LB)
1½ LB COD, HADDOCK, HAKE OR OTHER FIRM WHITE FISH FILLET

REFRIGERATED
6 CUPS WHOLE MILK
8 TBSP BUTTER
1 TUB (15 OZ) PART-SKIM RICOTTA
12 OZ SHREDDED PART-SKIM MOZZARELLA
EGGS (2 LARGE)
1 PKG (10 OZ) PREBAKED THIN PIZZA CRUST

GROCERY
2 CANS (11 OZ) VACUUM-PACKED CORN
1 CAN (5 OZ) EVAPORATED MILK (NOT SWEETENED CONDENSED MILK)
¾ CUP PASTA SAUCE (360 MG SODIUM OR LESS PER ½ CUP)
¼ CUP JARRED ROASTED RED PEPPERS
½ CUP KETCHUP OR TOMATO CHILI SAUCE
9 OVEN-READY LASAGNA NOODLES (FROM AN 8-OZ BOX)
LIGHT MAYONNAISE
1 PKT (1.8 OZ) WHITE SAUCE MIX
OLD BAY SEASONING
2 CHICKEN BROTH CUBES
1 PKG (10 OZ) PREBAKED THIN PIZZA CRUST
½ CUP SWEET OR BITTER ORANGE MARMALADE
⅓ CUP DRY WHITE WINE

PANTRY
SALT
PEPPER
OLIVE OIL
FLOUR
DIJON MUSTARD
CHILI POWDER (MILD, HOT OR A MIX OF BOTH)
GROUND CUMIN
GROUND NUTMEG
GROUND MIXED PEPPERCORNS OR BLACK PEPPERCORNS
DRIED BASIL
DRIED TARRAGON

Week 2
DECEMBER 8 TO DECEMBER 14

PRODUCE
1 LARGE GRANNY SMITH APPLE
1 LEMON
5 MEDIUM ONIONS
1 HEAD GARLIC (8 CLOVES)
2 MEDIUM SWEET POTATOES (1¼ LB)
3 SMALL PARSNIPS OR CARROTS
6 CARROTS
3 MEDIUM ZUCCHINI (ABOUT 1½ LB)
8 OZ GREEN BEANS
3 OZ BABY SPINACH
1 BUNCH CILANTRO

DELI
8 SLICES BACON

MEAT/POULTRY/FISH
4 THIN-CUT LOIN PORK CHOPS (1¼ LB)
2-LB BONELESS PORK SHOULDER
2-LB BONELESS LAMB SHOULDER
3 CUPS BITE-SIZE PIECES COOKED CHICKEN
1 LB COD OR SCROD FILLET

FROZEN
1 PKG (10 OZ) PEAS
1 BOX (10 OZ) CHOPPED KALE
1 SHEET PUFF PASTRY (FROM A 17.25-OZ BOX)

REFRIGERATED
1 CUP HALF-AND-HALF
2 TBSP BUTTER OR MARGARINE
CRUMBLED FETA CHEESE
EGG (1)
1 CUP APPLE CIDER

GROCERY
1 CAN (14.5 OZ) CHICKEN BROTH
2 CANS (15.5 OZ EACH) BLACK BEANS
1 CAN (14.5 OZ) DICED TOMATOES
1 CAN (14.5 OZ) SALSA-STYLE TOMATOES
1 CAN (19 OZ) CANNELLINI BEANS
1 CAN (19 OZ) CHICKPEAS
1 CAN (13.75 OZ) WHOLE ARTICHOKE HEARTS
1 JAR (14 OZ) SPAGHETTI SAUCE
1 CUP ALFREDO SAUCE
12 OZ FUSILLI PASTA
2 BOXES (8 OZ) YELLOW-RICE MIX
GREEK HERB SEASONING
1 CHICKEN BOUILLON CUBE
¼ CUP SLICED OR SLIVERED ALMONDS
¼ CUP GOLDEN RAISINS

PANTRY
SALT
PEPPER
VEGETABLE OIL
DIJON MUSTARD
FLOUR
GROUND CUMIN

GROUND CINNAMON
CRUSHED RED PEPPER
SMOKED PAPRIKA
DRIED THYME
DRIED SAGE

Week 3

DECEMBER 15 TO DECEMBER 22

PRODUCE
2 LEMONS
2 LARGE ONIONS
2 MEDIUM ONIONS
4 HEADS GARLIC (24 CLOVES)
4 LARGE RIPE TOMATOES
3 PLUM TOMATOES
2 MEDIUM CARROTS
1 LB ZUCCHINI OR YELLOW SQUASH
1 MEDIUM ZUCCHINI (ABOUT 6 OZ)
1 MEDIUM EGGPLANT
1 BAG (10 OZ) FRESH SPINACH
1 BUNCH BASIL
FRESH ROSEMARY

MEAT/POULTRY/FISH
1 BONELESS BEEF CHUCK ROAST (5 LB)
1 LB CHUCK STEW MEAT
8 CHICKEN THIGHS (2 LB)
2 TURKEY BREAST TENDERLOINS (ABOUT 2 LB)
2 TURKEY THIGHS (ABOUT 2 LB)
1½ LB HALIBUT, HAKE OR COD FILLET
4 FLOUNDER FILLETS (ABOUT 6 OZ EACH)

REFRIGERATED
2 TBSP BUTTER OR MARGARINE
GRATED PARMESAN
1 PKG (14 OZ) FIRM TOFU

GROCERY
1 CAN (14.5 OZ) CHICKEN BROTH
1 CAN (28 OZ) FIRE-ROASTED DICED TOMATOES
1 CAN (14.5 OZ) PETITE DICED TOMATOES WITH GARLIC AND ONION OR ITALIAN-SEASONED
1 CAN (15 OZ) RED KIDNEY BEANS
1 CAN (15 OZ) BLACK BEANS
1 CAN (15 OZ) PINTO BEANS
1 CAN (11 OZ) MEXICAN-STYLE CORN
1 CAN (4.5 OZ) CHOPPED GREEN CHILES
1 LB LINGUINE OR SPAGHETTI
1 BOX (5.8 OZ) ROASTED GARLIC AND OLIVE OIL FLAVORED COUSCOUS
½ CUP LIGHT MAYONNAISE
⅓ CUP WASABI MAYONNAISE
⅓ CUP CORNFLAKE CRUMBS
1 CUP DRY RED WINE, OR 1 CUP CHICKEN BROTH PLUS 1 TBSP RED-WINE VINEGAR

PANTRY
SALT
PEPPER
OLIVE OIL
VEGETABLE OIL
NONSTICK SPRAY
FLOUR
GROUND CUMIN
GARLIC SALT
DRIED ROSEMARY
DRIED SAGE
DRIED THYME

Week 4

DECEMBER 23 TO DECEMBER 31

PRODUCE
1 LEMON
2 LIMES
4 MEDIUM ONIONS
1 HEAD GARLIC (6 CLOVES)
1 LB RED-SKINNED POTATOES
2 RIPE TOMATOES
2 LARGE RIPE PLUM TOMATOES
1 PT CHERRY TOMATOES
1 MEDIUM RED BELL PEPPER
1 BUNCH (ABOUT 1 LB) BROCCOLI FLORETS
1 BAG (5 OZ) BABY ARUGULA BLEND OR OTHER SALAD MIX
1 BAG (12 OZ) FRESH SPINACH
1 BUNCH PARSLEY
1 BUNCH CILANTRO
1 BUNCH BASIL

DELI
14 SLICES BACON
16 SMALL SLICES 70%-LESS-FAT TURKEY PEPPERONI (SUCH AS HORMEL)

MEAT/POULTRY/FISH
12-OZ FLANK STEAK
FOUR 4-OZ BONELESS THIN-CUT PORK CHOPS
1 FULLY COOKED 7- TO 8-LB SPIRAL-SLICED BONE-IN HALF-HAM
1 LB CHICKEN THIGHS
1¼ LB GROUND TURKEY
1 LB RAW MEDIUM SHRIMP
1 LB SEA, BAY OR CALICO SCALLOPS

FROZEN
1 BOX (8 OZ) VIDALIA ONION RINGS
TEXAS TOAST (½ AN 11.25-OZ BOX)

REFRIGERATED
2 CUPS WHOLE MILK
2 TBSP BUTTER OR MARGARINE
½ CUP SHREDDED ITALIAN 6-CHEESE BLEND
½ CUP GARLIC-AND-HERB SPREADABLE CHEESE (SUCH AS ALOUETTE)
GRATED PARMESAN
EGG (1 LARGE)
2 CUPS POMEGRANATE JUICE

GROCERY
3 CANS (14.5 OZ) CHICKEN BROTH
2 CANS (14.5 OZ EACH) FAT-FREE REDUCED-SODIUM CHICKEN BROTH
1 CAN (14.5 OZ) DICED TOMATOES WITH GREEN CHILES
1 CAN (15 OZ) BLACK BEANS
1 CAN (15 OZ) CANNELLINI OR OTHER WHITE BEANS
1 CAN (10 OZ) CHICKPEAS
1 CAN (15.25 OZ) WHOLE-KERNEL CORN
1 CAN (14.5 OZ) WHOLE-KERNEL CORN
1 CAN (5 OZ) SOLID LIGHT TUNA IN OLIVE OIL
1 JAR (12 OZ) ROASTED PEPPERS, PREFERABLY RED AND YELLOW
½ CUP JARRED ROASTED YELLOW OR RED PEPPERS
1 JAR (4 OZ) SLICED PIMIENTOS
¼ CUP SLICED OLIVES (PREFERABLY PIMIENTO-STUFFED)
2½ CUPS MARINARA SAUCE
1 LB BOW-TIE PASTA
12 OZ PASTA (ANY SHAPE)
COARSE-GRAIN MUSTARD
1 BAG (9 OZ) TORTILLA CHIPS
¾ CUP ITALIAN-SEASONED DRIED BREAD CRUMBS
¾ CUP MAPLE OR PANCAKE SYRUP
2 TBSP RAISINS (OPTIONAL)

PANTRY
SALT
PEPPER
OLIVE OIL
VEGETABLE OIL
RED-WINE VINAIGRETTE
FLOUR
CORNSTARCH
GROUND CUMIN
DRIED OREGANO
DRIED THYME

FISH & VEGGIE CHOWDER

5 STRIPS THIN-SLICED **BACON**

2 LB **RED POTATOES**, SCRUBBED AND CUBED

2 CUPS EACH CHOPPED **ONIONS** AND SLICED **CARROTS**

1 CUP SLICED **CELERY**

1 TBSP **OLD BAY SEASONING**

2 CUPS **WATER**

2 **CHICKEN BROTH CUBES**

2 CANS (11 OZ EACH) **VACUUM-PACKED CORN**

1½ LB **COD, HADDOCK, HAKE OR OTHER FIRM WHITE FISH FILLET**, CUT IN 1-IN. CHUNKS, BONES REMOVED

5 CUPS **WHOLE MILK**

⅓ CUP **FLOUR**

1 TSP **SALT**

YIELD
8 servings

ACTIVE
40 minutes

TOTAL
40 minutes

Fry bacon in a 5-qt pot until crisp; drain on paper towels, then crumble. Discard all but 1 Tbsp fat.

Add potatoes, onions, carrots and celery to pot. Sauté over medium-high heat 4 minutes or until onions wilt. Add seasoning, water and broth cubes. Bring to a boil, reduce heat, cover and simmer 6 to 8 minutes until vegetables are tender.

Add corn, fish and 4 cups milk to pot; return to a simmer. Whisk flour into remaining 1 cup milk until blended. Stir into chowder; add salt. Cook, stirring gently, 4 to 6 minutes until fish is cooked and chowder thickens slightly. Ladle into bowls; sprinkle with bacon.

PER SERVING
CALORIES 376 **TOTAL FAT** 10G **SATURATED FAT** 4G **CHOLESTEROL** 62MG **SODIUM** 1,099MG
TOTAL CARBOHYDRATES 47G **DIETARY FIBER** 5G **PROTEIN** 27G

HOT & CHILI CHICKEN

½ CUP SWEET OR BITTER **ORANGE MARMALADE**

2 TBSP **CHILI POWDER** (MILD, HOT OR A MIX OF BOTH)

½ TSP **SALT**

8 **CHICKEN DRUMSTICKS** (2¼ LB)

YIELD
4 servings

ACTIVE
5 minutes

TOTAL
35 minutes

SIDE SUGGESTION
Sautéed zucchini

Heat oven to 400°F. Line a rimmed baking sheet with nonstick foil.

Mix marmalade, chili powder and salt in a large ziptop bag. Add chicken; seal bag. Turn and squeeze bag to coat drumsticks. Remove and arrange on lined baking sheet, spooning on any excess marmalade mixture from bag.

Bake 25 to 30 minutes until cooked through and an instant-read thermometer inserted in thickest part of meat, not touching bone, registers 180°F.

PER SERVING
CALORIES 370 **TOTAL FAT** 14G **SATURATED FAT** 4G **CHOLESTEROL** 109MG **SODIUM** 458MG
TOTAL CARBOHYDRATES 29G **DIETARY FIBER** 1G **PROTEIN** 33G

SAVORY MEAT LOAF

YIELD
14 servings

ACTIVE
10 minutes

TOTAL
1 hour 50 minutes

1½ LB EACH **LEAN GROUND BEEF** AND **LEAN GROUND PORK**

2 CUPS FINE FRESH BREAD CRUMBS (FROM 4 SLICES **FIRM WHITE BREAD**)

1 CAN (5 OZ) **EVAPORATED MILK** (NOT SWEETENED CONDENSED MILK)

½ CUP **KETCHUP** *OR* **TOMATO CHILI SAUCE**

½ CUP THINLY SLICED **SCALLIONS**

2 LARGE **EGGS**

½ CUP FINELY CHOPPED **RED BELL PEPPER**

1 TBSP MINCED **GARLIC**

1 TSP EACH **GROUND CUMIN**, **SALT** AND **PEPPER**

¼ TSP **GROUND NUTMEG**

Heat oven to 350°F. In a large bowl, mix all ingredients with hands or wooden spoon until well blended. Pack into a 9 x 5 x 3-in. loaf pan.

Bake 1 hour 40 minutes or until no longer pink in middle and meat thermometer inserted in center of loaf registers 160°F.

Let stand 10 minutes before slicing and serving, or pour off juices in pan, cover tightly with foil and refrigerate up to 5 days.

PER SERVING
CALORIES 314 **TOTAL FAT** 22G **SATURATED FAT** 0G **CHOLESTEROL** 105MG **SODIUM** 375MG
TOTAL CARBOHYDRATES 8G **DIETARY FIBER** 0G **PROTEIN** 19G

VEGETABLE LASAGNA

1 TBSP **OLIVE OIL**

4 CUPS SLICED **ONIONS**

1 LB **FRESH KALE**, STEMS REMOVED, LEAVES WASHED, DRIED AND CHOPPED

¼ TSP **SALT**

¼ TSP **PEPPER**

1 PKT (1.8 OZ) **WHITE SAUCE MIX**, PREPARED WITH **MILK** AS PKG DIRECTS AND ADDING 1 TBSP MINCED **GARLIC**

9 **OVEN-READY LASAGNA NOODLES** (FROM AN 8-OZ BOX)

1 TUB (15 OZ) **PART-SKIM RICOTTA**

1 PT **CHERRY OR GRAPE TOMATOES**, HALVED

1 PKG (8 OZ) SHREDDED **PART-SKIM MOZZARELLA**

YIELD
6 servings

ACTIVE
30 minutes

TOTAL
1 hour 30 minutes

NOTE
Insert the tip of a knife in the center for 30 seconds. If tip feels hot when removed, the lasagna is done.

Heat oven to 375°F. Grease a 13 x 9 x 2-in. baking dish.

Heat oil in a large saucepan. Add onions; sauté until golden. Stir in kale, salt and pepper; cook 4 minutes or until kale wilts.

Spoon a thin layer of white sauce in baking dish. Top with 3 noodles, not overlapping. Spread with half the ricotta cheese, covering noodles completely. Top with layers of half the kale, half the tomatoes and ⅓ the remaining sauce. Sprinkle with ⅓ the mozzarella. Repeat layers once. Top with remaining 3 noodles; cover completely with remaining sauce and sprinkle with remaining cheese. Cover with nonstick foil.

Bake 50 minutes. Uncover and bake 10 minutes longer until center is hot (see note).

PER SERVING
CALORIES 459 **TOTAL FAT** 17G **SATURATED FAT** 9G **CHOLESTEROL** 48MG **SODIUM** 732MG
TOTAL CARBOHYDRATES 27G **DIETARY FIBER** 4G **PROTEIN** 27G

PEPPER-COATED ROAST BEEF WITH RED PEPPER–BASIL BUTTER

YIELD
12 servings

ACTIVE
15 minutes

TOTAL
1 hour 10 minutes

BEEF

ONE 4-LB **EYE-ROUND BEEF ROAST**

1/3 CUP **DIJON MUSTARD**

3 TBSP COARSELY GROUND **MIXED PEPPERCORNS OR BLACK PEPPERCORNS**

RED PEPPER BUTTER

6 TBSP **BUTTER**, SOFTENED

1/4 CUP **JARRED ROASTED RED PEPPERS**, DRIED ON PAPER TOWELS, THEN MINCED

1 1/2 TBSP MINCED **FRESH BASIL** OR 1 TSP DRIED

1 1/2 TBSP MINCED **FRESH PARSLEY**

BEEF Heat oven to 425°F. Set a wire rack into a shallow roasting pan.

Rub roast with mustard; sprinkle with pepper. Place on rack in pan.

Roast 45 to 55 minutes or until a meat thermometer inserted in center registers 145°F. Remove roast to carving board, cover loosely with foil and let rest about 10 minutes. (Temperature will rise about 5 degrees to 150°F for medium-rare.)

Meanwhile, make **RED PEPPER BUTTER**: Beat butter in a small bowl with a wooden spoon until fluffy. Stir in remaining ingredients.

TO SERVE Thinly slice roast beef and arrange on a platter. Serve with the flavored butter to spread over the meat.

PER SERVING
CALORIES 316 **TOTAL FAT** 20G **SATURATED FAT** 9G **CHOLESTEROL** 95MG **SODIUM** 288MG
TOTAL CARBOHYDRATES 1G **DIETARY FIBER** 0G **PROTEIN** 30G

BLT PIZZA

1 PKG (10 OZ) **PREBAKED THIN PIZZA CRUST**

¾ CUP **PASTA SAUCE** (360 MG SODIUM OR LESS PER ½ CUP)

5 STRIPS **TURKEY BACON**, COOKED AS PKG DIRECTS, CRUMBLED

1 CUP **SHREDDED REDUCED-FAT MOZZARELLA**

3 CUPS SHREDDED **ROMAINE LETTUCE**

2 **PLUM TOMATOES**, CUT IN THIN WEDGES

1 TBSP **LIGHT MAYONNAISE**

YIELD
5 servings

ACTIVE
10 minutes

TOTAL
20 minutes

Heat oven to 450°F. Place the pizza crust on a baking sheet.

Spread sauce on crust and sprinkle with bacon and cheese.

Bake 8 to 10 minutes until crust is crisp and lightly browned at the edges.

Meanwhile, mix remaining ingredients in a bowl. Spread over pizza; serve immediately.

PER SERVING
CALORIES 287 **TOTAL FAT** 9G **SATURATED FAT** 3G **CHOLESTEROL** 19MG **SODIUM** 829MG
TOTAL CARBOHYDRATES 34G **DIETARY FIBER** 3G **PROTEIN** 15G

CHICKEN BREASTS WITH TARRAGON

YIELD
4 servings

ACTIVE
7 minutes

TOTAL
20 minutes

4 **BONELESS, SKINLESS CHICKEN BREASTS** (ABOUT 5 OZ EACH)

¼ TSP **SALT**

⅛ TSP FRESHLY GROUND **PEPPER**, OR TO TASTE

2 TBSP **BUTTER OR MARGARINE**

1 TSP FINELY SNIPPED **CHIVES** *OR* GREEN PART OF A **SCALLION**

2 TBSP FINELY CHOPPED **PARSLEY**

⅓ CUP **DRY WHITE WINE**

2 TBSP FINELY CHOPPED **FRESH TARRAGON** LEAVES *OR* 2 TSP **DRIED**, CRUMBLED

Place chicken breasts between 2 sheets of wax paper and gently pound with a meat mallet or bottom of a heavy skillet until about ½ in. thick. Season with salt and pepper.

Heat butter in a large, heavy nonstick skillet over medium heat until bubbly. Add chicken and cook about 10 minutes, turning occasionally, or until almost opaque in center and golden on both sides. Remove to serving plates. Sprinkle with chives and parsley.

Add wine (and tarragon, if using dried) to skillet and cook over high heat, stirring in any brown bits on bottom, until reduced to about 3 Tbsp. Stir in fresh tarragon. Spoon over chicken.

PER SERVING
CALORIES 211 **TOTAL FAT** 8G **SATURATED FAT** 0G **CHOLESTEROL** 98MG **SODIUM** 288MG **TOTAL CARBOHYDRATES** 1G **DIETARY FIBER** 0G **PROTEIN** 33G

SALSA PORK DINNER

YIELD
4 servings

ACTIVE
5 minutes

TOTAL
30 minutes

1 BOX (8 OZ) **YELLOW RICE MIX**

2 TSP **VEGETABLE OIL**

4 **THIN-CUT LOIN PORK CHOPS** (1¼ LB)

1 CAN (14.5 OZ) **SALSA-STYLE TOMATOES**

¼ CUP CHOPPED **CILANTRO**

Cook rice in a medium-size saucepan according to package directions, omitting butter, oil or margarine.

After rice has cooked 18 to 19 minutes, heat oil in a large nonstick skillet over medium-high heat. Add pork chops and cook 2 minutes per side or until no longer pink at center. Remove to one side of a serving platter.

Put tomatoes in skillet and heat through.

To serve, mound rice on serving platter. Top with pork chops. Spoon on tomatoes and sprinkle cilantro over all.

PER SERVING
CALORIES 415 **TOTAL FAT** 19G **SATURATED FAT** 0G **CHOLESTEROL** 66MG **SODIUM** 1,058MG
TOTAL CARBOHYDRATES 46G **DIETARY FIBER** 0G **PROTEIN** 25G

GREEK LAMB & SPINACH STEW

YIELD
6 servings

ACTIVE
10 minutes

TOTAL
7 to 9 hours on low plus 15 minutes on high

2-LB **BONELESS LAMB SHOULDER**, VISIBLE FAT TRIMMED, CUT IN 1-IN. PIECES

1 CAN (14.5 OZ) **DICED TOMATOES**

½ CUP CHOPPED **ONION**

1 TBSP MINCED **GARLIC**

½ TSP EACH **GREEK HERB SEASONING** AND **SALT**

¼ TSP **PEPPER**

1 CAN (19 OZ) **CANNELLINI BEANS**, RINSED

1 CAN (13.75 OZ) **WHOLE ARTICHOKE HEARTS**, CUT IN HALF

3 CUPS **BABY SPINACH** (3 OZ)

2 TSP GRATED **LEMON ZEST**

TOPPING: CRUMBLED **FETA CHEESE**

Mix lamb pieces, tomatoes, onion, garlic, Greek seasoning, salt and pepper in a 3½-qt or larger slow cooker.

Cover and cook on low 7 to 9 hours or until lamb is tender when pierced.

Mash 1 cup beans. Stir mashed and whole beans, artichoke hearts and spinach into cooker.

Cover and cook on high 15 minutes or until spinach wilts and mixture is hot.

Stir in lemon zest; sprinkle with feta.

PER SERVING
CALORIES 325 **TOTAL FAT** 11G **SATURATED FAT** 4G **CHOLESTEROL** 100MG **SODIUM** 619MG
TOTAL CARBOHYDRATES 19G **DIETARY FIBER** 6G **PROTEIN** 36G

FUSILLI WITH ALFREDO SAUCE, PEAS & BACON

- 12 OZ **FUSILLI PASTA**
- 8 STRIPS **BACON**
- 1 CUP SHREDDED **CARROTS**
- 2 CUPS **FROZEN PEAS**
- 1 CUP **ALFREDO SAUCE**
- 1½ TSP EACH CHOPPED **GARLIC** AND **DIJON MUSTARD**
- FRESHLY GROUND **PEPPER**, TO TASTE

YIELD
4 servings

ACTIVE
5 minutes

TOTAL
10 minutes

Boil fusilli as package directs, reserving 1 cup cooking water before draining.

Meanwhile, panfry bacon in a large nonstick skillet until crisp. Drain on paper towels; coarsely crumble. Pour off all but 1 tsp fat from skillet.

Heat skillet; add shredded carrots and sauté 1 minute or until almost tender. Add frozen peas, Alfredo sauce, garlic and mustard, and pepper to taste. Bring to a simmer.

Toss with drained pasta, bacon and reserved cooking water as needed.

PER SERVING
CALORIES 570 **TOTAL FAT** 17G **SATURATED FAT** 8G **CHOLESTEROL** 37MG **SODIUM** 729MG **TOTAL CARBOHYDRATES** 80G **DIETARY FIBER** 7G **PROTEIN** 23G

SPICY COD WITH ZUCCHINI

YIELD
4 servings

ACTIVE
10 minutes

TOTAL
41 minutes

¼ CUP **SLICED OR SLIVERED ALMONDS**

1 TSP **VEGETABLE OIL**

3 MEDIUM **ZUCCHINI** (ABOUT 1½ LB), CUT IN 1½-IN. CHUNKS

1 MEDIUM **ONION**, THINLY SLICED

1 CAN (19 OZ) **CHICKPEAS**, RINSED

1 JAR (14 OZ) **SPAGHETTI SAUCE** (ABOUT 1¾ CUPS)

¼ CUP **GOLDEN RAISINS**

1 TSP **GROUND CUMIN**

½ TSP **GROUND CINNAMON**

¼ TSP **CRUSHED RED PEPPER**

1 LB **COD OR SCROD FILLET**, CUT IN 4 PIECES

SIDE SUGGESTION
Couscous or rice

Lightly toast almonds in a large nonstick skillet over medium heat, stirring often, 3 to 4 minutes. Remove from pan.

Heat oil in same skillet. Add zucchini and onion and cook, stirring often, 4 to 5 minutes until onion is limp.

Stir in chickpeas, spaghetti sauce, raisins, cumin, cinnamon and crushed pepper. Simmer uncovered 8 to 10 minutes to develop flavors.

Top with fish in a single layer. Cover and simmer 10 to 12 minutes until fish is opaque in center. Sprinkle with toasted almonds.

NOTE
This recipe has a distinctive Middle Eastern flavor.

PER SERVING
CALORIES 408 **TOTAL FAT** 12G **SATURATED FAT** 0G **CHOLESTEROL** 49MG **SODIUM** 711MG
TOTAL CARBOHYDRATES 47G **DIETARY FIBER** 0G **PROTEIN** 31G

BLACK BEANS ON RICE

YIELD
4 servings

ACTIVE
20 minutes

TOTAL
20 minutes

1 BOX (8 OZ) **YELLOW RICE MIX**

2 TSP **OIL**

1 CUP CHOPPED **ONION**

1 TBSP MINCED **GARLIC**

1 CUP **WATER**

1 **CHICKEN BOUILLON CUBE**

1 BOX (10 OZ) **FROZEN CHOPPED KALE**

2 CANS (15.5 OZ EACH) **BLACK BEANS**, RINSED

2 TSP **SMOKED PAPRIKA**

1 TSP EACH **DRIED THYME** AND **GROUND CUMIN**

Cook rice as package directs.

Heat oil in a 3-qt saucepan over medium heat. Add onion and sauté 2 to 3 minutes until translucent. Stir in garlic; cook 30 seconds or until mixture is fragrant.

Add water, the bouillon cube and kale. Bring to a boil, reduce heat, cover and simmer, stirring occasionally, 5 to 6 minutes until kale thaws. Add beans, paprika, thyme and cumin; simmer 5 minutes. Serve over rice.

PER SERVING
CALORIES 516 **TOTAL FAT** 8G **SATURATED FAT** 1G **CHOLESTEROL** 0MG **SODIUM** 1,933MG
TOTAL CARBOHYDRATES 92G **DIETARY FIBER** 20G **PROTEIN** 21G

BLUE-RIBBON CHICKEN POTPIE

YIELD
6 servings

ACTIVE
15 minutes

TOTAL
1 hour

1 SHEET **FROZEN PUFF PASTRY** (FROM A 17.25-OZ BOX), THAWED ACCORDING TO PACKAGE DIRECTIONS

1 CUP **CHICKEN BROTH**

3 MEDIUM **CARROTS**, THINLY SLICED

8 OZ **GREEN BEANS**, CUT IN 1-IN. PIECES

2 TBSP **BUTTER** *OR* **MARGARINE**

1 CUP CHOPPED **ONION**

2 TBSP **ALL-PURPOSE FLOUR**

1 CUP **HALF-AND-HALF**

1½ TSP COARSELY CHOPPED **FRESH THYME** *OR* ½ TSP **DRIED**

½ TSP **SALT**

½ TSP **PEPPER**

3 CUPS BITE-SIZE PIECES **COOKED CHICKEN**

1 **EGG**, SLIGHTLY BEATEN

Using a deep 2-quart soufflé dish, or other round casserole about 7 in. across the top and 3 in. deep, as a guide, trim pastry with kitchen scissors into a circle, leaving a 1-in. border. Discard trimmings. Refrigerate pastry on a large plate or cookie sheet until firm.

In a large saucepan, bring broth to a simmer. Add carrots and green beans, cover and cook over medium heat just until tender, about 5 minutes. Drain, reserving vegetables and broth in separate bowls.

Return saucepan to medium heat. Add butter, and when melted, add onion. Cook, stirring occasionally, 3 to 5 minutes until soft. Stir in flour and cook 2 minutes. Gradually whisk in reserved broth, then half-and-half, thyme, salt and pepper. Cook, stirring often, until thick and hot, about 5 minutes. Remove from heat; stir in chicken and cooked vegetables.

Heat oven to 375°F.

Scrape chicken mixture into soufflé dish, cover with foil and bake 30 minutes or until warm throughout. Brush 1 in. border of pastry circle with beaten egg. Invert carefully over hot casserole. Gently press edge of pastry to dish until it sticks, then brush all over with more egg. Cut 2 vents in middle of pastry for steam to escape. Bake 20 to 25 minutes until puffed and browned. Let cool slightly before serving.

PER SERVING
CALORIES 430 **TOTAL FAT** 25G **SATURATED FAT** 0G **CHOLESTEROL** 123MG **SODIUM** 557MG **TOTAL CARBOHYDRATES** 24G **DIETARY FIBER** 0G **PROTEIN** 26G

PORK & CIDER STEW

2 MEDIUM **SWEET POTATOES** (1¼ LB), PEELED AND CUT IN ¾-IN. PIECES

3 SMALL **PARSNIPS** *OR* **CARROTS**, PEELED AND CUT IN ½-IN.-THICK SLICES

1 CUP CHOPPED **ONION**

2-LB **BONELESS PORK SHOULDER**, CUT IN 1-IN. PIECES

1 LARGE **GRANNY SMITH APPLE**, PEELED, CORED AND COARSELY CHOPPED

¼ CUP **FLOUR**

¾ TSP **SALT**

½ TSP EACH **DRIED SAGE** AND **THYME**

¼ TSP **PEPPER**

1 CUP **APPLE CIDER**

YIELD
5 servings

ACTIVE
15 minutes

TOTAL
7 to 9 hours on low

Layer sweet potatoes, parsnips, onion, pork and apple in a 3½-qt or larger slow cooker.

Stir flour, salt, sage, thyme and pepper in a small bowl to mix. Add cider; stir until smooth. Pour over meat and vegetables.

Cover and cook on low 7 to 9 hours or until pork and sweet potatoes are tender when pierced.

PER SERVING
CALORIES 631 **TOTAL FAT** 33G **SATURATED FAT** 11G **CHOLESTEROL** 129MG **SODIUM** 485MG
TOTAL CARBOHYDRATES 47G **DIETARY FIBER** 6G **PROTEIN** 34G

GRILLED TURKEY TENDERS & VEGETABLES

MARINADE

2 TSP GRATED **LEMON ZEST**

¼ CUP **LEMON JUICE**

2 TBSP **OLIVE OIL**

1 TBSP CHOPPED **GARLIC**

1 TBSP CHOPPED **FRESH ROSEMARY**

¼ TSP **SALT**

⅛ TSP **PEPPER**

2 **TURKEY BREAST TENDERLOINS** (ABOUT 2 LB)

1 MEDIUM **EGGPLANT** (1 LB)

1 LB **ZUCCHINI** *OR* **YELLOW SQUASH**

3 **PLUM TOMATOES**, CUT IN HALF

NONSTICK SPRAY

YIELD
6 servings

ACTIVE
5 minutes

TOTAL
1 hour 5 minutes

Line a rimmed baking sheet with foil.

MARINADE Whisk ingredients in a bowl. Put 6 Tbsp and the turkey in a large ziptop bag and seal; turn to coat. Refrigerate 45 minutes.

Meanwhile, slice eggplant and squash lengthwise ½ in. thick. Place with tomatoes on baking sheet; coat with nonstick spray.

Heat stovetop grill pan.

Put turkey on grill (discard bag with marinade). Grill 7 to 9 minutes per side until an instant-read thermometer inserted from side to middle registers 160°F. Remove; cover loosely with foil.

Grill eggplant and zucchini 4 minutes per side until just tender; grill tomatoes 2 minutes per side until charred but not soft. Cut vegetables bite-size; toss gently with remaining marinade. Serve with sliced turkey.

PER SERVING
CALORIES 243 **TOTAL FAT** 6G **SATURATED FAT** 1G **CHOLESTEROL** 94MG **SODIUM** 159MG **TOTAL CARBOHYDRATES** 10G **DIETARY FIBER** 2G **PROTEIN** 39G

WASABI-BAKED HALIBUT

YIELD
4 servings

ACTIVE
5 minutes

TOTAL
20 minutes

1½ LB **HALIBUT, HAKE OR COD FILLET,** CUT IN 4 EQUAL PIECES

⅓ CUP **WASABI MAYONNAISE**

⅓ CUP **CORNFLAKE CRUMBS**

SIDE SUGGESTION
Mixed greens salad

Heat oven to 425°F. Line a rimmed baking sheet with nonstick foil.

Arrange fillet pieces on foil. Spread top of fish with mayonnaise, then sprinkle with cornflake crumbs.

Bake 15 minutes or until fish is opaque at centers and crumbs just begin to brown.

DIFFERENT TAKES

- Top fish with crushed potato chips instead of cornflake crumbs.
- Add ⅓ cup chopped cilantro to the wasabi mayonnaise.
- Serve with lime wedges.

PER SERVING
CALORIES 290 **TOTAL FAT** 10G **SATURATED FAT** 0G **CHOLESTEROL** 68MG **SODIUM** 360MG
TOTAL CARBOHYDRATES 11G **DIETARY FIBER** 0G **PROTEIN** 36G

TEXAS-STYLE CHILI

2 TSP **OIL**

1 LB **CHUCK STEW MEAT**, CUT INTO ½-IN. CHUNKS

1 MEDIUM **ONION**, CHOPPED

2 MEDIUM **CARROTS**, SHREDDED

2 TSP **GROUND CUMIN**

1 CAN (4.5 OZ) **CHOPPED GREEN CHILES**

1 CAN (14.5 OZ) **CHICKEN BROTH**

1 CAN (28 OZ) **FIRE-ROASTED DICED TOMATOES**

1 CAN (15 OZ) EACH **RED KIDNEY**, **BLACK** AND **PINTO BEANS**, RINSED AND DRAINED

1 CAN (11 OZ) **MEXICAN-STYLE CORN**, DRAINED

YIELD
6 servings

ACTIVE
15 minutes

TOTAL
1 hour 10 minutes

Heat oil in a large nonstick skillet over medium-high heat. Add beef and sauté 4 minutes or until browned. Add onion and sauté 5 minutes. Stir in carrots and cumin; cook 1 minute.

Add chiles, broth and tomatoes. Heat just to a boil, cover and reduce heat to medium-low. Cook 1 hour, stirring occasionally, or until beef is tender. Stir in remaining ingredients and cook to heat through.

PER SERVING
CALORIES 483 **TOTAL FAT** 16G **SATURATED FAT** 6G **CHOLESTEROL** 50MG **SODIUM** 1,161MG **TOTAL CARBOHYDRATES** 52G **DIETARY FIBER** 16G **PROTEIN** 29G

SLOW COOKER TURKEY THIGHS

2 **TURKEY THIGHS** (ABOUT 2 LB), SKIN AND EXCESS FAT REMOVED

1 CUP **DRY RED WINE**, *OR* 1 CUP CHICKEN BROTH PLUS 1 TBSP RED-WINE VINEGAR

1 CUP THINLY SLICED **ONIONS**

2 TSP MINCED **GARLIC**

½ TSP EACH **DRIED ROSEMARY**, **SAGE**, **THYME** AND **SALT**

GRAVY

3 TBSP **FLOUR**

¼ CUP **WATER**

YIELD
4 servings

ACTIVE
10 minutes

TOTAL
4 to 5 hours on high *or* 8 to 10 hours on low

SIDE SUGGESTION
Mashed sweet potatoes and green beans

Eight to 12 hours before cooking, put all except Gravy ingredients in a 3½-qt or larger slow cooker. Cover and refrigerate.

Cook on high 4 to 5 hours or on low 8 to 10 hours until turkey is tender.

Remove turkey thighs to cutting board and cover loosely with foil.

GRAVY Set cooker to high and cover. Whisk flour and water until well blended. Whisk into liquid in cooker. Cover and cook, stirring once, 15 minutes or until thickened.

Cut meat in large pieces from both sides of each thigh bone to give you 4 pieces. Arrange on serving plates; spoon on some gravy. Serve remaining gravy from a sauceboat.

PER SERVING
CALORIES 286 **TOTAL FAT** 9G **SATURATED FAT** 3G **CHOLESTEROL** 113MG **SODIUM** 432MG
TOTAL CARBOHYDRATES 10G **DIETARY FIBER** 1G **PROTEIN** 38G

POT ROAST WITH ONION GRAVY

YIELD
10 servings

ACTIVE
15 minutes

TOTAL
3 hours 25 minutes

1 TBSP **VEGETABLE OIL**

1 **BONELESS BEEF CHUCK ROAST** (5 LB)

1 TSP **GARLIC SALT**

½ TSP **PEPPER**

4 CUPS SLICED **ONIONS**

½ CUP COLD **WATER** MIXED WITH
2 TBSP **ALL-PURPOSE FLOUR**

SIDE SUGGESTION
Steamed potatoes

Heat oven to 325°F. Heat oil in a 4- to 5-quart ovenproof pot or Dutch oven over medium-high heat. Add roast and brown on all sides, about 8 minutes.

Sprinkle with garlic salt and pepper. Add onions and cover with tight-fitting lid (if lid doesn't fit tightly, cover first with foil, then lid). Bake 3 hours or until tender.

Transfer beef to a cutting board, cover loosely with foil and let stand 10 minutes before carving.

Meanwhile, make gravy. Skim fat from liquid in pot and discard. Bring liquid to a gentle boil. Mix cold water with flour until blended. Whisk into liquid and boil 2 minutes, stirring constantly, until slightly thickened.

Thinly slice meat across the grain. Arrange slices on serving platter. Spoon some gravy over meat. Serve remaining gravy at the table.

NOTE Pot roasts can easily be made two or three days before serving, and they're actually better that way. Also, any fat in the gravy will rise and harden, making it easy to remove. To serve, slice the pot roast and heat it in the gravy over medium-low heat.

PER SERVING
CALORIES 303 **TOTAL FAT** 14G **SATURATED FAT** 0G **CHOLESTEROL** 114MG **SODIUM** 281MG
TOTAL CARBOHYDRATES 7G **DIETARY FIBER** 40G **PROTEIN** 35G

LINGUINE WITH TOMATOES & TOFU

YIELD
6 servings

ACTIVE
20 minutes

TOTAL
30 minutes

- 1 LB **LINGUINE OR SPAGHETTI PASTA**
- 4 LARGE RIPE **TOMATOES**, CUT IN CHUNKS
- ½ CUP **FRESH BASIL**, CHOPPED
- 3 TBSP **OLIVE OIL**
- 2 TBSP MINCED **GARLIC**
- ½ TSP EACH **SALT** AND **PEPPER**
- 1 PKG (14 OZ) **FIRM TOFU**, DRAINED, PATTED DRY AND CUT IN ¾-IN. CUBES
- 1 BAG (10 OZ) **FRESH SPINACH**, TOUGH STEMS REMOVED, LEAVES CHOPPED
- 1 TBSP **WATER**

SERVE WITH
Grated Parmesan

Cook pasta as package directs; drain, reserving ⅓ cup cooking water. Return pasta to pot.

While pasta cooks, stir tomatoes, basil, 1 Tbsp each oil and garlic, and the salt and pepper in a bowl to mix.

Heat remaining 2 Tbsp oil in a large nonstick skillet over medium-high heat. Add tofu and sauté 4 to 5 minutes until lightly golden. Add remaining 1 Tbsp garlic; sauté 30 seconds or until aromatic. Add spinach and reserved cooking water. Cover and cook 2 to 3 minutes until wilted.

Toss pasta with tomato and tofu mixtures and up to ⅓ cup reserved cooking water to loosen pasta.

PER SERVING
CALORIES 433 **TOTAL FAT** 11G **SATURATED FAT** 2G **CHOLESTEROL** 0MG **SODIUM** 248MG
TOTAL CARBOHYDRATES 67G **DIETARY FIBER** 6G **PROTEIN** 18G

GOLDEN FLOUNDER WITH ZUCCHINI COUSCOUS

YIELD
4 servings

ACTIVE
3 minutes

TOTAL
10 minutes

½ CUP **LIGHT MAYONNAISE**

⅓ CUP **GRATED PARMESAN**

1 TO 2 TBSP PLUS ½ CUP **WATER**

4 **FLOUNDER FILLETS** (ABOUT 6 OZ EACH)

2 TSP **OLIVE OIL**

1 MEDIUM **ZUCCHINI** (ABOUT 6 OZ), HALVED LENGTHWISE, CUT IN ½-IN.-THICK SLICES

1 CAN (14.5 OZ) **PETITE DICED TOMATOES WITH GARLIC AND ONION OR ITALIAN-FLAVORED**

1 BOX (5.8 OZ) **ROASTED GARLIC AND OLIVE OIL FLAVORED COUSCOUS**

Heat oven to 450°F. Line a 15½ x 10½-in. rimmed baking sheet with foil.

Mix mayonnaise and cheese in a small bowl. Stir in 1 to 2 Tbsp water until spreadable. Place fish on lined sheet; fold thin edge of fillets under fish. Spread top of each with about 2 Tbsp mayonnaise mixture.

Bake 7 to 8 minutes until topping is golden and fish is cooked through.

Meanwhile, heat oil in a large skillet over medium-high heat. Add zucchini; sauté 3 minutes. Add tomatoes with their juices, ½ cup water, the couscous and its seasoning packet. Cover, remove from heat and let stand until couscous is cooked. Stir before serving.

PER SERVING
CALORIES 477 **TOTAL FAT** 17G **SATURATED FAT** 4G **CHOLESTEROL** 97MG **SODIUM** 1,329MG **TOTAL CARBOHYDRATES** 37G **DIETARY FIBER** 2G **PROTEIN** 41G

GARLIC-CUMIN CHICKEN THIGHS

YIELD
4 servings

ACTIVE
8 minutes

TOTAL
41 minutes

8 **CHICKEN THIGHS** (2 LB TOTAL), SKIN AND VISIBLE FAT REMOVED (SEE NOTE)

½ TSP **SALT**

½ TSP FRESHLY GROUND **PEPPER**

2 TBSP **BUTTER OR MARGARINE**

16 LARGE CLOVES **GARLIC**, PEELED

1 TBSP **GROUND CUMIN**

⅓ CUP FINELY CHOPPED **PARSLEY**

4 **LEMON WEDGES**

SIDE SUGGESTION
Mexican-style corn, tossed green salad

Season chicken with salt and pepper. Heat butter in a large, heavy nonstick skillet until bubbly.

Add thighs and brown on one side, about 5 minutes. Turn, add garlic, cover and cook over medium-low heat 20 to 23 minutes, turning several times, until brown on both sides and opaque at the bone. Sprinkle both sides with cumin, increase heat to medium-high and cook, uncovered, 3 to 5 minutes, turning once, until drippings and chicken are crisp.

Remove chicken to serving plates. Spoon on garlic and crisp drippings. Sprinkle with chopped parsley and serve with lemon wedges.

NOTE To trim the fat, especially from the boned side of thighs, snip it off with kitchen scissors.

PER SERVING
CALORIES 234 **TOTAL FAT** 11G **SATURATED FAT** 5G **CHOLESTEROL** 123MG **SODIUM** 451MG
TOTAL CARBOHYDRATES 6G **DIETARY FIBER** 1G **PROTEIN** 27G

SICILIAN PASTA

YIELD
4 servings

ACTIVE
10 minutes

TOTAL
25 minutes

12 OZ **PASTA (ANY SHAPE)**

1½ TSP **OLIVE OIL**

1 MEDIUM **ONION**, CHOPPED

1½ CUPS **MARINARA SAUCE**

2 TBSP **RAISINS** (OPTIONAL)

1 CAN (5 OZ) **SOLID LIGHT TUNA IN OLIVE OIL**, DRAINED

¼ CUP SLICED **OLIVES (PREFERABLY PIMIENTO-STUFFED)**

Bring a large pot of lightly salted water to a boil. Add pasta and cook as package directs, removing and reserving ½ cup water before draining.

Meanwhile, heat oil in a large nonstick skillet. Add onion; sauté 10 minutes or until golden and tender. Add marinara sauce and the raisins, if desired; bring to a simmer. Stir in tuna and olives and heat through.

Toss pasta, sauce and reserved cooking water to mix and coat.

PER SERVING
CALORIES 498 **TOTAL FAT** 9G **SATURATED FAT** 2G **CHOLESTEROL** 20MG **SODIUM** 795MG
TOTAL CARBOHYDRATES 81G **DIETARY FIBER** 6G **PROTEIN** 21G

8-MINUTE SCALLOP SAUTÉ

YIELD
4 servings

ACTIVE
3 minutes

TOTAL
8 minutes

2 TBSP **BUTTER** *OR* **MARGARINE**

½ TSP MINCED **GARLIC**

1 LB **SEA, BAY OR CALICO SCALLOPS**

2 CUPS COARSELY CHOPPED RIPE **TOMATOES**

¼ TSP **SALT**

2 TBSP CHOPPED **PARSLEY**

Melt 1 Tbsp of the butter in a medium-size skillet. Add garlic and cook over low heat 1 minute.

Stir in scallops, tomatoes and salt. Cover and cook 2 to 4 minutes, stirring once or twice, until scallops are opaque at centers. Stir in remaining butter.

Remove from heat and stir in parsley.

PER SERVING
CALORIES 171 **TOTAL FAT** 7G **SATURATED FAT** 0G **CHOLESTEROL** 53MG **SODIUM** 385MG
TOTAL CARBOHYDRATES 7G **DIETARY FIBER** 0G **PROTEIN** 20G

MAPLE-POMEGRANATE GLAZED HAM

YIELD
12 (3-oz) servings with leftovers

ACTIVE
15 minutes

TOTAL
1 hour

2 CUPS **POMEGRANATE JUICE**

3 TBSP **CORNSTARCH**

¾ CUP **MAPLE OR PANCAKE SYRUP**

⅓ CUP **COARSE-GRAIN MUSTARD**

1 FULLY COOKED 7- TO 8-LB **SPIRAL-SLICED BONE-IN HALF-HAM**
(WE USED SMITHFIELD MARKETPLACE)

SIDE SUGGESTION
Roasted potatoes, corn pudding, steamed asparagus, roasted butternut squash

Heat oven to 325°F. Line a roasting pan with nonstick foil.

Whisk pomegranate juice and cornstarch in a medium saucepan until blended. Bring to a boil over medium-high heat, stirring frequently. Reduce heat and simmer 1 minute or until slightly thickened and clear. Remove from heat; stir in syrup and mustard.

Place ham in roasting pan. Brush on some of the glaze. Cover loosely with nonstick foil and bake according to package directions, brushing on more glaze 2 or 3 times during baking time.

Serve ham with remaining glaze to drizzle over slices.

PLANNING TIP The glaze can be made and refrigerated up to 5 days ahead.

PER SERVING
CALORIES 200 **TOTAL FAT** 8G **SATURATED FAT** 3G **CHOLESTEROL** 50MG **SODIUM** 1,346MG
TOTAL CARBOHYDRATES 13G **DIETARY FIBER** 0G **PROTEIN** 19G

THE ULTIMATE STEAK SANDWICH WITH SALAD ITALIENNE

1 BOX (8 OZ) **FROZEN VIDALIA ONION RINGS**

4 SLICES **FROZEN TEXAS TOAST** (½ AN 11.25-OZ BOX)

12-OZ **FLANK STEAK**

½ TSP **SALT**

½ TSP **PEPPER**

2 LARGE RIPE **PLUM TOMATOES**, SLICED

SALAD

1 BAG (5 OZ) **BABY ARUGULA BLEND OR OTHER SALAD MIX**

1 JAR (12 OZ) **ROASTED PEPPERS, PREFERABLY RED AND YELLOW**, CUT UP

1 CAN (10 OZ) **CHICKPEAS**, RINSED

¼ CUP **RED-WINE VINAIGRETTE**

YIELD
4 servings

ACTIVE
4 minutes

TOTAL
18 minutes

Heat oven to 475°F. Line a large rimmed baking sheet with foil (for easy cleanup). Spread onion rings in a single layer on half the lined pan and bake 5 minutes. Put Texas Toast on other side of pan. Bake 6 to 9 minutes, turning once, until onion rings and toast are golden and crisp.

Meanwhile, heat a large nonstick skillet over medium-high heat. Season steak with salt and pepper, place in skillet and cook, turning once, 7 to 9 minutes, until an instant-read thermometer inserted from side to middle registers 155°F. Remove to a cutting board, cover loosely with foil and let rest. (Temperature will rise to 160°F for medium doneness.)

Meanwhile, make **SALAD**: Mix ingredients in a large bowl.

Slice steak thinly across the grain. Put 1 slice toast on each of 4 plates. Top with tomatoes, steak, then onion rings; serve with the salad.

PER SERVING
CALORIES 555 **TOTAL FAT** 31G **SATURATED FAT** 7G **CHOLESTEROL** 44MG **SODIUM** 1,155MG **TOTAL CARBOHYDRATES** 43G **DIETARY FIBER** 4G **PROTEIN** 25G

BOW-TIES WITH WHITE BEANS & BROCCOLI

YIELD
6 servings

ACTIVE
10 minutes

TOTAL
28 minutes

1 LB **BOW-TIE PASTA**

1 TBSP **VEGETABLE OIL**

1 BUNCH (ABOUT 1 LB) **BROCCOLI FLORETS**, CUT SMALL, STEMS PEELED AND CUT IN SMALL PIECES

1 TBSP MINCED **GARLIC**

2 CUPS **CHICKEN BROTH**

1 CAN (15 OZ) **CANNELLINI OR OTHER WHITE BEANS**, RINSED

1 TSP FRESHLY GRATED **LEMON ZEST**

1 TBSP **FRESH LEMON JUICE**

⅓ CUP **GRATED PARMESAN**

Bring a large pot of lightly salted water to a boil. Add pasta and cook according to package directions.

While pasta cooks, heat oil in a large nonstick skillet. Add broccoli and garlic; stir over medium heat 3 to 4 minutes until broccoli is bright green. Add broth and cook 2 to 3 minutes until broccoli is crisp-tender. Stir in beans and lemon zest and juice.

Drain pasta and put into a warmed large serving bowl. Add broccoli mixture; sprinkle with cheese. Toss to mix well.

PER SERVING
CALORIES 397 **TOTAL FAT** 6G **SATURATED FAT** 0G **CHOLESTEROL** 3MG **SODIUM** 780MG
TOTAL CARBOHYDRATES 68G **DIETARY FIBER** 0G **PROTEIN** 17G

CHICKEN TORTILLA SOUP

1 LB **CHICKEN THIGHS**, SKIN REMOVED

3 CUPS **WATER**

2 CANS (14.5 OZ EACH) **FAT-FREE REDUCED-SODIUM CHICKEN BROTH**

1 CAN (15 OZ) **BLACK BEANS**, RINSED

1 CAN (15.25 OZ) **WHOLE-KERNEL CORN**

1 CAN (14.5 OZ) **DICED TOMATOES WITH GREEN CHILES**

½ TSP EACH **GROUND CUMIN** AND **DRIED OREGANO**

1 CUP CRUMBLED **TORTILLA CHIPS**

½ CUP CHOPPED **CILANTRO**

GARNISH: **LIME WEDGES, TORTILLA CHIPS**

YIELD
6 servings

ACTIVE
10 minutes

TOTAL
45 minutes

Bring chicken and water to a boil in a large saucepan. Reduce heat, cover and simmer 25 minutes or until chicken is cooked. Remove chicken to cutting board; let cool slightly.

Meanwhile, add broth to pot; bring to a boil. Stir in beans, corn, tomatoes, cumin and oregano, and bring to a simmer. Simmer 5 minutes for flavors to blend.

Meanwhile, pull chicken meat from bones and shred.

Stir chicken and tortilla chips into soup; cook 1 minute to slightly soften chips. Remove from heat and stir in cilantro. Garnish with lime wedges and additional tortilla chips.

PER SERVING
CALORIES 249 **TOTAL FAT** 7G **SATURATED FAT** 2G **CHOLESTEROL** 36MG **SODIUM** 1,038MG **TOTAL CARBOHYDRATES** 33G **DIETARY FIBER** 7G **PROTEIN** 16G

PEPPERONI PIZZA TURKEY MEAT LOAF

1¼ LB **GROUND TURKEY**

1 CUP **BOTTLED MARINARA SAUCE**

½ CUP **JARRED ROASTED YELLOW OR RED PEPPERS**, SLICED

½ CUP **SHREDDED ITALIAN 6-CHEESE BLEND**

½ CUP **ITALIAN-SEASONED DRIED BREAD CRUMBS**

½ CUP FINELY CHOPPED **ONION**

16 SMALL SLICES **70%-LESS-FAT TURKEY PEPPERONI** (SUCH AS HORMEL), 8 SLICES DICED

1 LARGE **EGG**

2 TSP MINCED **GARLIC**

¼ TSP **SALT**

GARNISH: **FRESH BASIL LEAVES**

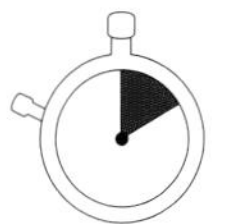

YIELD
4 servings

ACTIVE
10 minutes

TOTAL
4 to 6 hours on low

SIDE SUGGESTION
Steamed green beans, farfalle pasta

In a medium bowl, using your hands or a wooden spoon, mix ground turkey, ½ cup marinara sauce, ¼ cup each peppers and cheese blend, the bread crumbs and onion, diced pepperoni (reserve sliced), egg, garlic and salt until blended. Pat mixture over bottom of a 3½-qt slow cooker (if using a larger cooker, pat mixture into an 8-in. round). Spread top with ¼ cup marinara sauce.

Cover and cook on low 4 to 6 hours or until a meat thermometer (preferably instant-read) inserted in center of loaf registers 165°F.

Spread with remaining sauce, sprinkle with remaining cheese, then top with remaining pepperoni and peppers. Cover and cook 5 minutes or until cheese melts. Sprinkle with basil; cut into wedges.

PER SERVING
CALORIES 443 **TOTAL FAT** 22G **SATURATED FAT** 8G **CHOLESTEROL** 186MG **SODIUM** 1,458MG
TOTAL CARBOHYDRATES 22G **DIETARY FIBER** 2G **PROTEIN** 39G

PORK CUTLETS WITH CREAMY GARLIC SAUCE & SPINACH

YIELD
4 servings

ACTIVE
13 minutes

TOTAL
13 minutes

3 TBSP **SEASONED DRIED BREAD CRUMBS**

FOUR 4-OZ **BONELESS THIN-CUT PORK CHOPS**

1 TBSP **OLIVE OIL**

1 BAG (12 OZ) **FRESH SPINACH**

1 PT **CHERRY TOMATOES**

½ CUP **GARLIC-AND-HERB SPREADABLE CHEESE** (SUCH AS ALOUETTE)

1 TBSP **WATER**

1 JAR (4 OZ) **SLICED PIMIENTOS**, DRAINED

1 TBSP CHOPPED **PARSLEY** (OPTIONAL)

Spread bread crumbs on wax paper; dip cutlets in crumbs to coat on both sides.

Heat oil in a large nonstick skillet. Add cutlets; cook over medium-high heat 5 minutes, turning once, until cooked through. Remove to a plate; cover to keep warm.

Add half the spinach and the tomatoes to skillet. Cook, tossing often, 1 minute or until spinach starts to cook down. Add rest of spinach; cook, tossing, 2 minutes or until spinach wilts and tomato skins begin to split.

Microwave cheese and water in a covered small bowl on high 45 seconds or until melted. Stir in pimientos and parsley; drizzle over pork. Serve with spinach and tomatoes.

PER SERVING
CALORIES 413 **TOTAL FAT** 27G **SATURATED FAT** 12G **CHOLESTEROL** 101MG **SODIUM** 475MG **TOTAL CARBOHYDRATES** 12G **DIETARY FIBER** 3G **PROTEIN** 29G

HEARTY SHRIMP & CORN CHOWDER

14 STRIPS **BACON**, STACKED AND DICED

1 EACH MEDIUM **ONION** AND **RED PEPPER**, DICED

3 TBSP **FLOUR**

1 LB **RED-SKINNED POTATOES**, CUT IN ½-IN. CHUNKS (3 CUPS)

2 CUPS **WHOLE MILK**

1 CAN (14.5 OZ) **CHICKEN BROTH**

1 CAN (14.5 OZ) **WHOLE-KERNEL CORN**, DRAINED

1 TBSP **FRESH THYME LEAVES** (OR 1 TSP DRIED)

¾ TSP **SALT**

½ TSP **PEPPER**

1 LB **RAW MEDIUM SHRIMP**, PEELED, DEVEINED AND CUT BITE-SIZE

YIELD
4 servings

ACTIVE
25 minutes

TOTAL
50 minutes

Heat a 3- to 4-qt saucepan over medium heat. Add bacon; cook until crisp. Remove with a slotted spoon, drain well on paper towels and reserve.

Drain off all but 1 Tbsp fat. Add onion and red pepper and cook, stirring as needed, 5 minutes or until soft. Add flour; stir until blended with fat. Stir in remaining ingredients except shrimp.

Bring to a boil, stirring bottom of saucepan and taking care to get into corners. Reduce heat, partially cover and simmer, stirring occasionally, 10 minutes or until potatoes are tender.

Add the shrimp and simmer 1 to 2 minutes or until cooked through. Ladle into soup plates, sprinkle with bacon and serve immediately.

PER SERVING
CALORIES 436 **TOTAL FAT** 13G **SATURATED FAT** 5G **CHOLESTEROL** 164MG **SODIUM** 1,337MG
TOTAL CARBOHYDRATES 50G **DIETARY FIBER** 5G **PROTEIN** 31G

APPENDIX

WEIGHTS & MEASURES

TABLE OF EQUIVALENTS

ABBREVIATIONS

OUNCE = OZ
POUND = LB
QUART = QT
INCH = IN.
FOOT = FT
TEASPOON = TSP
TABLESPOON = TBSP
MILLILITER = ML
LITER = L
GRAM = G
KILOGRAM = KG
MILLIMETER = MM
CENTIMETER = CM

WEIGHTS

U.S. / U.K.	METRIC
.035 oz	1 g
¼oz	7 g
½ oz	14 g
¾ oz	21 g
1 oz	28 g
1½ oz	42.5 g
2 oz	57 g
3 oz	85 g
4 oz	113 g
5 oz	142 g
6 oz	170 g
7 oz	198 g
8 oz (½ lb)	227 g
10 oz	315 g
12 oz (¾ lb)	375 g
14 oz	440 g
16 oz (1 lb)	454 g
2.2 lbs	1 kg

LENGTH MEASURES

U.S. / U.K.	METRIC
⅛ in.	3 mm
¼ in.	6 mm
½ in.	12 mm
1 in.	2.5 cm
2 in.	5 cm
3 in.	7.5 cm
4 in.	10 cm
12 in.	30 cm

VOLUME

U.S.	METRIC
¼ tsp	1 ml
½ tsp	2.5 ml
¾ tsp	4 ml
1 tsp	5 ml
1¼ tsp	6 ml
1½ tsp	7.5 ml
1¾ tsp	8.5 ml
2 tsp	10 ml
1 Tbsp	15 ml
2 Tbsp	30 ml
¼ cup	60 ml
⅓ cup	80 ml
½ cup	120 ml
⅔ cup	160 ml
¾ cup	180 ml
1 cup	240 ml
1½ cups	355 ml
2 cups (1 pint)	475 ml
3 cups	710 ml
4 cups (1 quart)	.95 l
1.06 quart	1 l
4 quarts (1 gallon)	3.8 l

OVEN TEMPERATURES

FAHRENHEIT	CELSIUS	GAS
250	120	½
275	140	1
300	150	2
325	160	3
350	180	4
375	190	5
400	200	6
425	220	7
450	230	8
475	240	9
500	260	10

The following information often comes in handy. You might be surprised at how many professionals don't know that there are 3 teaspoons (tsp) in 1 tablespoon (Tbsp).

TEASPOONS, TABLESPOONS, CUPS, PINTS, QUARTS AND GALLONS

3 TSP = 1 TBSP
4 TBSP = ¼ CUP
8 TBSP = ½ CUP
5 TBSP PLUS 1 TSP = 1/3 CUP
2 CUPS = 1 PT (16 FLUID OZ)
4 CUPS = 1 QUART (2 PT, 32 FLUID OZ)
4 QT = 1 GALLON (16 CUPS, 128 FLUID OZ)

ELECTRONIC SCALE EQUIVALENTS

While recipes specify the amount of some ingredients (such as meat or produce) in pounds and ounces, most stores use electronic scales, which display (and print out on labels) ounces as fractions of pounds. Electronic scales are digital so a weight will seldom read any of the following figures exactly. Use them as a guide to make sure you buy what you need.

WHEN A RECIPE CALLS FOR	A DIGITAL PRINTOUT WILL READ
4 OZ (¼ LB)	.25 LB
8 OZ (½ LB)	.50 LB
12 OZ (¾ LB)	.75 LB
1 LB (16 OZ)	1.00 LB
1 LB 4 OZ (1¼ LB)	1.25 LB

DRY WEIGHT AND FLUID MEASURE, POUNDS AND OUNCES VERSUS METRIC

The labels of most packaged food and beverages now show contents in metric as well as avoirdupois. For the metrically impaired, liquids are given in fluid ounces (fl oz) or liters (l); solids in pounds and ounces (lb and oz) or grams (g). usually minor confusions can occur in semi-solid products such as jam; the label may say "Net weight 12 oz," and you may think that is 1½ cups, just what the recipe calls for, but in fact a 12-oz jar of jam is only about 1 cup.

MEASURING

With a stew or a pasta dish, a little more or a little less meat, onion or broth isn't going to make or break the results. But when it comes to baking, accurate measuring of ingredients is essential to success.
For dry ingredients, including flour, sugar, baking powder and spices (also for small amounts of liquids such as vanilla and lemon juice), use nested measures that come in sets and are sized to the rim: ¼, ⅓, ½ and 1 cup; ⅛, ¼, ½, 1 teaspoon (tsp) and 1 tablespoon (Tbsp).

Buy good quality metal or plastic nested cups with sturdy handles that are clearly marked with the amount they hold. Have at least two sets of measuring cups and spoons (for ease). When you bake, especially if you are on the learning track, there are lots of distractions in your home or you are trying a recipe for the first time, measure all the ingredients before you begin and set them out, still in the measuring cups or spoons, on a tray or baking sheet. Do a final check against the recipe before you start mixing. That way, if you do get distracted, you can quickly tell whether or not you have added the baking powder to a cake batter.

FLOUR: If the recipe calls for ¾ cup flour, take a ½-cup measure and a ¼ cup. Put a strip of wax paper on the counter. Stir the flour in the bag or canister. Working over the wax paper (or the bag or canister), spoon flour lightly into the ½-cup measure until it is overflowing. Do not tap the cup on the counter, or press down the flour. Then take a metal spatula (or any straight edge) and sweep off the excess. Measure the ¼ cup in the same way. Use the wax paper to pour the spilled flour back into the bag.

Use this method also for measuring cocoa, confectioners' sugar and cornstarch.

SUGAR: Scoop up the sugar in the appropriate cup measure(s) and level off the surface. Use this method for other compact ingredients such as cornmeal and rice.

BROWN SUGAR: Since brown sugar does not find its own level if scooped or spooned, pack it firmly into a cup measure until level with the rim.

SPICES, BAKING POWDER, BAKING SODA: Use nested teaspoon/tablespoons to measure. Slip measuring spoon into container of baking powder or baking soda, then level off excess with a small metal spatula or other straight edge. If the neck of a spice jar is too narrow for a measuring spoon to pass through, pour the spice into the spoon over a small piece of wax paper until spoon is overflowing. Then sweep off the excess. Use the piece of wax paper to pour the excess spice back into the jar.

MILK, WATER AND OTHER LIQUIDS: Use a stainless

steel or clear polycarbonate angled measuring cup that allows you to check the liquid level from the top. Or use clear glass or plastic measures and check the liquid level by looking through the side of the measure.

SOUR CREAM, YOGURT AND OTHER SEMISOLIDS: Use the nested cups. It's hard to get a level surface of sour cream in a glass or plastic measure.

BUTTER: To measure butter, use the marks on the paper each stick is wrapped in. If the wrapper is off center and you need to measure accurately for a cake or cookies, unfold it and reposition the butter before cutting.

HERBS & SPICES

While herbs are usually the leaves from grassy plants (herba is the Latin for grass), spices can be from bark (cinnamon), buds (cloves), fruit (allspice, cardamom, vanilla), roots or rhizomes (galangal, ginger, turmeric) or seeds (anise, caraway, cumin, fennel, mustard, nutmeg). Many home cooks grow and cultivate their own herbs; few of us grow our own spices.

Herbs include familiar specimens such as basil, cilantro, parsley, rosemary, tarragon and thyme. Fresh herbs are increasingly accessible all year in large super-markets, produce markets and specialty stores, and the variety goes way beyond big bunches of parsley and cilantro to include just several sprigs of rosemary, thyme, sage or other fresh herbs packed in rigid containers. Look for moist (but not wet), fresh-looking herbs without drooping leaves or black spots. If the herb has thick stems (rosemary, thyme and oregano are examples), discard the stems and use only the leaves. Fresh herbs are usually chopped to release the flavor before being added to a dish.

Many herbs grow year round in flowerpots set on sunny kitchen windowsills. During warm months, they are easy to grow in containers on decks or planted in gardens. Nothing compares to the flavor and aroma of an herb snipped moments before use. But dried herbs add excellent flavors to dishes, too. In most instances, a teaspoon of dried herb can be used in place of a tablespoon of a chopped fresh herb—which translates to one-third the amount. It's a good idea to rub the dried herb between your fingertips before adding it to the dish to help release the herb's essential oils and flavors. Store dried herbs in their containers, in a cool, dark cupboard, away from the warmth of the stove.

Like dried herbs, spices should be stored in a cool, dark cupboard. Whole, unground spices (such as cloves, nutmeg, peppercorns, coriander and anise) will keep indefinitely. But write the date on jars of ground spices when you open them and be ruthless: Toss those that have been open for a year. (Or put them in a bowl and enjoy the last vestiges of aroma as a potpourri.) If you won't be using a spice often, buy it in small quantities. For example, depending on your cooking interests, you may prefer large containers of cinnamon and pepper but small ones of poppy seeds and cardamom.

PRESERVING FRESH HERBS

Most fresh herbs can be dried or frozen and used later, with little loss of flavor or aroma. Cilantro is an exception.

TO DRY HERBS

Tie the washed herbs in a bunch at the stem end and hang them, stem ends up, in a warm, dry, well-ventilated section of the kitchen or pantry. Or you can dry them by laying them on a screen and leaving them in a dry, well-ventilated place, indoors or out (protect them from morning dew and evening moisture). Depending on the size and type of herb, it will dry in one to two weeks. Make sure the herbs are completely dry before storing them in a glass or rigid plastic container. If not completely dry, mold may grow.

TO FREEZE HERBS

Dill, parsley, chervil and fennel freeze well. Wash and dry them thoroughly. Discard large stems. Put the herbs in an airtight, rigid plastic container and freeze them. Date the container and use the herbs within a year, using them as you would fresh herbs (no need to defrost). Basil also freezes beautifully and many people like to make and freeze huge amounts of basil pesto when basil is at its best. At the least, purée the basil with olive oil and a little salt before freezing it.

HERBS

BASIL: Sweet and aromatic with a faint licorice flavor, basil is found most often in Italian and Mediterranean cooking but is also important in Thai cooking. Its marriage with tomatoes is legendary, and its presence in pesto imperative. Basil may have large or small leaves and may be green or purplish-red. All sizes and colors are equally aromatic. Fresh basil is easy to find all year long. Store-bought basil that has been washed and packaged is often a good bet. If you buy bunches of basil at a farmer's market, plan to use them promptly, especially if they are wet from rain. Pluck leaves from stems, then wash and drain them. Dry the leaves in a salad spinner, or wrap in kitchen towels or paper towels. Refrigerate until ready to use. Fresh basil is best for serving with sliced fresh tomatoes and mozzarella cheese, or to top a pizza. You can chop the leaves in the usual way like parsley, but to decrease bruising with the knife, stack several leaves and cut them across in thin strips. Dried basil is usually added to cooked preparations such as tomato sauces, soups and stews.

BAY LEAVES: Bay leaves are also called bay laurel and sweet bay. They are slightly spicy, very aromatic and one of the three herbs used (with parsley and thyme) in a classic bouquet garni. Bay leaves, which are fairly large, grayish-green specimens, are usually sold dried, and are added to stews and other savory dishes. They should be discarded before serving. Turkish leaves are greatly preferable to the Californian variety.

CHIVES: Long, green and grassy-looking, chives are a member of the onion family and are available fresh all year long. Freeze-dried chives are not as flavorful as fresh. Chives' mild onion flavor is delicious in salads and sprinkled on top of chilled soups or mixed into creamy dips and spreads.

CILANTRO/FRESH CORIANDER: Fresh cilantro resembles flat-leaf parsley and is also called fresh coriander and even Chinese parsley. Cilantro finds its way into Mexican, Indian, Asian, North African and Caribbean cooking, where the roots, stems and leaves are often used. Some call cilantro the love-it-or-hate-it herb. Its distinctive, pungent flavor is easy to discern in salsa and other uncooked preparations. It is less powerful when cooked. Cilantro has little flavor when dried. Coriander seeds (page 469) come from the same plant but impart a very different flavor.

DILL WEED: Fragrant, fresh dill has a sharp lemony flavor; dried dill imparts a similar flavor. Dill weed is used in German, Scandinavian and Middle Eastern cooking often with fish or lamb. It's very good with potato soups and rice salad as well as with cream cheese for a spread. Greeks use it to flavor stuffed grape leaves. See also dill seed (page 470): same plant, very different flavor.

MARJORAM: Sometimes called sweet marjoram, it is sold both fresh and dried. Its flavor somewhat resembles oregano and it may be used in place of it in many dishes. Fresh marjoram leaves are small and grayish-green.

MINT: Mint is one of the most common and recognizable herbs; it is also the easiest to grow and can often take over a garden. Mint's cool, fresh flavor adds to lemonade, iced tea, mint juleps, desserts, chocolate and lamb dishes. It is also used very often for garnish. Mint is easy to buy fresh, but spearmint is also sold dried.

OREGANO: Oregano is most readily associated with Italian, Greek and Mexican cooking and blends well with meat, vegetables and legumes. It has a pungent flavor and aroma and is available both fresh and dried. Fresh oregano has medium-sized dark green leaves.

PARSLEY: Whether curly- or flat-leafed, parsley is our most common herb, but is much more than just a finishing sprig. Parsley, with bay leaves and thyme, makes up traditional bouquet garni, herb flavoring for long-simmering pot roasts and rich stews. Parsley, with lemon juice and a little bulgur wheat, makes tabbouleh, the delicious Middle-Eastern salad. Mixed with garlic and butter it flavors baked snails; with garlic, clams and olive oil it is a great sauce for pasta. Parsley again teams with garlic in Argentinian chimichurri sauce, served with beef and chicken. Parsley is nearly always best used fresh, although it is sold dried.

ROSEMARY: Rosemary is characteristically found in Mediterranean cooking, where its spicy flavor and fragrant scent lend themselves to roast chicken and lamb. Rosemary and olives add delicious flavor to bread. But rosemary also has an unexpected sweet side. Rosemary is sold both fresh and dried. If purchased fresh, pull the leaves off the hard stems before chopping them.

SAGE: Sage's fuzzy gray-green leaves are easy to spot among the fresh herbs; its strong, slightly musty flavor is easy to recognize in pork sausage, sage and onion stuffing and other meat and poultry dishes. Dried sage comes in two forms: cut sage, when you want the leaf to show, and ground, which is closer to a powder. Ground sage loses its flavor much more quickly than do the leaves.

TARRAGON: Pleasantly aromatic and tasting of licorice, tarragon's slender and somewhat spiky dark green leaves make it easily recognizable. Tarragon is used extensively in French cooking, in béarnaise sauce, with fish and with chicken (poulet à l'estragon) and is a common flavoring for vinegar. Tarragon is available both fresh and dried.

THYME: Thyme is one of the three herbs found in a classic bouquet garni (with bay leaves and parsley), a bundle of herbs used to flavor soups, stews and stocks. Its slightly strong pungent taste and spicy aroma are also frequently used to flavor chicken and other poultry dishes, including traditional bread stuffing. Thyme, readily available both fresh and dried, has tiny, dark green leaves.

SPICES

ALLSPICE: Allspice is sold as whole berries or ground. It comes from the seed of a tree indigenous to the Western Hemisphere, which makes it unusual in the world of spices, most of which originate in Asia. It earned the name "allspice" because its flavor represents a combination of cinnamon, cloves and nutmeg. Allspice is used in fruit desserts, chutneys and pickles (it's a frequent ingredient in pickling spices). Allspice is essential in Jamaican jerk seasoning.

CARAWAY SEEDS: Caraway seeds taste sweet and nutty and are used to flavor breads, cheeses, coleslaw, sauerkraut, sausages and vegetable dishes. They are one of the oldest known spices and as such are integral to European and Asian cooking. Caraway seeds are available either whole or ground.

CARDAMOM: Cardamom is the dried, unripened fruit of a perennial. Enclosed in green, white or black pods are a dozen or so tiny, brownish-black aromatic seeds. Cardamom is available in the pod or ground, and is widely used in Scandinavian, Indian and Arab cuisines. In Scandinavia it is more popular than cinnamon for baked goods. Cardamom is an essential ingredient in dishes as diverse as Indian garam masala seasoning and Swedish meatballs and breads. The Arabs often flavor coffee with cardamom, a drink considered a symbol of hospitality. Cardamom is the third most costly spice—after saffron and vanilla.

CAYENNE: Cayenne, more properly called ground red pepper, is ground red chiles and adds noticeably spicy heat to dishes such as chilies and curries and in spice rubs for meats to be grilled. Use it sparingly at first. Cayenne is only available ground.

CHILI POWDER: Chili powder is deep red, ground seasoning mix that combines chiles, spices, herbs, garlic and salt. It may be mild, somewhat hot or fiery hot. Chili powder is used to flavor chilies and other Mexican and Southwestern dishes.

CINNAMON: Cinnamon, native to Sri Lanka, is a treasured spice used around the world to flavor desserts, baked goods and some meat dishes. Its warm, sweet flavor is recognizable to nearly everyone. Cinnamon is sold in rolled sticks in various lengths (part of the actual bark of a plant) or ground.

CLOVES: Cloves are the buds of furled flowers of an evergreen tree. The name comes from the French "clou," meaning nail, which whole cloves resemble. We think of them as something to stud ham with and as flavoring for cookies, but cloves are also an important flavor factor in tomato ketchup and Worcestershire sauce. Cloves are an important ingredient in the spice blends of Sri Lanka, North India (garam masala) and the Caribbean. Cloves are also use in Chinese and German cooking.

CORIANDER SEEDS: Coriander seeds are aromatic and sweet and are used extensively in North African,

Mediterranean, Mexican, Indian and Southeast Asian cuisines. Whole coriander seeds are often found in pickling spice. Ground coriander is found in many spice blends including chili powder, garam masala, curry powder and Ethiopian berbere. It is often included in hot dogs and other sausages, as well as in pastries.

CUMIN: Cumin imparts a strong, aromatic, somewhat bitter flavor to foods. It is an essential ingredient in most chili powders and can also be found in curries, vegetable dishes, breads, soups and pickles. Cumin is available whole or ground.

CURRY POWDER: Curry powder is a blend of several spices and is used to flavor many dishes, particularly those referred to as curries inspired by Indian cooking. Not all curry powder blends are identical, but most commercially available in the United States include ginger, cumin, turmeric, black pepper, cayenne and coriander. Look in the Thai foods section of your market for red, yellow and green curry bases.

DILL SEED: Dill seed is used most often as a pickling spice, although it is also popular in breads and potato and vegetable dishes. Dill seeds are sold whole or ground.

FENNEL SEEDS: Fennel seeds taste of licorice and are used to flavor breads, fish dishes, soups and sweet pickles. They are available whole or ground. Fennel is the dominant flavor in Italian sausage.

GINGER: Ginger is sold fresh or ground. When fresh, it comes as gingerroot, a knobby, woody root (actually a rhizome) that is peeled and grated, sliced or chopped before being used. Ginger is used to flavor both savory and sweet dishes, including meat, poultry, fish, curries, winter squash, carrots and sweet potatoes. Ginger is essential to many Asian, Indian and African dishes. It is also used to flavor fruit, syrups and desserts. Crystallized ginger is candied ginger; it may be chopped and added to gingerbread or crème brulée, or enjoyed on its own.

MUSTARD SEEDS: The seeds of the mustard plant are sold whole or ground into powder and are used to flavor coleslaw, curry, dressings and pickles, to say nothing of the yellow mustard that we slather on hot dogs. The most common mustard seeds are white, yellow or brown. Black mustard seeds, which are more pungent, are used in Indian cooking. White mustard seeds are used to make commercially prepared American mustards and some English mustards. Brown mustard seeds are used for Dijon mustards.

NUTMEG: Nutmeg is a favorite among spices and finds its way into any number of baked goods, sauces, fruit desserts and puddings. Eggnog is not official until it is topped with a sprinkling of nutmeg. Nutmeg is sold ground or whole, but for the best flavor it is advisable to buy the whole seed and grate it as needed. It grates very easily and can even be scraped with a small paring knife. Whole nutmegs keep their flavor almost indefinitely so grating it as you need it eliminates the pressure to toss opened ground spices after a year.

PAPRIKA: To those who know, paprika is not just a pretty red powder sprinkled on food as decoration. It is serious spice. Hungarians, for example, use lavish amount of paprika in many national favorites, including goulash soup and chicken paprikash. And paprika is used in seasoning blends for barbecue and chili. It is also essential to the cooking of India, Morocco and the Middle East. Paprika is made by grinding dried spicy red peppers to powder. Hungarian rose paprika ranges from mild and full-bodied to hot and spicy; Spanish paprika, ground from dried pimientos, is always mild.

PEPPER: Pepper is our most popular spice and accounts for 25% of the world's spice trade. The most common pepper is ground from black peppercorns, although white, red and dried green peppercorns are available and are often sold as a mixture. Some recipes specify white pepper because it does not add dark specks to the food. Although pepper is sold already ground, it tastes best when ground in a peppermill just before using. Pink peppercorns are dried berries of a rose plant and not true peppercorns.

SAFFRON: Saffron, the threadlike stigmas from a variety of Spanish crocus, is the world's most expensive spice. The stigmas must be plucked from the flowers by hand—and it takes 225,000 of them to make 1 pound of saffron. Saffron imparts a strong aroma and distinctive bitter honey-like taste to food as well as a deep yellow color. It is used for paella, for the rich French fish soup called bouillabaisse, and for chicken and fish dishes in Moroccan cooking. Saffron is also used in some sweet pastries. Saffron is sold whole and ground. Whole is the better way. A few stamens are usually soaked for a few minutes in warm water before being added to the dish.

SESAME SEEDS: Also known as benne seeds, sesame seeds were introduced to the Americas by African slaves. Sesame seeds are integral to African, Asian and Indian cooking and are used in the United States in baked goods. Favored for their nutty flavor, sesame seeds are also used to make the candy called halva. The white variety of sesame seed is the most common.

TURMERIC: A member of the ginger family, turmeric is ground into a bright yellow-orange powder and is used to flavor curries as well as vegetable, egg and fish dishes. Turmeric is a significant ingredient in curry powder and prepared mustard, and is also used in pickling. It gives food a pleasantly bitter, mild flavor.

INDEX

C

I

J

K

L

M

T

V

PHOTOGRAPHY CREDITS

Lucas Allen: 408.
Caren Alpert: 77, 175, 190, 206, 220, 229, 250, 292, 327.
Sang An: 45, 134, 153, 231, 297, 309, 386.
Australian Lamb: 397.
Quentin Bacon: 136, 286.
Iain Bagwell: 36, 109, 147, 182, 189, 218, 226, 320, 325, 378, 392, 454.
James Baigrie: 61, 88, 359.
Mary Ellen Bartley: 53, 54, 102, 133, 155, 178, 184, 214, 223, 228, 235, 249, 258, 278, 290, 298, 363, 371, 423, 447.
John Blais: 143.
Tony Cenicola: 255.
Gemma Coates: 39.
Joey De Leo: 144.
Tara Donne: 15, 40, 279, 300, 311, 336.
Philip Ficks: 51.
Stephanie Foley: 253, 304.
Jim Franco: 20, 42, 67, 96, 204, 210, 322, 329, 404, 416, 460.
Dennis Gottlieb: 33.
Brian Hagiwara: 333.
Paula Hible: 193.
Jacqueline Hopkins: 28, 44, 58, 90, 110, 114, 130, 261, 266, 287, 291, 382, 402, 414, 431.
Lisa Hubbard: 26.
Frances Janisch: 41, 89, 181, 194, 328, 340, 349, 440.
Jeff McNamara: 25.
Tom McWilliam: 24, 140, 308.
Rita Maas: 168, 188, 208, 330, 373, 374.
Anastassios Mentis: 132, 171, 212, 216, 225, 245, 254, 360, 362, 413.
Alison Miksch: 99, 111, 131, 148, 262, 285, 306, 394.
Ellie Miller: 150, 248, 331, 372, 406.
Laura Moss: 187, 299, 342.
Kana Okada: 12, 55, 62, 70, 98, 156.
Con Poulos: 92, 118, 121, 246, 289, 303.
Alan Richardson: 95, 108, 151, 356.
Sea Pack Shrimp Co.: 383.
Kate Sears: 17, 172, 180, 205, 213, 219, 270, 424.
Charles Schiller: 19, 22, 31, 35, 56, 60, 68, 69, 73, 74, 97, 106, 141, 160, 207, 222, 243, 251, 264, 267, 272, 294, 296, 305, 310, 321, 338, 341, 344, 346, 366, 367, 376, 379, 380, 415, 449.
Ellen Silverman: 176, 339, 384, 407, 421.
Amy Kalyn Sims: 100, 119, 398, 401.
Shaffer Smith: 91, 183.
Ann Stratton: 30, 32, 52, 80, 152, 170, 177, 197, 217, 280, 435.
Mark Thomas: 59, 66, 78, 116, 135, 192, 224, 230, 282, 319, 354, 364, 433.
John Uher: 57, 64, 76, 79, 86, 93, 101, 126, 146, 198, 227, 241, 271, 316, 361, 430, 451, 458, 463.
Jonny Valiant: 6, 14, 38, 81, 157, 195, 317, 335, 368, 410, 448, 456.
Elizabeth Watt: 129.
Wendell Webber: 166, 232, 387.
Dasha Wright: 87, 104, 128, 186, 242, 260, 357, 438, 443, 445, 446.

ACKNOWLEDGMENTS

Producing the food photographs that grace the pages of *Woman's Day* involves many skills. The food stylists are almost always the people who develop the recipes. The 365 featured in this book were created by Nancy Dell'Aria, Terry Grieco Kenny, Susan F. Kadel, Christine Makuch, Donna Meadow, Frank P. Melodia, Kate Merker and Jackie Plant.